Reviewer Quotes

'*Teaching Early Years* is very comprehensive and covers all areas of curriculum. It also provides an overview of the early childhood context and important aspects such as leadership and communities of learners. It is exciting to see such a wide range of writers brought together.'

Dr Leonie Arthur, Senior Lecturer, Early Childhood Education, University of Western Sydney

'*Teaching Early Years: Curriculum, pedagogy and assessment* is comprehensive and pertinent. Its strength lies in the diversity of the chapters and its reference to evidence based research which pre-service teachers and early childhood professionals can apply to their practice. It brings together the expertise of specialists in each area, and it provides a strong professional knowledge base which targets key areas generally covered in undergraduate and post-graduate early childhood education courses.'

Dr Elizabeth Stamopoulos, Senior Lecturer, School of Education, Edith Cowan University

This book is dedicated to our families.
We particularly dedicate this to the young people in our families.

Kyrra, Bess, Blyton, Zeke and Bader
and
James

Teaching
EARLY YEARS

Curriculum, pedagogy and assessment

EDITED BY DONNA PENDERGAST AND SUSANNE GARVIS

ALLEN&UNWIN
SYDNEY • MELBOURNE • AUCKLAND • LONDON

First published in Australia by Allen & Unwin in 2013

Allen & Unwin
Sydney, Melbourne, Auckland, London

83 Alexander Street
Crows Nest NSW 2065
Australia
Phone: (61 2) 8425 0100
Email: info@allenandunwin.com
Web: www.allenandunwin.com

Cataloguing-in-Publication details are available
from the National Library of Australia
www.trove.nla.gov.au

ISBN 978 1 74237 995 1

Set in 11/14 pt Minion Pro by Midland Typesetters, Australia
Printed by Phoenix Print Media, Singapore.

10 9 8 7 6 5 4 3 2 1

Contents

List of tables and figures

Tables

Figures

Contributors

Donna Pendergast is Dean and Head of the School of Education and Professional Studies at Griffith University. She has undertaken extensive research and published widely in the fields of early years and middle years education.

Susanne Garvis is an early childhood lecturer at Griffith University. Her research interests include early childhood arts education and policy reform. Dr Garvis has been a visiting scholar in Norway and Sweden. She has published in national and international journals and scholarly books.

Wendi Beamish is a special educator with a strong practitioner background. She has over 30 years' experience working with young children with disabilities and their families. She currently lectures at Griffith University in the areas of early childhood intervention, behavioural support and social-emotional competence.

Gillian Busch has experience as an early childhood educator working as an early childhood teacher and more recently as a lecturer at Central Queensland University. Her research interests include social interaction, social and moral orders, children's disputes and leadership. Her recent research has examined the social orders of family mealtimes.

Carmen Dalli is Professor of Early Childhood Education and Director of the Institute for Early Childhood Studies at Victoria University of Wellington, New Zealand. Her research relates to issues of quality and professionalism in early childhood education, and the intersection of policy and pedagogy in children's experiences in early childhood settings.

Marjory Ebbeck is a well-known academic with expertise in early childhood curriculum research methods who has published texts that are used in Australia and overseas. She continues to work at the University of South Australia, supervising PhD students, and is currently senior academic adviser with the SEED Institute in Singapore.

Glenn Finger is Dean (Learning and Teaching) in the Arts, Education and Law Group at Griffith University. He has extensively researched, published and provided consultancies in creating transformational stories about the use of Information and Communication Technologies (ICT) to enhance learning.

Scott Harrison is Deputy Director (Research) at the Queensland Conservatorium, Griffith University and a recipient of an Australian Award for Teaching Excellence. Current research and teaching focus on the interface of music with health, gender and identity.

Ian Hay is the Executive Dean of the Faculty of Education, University of Tasmania. He has published some 200 scholarly publications. His main research interests are in the domain of children's early literacy development, the role of motivation in learning and students' cognitive development.

Kate Highfield is an academic at the Institute of Early Childhood, Macquarie University. Kate's teaching focuses on technology use in mathematics and science. Her current research investigates young children's engagement with technology, including techno-toys, screen-based games, creative play with technology and robotics in problem-solving and play.

Karin Ishimine is currently an Australian Research Council Postdoctoral Fellow in the Melbourne Graduate School of Education at the University of Melbourne. Her research interests are the quality of early childhood education, assessments of children's developmental outcomes and evidence-based policy.

Robyn Jorgensen currently lectures at Griffith University and has worked in many contexts in education, including early childhood. Her interest is in identifying contexts that offer new potential for learning. She attempts to disrupt traditional methods and approaches to find new ways of engaging learning and learners.

Christopher Klopper is a Senior Lecturer in Arts Education at Griffith University. He publishes in the field of pre-service arts education, intentional provision of music in early childhood settings and intercultural musical communication.

Susan Krieg is the Program Coordinator of the Early Childhood programs at Flinders University. Her educational leadership and teaching within the university context focus on social justice and repositioning children in the learning process as a way of achieving more equitable outcomes in early childhood education.

Lai Wan Maria Lee is the Vice-chairperson of the Pacific Early Childhood Education Research Association (Hong Kong) and a panel member of the Child Fatality Review. Her interests include Reggio Emilia, early literacy, storytelling and moral education.

Narelle Lemon is a Lecturer at Royal Melbourne Institute of Technology. She publishes in image-based research methods where young people are seen as co-researchers, as well as arts education and meaningful embedding of digital technologies to support meaning making.

Katherine Main is a Lecturer at Griffith University specialising in the middle years and primary education. Her main research interests include the formation, development and maintenance of effective collaborative practices, teacher efficacy, middle school reform and improving the personal literacy levels of pre-service teachers.

Joanne Mulligan leads research projects, teaches mathematics education in undergraduate programs and supervises research students in the Department of Education, Faculty of Human Sciences at Macquarie University. Joanne is internationally renowned for research in early mathematical development.

Michael Nagel teaches and researches in the areas of human development, educational psychology, behaviour and learning in the School of Science and Education at the University of the Sunshine Coast.

Karuppiah Nirmala is a Lecturer at the Department of Early Childhood and Special Education, National Institute of Education, Singapore. She has conducted talks for parents and workshops for teachers both in and outside Singapore. Her areas of research interests include diversity, adult–child interactions and teaching-learning processes.

Marina Papic is the Head of the Institute of Early Childhood, Macquarie University. Her specialisations include early mathematics learning, curriculum and assessment, patterning and early algebraic thinking. She currently leads the ARC Project Improving numeracy outcomes for young Indigenous children through the Patterns and Early Algebra Preschool Professional Development Program.

Anne Petriwskyj lectures in early years science and technology education in the School of Early Childhood, Faculty of Education, Queensland University of Technology. Her professional background includes prior-to-school, early school, inclusive and Indigenous education, particularly in rural and regional locations.

Bridie Raban conducts research and development in the field of early childhood education. Bridie is a Senior Research Fellow in the Australian Council for Educational Research's Teaching, Learning and Transitions research program and an Honorary Professorial Research Fellow (Early Childhood) at the Melbourne Graduate School of Education.

Beth Saggers currently works as a Senior Lecturer in the School of Learning and Professional Studies at Queensland University of Technology, lecturing in supporting students with Autism Spectrum Disorders, catering for diversity and behaviour support.

Janet Scull is a senior lecturer in language and literacy education at the University of Melbourne. Her research interests focus on literacy acquisition, particularly the relationships between language, literacy and teaching interactions.

Margaret Sims is Professor of Early Childhood at the University of New England. Her research interests and experience are in a range of community-based services for children and families. She has recently published texts on working with infants and toddlers, social inclusion and the Early Years Learning Framework, and integrated early childhood service delivery.

Collette Tayler holds the Chair in Early Childhood Education and Care at the University of Melbourne, where she researches child learning and development, program effectiveness, policy and strategy, and leads the Master of Teaching Early Childhood. Collette conducts numerous program and policy implementation activities in the field.

Maryanne Theobald is a Lecturer at Queensland University of Technology. Her research interests include children's talk and interaction, social and moral orders and children's rights. Dr Theobald's recent research has investigated child participation and the teacher's management of children's disputes in the school playground.

Kate Thornton currently works in the School of Education Policy and Implementation in the Faculty of Education at the Victoria University of Wellington, New Zealand. Her research interests include educational leadership and leadership development, blended learning, mentoring and coaching.

Danielle Twigg is an early childhood educator and researcher at Griffith University. Her research interests are eclectic, and include leadership in early childhood education, health and well-being practices in schools, phenomenology and professional learning.

Gary Woolley has taught primary and secondary school children in public and private school systems for over 30 years. He currently lectures at Griffith University and researches in the field of literacy and learning difficulties. His professional interests include reading difficulties, memory, cognition, learning engagement and professional development.

Hoi Yin Bonnie Yim is a Senior Lecturer at Deakin University, and has special research interests in early childhood curriculum, cultural diversity in learning, music education and research methods. Dr Yim is an early years consultant in Australia, Singapore, Hong Kong and Indonesia.

Foreword

High-quality early childhood education and care are important to allow all young Australians to meet their potential and become valued members of our community. The early years learning frameworks in Australia create exciting possibilities for the care and education of young children. However, to engage with these new challenges, educators need a broad understanding of the current approaches and debates. There is a need for an integrated Australian approach to early childhood education and care regarding its practices, theories, critical themes and research, especially because of the great diversity in forms of provision and approaches to professional development.

The Early Childhood Teachers' Association (ECTA) advocates for high-quality education and care through supporting professional development and collegiate support between educators working with young children. ECTA promotes collaboration and professional development within and across early childhood sectors, including tertiary educators, early years health professionals, early years teachers, educators working in before-school services and outside school hours professionals.

This new early childhood text provides a comprehensive overview of early childhood education in Australia for children aged from birth to eight years. The book closely aligns with ECTA key priorities of:

- the importance of active, inquiry-based learning nurtured through early childhood teaching pedagogy
- an acknowledgement that children learn best when both children and adults share responsibility for learning and decision-making
- a commitment to early childhood learning environments reflecting the rights of children and families to be active participants in the learning process

- a belief that teaching and learning should be characterised by opportunities for children to engage in play in all its forms, including children initiating and undertaking investigations around topics of their own interest
- a respect for the diverse social, cultural and learning needs of all children.

We encourage you to read this publication carefully and to share it with others, including early childhood professionals and the wider community. It reports on a wide variety of significant early childhood topics and is written in a style directed towards early childhood professionals. Now is the time to support young children in their development so they can reach their full potential. The young children with whom we live and work on a daily basis deserve nothing less.

Kim Walters
President, Early Childhood Teachers' Association

Preface

Donna Pendergast and Susanne Garvis

The early years of care and learning are recognised as crucial, with significant consequences for ongoing educational success and future participation in society. Early childhood professionals in this critical phase need specialist preparation and to have the skills and knowledge to understand and manage issues related to early years learners.

This book will assist child-care centres, kindergartens, pre-schools, schools, academics, pre-service student teachers and teachers in their quest to successfully develop early years curriculum, pedagogy and assessment to meet the needs of today's early years learners. The book brings together the expertise of academics in the early years field. It is not exhaustive in its coverage—several books would be required to document and detail all of the relevant aspects of early years learning, and each chapter could easily be expanded into a book in its own right.

The organisation of the book reflects the key priorities for the early years— that is, reform in curriculum, pedagogy and assessment. It commences with a platform about the early years, before addressing reform in practices grouped around curriculum, pedagogy and assessment, with a final section focusing on the key imperatives facing the early years. Each chapter concludes with questions that guide reflection on the concepts developed in the chapter. In addition to meeting editorial requirements, each chapter has been peer reviewed. The book is a collaborative effort, drawn from a range of scholars and practitioners who responded to an open call for contributions made by the editors in 2011. The book fills a gap in the resources available for the early years, bringing together sound scholarly debates and practical applications.

Acknowledgements

The editors wish to thank Joy Reynolds for her administrative contribution to this book. We also acknowledge the enthusiastic response of our colleagues who replied to the call for chapter abstracts, many of whom we reluctantly were unable to include given the overwhelming response. We thank the reviewers for their insightful comments and the publishers for their confidence in this project.

PART I

The context of early years learning

1

Early years in Australia

Donna Pendergast and Susanne Garvis

Introduction

In recent years, there has been a trend towards the increased use of early child-hood formal education and care settings, including in Australia. With this trend, the importance of acceptable standards of provision of services has come to the forefront of policy interest. Federal, state and territory governments have responded with agendas designed to improve the quality of early childhood education and care. The current agendas apply to children from birth to eight years, and aim to both achieve consistency and improve the health, safety, early learning and well-being of all children, as well as to provide better support for disadvantaged children in order to reduce inequalities.

This chapter provides an overview of the current agendas in the early years, and explores national and state initiatives. It is linked to a change model that was developed some years ago to provide a realistic insight into the time and sequenc-ing necessary to undertake successful change. The implementation of the early years agenda is discussed, and the chapter outlines how systems in Australia are currently moving from the early stages of understanding the need for and nature of the National Quality Framework for Early Childhood Education and Care, to widespread implementation. It is argued that the current Australian early years agenda will take some seven to ten years to reach the point of full and sustainable implementation with the opportunity for ongoing refinement.

The early years: What are we talking about?

Early childhood education and care has been a concern of many countries in recent times. The Organization for Economic Cooperation and Development (OECD) describes the growing consensus in OECD countries that 'care' and 'education' are inseparable concepts, defining early childhood education and care (ECEC) as:

> an integrated and coherent approach to policy and provision which is inclusive of all children and all parents regardless of their employment status or socioeconomic status. This approach recognizes that such arrangements may fulfil a wide range of objectives including care, learning and social support. (OECD, 2001, p. 14)

At a practical level, this definition of ECEC includes both child-care centres and other 'care' services like family day care, and programs with the primary purpose of 'early childhood education' like kindergartens and child care. These programs are all intended to enhance child development and well-being, and to support parents in a variety of ways, both within and outside the paid workforce.

In Australia, there are various early childhood education and care facilities for children prior to the formal years of schooling. These include:

- long day care
- family day care
- occasional care
- kindergarten/preschool (the year prior to formal schooling).

Children can enter into some of the settings listed above at six weeks of age. The end of the early years in schooling is considered to be age eight. Early years is therefore defined as children from birth to eight years of age.

Over the past decade, there has been a growth in early childhood formal education and care settings in most countries around the world. This growth has occurred largely in the prior to formal schooling child-care sector, especially in OECD countries (children aged from birth to six years). On average across OECD countries, 30 per cent of children under the age of two used child-care facilities in 2008 (OECD, 2011). However, whereas enrolment rates of young children were less than 10 per cent in Chile, the Czech Republic, Hungary, Mexico, Poland and the Slovak Republic, more than 50 per cent of children in this age group were enrolled in formal childcare in Denmark, Iceland, The Netherlands and Norway (OECD, 2011). For children aged three to five years, the rate was significantly higher, with 77 per cent on average in early childhood programs.

In Australia, 9 per cent of children under one year of age attended formal care during 2008 (ABS, 2008). Some 35 per cent of children at one year of age attended formal care, with the number growing to 48 per cent at two years of age and 50 per cent at three years of age (ABS, 2008). Early years education in Australia also includes the early years of formal schooling (children aged five to eight years). This period in primary school is recognised as a distinct sub-set of early years education.

As the participation of children in formal early childhood, education and care settings continues to grow around the world, greater interest is focused on improving the quality of services for young children. Many governments are interested in how to enhance child development and potential in these formalised settings.

Quality of early childhood education and care

The quality of early childhood education and care can be considered in terms of structural and process quality. The structural aspects of quality are relatively fixed and easily measured, such as the adult:child ratio, staff qualifications and group size. Process quality is the nature of the daily interactions and experiences of children and is not so easily measured, but techniques are available. International research shows that ECEC of high quality can affect child outcomes in a short and long time perspective (e.g. OECD, 2010; Dalli et al., 2011).

Melhuish (2004) concludes that research indicates the following factors are most important for enhancing children's development:

- adult-child interaction that is responsive, affectionate and readily available
- well-trained staff who are committed to their work with children
- facilities that are safe and sanitary, and accessible to parents
- ratios and group sizes that allow staff to interact appropriately with children
- supervision that maintains consistency
- staff development that ensures continuity, stability and improving quality
- a developmentally appropriate curriculum with educational content.

Similar conclusions are reached in a number of reviews, including a recent study of quality early childhood education for children aged under two in New Zealand (Dalli et al., 2011). Some aspects are particularly important—for instance, teaching style, educational ideology, and teacher competence (NAEYC, 1991; Sheridan et al., 2009). The Effective Provision of Pre-School Education (EPPE) project in the United Kingdom found that persistent long-term interactions with a teacher supporting 'shared sustained thinking' was a particularly important context of learning for children. It means that child and teacher focus and communicate on common content (Siraj-Blatchford et al., 2003). In Swedish studies, being aware of how to challenge children's meaning-making, creativity and playfulness, and the integration of play and learning, were found to be important (Johansson & Pramling Samuelsson, 2009; Pramling Samuelsson & Asplund Carlsson, 2009). The role of the educator is to stimulate learning, as well as cognitive and communicative development, and to ensure activities are related to development and experiences (Johansson, 2004). Consequently, early childhood services need clear goals and intentions that result in a progression in child learning (Alvestad, 2004).

A new Australian longitudinal funded study, 'E4Kids Effective Early Educational Experiences' (see <www.e4kids.org.au>), is currently assessing the impact of participation in child care and kindergarten on 2600 young children's outcomes over five years. The E4Kids research program has been developed to provide an evidence base to determine the best ways to support higher quality in our child-care and kindergarten settings—an essential element in providing young children with a good start in life. This study is one of the first longitudinal studies for early childhood education and care in Australia, and there is much anticipation about the contribution the findings will make to better understanding the sector.

The early years in Australia

Over the past decade and a half, rapid growth has occurred in early childhood education and care provisions in Australia. There has also been increased attention from governments around the world to investing in the years before compulsory schooling, based on research claims that increased spending in the before-school sector reduces later costs to society. In 2007, the Commonwealth government responded with a higher level commitment (Australian Government, 2009) to improve quality and provision. Following are some key elements of the National Early Childhood Development Strategy: Investing in the Early Years.

National Early Childhood Development Strategy: Investing in the Early Years

A key initiative was the endorsement of the National Early Childhood Development Strategy: Investing in the Early Years by the Council of Australian Governments (COAG) in 2009. The strategy is a 'collaborative effort between the Commonwealth and the state and territory governments to ensure that by 2020 all children have the best start in life to create a better future for themselves and for the nation' (COAG, 2009). The strategy proposed six priority areas for change to be further developed for COAG in 2010, recognising the different starting points of states and territories as resources allow (DEEWR, 2011):

- strengthening universal maternal, child and family health services
- supporting vulnerable children
- engaging parents and the community in understanding the importance of early childhood development
- improving early childhood infrastructure
- strengthening the workforce across early childhood development and family-support services, and
- building better information and a solid evidence base.

National Quality Framework for Early Childhood Education and Care

The Council of Australian Governments also agreed to a National Quality Framework for Early Childhood Education and Care in 2010. It puts in place a National Quality Standard from 2012 to ensure a high quality that is consistent across all states and territories. The National Quality Standard will improve quality through (DEEWR, 2011):

- improved staff to child ratios to ensure each child gets more individual care and attention
- new staff qualification requirements to ensure staff have the skills to help children learn and develop
- a new quality rating system to ensure Australian families have access to transparent information relating to the quality of early childhood education and care services

- the establishment of a new national body, known as the Australian Children's Education and Care Quality Authority (ACECQA), to ensure early childhood education and care are of a high quality.

A new rating system is being implemented as part of the National Quality Standard. Each early years service will be assessed on its performance across seven quality areas. All services will need to display their approval and rating information. Ratings will also be available online. The five-point rating scale is represented below in Table 1.1 (DEEWR, 2011).

Table 1.1   Rating scales

Level	Description
Significant improvement required	Indicates that a service is not meeting the National Quality Standard and the regulator is working closely with the service to immediately improve its quality (otherwise the service's approval to operate will be withdrawn).
Working towards National Quality Standard	Indicates that a service is working towards meeting the National Quality Standard.
Meets National Quality Standard	Indicates that a service is meeting the National Quality Standard.
Exceeds National Quality Standard	Indicates that a service is exceeding the National Quality Standard.
Excellent	Indicates that a service demonstrates excellence and is recognised as a sector leader.

Belonging, Being and Becoming: The Early Years Learning Framework for Australia

Belonging, Being and Becoming: The Early Years Learning Framework for Australia (the Framework) is part of the Council of Australian Government's (COAG's) agenda for early childhood education and care, and is a key component of the Australian government's National Quality Framework for Early Childhood Education and Care for early childhood education and care. It underpins universal access to early childhood education, and will be incorporated in the National Quality Standard. Universal access means *all* children.

The Framework describes the principles, practices and outcomes essential to support and enhance young children's learning from birth to five years of age. It has a strong emphasis on play-based learning as the best vehicle for children's learning and development. The Framework also recognises the importance of communication and language, and of social and emotional development.

Universal access ensures that every child in Australia has access to a quality early childhood education program. The program is to be delivered by a four-year university-trained early childhood teacher for fifteen hours a week, 40 weeks of the year, in the year before formal schooling (often referred to as 'preschool' or 'kindergarten'). The commitment is to be fully implemented by mid-2013. Each state and territory has different arrangements for regulating, funding and delivering early childhood education services.

Aboriginal and Torres Strait Islander Universal Access Strategy

To help increase the number of Aboriginal and Torres Strait Islander children participating in preschool, the Australian, state and territory governments have developed and endorsed the Aboriginal and Torres Strait Islander Universal Access Strategy (DEEWR, 2011). This strategy outlines the participation of Aboriginal and Torres Strait Islander children in early childhood education in urban, regional and remote locations. Four key focus areas for the development of strategies and actions for improvement have been identified:

- increasing access to early childhood education
- positive community awareness and engagement
- quality early childhood programs and activities
- Aboriginal and Torres Strait Islander cultural awareness of teachers and support staff.

My Time, Our Place: Framework for School Age Care in Australia

My Time, Our Place: Framework for School Age Care in Australia will also be part of the National Quality Standard. This framework is intended to ensure that all children in school-age care have opportunities to engage in leisure and play-based experiences that are responsive to their needs and interests.

The framework is designed to support educators working with school-age children in outside school hours care, long day care, and family day care settings. It builds on the Early Years Learning Framework, and extends on the outcomes and principles to accommodate the age range of children in school-age care.

Early childhood workforce

An important area for change in the early years has been raising the standards of qualifications of early childhood educators. This was formalised in the National Quality Framework (2009). The requirements (to be implemented by 2014) are explicit:

- Half of all staff at every long day care centre or preschool must have (or be working towards) a diploma-level early childhood qualification. The remaining staff will all be required to have (or be working towards) a Certificate III-level early childhood education and care qualification.
- An early childhood teacher will be required in long day care and preschool services for 25 children or more. Additional early childhood teachers will be required for larger services by 2020.
- Family day care coordinators will need to have a diploma-level early childhood education and care qualification, and family day carers must have (or be working towards) a Certificate III.

A crucial component of the changes in the early years are the improved staff-to-child ratios, which are consistent nationally for the first time. Research has shown that improving staff-to-child ratios improves the quality of interactions with the child, improving the understanding of the child's learning and development. In a US Department of Health and Human Services-commissioned literature review (Fiene, 2002), findings showed that in centres where there were lower child:staff ratios:

- there was a reduction in the transmission of disease because caregivers were better able to monitor and promote healthy practices and behaviours
- there were fewer situations involving potential danger and child abuse
- caregivers were able to have more positive, nurturing interactions with children and provide children with more individualised attention
- infants displayed less apathy and distress, and greater social competence
- babies engaged in more talk and play, and displayed more gestural and vocal imitation than children in classrooms with higher child:staff ratios

- babies were more likely to have positive interactions with caregivers, be properly supervised and be engaged in activities rated as good or very good
- there was more developmentally appropriate caregiving and sensitivity, more contact (e.g. talking, playing, touching and laughing), more responsive and stimulating behaviour and less restriction of children's behaviour
- there were higher rates of secure attachments between toddlers and their caregivers
- there was more verbal communication between caregivers and children, which appeared to foster language development in children
- adults and children talked to one another more and caregivers engaged in more dialogues and fewer monologues
- caregivers engaged in more educational activities (e.g. teaching, promoting problem-solving) with children.

In Australia, the new ratios for long day care are a staff:child ratio of 1:4 for children aged under two years of age. In some states, this new regulation reduces the ratio (such as in New South Wales and Victoria) from five children to four.

Indigenous children

The Council of Australian Governments has agreed to a number of targets to improve outcomes for Indigenous people, especially children. The targets that relate to early childhood development are (DEEWR, 2011):

- halving the gap in mortality rates for Indigenous children under five within a decade
- ensuring all Indigenous four-year-olds in remote communities have access to early childhood education within five years
- ensuring every child will have access to a preschool program in the twelve months prior to full-time schooling by 2013
- halving the gap for Indigenous students in reading, writing and numeracy within a decade.

Part of the strategy includes the establishment of 38 Children and Family Centres across Australia by June 2013. The Children and Family Centres are targeted at addressing the needs of Indigenous families and their young children (the distribution of the centres across states and territories is shown in Table 1.2).

Table 1.2   Distribution of Children and Family Centres across states and territories

Centres	NSW	QLD	VIC	SA	WA	TAS	NT	ACT
Regional/remote	4	6	1	3	4	1	4	0
Urban	5	4	1	1	1	1	1	1
Total	9	10	2	4	5	2	5	1

The centres will deliver integrated services, including early learning, child-care and family-support programs. The design and operation of the facilities will differ from centre to centre so that services meet local needs.

Early years education in schools

Significant changes have also occurred in the formal years of schooling for young learners in the early years. Two of the major changes have been the introduction of the new Australian Curriculum and the National Assessment Program (NAP).

The Australian Curriculum

The Australian Curriculum provides a national curriculum for all states and territories in Australia from Foundation Year to Year 12. The term 'Foundation Year' has been used as a nationally consistent term for the year of schooling prior to Year 1 for the purpose of the Australian Curriculum. It does not replace the equivalent terms used in states and territories—Kindergarten (NSW/ACT), Preparatory (Qld/Vic/Tas), Pre-primary (WA), Reception (SA) and Transition (NT) (ACARA, 2011). The curriculum implementation in schools has been undertaken over three phases:

- *Phase 1:* development of the Australian Curriculum for English, mathematics, science and history (Foundation—Year 10 published 2010; Years 11–12 in development)
- *Phase 2:* development of the Australian Curriculum for geography, languages and the arts (in development from 2010)

- *Phase 3*: development of the Australian Curriculum for the remaining areas identified in the Melbourne Declaration on Educational Goals for Young Australians (in development from 2011).

The Australian Curriculum will be available to all young children in Australia, regardless of location or socio-economic status. The Australia Curriculum is guided by two key documents: the Melbourne Declaration on Education Goals for Young Australians (Ministerial Council on Education, Employment, Training and Youth Affairs, 2008) and The Shape of the Australian Curriculum (ACARA, 2010). Key messages from each document are highlighted in Box 1.1.

Box 1.1 Key messages: Melbourne Declaration on Education Goals for Young Australians and Shape of the Australian Curriculum

Goal 1: Australian schooling promotes equity and excellence.
Goal 2: All young Australians become:

- successful learners
- confident and creative individuals
- active and informed citizens.

Achieving these educational goals is the collective responsibility of governments, school sectors and individual schools as well as parents and carers, young Australians, families, other education and training providers, business and the broader community. (MCEETYA, 2008 p. 6)

Education plays a critical role in shaping the lives of the nation's future citizens. To play this role effectively, the intellectual, personal, social and educational needs of young Australians must be addressed at a time when ideas about the goals of education are changing and will continue to evolve. (ACARA, 2010, p. 5)

The commitment to develop a national curriculum reflects a willingness to work together, across geographical and school-sector boundaries, to provide a world-class education for all young Australians. Working nationally makes it possible to harness collective expertise and effort in the pursuit of this common goal. It also offers the potential of economies of scale and a substantial reduction in the duplication of time, effort and resources. (ACARA, 2010, p. 6)

The Australian Curriculum also means that all young Australians can learn about the histories and cultures of Aboriginal and Torres Strait Islander peoples, of their contribution to Australia, and of the consequences of colonial settlement for Indigenous communities, past and present. For Aboriginal people and Torres Strait Islanders, the Australian Curriculum promotes the importance of pursuing excellence within education settings which respect and promote their cultural identity. (ACARA, 2010, p. 6)

National Assessment Program
The National Assessment Program (NAP) is the measure through which governments, education authorities and schools can determine whether young Australians are meeting important educational outcomes. It includes a battery of assessments, including:

- the National Assessment Program—Literacy and Numeracy (NAPLAN)
- three-yearly NAP Sample Assessments in Science Literacy; Civics and Citizenship; and Information and Communication Technology (ICT) Literacy, and
- international sample assessments.

NAPLAN comprises the standardised assessment items that are relevant to the early years of formal schooling. All students in Year 3 across Australia take part in standardised testing every year to engage current competency levels for reading, writing, language conventions and numeracy.

A change model: Towards sustainability

As evidenced in this chapter, the context of early years education is one of considerable interest at this time in Australia. In order to better understand the nature and sequence of change, it is helpful to utilise a model that provides a general understanding of the timelines and commitments necessary to promote change to a sector. The Educational Change Model developed originally for reform processes in Australian middle schooling (Pendergast et al., 2005; Pendergast, 2006) can be used for this purpose. This model has been drawn from an educational scenario; however, the principles underpinning the model are equally applicable to business, industry and community settings. The model has value for an individual, for a site or setting, and at a systemic level. At the individual level, it can be used to assist individuals to determine the stage of change at which they are operating by reflecting on their understandings and practices. Similarly, in a specific site, the phase of change can be determined by auditing the evidence presented across the site. At a systemic level, the guidance required to scaffold individuals and sites to achieve change can be tailored by utilising the components of the phases as an audit tool. Hence the adoption of the Educational Change Model (the Model) is applicable to the changes in the early childhood sector.

The Model proposes that agendas of proposed change typically progress through three phases, gradually introducing particular core component changes, spanning a minimum of about eight years, and stretching out beyond this depending upon circumstances. The Model, together with the relevant literature, also recognises that educational change takes longer than usually expected or normally allowed for in agenda schedules.

The three broad phases can be mapped on to any major agenda initiative, and feature indications of time taken to achieve each phase (see Figure 1.1). The Initiation phase typically occupies the first year or two; the Development phase typically consumes the next two to five years; and the Consolidation phase can last over a further five to ten years. The time periods associated with each of the three phases are indicative only and can be accelerated through the alignment of enablers. Similarly, inhibitors can lead to dips in the agenda, adding extra time to the overall change process.

During the Initiation phase organisations are characterised by activities that include goal setting (e.g., development of vision statements), developing buy-in and information dissemination of the new agenda, what they entail and how they will be achieved (Pendergast, 2006). The focus for individuals is on understanding the new agenda and the implications for changes to their thinking, language and practices.

Figure 1.1   The Educational Change Model mapped against a typical reform curve

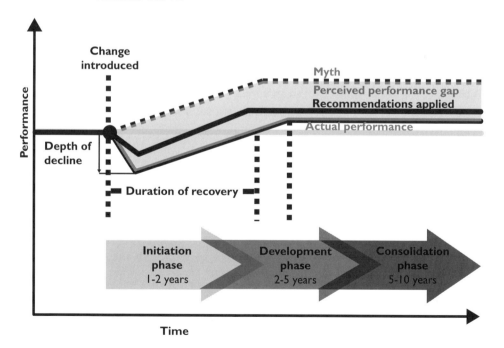

During the Development phase, individuals and groups are deepening their understanding of the agendas and are implementing more and more new practices in accordance with the new agendas. This stage of exploration and experimentation yields many successes, but inevitably leads to some failed trials and experiments. This can sometimes result in frustration, despair and despondency with the new agendas and is accompanied by decreases in performance and perceived efficacy. This is identified in the literature as an implementation dip (Pendergast & Main, 2011).

Factors that cause, exacerbate and/or lengthen the dip are known as inhibitors, while enablers are factors that aid effective implementation and shorten the dip. Pendergast et al. (2005) identify thirteen inhibitors of reform in educational settings, including weak or inconsistent leadership, poorly conceived vision statements, insufficient funding and resistance from the community. Typically, the organisational focus is starting to turn away from the agenda efforts, with a corresponding drop in funding. Sustained commitment beyond the life of the initial change notification is required to ensure continuity of focus.

During the Consolidation phase, individual and group understanding of the agenda is much more closely aligned and practices have largely been bedded down. Organisations are further deepening their knowledge, and the language and practices are becoming more automatic and widespread within the organisation. Individual reliance on experts and leadership decreases as their own expertise increases. Agenda efforts largely have disappeared by this phase, with the expectation that individuals are able to continuously improve independent of external assistance as individuals move towards more expert knowledge and to a stronger practice base.

As individuals and groups progress along a change trajectory, their understanding and ability to implement the changes improves over time. Because of these changes, the implementation activities must conform to the needs of the group during that particular phase. The more closely aligned the activities are with the needs of the individual, the more likely (and more quickly) they are to move on a continuum towards full implementation.

Early years agendas in Australia are currently moving into the development phase. The initiative phase occurred between 2009 and 2011. While early years services are at different levels of implementation, as a whole the early years sector has moved into a stage that is focused on realising the vision of early years practice in services.

The journey of change is a long one, and the policy frameworks in place provide an excellent platform from which it might be achieved. Ongoing commitment through resourcing, education and leadership will be critical to achieve what are valued and valuable goals to change the early years sector in Australia.

Summary

- Significant change has occurred in Australian early childhood and care since the introduction of Australian early years agenda in 2009.
- Current changes will take at least seven years for complete implementation. Many individuals and early childhood services are currently moving into the second stage of implementation, known as 'development'.
- The National Quality Framework for Early Childhood Education and Care has a key focus on improving outcomes for Indigenous children.
- Changes in early childhood education and care have also occurred for children in the formal years of schooling across Australia.

Discussion questions

1.1 What do you think early years education and child care will be like in Australia in 2020?

1.2 Do you know of any early years services? Looking at the change model, what stage of implementation do you think they are up to?

1.3 Part of being an early childhood educator is the concept of continual improvement. What can you do to make sure you are engaged in 'continual improvement' with your early years practice?

References

Alvestad, M. (2004). Preschool teachers' understanding of some aspects of educational planning and practice related to the National Curricula in Norway. *International Journal of Early Years Education*, *12*(2), 83–97.

Anderson, S.E. (1997). Understanding teacher change: Revisiting the Concerns Based Adoption Model. *Curriculum Inquiry, 27*(3), 331–67.

Australian Bureau of Statistics (ABS) (2008). *4402.0—Childhood Education and Care, Australia, June 2008 (Reissue)*. Retrieved 29 December 2011 from <www.abs.gov.au/ausstats/abs@.nsf/mf/4402.0>.

Australian Curriculum, Assessment and Reporting Authority (ACARA) (2010). *The shape of the Australian curriculum*. Sydney: ACARA.

Australian Government Department of Education, Employment and Workplace Relations for the Council of Australian Governments (2009). *National Quality Framework for Early Childhood Education and Care.* Canberra: Council of Australian Governments.

Council of Australian Governments (COAG) Early Childhood Development Steering Committee (2009). *National Quality Standard for Early Childhood Education and Care and School Age Care.* Canberra: Council of Australian Governments.

Dalli, C., White, J., Rockel, J. & Duhn, I., with Buchanan, E., Davidson, S., Ganly, S., Kus, L. & Wang, B. (2011). *Quality early childhood education for under-two-year-olds: What should it look like? A literature review.* Wellington: New Zealand Ministry of Education.

Department of Education, Employment and Workplace Relations (DEEWR) (2009). *Belonging, being and becoming: The Early Years Learning Framework for Australia.* Canberra: Commonwealth of Australia.

—— (2011). *Early Childhood Policy Agenda.* Retrieved 9 September 2011 from <www.deewr.gov.au/Earlychildhood/Policy_Agenda/Pages/home.aspx>.

Easton, L. (2008). Context: Establishing the environment for professional development. In L. Easton (ed.), *Powerful designs for professional learning* (pp. 1–19). Oxford, OH: National Staff Development Council.

Fiene, R. (2002). *Thirteen indicators of quality child care: Research update.* Washington, DC: Office of the Assistant Secretary for Planning and Evaluation and Health Resources and Services Administration/Maternal and Child Health Bureau, US Department of Health and Human Services.

Hall, G. & Hord, S. (2001). *Implementing change: Pattern, principles and potholes.* Needham Heights, MA: Allyn & Bacon.

Hargreaves, A. & Shirley, D. (2007). *The long and short of raising achievement: Final report of the Evaluation of the Raising Achievement Transformation Learning.* Chestnut Hill, UK: Specialist Schools and Academies Trust.

Johansson, E. (2004). Learning encounters in preschool: Interaction between atmosphere, view of children and of learning. *International Journal of Early Childhood, 1*(36), 9–26.

Johansson, E. & Pramling Samuelsson, I. (2009). To weave together: Play and learning in early childhood education. *Journal of Australian Research in Early Childhood Education, 16*(1), 33–48.

Little, J. (2001). Professional development in pursuit of school reform. In A. Lieberman & L. Miller (eds), *Teachers caught in the action: Professional development that matters* (pp. 23–44). New York: Teachers College Press.

Melhuish, E.C. (2004). *A literature review of the impact of early years provision upon young children, with emphasis given to children from disadvantaged backgrounds: Report to the Comptroller and Auditor General.* London: National Audit Office. Retrieved 10 September 2011 from <www.nao.org.uk/publications/0304/early_years_progress.aspx>.

Ministerial Council on Education, Employment, Training and Youth Affairs (MCEETYA) (2008). *Melbourne Declaration on Educational Goals for Young Australians.* Retrieved 9 September 2011 from <www.curriculum.edu.au/verve/_resources/National_Declaration_on_the_Educational_Goals_for_Young_Australians.pdf>.

National Association for the Education of Young Children (NAEYC) (1991). *Accreditation criteria and procedures.* Washington DC: National Association for the Education of Young Children.

Organization for Economic and Co-operative Development (OECD) (2001). *Starting strong: Early childhood education and care*. Paris: OECD.

—— (2006). *Starting strong II: Early childhood education and care*. Retrieved 9 September 2011 from <www.oecd.org/dataoecd/14/32/37425999.pdf>.

—— (2010). *PISA 2009 results: Volumes II and IV, Overcoming social background: Equity in learning opportunities and outcomes*. Retrieved 9 September 2011 from >www.pisa.oecd.org/document/24/0,3746,en_32252351_46584327_46609752_1_1_1_1,00.html>.

—— (2011). *PF3.2: Enrolment in childcare and pre-schools*. Retrieved 29 December 2011 from <www.oecd.org/dataoecd/46/13/37864698.pdf>.

Pendergast, D. (2006). Fast-tracking middle schooling reform: A model for sustainability. *Australian Journal of Middle Schooling*, 6(2), 13–18.

Pendergast, D., Flanagan, R., Land, R., Bahr, M., Mitchell, J., Weir, K., Noblett, G., Cain, M., Misich, T., Carrington, V. & Smith, J. (2005). *Developing lifelong learners in the middle years of schooling: A report about the practices, process, strategies and structures that best promote 'lifelong learning' and the development of 'lifelong learners' in the middle years of schooling*. Brisbane: University of Queensland.

Pendergast, D. & Main, K. (2011). Middle school reform: Constructing an audit tool for practical purposes. *Australian Journal of Middle Schooling*, 11(2), 4–10.

Pramling Samuelsson, I. & Asplund Carlsson, M. (2009). The playing learning child: Towards a pedagogy of early childhood. *Scandinavian Journal of Education*, 52(6), 623–41.

Rogers, E.M. (2003). *Diffusion of initiatives* (5th ed.). New York: Free Press.

Rusch, E. (2005). Institutional barriers to organizational learning in school systems: The power of silence. *Educational Administration Quarterly*, 41, 83–120.

Sheridan, S., Pramling Samuelsson, I. & Johansson, E. (2009). *Barns tidiga lärande: En tvärsnittsstudie av förskolan som miljö förbarns lärande* [Children's early learning in ECEC]. Göteborg: Acta Universitatis Gothenburgensis.

Siraj-Blatchford, I., Sylva, K., Taggart, B. Sammons, P., Melhuish, E. & Elliot, K. (2003). *Intensive case studies of practice across the foundation stage*. The Effective Provision of Pre-School Education (EPPE) project, Technical Paper 10. London: Institute of Education/DfES.

Stroll, L. & Fink, D. (1996). *Changing our schools*. Buckingham: Open University Press.

Walsh, G. & Gardiner, J. (2006). Teachers' readiness to embrace change in the early years of schooling: A Northern Ireland perspective. *European Early Childhood Education Research Journal*, 14(2), 127–40.

2

The importance of early years education

Margaret Sims

Introduction

International definitions vary, but there is general agreement that early childhood consists of the time from birth until at least entry into primary schooling, although a number of states include children up until the age of eight years in the definition. Early childhood services are also subject to variations in definition, and are often given the name Early Childhood Education and Care (ECEC) services to reflect their holistic nature. The United Nations argues that 'ECEC services and programmes support children's survival, growth, development and learning–including health, nutrition and hygiene, and cognitive, social, emotional and physical development . . .' (UNESCO, 2010, p. 3). This is a broader view than that taken traditionally, where early childhood was often positioned as:

> a contentious add-on to education, rather than an integral part of it; and even more so for childcare because it is intimately tied with cultural notions of women's roles and rights, as well as with views about the robustness of young children and what they might need. (Penn, 2009, p. 22)

Despite this perception, there is growing recognition that early childhood is critical in shaping future outcomes, not just for individual children but, in their roles as future citizens, the long-term well-being of the state. The United Nations recently positioned early childhood as 'a serious education and human capital development issue' (UNESCO, 2010, p. 3). In recognition of this, the Australian government has invested in a range of policy initiatives aimed at enhancing service provision in the early years. These initiatives include the development of national quality standards for early childhood, a child protection framework, a national early childhood development strategy, a plan for Indigenous children and the Early Years Learning Framework. The aim of these initiatives is to guide a 'National effort to improve child outcomes (which) will in turn contribute to increased social inclusion, human capital and productivity in Australia' (COAG, 2009, p. 4). The following sections review the evidence upon which this claim is based.

Experiences in the early years impact on later academic outcomes

Early years experiences are important because they shape long-term academic outcomes. High-quality learning experiences in the early years of life enhance children's cognitive and language skills. These learning experiences may take place in the home or in out-of-home settings. In home settings, it has been found that children experiencing higher quality interactions with their mothers, and who had more literacy resources available to them, performed better in literacy and vocabulary measures at age five (Rodriguez & Tamis-LeMonda, 2011). Education levels of mothers (more than fathers) impact on children's English and maths achievements at age eleven (Melhuish et al., 2010). Melhuish et al. also report that children from families with a higher socio-economic background consistently do better, and children from more affluent neighbourhoods (irrespective of socio-economic status) also do better academically at four and five years of age.

In the out-of-home setting, research confirms that children attending higher quality public kindergartens have better academic, language and social skills than those attending poorer quality kindergartens (Mashburn et al., 2008). Children who have attended early childhood programs tend to perform better in school. The large EPPE study in the United Kingdom (summarised in Sylva et al., 2010) has found that the earlier children attended preschool (under age three), the better their intellectual outcomes (especially in language) when they attended school, and that these benefits accrued irrespective of full-time or part-time attendance. Children attending higher-quality programs (with staff who had higher qualifications) showed greater benefits. These benefits were long lasting, remaining statistically significant after taking into account background factors, until the most recent reports (when the children were aged eleven). Children attending low-quality preschools did not show any advantages in maths and English achievement compared with those who had no preschool experience, but continued to demonstrate better pro-social skills. Children from disadvantaged backgrounds demonstrated the greater gains in achievement. Attendance at a high-quality preschool helped to some extent in buffering children against the negative impacts of attending a lower-quality primary school. A review across ten countries identified consistently that children's language at age seven was better when they had child-directed learning opportunities with more highly qualified adults (Montie et al., 2006).

Experiences in the early years impact on later health and well-being outcomes

Early years experiences are important because they contribute significantly to shaping long-term health and well-being outcomes. Kendall and colleagues (2009) argue that social gradients in children's health and development are so significant that they should be regarded as important as issues such as climate change.

'Social gradients' is a term used in the health literature to identify socio-economic differences in outcomes—specifically, children who are disadvantaged have poorer outcomes than children who are advantaged. For example, research has identified that cardiovascular disease in adulthood is linked to nutritional deficits (commonly associated with reduced access to resources) and subsequent growth impairment in utero (Shonkoff et al., 2009). Social gradients were demonstrated in the Western Australian Raine study (Kendall et al., 2009), where it was shown that experiences of stressful life events in the early years (such as poverty, unemployment and dysfunctional relationships) increased the risk of clinically significant mental health problems. Risk was almost doubled when children were exposed to stressful life events both in utero and in their early years. Experiencing seven or more stressful life events is estimated to create a level of stress similar to that generated by living in a war zone (Silburn et al., 2006), with equally negative outcomes. These experiences of stress in the early years are linked to adult coronary artery disease, chronic pulmonary disease, cancer, alcoholism, depression and drug abuse, mental health problems and cardiovascular risk factors such as obesity. A key stressful life event is associated with membership in a minority group. Minority group placement is associated with an increased risk for chronic health problems (Paradies, 2006), and systemic racism is linked with mental health problems, maladaptive behaviours (such as smoking and substance abuse) and physical health problems (such as hypertension) (Paradies & Williams, 2008).

Considerable focus is now placed on experiences in utero, and how these impact on long-term outcomes. For example, we now know that excessive maternal weight gain in pregnancy increases the risk of offspring obesity in later life. In contrast, children born to mothers who were obese, but had anti-obesity surgery before the pregnancy, were much more likely to have normal weights later in life (Paul, 2010). Foetuses exposed to high levels of air pollution (as in a large city) were more at risk for a range of problems, including heart problems and increased risk of cancer (Paul, 2010). Children whose mothers smoked during pregnancy were at greater risk for substance abuse themselves later in life (Tremblay, 2010). Foetuses of mothers directly exposed to the collapse of the World Trade Center in 2001, and who showed symptoms of post traumatic stress disorder as a result, were found at one year of age to have atypical cortisol levels, increasing the risk that they would later develop PTSD (Yehuda et al., 2005).

High-quality experiences in the early years reduce later disadvantage/social exclusion

Early years experiences are important because key outcomes combine to result in more than improvements in academic, health and well-being. While these outcomes are very important on their own, together they contribute towards reducing social exclusion and disadvantage.

Classic early intervention research, such as that undertaken by Schweinhart and colleagues in the Perry High/Scope intervention (Schweinhart et al., 2005), reports that children attending the early childhood education program provided were, by age 40, more likely to be employed, to have remained in school longer and to have achieved post-school qualifications, to be healthy and to own their own homes. They were less likely to be on welfare, to have committed criminal offences, to have required special education support, to have become pregnant as teenagers or to have used illegal drugs.

The Chicago Child–Parent Centres offered preschool education to low-income children from the age of three, with ongoing support offered up until age nine. The program demonstrates similar outcomes, with increased rates of school completion by age 20 and lower rates of juvenile delinquency. Longer periods of intervention (into the early primary years) were associated with better school achievement (Reynolds et al., 2011). Preschool appeared to advantage children through improving cognitive abilities, offering family and school support, creating a motivational advantage and addressing issues of social adjustment (Reynolds & Ou, 2011).

David Olds' nurse home visiting program is different from a number of the early intervention programs because it begins before the birth of the child. Nurses visit disadvantaged mothers fortnightly in the latter stages of their pregnancy and for the first two years of the infants' lives (Olds et al., 1998). The focus is on both the health and well-being of the family, as well as those of the infant. The program has had a significant impact in improving maternal prenatal health-related behaviours and reducing the risk of child abuse and neglect. Mothers are less likely to have successive unintended pregnancies, and to engage in substance abuse and criminal behaviours. They are also more likely to obtain employment, making them less likely to be welfare dependent.

Social disadvantage and exclusion have an impact not just on the family and the target children but potentially on the descendants of the target children. Najman and colleagues (2004) show that grandfathers' occupation impacted on the cognitive development of children in the Mater Hospital–University of Queensland Study of Pregnancy. They argue that socio-economic status creates a context where children have less opportunity to engage in health-promoting and learning behaviours. The Western Australian Indigenous Child Health Survey found that grandchildren of Stolen Generations children were more likely to have impaired health compared with Indigenous children who did not have a 'stolen child' in their immediate ancestry (Silburn et al., 2006). Children growing up in disadvantaged circumstances become adults who were less able to provide these opportunities for their own children, thus transmitting disadvantage across the generations. Recent epigenetic research provides a possible explanation for such transmission, and this is discussed below.

Quality experiences in the early years are cost-effective

Early years experiences are important because they are cost-effective: changes can easily be made in the early years that have a dramatic impact on long-term outcomes. Cost-benefit analyses identify the outcomes of early education experiences (for example, in monetary terms these include higher tax income and lower welfare costs for the state arising from higher rates of employment). Detailed explanations as to how cost-benefit calculations are made can be found in a recent report from HighScope (2010).

One of the earlier examples of cost-benefit analysis is associated with the Perry High/Scope evaluations. By the time graduates were 40 years of age, the return on investment was calculated at 17:1 (Schweinhart et al., 2005)—that is, for every dollar spent (brought up to today's value) the state benefited by $17 (based on reduced welfare, education, justice and health costs, and increased revenue through employment).

Reynolds and colleagues (2011) reported on the cost-benefit analysis undertaken for the Chicago Child–Parent Centres. The preschool program offered a return on investment of $7.14 for every $1 spent, calculated when the graduates were 20 years of age. Where the intervention program was extended over four to six years, the return on investment was slightly lower (reflecting higher delivery costs of the intervention) at $6.11 per $1 spent. Higher return on investment resulted with a longer-term view of outcomes. When graduates were 26, return on investment was calculated as $10.83 per dollar invested (18 per cent annual return). Males and children from the most disadvantaged families were shown to benefit the most (Reynolds et al., 2011).

The nurse home visiting program recoups the cost of the intervention by the time children are four years of age, mainly through reduced costs associated with ongoing reliance on welfare and subsequent pregnancies. When the focus is on children from disadvantaged backgrounds (who make the most gains as a result of the intervention), costs are recouped four times by the time the children are fifteen years of age (Karoly et al., 2005).

More recently, researchers have investigated the impact of different models of early childhood education on outcomes (HighScope, 2010). In the High/Scope study, a comparison was made between those children who received direct instruction, a High/Scope curriculum and a traditional nursery curriculum. By age fifteen, those who had experienced the High/Scope curriculum were more likely to plan to stay in school longer and less likely to be involved in juvenile delinquency than those who had received direct instruction. Those in the nursery school group were, by age 22, more likely than the direct instruction group to have been arrested or be suspended from work. These results are interpreted to support the need for a child-focused approach (for example, learning through play as identified in the Australian Early Years Learning Framework) rather than a direct instruction approach in early intervention programs.

James Heckman, a Nobel Prize–winning economist, produced a graph illustrating the changing returns on investment based on the timing of the intervention (see <www.heckmanequation.org/content/heckman–101>). This graph is used widely around the world by those arguing the importance of investing in early childhood, as it clearly demonstrates much greater long-term gains achieved by earlier investment (Heckman, 2008). While many agree that earlier investment is more cost-effective in the long term, there is also concern that states do not have the funding to continue existing programs (such as schooling, employment preparation programs and so on) and, at the same time, direct additional funds to early childhood programs. It can, however, be argued that funding early childhood programs is not a matter of finding more money, but simply a matter of reprioritising spending (Sims & Hutchins, 2011). Many years ago now, Arias (2000/01) demonstrated that only 5 per cent of the money spent internationally on military technology and training could have provided basic education, health care, food and water for every human on the planet. That we choose not to spend money in this way is a telling comment on the value accorded to children in our society.

Quality experiences in the early years honour children's rights

Early years experiences are important because it is our obligation, as ethical human beings, to ensure that those who are vulnerable are supported in the best way possible. As a signatory to the UN Convention on the Rights of the Child (CROC), the Australian state has made a commitment to honour children's rights: 'Considering that the child should be fully prepared to live an individual life in society, and brought up in the spirit of the ideals proclaimed in the Charter of the United Nations, and in particular in the spirit of peace, dignity, tolerance, freedom, equality and solidarity . . .' (United Nations, 1989, Preamble). CROC sets out a number of requirements for states to ensure the health, well-being and education of children; as a signatory to the convention, Australia is committed to meeting these requirements (United Nations, 1989):

Article 6: States Parties shall ensure to the maximum extent possible the survival and development of the child.

Article 21(2): The parent(s) or others responsible for the child have the primary responsibility to secure, within their abilities and financial capacities, the conditions of living necessary for the child's development. (3) States Parties, in accordance with national conditions and within their means, shall take appropriate measures to assist parents and others responsible for the child to implement this right and shall in case of need provide material assistance and support programmes, particularly with regard to nutrition, clothing and housing.

Article 24: States Parties recognize the right of the child to the enjoyment of the highest attainable standard of health and to facilities for the treatment of illness and rehabilitation of health. States Parties shall strive to ensure that no child is deprived of his or her right of access to such health care services.

Article 28: States Parties recognize the right of the child to education, and with a view to achieving this right progressively and on the basis of equal opportunity . . .

Article 29: 1. States Parties agree that the education of the child shall be directed to the development of the child's personality, talents and mental and physical abilities to their fullest potential; (b) The development of respect for human rights and fundamental freedoms, and for the principles enshrined in the Charter of the United Nations; (c) The development of respect for the child's parents, his or her own cultural identity, language and values, for the national values of the country in which the child is living; the country from which he or she may originate, and for civilizations different from his or her own; (d) The preparation of the child for responsible life in a free society, in the spirit of understanding, peace, tolerance, equality of sexes, and friendship among all peoples, ethnic, national and religious groups and persons of indigenous origin; (e) The development of respect for the natural environment.

The neurobiological/epigenetic pathway linking the environment and children's outcomes

Early years experiences are important because they impact on the genome, not only shaping the child as a future adult, but also shaping the descendants of the child as well. The study of the relationship between these experiences and their impact on the genome is called epigenetics. Perry and Hambrick (2008, p. 40) argue that:

> of all the experiences throughout the life of an individual, the organising experiences of early childhood have the most powerful and enduring effects on brain organisation and functioning . . . early childhood trauma or maltreatment has a disproportionate capacity to cause significant dysfunction, in comparison with similar trauma or maltreatment later in life.

Early experiences create chemical changes in the body that ultimately result in other chemicals attaching to, or detaching from, the outside of the DNA, altering the expression of the DNA. 'The epigenome is innately plastic and can be programmed or reprogrammed by environmental experiences such as nutrition and stress. (Francis, 2009, p. S197). The chemical pathways involved are those associated with the stress response, which is triggered by a complex array of stressors (such as emotional reactions/fear/anxiety, hunger, thirst, pain, pollutants, drugs/alcohol). Chronic activation of the stress response leads to poor adult outcomes, including poorer health (immune system problems, hypertension problems), shorter life expectancy, behaviour problems (internalising and externalising problems, and the social consequences of these, including drug/alcohol addiction, juvenile delinquency, early school drop-out) and mental health problems (including depression, suicide) (Marshall & Kenney, 2009).

Secure and nurturing relationships have been shown to reduce these stress responses—see Figure 2.1. Research undertaken by Meaney and colleagues with rats illustrates this link. Although we cannot apply research with rats directly to human populations, chemical reactions are universal and their implications for human outcomes are suggestive. Meaney (2001, 2010) showed that rat pups separated from their mothers for long periods of time each day in the first few weeks of life showed significantly greater stress responses in adulthood. Offspring of highly nurturing rat mothers showed a lower stress response throughout life than offspring of low-nurturing mothers. The latter offspring were less healthy in adulthood, had shorter life spans, were less effective problem-solvers and were themselves less-nurturing mothers. Pups born to high-nurturing mothers, but fostered from birth with low-nurturing mothers, grow up to be indistinguishable in their behaviour and characteristics from those pups born to low-nurturing mothers. Conversely, pups born to low-nurturing mothers but fostered at birth with high-nurturing mothers demonstrated positive long-term outcomes. Meaney's work demonstrates the impact of the environment on the genome—the way in which nurturing experiences in the early years impact on lifelong outcomes.

The environment itself contains stressors that impact on parents' ability to offer nurturing experiences to their children. Rats living in highly stressful environments (high levels of predation, poor nutrition) were more likely to be anxious and to be less-nurturing parents, resulting in offspring that themselves were highly anxious and less nurturing. 'Chronic stress increases anxiety and fearfulness and, thus, decreases maternal responsivity, which in turn influences the development of stress reactivity in the offspring' (Meaney, 2001, p. 1181). Many human mothers live in contexts of high stress (poverty, poor nutrition, family violence, drug/alcohol addiction), and the impact of these on their children's neurobiology is significant.

Perry and Hambrick (2008) propose a therapeutic model for working with such children based on an understanding of this impact on neural development. They argue that the heightened stress response evident in children growing up in stressful environments ensures they are in a chronic state of high stress arousal:

> Neglected children can change; however, the process is long, and it requires patience and an understanding of development . . . enrichment or therapeutic services for maltreated children need to be consistent, predictable, patterned and frequent. (Perry & Hambrick, 2008, pp. 37, 38)

Figure 2.1: The epigenetic story

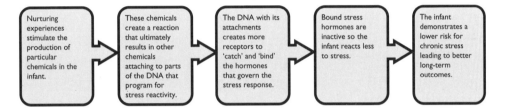

Summary

- The early childhood years increasingly are being recognised as important, and governments around the world are beginning to focus their attention on developing policy and programs to enhance early childhood development. Their reasons for doing so vary, but are generally based on a combination of the following understandings.
- Academic outcomes into adulthood are shaped by experiences in the early years—children growing up in environments rich in learning opportunities do better.
- Health and well-being outcomes into adulthood are shaped by experiences in the early years. Children growing up in health-promoting environments become healthier and better functioning adults.
- Social disadvantage/social exclusion can effectively be addressed by early intervention. The well-being of a nation may best be identified by the well-being of the nation's children.

- Social disadvantage is transmitted across generations, thus intervening to break the transmission impacts on the future well-being of the nation.
- For the state, providing high-quality early intervention is less expensive in the long term than managing the adult problems that arise from poor quality early years experiences. Value for money is particularly evident when early intervention is available to those young children who are most disadvantaged.
- As a signatory to the United Nations Convention on the Rights of the Child, Australia is obligated to ensure that all young children in Australia have appropriate, high-quality experiences in their early years of life. Young children have a right to expect a healthy learning environment that maximises their academic, social, emotional, health and well-being outcomes.
- Neurobiological research, the science of epigenetics, is starting to build understanding of how experiences in the outside world modify the internal world of the child and shape outcomes across generations. Understanding how disadvantage impacts on the genome provides guidance about the most effective strategies for intervening and changing outcomes.

Discussion questions

2.1   How would you answer a politician who argued that the way to address growing disadvantage in your community was to have zero tolerance for crime?

2.2   How could you persuade parents that they are doing one of the most important jobs in the world in rearing their children?

2.3   How do you think you could inspire early childhood professionals to value the work they are doing with early years learners?

2.4   How do you think you might start changing community perceptions about the importance of the early years of life?

References

Arias, O. (2000/01). 2000 Conference Keynote Address: Dr Oscar Arias. *TASH Newsletter, 26/27*(12/1), 13–16.

Council of Australian Governments (COAG) (2009). *Investing in the early years: A national early childhood development strategy.* Canberra: Commonwealth of Australia.

Francis, D. (2009). Conceptualizing child health disparities: a role for developmental neurogenomics. *Pediatrics, 124,* S196–S202.

Heckman, J. (2008). *Schools, skills and synapses.* IZA Discussion Paper no 3515. Bonn: Institute for the Study of Labour (IZA).

HighScope (2010). *The cost-benefit analysis of the Preschool Curriculum Comparison Study through age 23. A final report to the John D. and Catherine T. MacArthur Foundation, Power of Measuring Social Benefits Research Initiative.* Ypsilanti, MI: HighScope.

Karoly, L., Kilburn, R. & Cannon, J. (2005). *Early childhood interventions: Proven results, future promises.* Santa Monica, CA: Rand Corporation.

Kendall, G., van Eekelen, A., Mattes, E. & Li, J. (2009). Children in harm's way: A global issue as important as climate change. *Forum on Public Policy, 1*, 1–17.

Marshall, P. & Kenney, J. (2009). Biological perspectives on the effects of early psychosocial experience. *Developmental Review, 29*, 96–119.

Mashburn, A., Pianta, R., Hamre, B., Downer, J., Barbarin, O., Bryant, D., et al. (2008). Measures of classroom quality in prekindergarten and children's development of academic, language, and social skills. *Child Development, 79*(3), 732–49.

Meaney, M. (2001). Maternal care, gene expression, and the transmission of individual differences in stress reactivity across generations. *Annual Review of Neuroscience, 24*, 1161–92.

—— (2010). Epigenetics and the biological definition of gene x environment interactions. *Child Development, 81*(1), 41–79.

Melhuish, E., Belsky, J. & Barnes, J. (2010). Evaluation and value of Sure Start. *Archives of Disease in Childhood, 95*, 159–61.

Montie, J., Xiang, Z. & Schweinhart, L. (2006). Preschool experience in 10 countries: Cognitive and language performance at age 7. *Early Childhood Research Quarterly, 21*, 313–31.

Najman, J., Aird, R., Bor, W., O'Callaghan, M., Williams, G. & Shuttlewood, G. (2004). The generational transmission of socioeconomic inequalities in child cognitive development and emotional health. *Social Science and Medicine, 58*(6), 1147–58.

Olds, D., Hill, P. & Rumsey, E. (1998). Prenatal and early childhood nurse home visitation. *Juvenile Justice Bulletin*, November, 1.

Paradies, Y. (2006). A review of psychosocial stress and chronic disease for 4th world indigenous peoples and African Americans. *Ethnicity and Disease, 16*(1), 295–308.

Paradies, Y. & Williams, D. (2008). Racism and health. In K. Heggenhougen & S. Quah (eds), *Encyclopedia of Public Health* (pp. 474–83). San Diego, CA: Academic Press.

Paul, A. (2010). Cancer. Heart Disease. Obesity. Depression. Scientists can now trace adult health to the nine months before birth. *Time*, 4 October, 28–33.

Penn, H. (2009). *Early childhood education and care: Key lessons from research for policy makers.* Brussels: European Commission for Education and Culture.

Perry, B. & Hambrick, E. (2008). The neuroseqential model of therapeutics. *Reclaiming Children and Youth, 17*(3), 38–43.

Reynolds, A. & Ou, S.-R. (2011). Paths of effects from preschool to adult well-being: A confirmatory analysis of the Child–Parent center Program. *Child Development, 82*(2), 555–82.

Reynolds, A., Temple, J., White, B., Ou, S.-R. & Robertson, D. (2011). Age 26 cost-benefit analysis of the Child–Parent Center Early Education Program. *Child Development, 82*(1), 379–404.

Rodriguez, E. & Tamis-LeMonda, C. (2011). Trajectories of the home learning environment across the first 5 years: Associations with children's vocabulary and literacy skills at prekindergarten. *Child Development, 82*(4), 1058–75.

Schweinhart, L., Montie, J., Xiang, Z., Barnett, W., Belfield, C. & Nores, M. (2005). *Lifetime effects: The High/Scope Perry Preschool Study through age 40.* Ypsilanti, MI: High/Scope Educational Research Foundation.

Shonkoff, J., Boyce, W. & McEwen, B. (2009). Neuroscience, molecular biology, and the childhood roots of health disparities: Building a new framework for health promotion and disease prevention. *Journal of the American Medical Association 301*(21), 2252–59.

Silburn, S., Zubrick, S., De Maio, J., Shepherd, C., Griffin, J., Mitrou, F., et al. (2006). *The Western Australian Aboriginal Child Health Survey: Strengthening the capacity of Aboriginal children, families and communities.* Perth: Curtin University of Technology and Telethon Institute for Child Health Research.

Sims, M. & Hutchins, T. (2011). *Program planning for infants and toddlers: In search of relationships.* Sydney: Pademelon Press.

Sylva, K., Melhuish, E., Sammons, P., Siraj-Blatchford, I. & Taggart, B. (eds) (2010). *Early childhood matters: Evidence from the Effective Pre-school and Primary Education Project.* London: Routledge.

Tremblay, R. (2010). Cash transfers, stress, DNA, methylation and health. *Bulletin on Early Childhood Development, 9*(2), 1.

United Nations (1989). *Convention on the Rights of the Child with Annex.* Retrieved 20 May 2012 from <http://sithi.org/admin/upload/law/Convention%20on%20the%20Rights%20of%20the%20Child.ENG.pdf>.

United Nations Educational Scientific and Cultural Organisation (UNESCO) (2010). *Concept Paper: The World Conference on Early Childhood Care and Education (ECCE) Building the Wealth of Nations.* Geneva: United Nations.

Yehuda, R., Engel, S., Brand, S., Seckl, J., Marcus, S. & Berkowitz, G. (2005). Transgenerational effects of Post Traumatic Stress Disorder in babies of mothers exposed to the World Trade Center attacks during pregnancy. *Journal of Clinical Endocrinology and Metabolism, 90*(7), 4115–18.

3

The nature of the early years learner

Michael Nagel

Introduction

Since the early 1990s, advances in technology have facilitated an exponential growth in our collective understanding of the human brain. Indeed, much of what we know about the brain has only been revealed in the last couple of decades. Furthermore, an increasingly diverse range of professions interested in child development, education and the way the mind works have offered new and exciting research focusing on how the brain grows, learns and operates. There is also growing consensus that research on brain development is relevant to educational and child-rearing contexts, given that it is now possible to look inside a human brain as it processes stimuli and 'thinks'. This chapter offers a rigorous and robust look at what neuroscience is telling us about the early years learner's brain. Specifically, the information provided details the development of the brain from infancy to the early school years and looks at the implications of this for those who work with young children in an educational context. The chapter also provides educators with a foundational look at the 'nature' of the early years learner in order to situate the best possible practices for nurturing these young minds.

Inside the brain and mind of a child before 'schooling'

As noted above, the last 20 years have seen phenomenal growth in the field of neuroscience and worldwide growth in research and literature on anything and everything about the brain. Many bookstores have numerous volumes of work related to the inner workings of the brain and all things associated with its structures and functions. Universities are now embedding aspects of neuroscience within pre-service teacher education programs. Furthermore, insights into the inner workings of the brain have altered many of our views on child development and learning, and by association aspects of education and 'schooling' (Carew & Magsamen, 2010). Arguably, the early years of learning offer one of the most important contexts for merging neuroscientific research with educational practice, given what is now known about the nature of the early years learner.

Before exploring what is known about neurodevelopment in children, it is significant to note that historically, and depending on the field of expertise, many individuals ardently believed that much brain development was entirely dependent on one's genetic inheritance. Contemporary understandings of the brain now tell us that the nature/nurture dichotomy is rather a moot point, given that brain development hinges on a complex interplay between the genes with which a child is born and his or her experiences, especially during the earliest stages of life (Brazelton & Greenspan, 2000; Healy, 2004; Herschkowitz & Herschkowitz, 2004; Shonkoff, 2010; Shonkoff & Levitt, 2010). This chapter focuses on how the brain grows and develops in the early years. Long before a child enters a formal educational setting, the brain has changed and matured in a number of ways. Much of this maturation occurs in utero, but that is beyond the context of this work. Instead, the following pages explore neural development during two stages: from birth to age four, and then from ages four to eight. The purpose of this approach is twofold. First, while much of the brain matures and changes in the earliest days of life, a child's brain is very 'plastic' and as such continues to mature and evolve as a child begins its formal educational journey. This suggests that educators would do well to understand how the brain might be maturing, given that learning and the brain are linked intimately. However, while the entry into formal schooling marks a major milestone in the life of a child, examining the first few years of growth and development prior to preschool provides a more holistic framework for understanding principles of behaviour and learning at school. Therefore, an appropriate place to begin the journey of looking at the nature of the early years learner is birth.

From the moment of conception to the initial and often tentative steps a child takes into its first formal learning environment, childhood development—and in particular brain development—takes place at a rate that exceeds that in any other stage of life. The brain is the only organ that is not completely developed at birth, and during the first few years of life its capacity to learn and absorb information and stimuli is simply astonishing. Some have described the brain as the most unimaginable thing imaginable, and it is perhaps the most functionally, best-organised and most complex 1.4 kilograms of matter in the universe (Hooper & Teresi, 1986; LeDoux, 1998).

On the eventful day when a child arrives in this world, one of its most obvious characteristics is the sheer size of its head, which is the largest part of the body. At birth, a child will have over 100 billion neurons that have already begun to connect through electrochemical impulses commonly referred to as synapses (Goswami, 2004). Moreover, in the first year of life a child's brain will triple in weight and require a great deal of energy in the form of glucose as it continues to develop its complex array of neural connections (Diamond & Hopson, 1999). These neural connections are formed as the brain responds to stimuli from the environment and lays down connections that, over time and through repetition, may become hardwired. Alternatively, connections that are not repeatedly used are discarded or 'pruned' away through a process known as 'apoptosis' (Diamond & Hopson, 1999; Ratey, 2001; Nagel, 2011). In this sense, 'hardwiring' of the brain may be described as a 'use it or lose it' process.

The hardwiring of the brain can be thought of as a cyclical process: neural connectivity occurs as the brain processes sensory stimulation, which in turn forms the foundation for a brain to continue to develop, and to act and react within the world around it. Harry Chugani (2004), one of the world's leading authorities in neurology and developmental paediatrics, compares the wiring of the brain in the early years of life to that of the early roots of a plant, whereby the sun and rain (environment) help to draw out the unique talents and traits of the individual and a healthy environment ensures continued and vibrant growth. Vibrant growth for a human brain occurs when neural connections are influenced by individual experience. The more repetitive an experience, the greater the opportunity to permanently hardwire those connections. From a neurological standpoint, this process could be thought of as the essence of learning, and overall it is actually a lifelong journey. However, most of the necessary hardwiring for 'normal' functioning occurs naturally in the first four years of life as infants and toddlers engage with the world around them through their five senses (Eliot, 2000; Aamodt & Wang, 2011). For many parents, caregivers and early childhood practitioners, this information may attract only passing interest and beg the question of why this might be important to know in the context of raising and educating children. Quite simply, learning begins to flourish at birth as the brain builds neural pathways *vis-à-vis* experiences in the world; children of all ages therefore require particular stimuli to facilitate their learning and neurological development. The types of stimulation and/or the deprivation of such stimulation are explored in greater detail in the next chapter.

Notwithstanding the rapid development of the brain in the first year of life, it is noteworthy that by the age of two, the brains of toddlers are as active as those of adults, and at age three a child's brain is two and a half times more active than that of an adult, suggesting that young children appear to be biologically geared for learning (Restak, 2001; Howard, 2006). This activity sees the continued development of a complex array of interconnectivity linking important structural components within the brain and facilitating increasingly complex and advanced ways for a child to engage with the world. As the brain matures, so too do numerous other capacities, and the overall process of neural maturation maintains particular timelines and developmental pathways evident in the behaviour and cognitive capacities of early learners. It is therefore important to remember that any suggestion that a child's brain is just a smaller version of an adult brain is patently false. Indeed, such assumptions often contribute to numerous misunderstandings related to child development and educational endeavour—especially when considering overall brain development in the early years and how the structures of the brain operate and mature.

In itself, the human brain is part of the central nervous system, controlling many bodily functions including voluntary activities such as walking and speaking, and involuntary activities such as blinking and breathing. The two hemispheres of the brain are often referred to as the cerebrum, and comprise four lobes that occupy the same space across each hemisphere and surround the limbic system or emotional part of the brain. Although each lobe is specialised for particular functions, they are intimately connected. However, from an educational and learning perspective, the frontal lobes are arguably of more interest than the parietal, temporal and occipital lobes.

Perhaps one of the reasons the frontal lobes—and in particular the prefrontal lobes—attract so much attention with regard to understanding learning and behaviour is that these areas of the brain are widely regarded as the brain's thinking centre—they allow humans to be aware of their thoughts and actions and are also responsible for aspects of memory, higher order thought processes, problem-solving, decision-making, planning, creativity, judgement and language

(Carter, 2000; Goldberg, 2001, 2009; Howard, 2006; Best, Miller & Jones, 2009; Nagel, 2008, 2010). Many researchers suggest that this part of the brain is perhaps the most critical neural region; importantly, it does not fully mature until early adulthood (Giedd et al., 1999; Casey et al., 2000; Ratey, 2001; Sylwester, 2005). In other words, the most advanced mechanisms of the human brain are very immature in early learners, and as such the types of attributes and skills evident in the minds of adults are, for want of a better term, 'childlike'. This is one of the reasons why relying on a child's memory to tend to a list of tasks set out by a parent can often end up in frustration and/or tears.

The limbic system, in turn, sits above the brain stem and harbours our memories and processes emotions. It connects the lower regions of the brain responsible for motor and automatic functions with the higher regions responsible for cognitive thought, and initiates most of our urges that direct us to behave in ways that usually help us to survive (LeDoux, 1998, 2002; Sylwester, 2005; Bloom et al., 2006; Howard, 2006). The limbic system also plays a significant role in attention, sleep, hormones, regulation of bodily functions, smell and the production of most of the chemicals found in the brain (Jensen, 1998; LeDoux, 1998, 2002; Damasio, 1999, 2004; Carter, 2000; Nagel, 2008). The limbic system sits atop and is connected to the brain stem, which monitors many important functions including circulation and respiration but also engages 'fight or flight' mechanisms whenever a threatening situation occurs. It is significant to note that the brain's overall trajectory towards full maturation sees the brain stem and limbic system mature a great deal sooner than the higher order thinking processes found in the pre-frontal lobes of the cerebrum. In an evolutionary context, the fact that our 'fight or flight' mechanisms mature sooner than our higher order thinking tools has ensured human survival. In a day-to-day context, the maturational timeline of the brain also helps to explain why children often have difficulty in mediating heightened emotional responses to particular stimuli; when a child is hungry they may go to extreme emotional measures to ensure they are provided food at that given moment. Moreover, and as noted above, all of the structures of the brain are interconnected and these connections improve in efficiency as we grow older.

One of the reasons why the brain becomes increasingly efficient at moving information from one region to another has to do with an important material known as 'myelin'. Myelin is a white fatty material that grows as a sheath around the axons of neurons, and acts as an insulator and conduit for transmitting information from one neuron to another (Bloom et al., 2006; Howard, 2006). The growth of myelin via 'myelination' facilitates greater opportunities for neural information to be passed quickly, and at birth children have very few myelinated axons. This is one reason why visual acuity and motor coordination are so limited in the early stages of life: the neural networks responsible for facilitating vision and movement are not working fast enough. Furthermore, the brain is not completely myelinated until the third decade of life, and as we grow older different regions of the brain myelinate at different times. For example, when Broca's area—the region of the brain responsible for language production—myelinates, children are then able to develop speech and grammar. These times of myelination have become referred to by neuroscientists as 'learning windows', and importantly myelination does not happen all at once and a healthy brain knows which areas need to be myelinated first (Diamond & Hopson, 1999; Herschkowitz & Herschkowitz, 2004). Moreover, there isn't anything a parent or educator can do to speed this process along, and when each individual child begins his or her formal educational journey there is still a great deal of neural development that will occur.

The developing brain in school

The preceding section offered a cursory examination of important aspects of brain development prior to an early years learner's involvement in formal schooling. When a child enters school, the brain will continue to grow and change and so will a child's cognitive, affective, social and physical skills and attributes. Given a human brain's individual characteristics, dynamic nature and overall complexity, it is rather arduous—if not impossible—to delineate exactly when each structural and functional aspect of the brain will mature in each child. Instead, the following pages identify major neurodevelopmental milestones from ages four to eight, and any resultant advancement in abilities associated with those milestones. It is important to note, however, that while this approach may resemble previous models of stage development found throughout many child development and/or psychology texts, it does so only to highlight the recognised neurological changes in early learners, regardless of social or cultural context. The role of the environment and insights into the impact of nurturing on the brain of early years learners get greater attention in other chapters of this volume; however, it should be apparent from the information presented earlier that the brain changes a great deal from birth to age four. After a child's fourth birthday, neural maturation continues to advance rapidly, and specific capacities and abilities emerge that in turn serve to enhance learning.

By the time a child reaches their fourth birthday, storytelling, make-believe, counting and a range of physical skills are apparent. As they progress towards their fifth birthday, the brain continues to develop and mature, and so too do the skills noted above, as well as many others. Much of the growing advances in the capacities of an early years learner are attributable to changes and maturation of the brain. Table 3.1 presents a framework of changes in the brain from birth to age eight and the resultant changes in skill sets associated with neural maturation. It is important to note, however, that while the table demarcates age as a parameter for development, each child—and indeed each brain—is uniquely different. The information presented therefore offers a broad overview and not a prescription for age-specific attributes. In other words, there is the possibility of substantive overlap and differentiation across and between age groups and attributes whereby a four-year-old and six-year-old can demonstrate similar characteristics. Additionally, it is beyond the scope of this chapter to provide a comprehensive list of all changes from birth to age eight associated with brain maturation, so the table provides insights into those areas of greatest potential interest for educators of early years learners.

Table 3.1   Brain development, birth to eight years

Ages	Neural changes/activity	Associated skills/attributes
Birth to three	At birth the limbic system and brain stem are the most mature regions of the brain.	The brain stem regulates blood pressure, heart rate, body temperature and numerous other important physiological functions. The brain stem and limbic system also work in concert to maintain the survival mechanism known as fight-or-flight.
	Synaptic growth is rampant in the first year of life throughout all regions of the brain. In the first three years of life the brain will produce billions of cells and trillions of synaptic connections via stimulation from the environment.	All aspects of sensory development are enhanced while the sense of touch is most is most pronounced.
	Increased synaptic connections between regions of the limbic system and cerebral cortex become stronger.	The regulation of the numerous survival mechanisms that govern appetite, sleep, alertness, emotional reactivity, attachment, feelings being to develop over time while the emergence of various aspects of memory develop.

continued

Ages	Neural changes/activity	Associated skills/attributes
	The vestibular system and cerebellum develop as motor skills improve.	Development of the vestibular system allows for gradual improvements in balance, spatial orientation, visual gaze, movement and head and body posture. As the cerebellum develops so too does motor coordination, movement and cognition.
	Myelination occurs in key sensory regions of the brain while lateralisation and differentiation of the hemispheres becomes more specialised.	Visual acuity, among other senses, improves while messages from the muscles to the brain allow for the development of gross and then fine motor skills.
	Myelin growth and increased connectivity between the cerebellum and frontal and parietal lobes emerges.	Dramatic gains in visual-motor coordination and higher cognitive processes emerge from one to three years of age.
	Synaptic density between regions of the brain associated with various aspects of language increases.	Increased language skills, improved vocabulary and the emergence of higher order thinking is evident and advances exponentially between one and three years of age.
	Regions of the parietal lobe associated with mathematics begin to develop.	Four-year-olds are able to demonstrate counting, at times in the right order, and this continues to improve.
	Greater dendrite growth occurs in Broca's region in the left temporal lobe in conjunction with increased blood flow in the left hemisphere. Broca's region and Wernicke's area show greater connectivity.	Broca's region is the brain's grammar and syntax area while Wernicke's area is the comprehension centre. Sentences become more grammatically correct and syntax improves. Vocabulary also increases markedly.
	Myelination in the limbic system and frontal lobes continues to accelerate in conjunction with greater dendrite growth in both regions.	Emotions gain greater stability and a child begins to regulate emotions while also demonstrating improvements in memory. Greater connections in the frontal lobes see a growing capacity to link details to events.

Ages	Neural changes/activity	Associated skills/attributes
	Myelination is also continuing in the cerebellum in conjunction with growth changes in the frontal and parietal lobes.	Motor skills improve and visual-motor coordination is evident.
	Neurons that produce acetylcholine appear. The hippocampus and amygdala are creating greater connections within the limbic system and across other regions of the brain.	Acetylcholine is an amino acid that assists in long-term memory. The hippocampus and amygdala are also part of the brain's memory system and as such memories become clearer. After the fourth birthday the emotional part of the brain becomes better connected with the factual/rationale part of the brain (frontal lobes).
Four to six	Regions of the parietal lobe associated with maths begin to develop.	Four-year-olds are able to demonstrate counting, at times in the right order, and this continues to improve.
	Greater dendrite growth occurs in Broca's region in the left temporal lobe in conjunction with increased blood flow in the left hemisphere. Broca's region and Wernicke's area show greater connectivity. Broca's region is the brain's grammar and syntax area, while Wernicke's area is the comprehension centre.	Sentences become more grammatically correct and syntax improves. Vocabulary also increases markedly.
	Myelination in the limbic system and frontal lobes continues to accelerate in conjunction with greater dendrite growth in both regions.	Emotions gain greater stability and the child begins to regulate emotions while also demonstrating improvements in memory. Greater connections in the frontal lobes see a growing capacity to link details to events.
	Myelination is also continuing in the cerebellum in conjunction with growth changes in the frontal and parietal lobes.	Motor skills improve and visual-motor coordination is evident.
	Neurons that produce acetylcholine appear. The hippocampus and amygdala are creating greater connections within the limbic system	The hippocampus and amygdala are also part of the brain's memory system, so memories become clearer. After the fourth birthday,

continued

Ages	Neural changes/activity	Associated skills/attributes
	and across other regions of the brain. Acetylcholine is an amino acid that assists in long-term memory.	the emotional part of the brain becomes better connected with the factual/rationale part of the brain (frontal lobes).
	Dendrite growth continues to increase in Broca's area; however, near the age of six greater dendritic patterns and connections are emerging and become evident in the right hemisphere.	Language skills and vocabulary range continue to improve.
	Electrical activity in the brain as measured by electroencephalograms (EEGs) shows improvements in the synchronisation of neural activity, or what is referred to as 'coherence'.	Because of enhanced 'coherence', the brain is better able to integrate 'past' with 'present'. Children demonstrate a greater understanding of these concepts and begin to articulate that in their conversations.
	Myelination of the corpus callosum (the band of tissue linking the right and left hemispheres) continues, and increases in myelin (white matter) throughout the frontal lobes are evident.	Increases in white matter in children correlate with increased development in various cognitive functions and motor skills. Improvements in reading and comprehension are evident.
	Dopamine levels in the prefrontal cortex of the brain are nearly at the same levels found in adults. Dopamine is a neurotransmitter that assists in focus, concentration, attention and motivation.	Children begin to demonstrate an emerging capacity for setting long-term goals and the pre-frontal cortex plays a prominent role in this behaviour.
	The reticular activating system (RTS) is myelinating extensively and generating greater synaptic connections. The (RTS) performs many functions, but two of the most important are the maintaining of alertness and consciousness.	Improvements in attention and focus become evident.
	The brain uses about 30 per cent of a child's energy via glucose consumption. Highest levels of glucose consumption are evident in the pre-frontal lobes, suggesting that there is a great deal of growth and maturation taking place.	This also serves as a reminder that higher order thought processes such as abstract and analytical thinking will improve with age.

Ages	Neural changes/activity	Associated skills/attributes
Six to eight	The limbic system continues to show increased connectivity and levels of myelin.	Memory strategies begin to develop and six-year-olds begin to demonstrate specific strategies for remembering things rather than repeating information over and over again out loud, as is evident in younger children.
	Myelination is also increasing in the posterior (back) of the corpus callosum, where the temporal and parietal lobes are linked.	The connection between these lobes facilitates greater comprehension and word meaning skills. Significant improvements in reading and increasing vocabulary skills are evident.
	Around the age of seven, synaptic density in the frontal lobes peaks.	Connections between the frontal lobes and limbic system have multiplied significantly, leading to better impulse control, improved ability to plan, increased understanding and acceptance of responsibility, and greater independence. When a child enters adolescence, the frontal lobes undergo a second phase of development and greater refinement.
	After age six, growth in Broca's region in the right hemisphere surpasses that of the left hemisphere. The right hemisphere of the brain is often described as the artistic, creative and esoteric hemisphere.	Greater growth in Broca's region results in improvements in reading fluency, along with greater connections to the emotional and prosodic aspects of language; irony and sarcasm begin to be understood and used.
	Dopamine levels continue to rise and the brain continues to use a substantive amount of the body's energy stores.	As noted above, dopamine is important for motivation and attention and by age eight, goal-setting behaviour has improved and is readily used when appropriate.
	Many early experiences have now been encoded in long-term memory throughout various regions of the brain, so automaticity of early skills is evident.	Now that many skills have become automatic (e.g. decoding words and rudimentary writing), the brain is free to focus on content and comprehension. This leads to a greater development of and reliance on memory for learning new tasks.

continued

Ages	Neural changes/activity	Associated skills/attributes
	Accelerated growth of the pre-frontal cortex begins. The brain will reach about 90 per cent of its adult weight by age eight. Overall brain connectivity continues to increase, and by a child's eighth birthday much of a brain's interconnectivity is complete.	During the first eight years of life, brain maturation can be characterised as a slow and steady journey. Children will now have marked increases across all developmental areas. Motor maturity, emotional control and advanced cognitive functions are evident. The brain now prepares for a stage of refinement and restructuring through adolescence.

Sources: Adapted from the works of Chugani (1999); Diamond & Hopson (1999); Eliot (2000); Giedd et al. (1999); Casey et al. (2000); Bergen & Coscia (2001); Herschkowitz & Herschkowitz (2004); Hannaford (2005); Kagan & Herschkowitz (2005); Berk (2006); Sprenger (2008).

The information presented in Table 3.1 offers an overview of some of the major neurological developmental milestones children experience at a time when they begin to move through formal educational settings. The aim is to give the reader some understanding of the complex nature of the early years learner's brain development. An understanding of this sort of information provides a framework for considering how to maximise learning opportunities within an educational context. This approach also builds on a long history of work in developmental psychology and research conducted by numerous pre-eminent theorists, psychologists and educationalists, and supports those earlier works with contemporary neuroscientific findings. Arguably, in an era of increased understanding of the human brain, such information is not only invaluable for educators but may also be considered a fundamental platform for developing learning environments that match the needs and skills of the early years learner. This sentiment is encapsulated best by Berninger and Richards (2002, p. 3), who note that 'the mind is the brain at work . . . we suspect that educational practice might also become more effective if grounded in a scientifically supported conceptual framework integrating neural, cognitive, linguistic and developmental science rather than a theoretical pedagogical procedures'.

This chapter has focused on the 'nature' of the early years learner. The following chapter examines the interplay between genetics and the environment by looking at the 'nurture' of the early years learner.

Summary

- This chapter provided a general overview of brain development from birth to age eight.
- The chapter looked at some of the brain's most important structures and the highly complex nature of its neural hardwiring.
- An overview provided the reader with a more holistic understanding of how the brains, and by association minds, of early years learners grow and develop.
- Contemporary interdisciplinary research suggests that early childhood educators should have some understanding of the 'science' of early childhood development. This has occurred as a result of an explosion of research in neurobiology identifying the extensive interactions between nature and nurture, and the recognition of the need for a highly skilled workforce to enhance educational endeavour while supporting healthy overall development.

Discussion questions

3.1 For some, an understanding of brain development may appear to be outside the realm of the required expertise of an educator. Given the information provided in the chapter, can you construct an argument to the contrary, and identify how such knowledge may inform your practice?

3.2 With regard to a child's behaviour, what might be some of the implications of the fact that the survival and emotional part of the brain matures long before the higher order thinking regions of the brain? Can you think of some real-life examples where children's emotions override the thinking part of the brain that is not fully mature until adulthood?

3.3 Many developmental neuropsychologists suggest that one of the most important things parents and educators can do with regard to healthy brain development is maintain as many routines as possible. Do you agree or disagree? Please support your ideas using the information from the chapter.

3.4 Given the complex nature of the brain and how it changes from ages four to eight, it is not surprising that developmental trajectories show a great deal of variability across individuals of the same age. Discuss the implications of this when preparing a learning environment and/or planning any type of activity. As a start, you might begin by considering how an understanding of early brain development might assist you in developing your own repertoire of practices.

References

Aamodt, S. & Wang, S. (2011). *Welcome to your child's brain: How the mind grows from conception to college.* New York: Bloomsbury.

Bergen, D. & Coscia, J. (2001). *Brain research and childhood education: Implications for educators.* Olney, MD: Association for Childhood Education International.

Berk, L. (2006). *Child development,* 7th ed. Boston: Allyn & Bacon.

Berninger, V.W. & Richards, T.L. (2002). *Brain literacy for educators and psychologists.* San Diego, CA: Elsevier.

Best, J.R., Miller, P.H. & Jones, L.L. (2009). Executive function after age 5: Changes and correlates. *Developmental Review, 29*(3), 180–200.

Bloom, F.L., Beal, M.F. & Kupfer, D.J. (2006). *The DANA guide to brain health: A practical reference from medical experts.* New York: DANA Press.

Brazelton, T.B. & Greenspan, S.I. (2000). *The irreducible needs of children: What every child must have to grow, learn and flourish.* Cambridge, MA: Perseus.

Carew, T.J. & Magsamen, S.H. (2010). Neuroscience and education: An ideal partnership for producing evidence-based solutions to guide 21st century learning. *Neuron, 67*(5), 685–8.

Carter, R. (2000). *Mapping the mind.* London: Orion.

Casey, B.J., Giedd, J.N. & Thomas, K.M. (2000). Structural and functional brain development and its relation to cognitive development. *Biological Psychology, 54,* 241–57.

Chugani, H.T. (1999). PET scanning studies of human brain development and plasticity. *Developmental Neuropsychology, 16*(3), 379–81.

—— (2004). Fine tuning the baby brain. *Cerebrum, 6*(3), 1–14.

Damasio, A. (1999). *The feeling of what happens: Body and emotion in the making of consciousness.* New York: Harcourt.

——(2004). Emotions and feelings: A neurobiological perspective. In A.S.R. Manstead, N. Frijda & A. Fischer (eds), *Feelings and emotions: The Amsterdam Symposium (Studies in Emotion and Social Interaction)* (pp. 49–57). Cambridge: Cambridge University Press.

Diamond, M. & Hopson, J. (1999). *Magic trees of the mind: How to nurture your child's intelligence, creativity, and healthy emotions from birth through adolescence.* New York: Penguin Putnam.

Eliot, L. (2000). *What's going on in there? How the brain and mind develop in the first five years of life.* New York: Bantam.

Giedd, J.N., Blumenthal, J., Jeffries, N.O., Castellanos, F.X., Liu, H., Zijdenbos, A., Paus, T., Evans, C. & Rapoport, J.L. (1999). Brain development during childhood and adolescence: A longitudinal MRI study. *Nature Neuroscience, 2*(10), 861–3.

Goldberg, E. (2001). *The executive brain: Frontal lobes and the civilized mind.* Oxford: Oxford University Press.

——(2009). *The new executive brain: Frontal lobes in a complex world.* Oxford: Oxford University Press.

Goswami, U. (2004). Neuroscience and education. *British Journal of Educational Psychology, 74,* 1–14.

Hannaford, C. (2005). *Smart moves: Why learning is not all in your head,* 2nd ed. Salt Lake City, UT: Great River Books.

Healy, J. (2004). *Your child's growing mind: Brain development and learning from birth to adolescence.* New York: Broadway Books.

Herschkowitz, N. & Herschkowitz, E.C. (2004). *A good start to life: Understanding your child's brain and behaviour from birth to age 6.* New York: Dana Press.

Hooper, J. & Teresi, D. (1986). *The 3 pound universe: Revolutionary discoveries about the brain—from chemistry of the mind to the new frontiers of the soul.* New York: G.P. Putnam's Sons.

Howard, P.J. (2006). *The owner's manual for the brain: Everyday applications from mind-brain research,* 3rd ed. Austin, TX: Bard Press.

Jensen, E. (1998). *Teaching with the brain in mind.* Alexandria, VI: Association for Supervision and Curriculum Development.

Kagan, J. & Herschkowitz, N. (2005). *A young mind in a growing brain.* Mahwah, NJ: Lawrence Erlbaum.

LeDoux, J. (1998). *The emotional brain: The mysterious underpinnings of emotional life.* New York: Simon & Schuster.

—— (2002). *The synaptic self: How our brains become who we are.* New York: Penguin.

Nagel, M.C. (2008). *It's a girl thing.* Melbourne: Hawker-Brownlow Education.

—— (2010). The middle years learner's brain. In N. Bahr & D. Pendergast (eds), *Teaching middle years: Rethinking curriculum, pedagogy and assessment,* 2nd ed. (pp. 86–100). Sydney: Allen & Unwin.

—— (2011). Student learning. In R. Churchill, P. Ferguson, S. Godinho et al., *Teaching—Making a Difference* (pp. 68–105). Brisbane: John Wiley.

Ratey, J.J. (2001). *A User's Guide to the Brain: Perception, Attention and the Four Theatres of the Brain.* New York: Vintage.

Restak, R. (2001). *Mozart's brain and the fighter pilot: Unleashing your brain's potential.* New York: Three Rivers Press.

Shonkoff, J.P. (2010). Building a new biodevelopmental framework to guide the future of early childhood policy. *Child Development, 81*(1), 357–67.

Shonkoff, J.P. & Levitt P. (2010). Neuroscience and the future of early childhood policy: Moving from why to what and how, *Neuron, 67*(5), 689–91.

Sprenger, M. (2008). *The developing brain: Birth to age eight.* Thousand Oaks, CA: Corwin Press.

Sylwester, R. (2005). *How to explain a brain: An educator's handbook of brain terms and cognitive processes.* Thousand Oaks, CA: Corwin Press.

4

The nurture of the early years learner

Michael Nagel

Introduction

One of the most important concepts emerging from advances in neuroscience is the intimate role a child's environment has on overall development. For young children, all aspects of their development—including neurological, social, emotional, behavioural, physical and moral—evolve at the nexus of experience and environment. Evolving concurrently, and central to the role of the environment in nurturing the early years learner, are the myriad relationships children negotiate each day. This chapter aims to enhance educational environments for young children by bridging the nature/nurture dichotomy so often articulated as opposing forces. To achieve this, the chapter examines the wealth of contemporary evidence demonstrating the integral role healthy relationships play in a child's overall development and looks at how the interactive influences of genes and experience literally shape the architecture of the developing brain, which in turn shapes how children engage with the world. This approach acknowledges that healthy development is a foundation for community development and economic development, as capable children become the foundation of a prosperous and sustainable society. More importantly, this chapter embodies the beliefs of the esteemed developmental psychologist Urie Bronfenbrenner (2005), who notes that 'in order to develop normally, a child needs the enduring irrational involvement of one or more adults in care of and in joint activity with that child. In short, *somebody has got to be crazy about that kid.*' (2005, p. 262)

A neurodevelopmental understanding of nurture

> It is the most fantastic and provocative discovery to come out of the world's neuro-science laboratories. An infant's brain thrives on feedback from its environment. It wires itself into a thinking and emotional organ from things it experiences—the sounds, sights, touches, smells, and tastes that come its way, and the important give-and-take interactions with others. (Kotulak, 1997, p. ix)

The previous chapter provided an opportunity to look at how the human brain grows and matures from conception to age eight. However, other important considerations related to overall brain maturation and development lie within the context of how the environment can impact on neural development as a child gets older. In this chapter, the word 'environment' is taken to mean the familial, social and educational contexts in which children are immersed during the first eight years of their lives. In essence, a child's environment is their 'lifeworld,' and the interactions between a child and the environment facilitated through 'nurturing' are not simply an interesting feature of brain development but an integral and absolute requirement of such development. This is particularly important when considering that while the number of neurons in the brain remains relatively stable until a child enters pubescence, the number of synapses increases markedly in the first three to four years of life and much of this increase is related to the experiences a child has each day (Shore, 1997; Diamond & Hopson, 1999; Shonkoff & Phillips, 2000). Groundbreaking research conducted in the late 1980s revealed how important experiences are in terms of brain development, and showed that in the first few years of life the brain actually expects some types of experiences and depends on others (Greenough et al., 1987).

Since the publication of the findings in the research noted above, notions of the brain 'expecting' or 'depending on' particular experiences for neural stimulation have been well documented and have become widely accepted by both neuro-scientists and child development experts as fundamental and important aspects of synapses formation, overall brain development and learning (e.g. see Nelson, 1999, 2000; Eliot, 2000; Healy, 2004; Bjorkland, 2005; Kagan & Herschkowitz, 2005;

Bloom et al., 2006). Experience-expectant neural development relates to the types of sensory stimulation alluded to in the previous chapter, whereby the brain 'expects' what might be called ordinary experiences to hardwire for particular capacities. For example, barring any medical difficulties or physical impairments, a child's visual nervous system will develop normally from birth onwards as they look at people and objects each day. This type of stimulation (seeing things) is quite sufficient for ensuring that the brain's neural mechanisms for sight develop normally, and in fact it appears that newborns enter the world prewired for certain abilities requiring only certain stimuli to develop normally (Bjorkland, 2005). Conversely, depriving a child's brain of the stimulation it expects can result in long-term or permanent impairments (Nelson, 2000).

Unlike those experiences a child's brain expects, experience-dependent stimulation can best be described as those adaptive processes arising out of the specific contexts and unique features of an environment that contribute to the additional growth of synapses and neural hardwiring. More simply stated, experience-dependent processes are those things children learn as they engage with the world around them, which in turn give rise to individual differences across all development domains. Therefore, the fundamental difference between the two processes noted above is that experience-expectant processes will generally apply to all children, while experience-dependent processes can be far more individual-istic in type, frequency and duration (Greenough et al., 1987; Greenough & Black, 1992; Black et al., 1998; Bjorkland, 2005). Experience-dependent processes are the types of stimulation that may be described as 'learning' or 'nurturing' experiences, and they require greater elaboration in terms of 'normal' brain maturation. Such elaboration offers more informed understanding related to providing the optimum opportunities for nurturing the early years learner.

Providing opportunities for children to learn is arguably not as complex as it might seem, or as it is portrayed in some contexts. From birth onwards, children engage with the world in increasingly complex ways, and as they do they are actually 'feeding' their brains via sensory stimulation through the enriched environments provided to them. However, this basic understanding of the nexus between environmental stimulation and brain development has also become part of a worrying trend with regard to the word 'enriched'. In itself, the term 'enriched' does not mean to do more with, or to, a child or 'hyperstimulate' them on a pathway to improved academic performance. Indeed, there are many people and companies currently promoting educational toys, tools and learning programs as avenues for building 'better' brains or enhancing intellectual prowess *vis-à-vis* enrichment. Promotion and advocacy of this type of enrichment should continuously be scrutinised rather than embraced, given what we know about the brain, maturation and enrichment.

Understanding the emergence of an expanding marketplace with a focus on improving a child's brain and mind via environmental enrichment can be traced back to studies done with non-humans. In these studies, researchers found that rats who grew up in enriched environments had more noticeable changes in some neurotransmitters in the brain than those rats who did not have the same measures of stimulation; subsequently, enriched environments were shown to have helped to increase synaptic density and the overall size of the cerebral cortex in rats (Rosenzweig et al., 1962; Renner & Rosenzweig, 1987). However, an important consideration in this work is what the word 'enriched' might actually mean.

In the studies done with rats, enriched environments were cages with numerous toys, spinning wheels and tunnels—or what could be described as Disneyland for rodents. The other rats in those studies lived in dull cages without any of the opportunities to play with the toys or apparatuses mentioned. It is important to emphasise the word 'dull', as other studies indicate that rats that grow up in their natural environments—not 'enriched' or 'dull'—and experience the types of challenges they could only encounter outside of any cage have bigger brains with greater synaptic connectivity than lab-enriched rats (Healy, 2004). In other words, contrived enrichment produced better results than dull environments, but was not necessarily as 'enriching' as what had occurred in the 'natural' environment. Further to that, and in terms of 'enriching' a child's environment, the term 'enriched environment' is often used as a polemic to the inferior characteristics of an 'impoverished environment', without any consideration of what might lie within that continuum. Currently, the available evidence suggests that environments somewhere in between impoverished and enriched are perfectly adequate for normal healthy development and learning to occur. To date, there has been scant scientific evidence to support any notion that special 'stimulation' or 'enrichment' activities beyond normal growth-promoting experiences lead to some measure of 'advanced' brain development (Shonkoff & Phillips, 2000; Shonkoff, 2010). Therefore, in order to move beyond oversimplified notions of enrichment or agendas of increased stimulation—and bearing in mind that learning is indeed a lifelong process—it is important to examine the types of environments and experiences young children need as early years learners.

Nurturing the mind of the early years learner before formal 'schooling'

As noted above and in the preceding chapter, sensory stimulation is a very important aspect of neurodevelopment within the first year of life, and forms the basis of early nurturance. Whenever an infant hears, sees, touches, smells or tastes something for the first time, the brain sets about building neural connections related to that experience. Repeated sensory experiences then lend themselves to the hard-wiring of particular connections—or what might be referred to as 'learning'. For any measure of learning to occur, the brain requires varying forms and degrees of stimulation. At the risk of appearing repetitive, it is important to emphasise that the lack, omission or deprivation of early environmental stimuli has the potential for lifelong difficulties. Understandably, then, one might ask what constitutes an appropriate environment for brain development in the first year of life.

It may appear to be self-evident, but it is important to note from the outset that from birth—and indeed throughout childhood and adolescence—safe, secure, supportive and loving environments are integral to all aspects of development. While learning is an important feature of the brain, in the earliest years of life the brain's fundamental focus is survival, and as such responding to a child's needs is of paramount concern. Even the simple act of not providing adequate nutrition can have long-term ramifications. Indeed, good nutrition is perhaps one of the most fundamental priorities for healthy brain development. A child's brain is growing rapidly and requires a great deal of energy. The developing brain is also more vulnerable to nutrient insufficiency, and certain nutrients have greater effects on brain development than others. Recent studies, for example, have indicated that adequate iron is important for both myelination and for specific development of regions of the hippocampus that contribute to memory (Healy, 2004; see also Lozoff, 2000; Beard & Connor, 2003; Georgieff, 2007). There are numerous other nutrients that are important and, given how much energy the brain utilises, it is important that children receive a diet that is diverse in content and nutritionally rich.

Meeting survival needs through the provision of a safe and secure environment where the requisite necessities of life, including food and water, are of paramount importance resonates well with the works of child development specialists across many years of research. Importantly, the first few years of life rely on other important factors and practices, most of which have developed from trial and error, intuition and as a result of many generations of child-rearing. In an era of mind/

brain science, intuition increasingly is being supported by empirical studies that have provided further insights related to neural stimulation during the first four years of life, and the role of the five senses in this process.

As adults, many of us take our senses for granted without realising how important they were in the earliest stages of our lives. The most fundamental purpose of all of our senses is to detect and discriminate between the myriad sensations with which the human body is bombarded each day. This process is hugely important, as it assists in supporting vital life functions. While all of our senses are present at birth, they do require particular types and amounts of stimulation in order to develop fully. Generally speaking, sight, hearing, taste, touch and smell will all develop along a normal neurological and physiological trajectory through the everyday interactions infants and children have within their home and outside environments. A child's sense of touch will develop as it feels its way around and comes into contact with a variety of objects each day. Importantly, the brain appears to have an innate and predetermined program for the full development of a child's sensory system, and as long as this sensory road map is intact at birth it will continue to evolve through experience. Parents and caregivers play a role in this process through the day-to-day interactions they have with children. For example, attending and interacting with children by touching and talking will directly impact on language, emotion and overall cognitive development (Stamm, 2008; Medina, 2010; Aamodt & Wang, 2011). In other words, the foundations for nurturing a healthy mind are laid primarily through social interactions in environments that are safe, secure, consistent and predictable.

As noted above, a child develops, thrives and learns in a social context characterised as safe, secure, consistent and predictable. Emotional regulation, or the capacity to monitor one's own emotions and those of other individuals, has been associated with sensitivity to a child's needs, security, encouragement, meaningful praise, cognitive support, support for autonomous behaviour, a sense of predictability, structure and routine, while criticism, coldness, indifference to needs, physical or verbal control and a lack of structure or routine have been associated with poor emotional regulation (Stamm, 2008; Willingham, 2011). Concomitantly, social engagement fosters language development that is enhanced not only when adults talk to children but also when adults respond to children. Study after study tells us that from the earliest days of babbling to the construction of grammatically correct sentences, a child's language skills improve when those around them respond verbally and also non-verbally through facial mannerisms (e.g. see Kuhl, 2004, 2007; Faull & McLean-Oliver, 2010).

While engaging in conversations with children is an important nurturing activity, so too is the provision of opportunities for children to explore and play, given that the brain thrives on, and facilitates, movement. As a child's muscles grow and strengthen, they become more physically active in the world around them—which, in a cyclical fashion, enhances overall brain development. Motor skills are an integral tool for learning about the social and physical environment, and an environment that safely allows for all aspects of movement is one that enhances all aspects of development. Indeed, physical/motor development are key pillars for understanding and working with young children.

In itself, and compared with other mammals, motor maturation is a rather slow developmental process in humans because motor circuits in the human brain are incredibly complex (Eliot, 2000). As noted above, much of a child's early learning and development occurs through the human sensory system; however, a great proportion of the information infants and young children receive in the early stages of life is a one-way street of sensory stimulation and interpretation. A great deal of feedback from the environment as a child grows and begins to move about is necessary for the development of the motor circuits in the brain, and the pace of neuromuscular maturation sets important limits on when various motor skills emerge (Eliot, 2000; Hannaford, 2005). An important mind–body connection is evident in the fact that as muscles grow so too does myelin, which improves neural communication, allowing signals from the motor cortices of the brain to travel more rapidly and efficiently to muscles in the legs and hands (Herschkowitz & Herschkowitz, 2004). Between a child's first and second birthdays, a great deal of myelin growth occurs in areas that help connect the various nerve fibres which facilitate motor development and movement, and children begin to move from not being able to sit on their own to walking and exploring the world.

The importance of motor development and movement is not confined to something that only exercises the body but might literally exercise the brain as well. Advances in motor development at the nexus of brain maturation facilitate the development of the vestibular system and cerebellum (Sprenger, 2008). The vestibular system is a highly complex sensory system that continually bombards the brain with information to assist in balance, spatial orientation, visual gaze, movement, and maintaining head and body posture (Cullen & Roy, 2004; Hannaford, 2005; Smith et al., 2010). The cerebellum is another very important region of the brain that is responsible for a number of functions linked to motor coordination, movement and cognition (Diamond, 2000; Berninger & Richards, 2002; Herschkowitz & Herschkowitz, 2004; Sylwester, 2005). This is one of the reasons why people often comment that they do their best thinking when they go for a walk: not only are they exercising the body, but they are also exercising the mind via the cerebellum. It is also important to note that extended physical activity through regular exercise improves aerobic fitness. Importantly, studies have identified a positive correlation between aerobic fitness in children and improved perceptual skills, verbal ability, mathematical ability, school readiness, attention, self-control and aspects of memory, with some of the strongest correlations occurring in children between the ages of four and seven (Sibley & Etnier, 2003). This is an important reason for ensuring that children are provided with opportunities to move and explore the world, and this becomes increasingly important when children enter formal schooling and expand on the social interactions around them.

Nurturing the mind of the early years learner at school

It is important to note from the outset that in relation to nurturing the early years learner in school environments, the following discussion does not offer a prescription or template for pedagogic endeavour. Various other chapters in this volume attend to the pedagogical and didactic frameworks appropriate for children in the early years. What follows, then, is a look at what neuroscience tells us are important factors for ensuring that school environments offer the best possible opportunities for learning in the early years, and also what might hinder those same opportunities. These factors are important considerations for early learning centres, kindergartens, preschools and/or Foundation Year, and focus on important considerations related to the brain after four years of age.

At the risk of appearing somewhat repetitive, it is important to note that discussions related to how to positively nurture the minds of children must continually recognise that opportunities for learning expand considerably as children engage with new people and new environments. It is equally important, however, to remember that when a child enters any notion of formal 'schooling', they arrive ready to learn but must do so in developmentally appropriate ways that are structured around the best available evidence related to learning and teaching. Historically, various experts across a range of disciplines involved in child development have argued for developmentally appropriate educational endeavours. In a new era of mind-brain science, those positions are being reinforced and further informed. This is particularly important given current educational climates related to enrichment, accountability and standardisation of curriculum.

One of the most fascinating contributions neuroscientific research has provided to educationalists was touched on briefly in the previous chapter and is related to the white fatty material known as myelin. If you recall, the more myelin that is present, the better the brain communicates across various regions, and when a region of the brain is myelinating it is highly receptive to particular stimulation (otherwise referred to as 'learning windows'). For example, the window for learning a language opens prior to birth and continues until roughly eleven years of age. That is not to say that an adult cannot learn another language, given that the window never closes; however, if a particular education system believes that the acquisition of a second language is important, then the introduction and opportunities for engaging in another language should probably happen long before children are entering the last phases of primary school. The concept of learning windows is accessible in a wide range of studies and literature, is gaining growing recognition as part of children's developmental trajectory and may prove useful in terms of curriculum decision-making (e.g. see Herschkowitz & Herschkowitz, 2004; Hirsch-Pasek & Golinkoff, 2004; Nagel, 2011).

While learning windows are important, it is equally important to remember that, in themselves, learning windows should not be used as evidence or fodder for unsupported notions of enrichment. Misguided notions of enrichment were discussed earlier, but are worth revisiting in terms of overall educational endeavour. This is particularly true given the emergence of specific discourses suggesting that if experience and activity are indeed significant factors in neural development, then surely the earlier the stimulation via enrichment the greater the propensity for enhanced learning and academic success. However, while science continues to inform us that the environment helps shape the brain, it is also quick to note that each brain—and consequently each child—is unique, and that trying to force a learning window open too soon can be very problematic. Therefore, nurturing an early years learner in school must take into account individual differences, circumstances and outside influences. The esteemed psychologist Urie Bronfenbrenner offers a bioecological framework for taking into account the myriad influences that impact on child development that is beyond the context of this chapter but worthy of note here for further reference and exploration (Bronfenbrenner, 1979, 1989; see also Bronfenbrenner & Morris, 2006).

Another way of thinking about how enrichment might be problematic can be found anecdotally through a small experiment, and through considering what is likely to happen when children are introduced to writing utensils too early. First, and by way of demonstration, fold your arms across your chest as if showing some measure of dissatisfaction. Now reverse the position of your arms as quickly as you can. For most people this simple act is cumbersome and often requires not only some degree of manual dexterity but also some concerted thinking to reconfigure one's arms. The reason for this is that very early in life you would have found a way to fold your arms that has become habitual and potentially hardwired into your brain, and when asked to do something contrary it becomes problematic, difficult and may even be frustrating. Now think of what happens when a young child is asked to engage in writing activities and hold a pen or pencil designed for the manual dexterity of an adult and beyond the early motor skills of a child. Quite often, a child who is introduced to penmanship too early has 'incorrect' pencil grip neurologically hardwired to the extent that when an educator or parent aims to correct this it becomes very difficult, if not impossible. In this case, the brain is being asked to 'unlearn' something already programmed because the 'learning window' was forced open too early. Moreover, if something as simple as pencil grip can be hampered by engaging in activities too soon, it is also worth considering what might happen to children who, in the early years of their educational lives, engage in cognitive endeavours beyond the developmental timetable of their brain. An equally important consideration is what any misguided agendas of enrichment or acceleration might do to a child's emotional development.

It is not possible to enrich or accelerate any degree of emotional maturation, since the limbic system has its own developmental timeline. With that in mind, a further issue related to enrichment and academic excellence concerns how we ensure that enrichment activities do not engulf a child in undue stress beyond their young brain's capacity for coping with any pressure associated with such activity. For some children, too much too soon can lead to stress-related anxieties that actually turn off thinking processes. Such considerations must be part of the craft of each and every educator, ensuring that timing is everything and that experiences are developmentally appropriate for the positive nurturing of young minds.

In an educational context, the nurturing of an early years learner starts with the provision of an environment where children are afforded opportunities to explore freely, self-regulate their behaviour and encouraged to ask questions. Howard Gardner, renowned educator and Professor of Cognition and Education at the Harvard Graduate School of Education, advises that educators carefully observe students and that in the early stages of a child's school life they forget about any formal testing or assessment (Gardner, 2011). Observing also means allowing young children to experience learning through the random appropriation of bits and pieces of information. That is why 'play' is such an important component of formal and informal learning: individual experience fosters new brain growth and refines existing brain structures, and there is nothing more naturally individual for children than opportunities to learn via playing.

Across educational and child development fields, play generally is recognised as an important aspect of early childhood pedagogy. Chapter 11 is dedicated to exploring the contribution of play to the early years experience. However, the role of play is often misconstrued, and its importance in terms of overall neurological development is not well understood. In this regard, the word 'play' may not receive the elevated status it deserves, and in some circles it may be criticised as being devoid of academic rigour. It is therefore significant to identify the importance of play to overall development and once again note the potential limitations of having children engage in activities that are beyond their level of readiness.

One of the most prominent points related to play and overall development is the volume of research showing that children do better academically and socially throughout the school lives when they come from home and early learning environments that have provided a great deal of opportunity to explore and play (Eliot, 2000; Fisher et al., 2008). Studies also tell us that open-ended or self-directed play is linked to better language and problem-solving abilities, expanded creative endeavour, better social skills, enhanced memory capacities and less stress in children (Medina, 2010). From an educational and developmental perspective, then, one might ask how play can be so beneficial.

One of the simplest, and perhaps least acknowledged, aspects of the importance of play is that play, generally speaking, is fun. When children—and adults, for that matter—engage in playful behaviour, it is usually pleasurable; in turn, this activates a number of regions of the brain that lead to the release of powerful chemicals, which not only contribute to repetitive behaviours but also facilitate learning at a synaptic level (Stamm, 2008; Aamodt & Wang, 2011). The importance of repetition was noted in the previous chapter, but as a reminder it is significant to note that through repetition, synaptic connections are strengthened. Greater connectivity means the brain can spend greater energy on new learning and refinement of other synapses—practice not only makes perfect, it also makes permanent! Moreover, when children repeat particular activities due to pleasurable stimulation, they are more likely to remember and learn from those repetitive behaviours. Importantly, children also learn what they do and don't like through play. Trial and error, problem-solving, imagination and creative endeavour, language skills and most other aspects of overall development are enhanced through play. Importantly, though, some types of play appear to be more neurologically beneficial than others when it comes to learning and overall development.

As noted earlier, many studies have identified the importance of open-ended play and self-directed activities. It is also important to remember that play is a multi-dimensional construct that varies across age, time, culture and context, and various conceptualisations of play have led to research linking play activities to a diverse range of developmental benefits (Fisher et al., 2008). The social and emotional benefits of play are evident whenever you observe children at play. Children learn a variety of social parameters and norms through play, and they also develop various emotional characteristics (Kolb, 2009). In terms of specific aspects of cognitive development, the types of play that appear to be of most benefit are those activities that assist in the development of self-regulation (Medina, 2010; Willingham, 2011). Self-regulation refers to being able to control one's emotions, impulses and behaviour, and to control attention and other cognitive processes, which in turn appear to have enormous consequences for overall academic and social success (Blair, 2002; Bodrova & Leong, 2005; Diamond et al., 2007; Eisenberg et al., 2010; Willingham, 2011). And while some aspects of self-regulation are linked to overall brain maturation, particular types of play activities can help to nurture this important component of the mind.

Nurturing aspects of executive functioning related to self-regulation may seem somewhat antithetical to parameters surrounding developmentally appropriate activities for children, given how the brain matures. It is now widely accepted that the brain does not fully mature until the third decade of life, and that a tremendous amount of growth and maturation in the frontal lobes occurs after a child's sixth birthday (Giedd & Rapoport, 2010). However, studies conducted over the last couple of years have found that with the appropriate level of support and planning, self-regulation with regard to executive functioning can be enhanced before children enter their first year of primary school (Diamond et al., 2007). One program entitled 'Tools of the Mind' has shown particular success at enhancing self-regulatory behaviour, and a cornerstone of that program is mature dramatic play. Drawing on the works of the Russian psychologist Lev Vygotsky, Tools of the Mind presents mature dramatic play as the provision of opportunities for children to engage in extended make-believe scenarios lasting for long periods of time. Importantly, educators do not simply 'let' children play, but rather carefully plan, coordinate and support imaginary scenarios in which children selectively engage, whereby they fall into particular roles guided by social norms (Bodrova & Leong, 2007). This type of play contributes to self-regulation in that while pretending to be a store clerk, for example, a child must behave in ways that meet the social rules of the role, and rely on private or internal speech to help define that role while simultaneously curbing impulses in order to think about how a clerk might act and what they might say (Barnett et al., 2008). Studies examining the impact of this type of play-based learning have identified that engaging in the types of activities noted above improves self-regulation, enhances aspects of executive functioning, builds language capacities and improves school readiness (Diamond et al., 2007; Barnett et al., 2008).

Given the points above related to play and particular types of play, it is not surprising that purposeful play-based activities are an integral component of nurturing a child's developing mind. Aside from the pleasurable outcomes of play noted earlier, play also complements the rationale behind why institutionalised learning prior to Year 1 traditionally has been referred to as *preschool*. If you recall from the last chapter, it is only some time after a child's fifth birthday that their brain is emotionally and cognitively ready for the types of formal learning that occur from Year 1 and throughout primary school. As children move out of 'preschool' environments, they are better able to learn on demand and follow adult reasoning; using memory in a deliberate fashion, beginning to grasp abstract concepts and having enough self-control to sit for long periods of time and attend to what is being taught all become increasingly evident from age six onwards. From this point forward, nurturing the mind of the early years learner still requires a developmentally appropriate framework that is generally found in most systemic curricula, but it also necessitates consideration of one final important factor that can greatly influence learning.

At the beginning of this chapter, a great deal of attention was given to recognising the importance of safe, secure and supportive environments for infants and toddlers. This is also an important consideration for children as they grow older, and in particular it is a significant factor related to a child's overall emotional well-being and capacity to learn. While it is true that a child's cognitive capacities improve as they grow older, it is also true that the emotional part of the brain can directly impact on thinking, learning and overall development. It is therefore incumbent on schools to ensure that learning environments are not only founded on ensuring that children are safe and supported, but also as devoid of stress as possible. Children who learn in a more relaxed environment and who feel less overwhelmed have better brain function (Carew & Magsamen, 2010). This may appear to be a rather bold claim, and as noted earlier stress and emotional upheaval can literally impact on many aspects of cognitive functioning given that when the brain is stressed, its default mechanism shuts down thinking and prepares the body to react (Nagel, 2009). It is also noteworthy that children in learning environments nurtured by educators who are consistent, predictable, positive, warm and appropriately responsive to children's emotional cues show fewer negative behaviours, less time off task, more self-reliance and more self-regulatory behaviours (Rimm-Kaufman et al., 2002; Willingham, 2011). Once again, relationships—be they at home or at school—emerge as integral to emotional well-being, the learning process and the nurture of the early years learner. Emotions and relationships also bring this chapter full circle in that their importance at the nexus of neural stimulation, child development, experience and learning permeates our overall understanding of healthy neurological development from birth to the early years of primary school. If educators fail to appreciate the importance of emotions and relationships with regard to providing the appropriate developmental stimuli for children, then they fail to appreciate a critical force in nurturing.

Summary

- The chapter focused on building on the reader's understanding of the developing human brain as discussed in the previous chapter by looking at the impact of experience and the environment on such development.
- While plenty of grandiose claims exist related to enhancing the brain of an early years learner or speeding up learning through 'brain enrichment' programs, toys or technological devices, contemporary evidence tells us that the best enrichment an early years learner can have is through social relationships and opportunities to explore and play.
- As our current era of mind and brain science continues to expand, it is conceivable that scientists and researchers may unlock many more mysteries of the developing mind, which will inform educational practice.
- Until then, and arguably in spite of any such advancements, it is perhaps more beneficial to allow Bronfenbrenner's words to shape any thoughts on nurturing an early years learner: 'a child requires progressively more complex joint activity with one or more adults who have an irrational emotional relationship with the child'.

Discussion questions

4.1 Given how problematic stress can be to learning and development, and considering that an early years learner's lifeworld is a complex mix of

familial, social and communal interactions, can you identify potential stressors within each aspect of those interactions? Place them on a continuum
with regard to how much influence an educator can have on mediating or
counteracting those stressors, with one end denoting 'no influence' and the
other end 'significant influence'.

4.2 If the brain depends on particular experiences for learning to occur, can you
note developmentally appropriate experiences for children within the following age ranges: 0–2, 2–4, 4–6 and 6–8? You may wish to refer to the works of
Jean Piaget found in many child development or educational psychology texts
as a starting point.

4.3 How does the play of a two-year-old differ from that of a six-year-old? Note
how the social dynamics of play may differ between these two age groups, and
how each can be nurtured given the information presented above.

4.4 Positive relationships form the foundation of all aspects of healthy neurological development. What are some simple strategies you can use to foster
healthy relationships with, and within, the children with whom you work on
a daily basis?

References

Aamodt, S. & Wang, S. (2011). *Welcome to your child's brain: How the mind grows from conception to college.* New York: Bloomsbury.

Allred, L.W. (2007). *Piggyback rides and slippery slides: How to have fun raising first-rate children,* Springville, UT: Cedar Fort.

Barnett, W.S., Jung, K., Yarosz, D.J., Thomas, J., Hornbeck, A., Stechuk, R. & Burns, S. (2008). Educational effects of the Tools of the Mind curriculum: A randomized trial. *Early Childhood Research Quarterly, 23*(3), 299–313.

Beard J.L. & Connor J.R. (2003). Iron status and neural functioning. *Annual Review of Nutrition, 23,* 31–58.

Berninger, V.W. & Richards, T.L. (2002). *Brain literacy for educators and psychologists.* San Diego, CA: Elsevier.

Bjorkland, D.F. (2005). *Children's thinking: cognitive development and individual differences.* Belmont, CA: Wadsworth/Thomson Learning.

Black, J.E., Jones, T.A., Nelson, C.A. & Greenough, W.T. (1998). Neural plasticity and the developing brain. In J.D. Noshpitz, N.E. Alessi, J.T. Coyle, S.I. Harrison & S. Eth (eds), *Handbook of child and adolescent psychiatry—Vol. 6: Basic psychiatric science and treatment* (pp. 31–53). New York: Wiley.

Blair, C. (2002). School readiness: Integrating cognition and emotion in a neurobiological conceptual-
ization of children's functioning at school entry. *American Psychologist, 57*(2), 111–27.

Bloom, F.L., Beal, M.F. & Kupfer, D.J. (2006). *The DANA guide to brain health: a practical reference from medical experts.* New York: DANA Press.

Bodrova, E. & Leong, D.J. (2005). Self-regulation: A foundation for early learning. *Principal*, Sept/Oct, 30–5.

—— (2005). Uniquely preschool: What research tells us about the ways young children learn. *Educational Leadership*, *63*(1), 44–7.

—— (2007). *Tools of the mind: The Vygotskian approach to early childhood education*, 2nd ed. Columbus, OH: Prentice-Hall.

Bronfenbrenner, U. (1979). *The ecology of human development: Experiments by nature and design*. Cambridge, MA: Harvard University Press.

—— (1989). Ecological systems theory. In R. Vasta (ed.), *Annals of child development*, Vol. 6 (pp. 187–251). Greenwich, CN: JAI Press.

—— (2005). *Making human beings human: Bioecological perspectives on human development*. Thousand Oaks, CA: Sage.

Bronfenbrenner, U. & Morris, P.A. (2006). The ecology of developmental processes. In W. Damon & R. Lerner (eds), *Handbook of child psychology*, 6th ed., pp. 793–829. New York: John Wiley.

Carew, T.J. & Magsamen, S.H. (2010). Neuroscience and education: An ideal partnership for producing evidence-based solutions to guide 21st century learning. *Neuron*, *67*(5), 685–8.

Cullen, K.E. & Roy, J.E. (2004). Signal processing in the vestibular system during active versus passive head movements. *Journal of Neurophysiology*, *91*(5), 1919–33.

Department of Education, Employment and Workplace Relations (DEEWR) (2009). *Belonging, being and becoming: The early years learning framework for Australia*. Canberra: Commonwealth of Australia.

Diamond, A. (2000). Close interrelation of motor development and cognitive development and of the cerebellum and prefrontal cortex. *Child Development*, *71*(1), 44–56.

Diamond, A., Barnett, W.S., Thomas, J. & Munro, S. (2007). Preschool program improves cognitive control. *Science*, *318*(5855), 1387–8.

Diamond, M. & Hopson, J. (1999). *Magic trees of the mind: How to nurture your child's intelligence, creativity, and healthy emotions from birth through adolescence*. New York: Penguin Putnam.

Eisenberg, N., Valiente, C. & Eggum, N.D. (2010). Self-regulation and school readiness. *Early Education and Development*, *21*(5), 681–98.

Eliot, L. (2000). *What's going on in there? How the brain and mind develop in the first five years of life*. New York: Bantam.

Faull, J. & McLean-Oliver, J. (2010). *Amazing minds: The science of nurturing your child's developing mind with games, activities and more*. New York: Berkley Books.

Fisher, K.R., Hirsh-Pasek, K., Golinkoff, R.M. & Gryfe, S.G. (2008). Conceptual split? Parents' and experts' perceptions of play in the 21st century. *Journal of Applied Developmental Psychology*, *29*(4) 305–16.

Gardner, H. (2011). *The unschooled mind: How children think and how schools should teach*, 12th ed. New York: Basic Books.

Georgieff, M.K. (2007). Nutrition and the developing brain: Nutrient priorities and measurement. *The American Journal of Clinical Nutrition*, *85*(suppl): 614–20.

Giedd, J.N. & Rapoport, J.L. (2010). Structural MRI of pediatric brain development: What have we learned and where are we going? *Neuron*, *9*(5), 728–34.

Greenough, W.T. & Black, J.E. (1992). Induction of brain structure by experience substrates for cognitive development. In M.R. Gunnar & C.A. Nelson (eds), *Developmental behavioral neuroscience:*

The Minnesota Symposia on Child Psychology—Vol. 24 (pp. 155–200). Mahwah, NJ: Lawrence Erlbaum.

Greenough, W.T., Black, J.E. & Wallace, C.S. (1987). Experience and brain development. *Child Development, 58*(3), 539–59.

Hannaford, C. (2005). *Smart moves: Why learning is not all in your head*, 2nd ed. Salt Lake City, UT: Great River Books.

Healy, J. (2004). *Your child's growing mind: Brain development and learning from birth to adolescence.* New York: Broadway Books.

Herschkowitz, N. & Herschkowitz, E.C. (2004). *A good start to life: Understanding your child's brain and behaviour from birth to age 6.* New York: Dana Press.

Hirsch-Pasek, K. & Golinkoff, R.M. (2004). *Einstein never used flashcards: How our children really learn—and why they need to play more and memorize less.* New York: Rodale.

Howard, P.J. (2006). *The owner's manual for the brain: Everyday applications from mind-brain research,* 3rd ed. Austin, TX: Bard Press.

Kagan, J. & Herschkowitz, N. (2005). *A Young Mind in a Growing Brain.* Mahwah, NJ: Lawrence Erlbaum.

Kolb, B. (2009). Brain and behavioural plasticity in the developing brain: Neuroscience and public policy. *Paediatrics & Child Health, 14*(10), 651–2.

Kotulak, R. (1997). *Inside the brain: Revolutionary discoveries of how the mind works.* Kansas City, MO: Andrews McMeel.

Kuhl, P.K. (2004). Early language acquisition: Cracking the speech code. *Nature Reviews Neuroscience, 5*(11), 831–43.

—— (2007). Is speech learning 'gated' by the social brain? *Developmental Science, 10*(1), 110–20.

Lozoff, B. (2000). Perinatal iron deficiency and the developing brain. *Pediatric Research, 48*(2), 137–9.

Maslow, A. (1999). *Toward a psychology of being, 3rd ed.* New York: John Wiley.

Medina, J. (2010). *Brain rules for baby: How to raise a smart and happy child from zero to five.* Seattle, WA: Pear Press.

Nagel, M.C. (2009). Mind the mind: Understanding the links between stress, emotional well-being and learning in educational contexts. *The International Journal of Learning, 16*(2), 33–42.

—— (2011). Student learning. In R. Churchill, P. Ferguson, S. Godinho et al., *Teaching: Making a difference* (pp. 68–105). Brisbane: John Wiley.

Nelson, C.A. (1999). Neural plasticity and human development. *Current Directions in Psychological Science, 8*(2), 42–5.

—— (2000). Neural plasticity and human development: The role of early experience in sculpting memory systems. *Developmental Science, 3*(2), 115–36.

Renner, M.J. & Rosenzweig, M.R. (1987). *Enriched and impoverished environments: Effects on brain and behavior.* New York: Springer.

Rimm-Kaufman, S.E., Early, D.M., Cox, M.J., Saluja, G., Pianta, R.C., Bradley, R.H. & Payne, C. (2002). Early behavioral attributes and teachers' sensitivity as predictors of competent behavior in the kindergarten classroom. *Journal of Applied Developmental Psychology, 23*(4), 451–70.

Rosenzweig, M.R., Krech, D., Bennett, E.L. & Diamond, M.C. (1962). Effects of environmental complexity and training on brain chemistry and anatomy: A replication and extension. *Journal of Comparative and Physiological Psychology, 55*(4), 429–37.

Shonkoff, J.P. (2010). Building a new biodevelopmental framework to guide the future of early child-hood policy. *Child Development, 81*(1), 357–67.

Shonkoff, J.P. & Phillips, D.A. (eds) (2000). *From neurons to neighborhoods: The science of early childhood development.* Washington, DC: National Academy Press.

Shore, R. (1997). *Rethinking the brain: New insights into early development.* New York: Families and Work Institute.

Sibley, B.A. & Etnier, J.L. (2003). The relationship between physical activity and cognition in children: A meta-analysis. *Pediatric Exercise Science, 15*(3), 243–56.

Smith, P.F., Darlington, C.L. & Zheng, Y. (2010). Move it or lose it: Is stimulation of the vestibular system necessary for normal spatial memory? *Hippocampus, 20*(1), 36–43.

Sprenger, M. (2008). *The developing brain: Birth to age eight.* Thousand Oaks, CA: Corwin Press.

Stamm, J. (2008). *Bright from the start: The simple science-backed way to nurture your child's developing mind from birth to age 3.* New York: Gotham Books.

Sylwester, R. (2005). *How to explain a brain: An educator's handbook of brain terms and cognitive processes.* Thousand Oaks, CA: Corwin Press.

Willingham, D.T. (2011). Can teachers increase students' self-control? *American Educator, 35*(2), 22–7.

PART II

*Curriculum practices for
the early years*

5

Literacy

Bridie Raban and Janet Scull

Introduction

While reviewing the extensive literature available internationally on literacy for this chapter, we were struck by a recurring theme that draws the material together. There are constant reminders that literacy grows out of and alongside language development generally, and that both are characterised by audience, context and purpose. We use language—spoken or written—to communicate, and this presupposes an audience and a purpose to the communicative acts marked out by both spoken and written language activities. What this means for educators of early years learners is that every opportunity should be taken to contextualise speaking, reading and writing experiences so that there is a clearly understood meaning about why we speak, read and write, and how we do this for different purposes on different occasions.

Early literacy before school

Early language development
Early years learners learn language by interacting and communicating with others. From infancy, physical contact and talk engage babies and give them a sense of

'place' in the lives of others and their world. Language that is rich with meaning is concerned with immediate experiences and builds the infant's understanding that language is 'about' something—that it is connected with their experience of life. Language is not an arbitrary noise, like the air conditioner; it is about something. Importantly, early years learners learn their native language without direct instruction—they do not learn by imitation. What infants, toddlers and early years learners require is a mature conversational partner who engages with them, talks about what is going on, draws them into conversations and generally acts as a resource. Mature speakers provide models of appropriateness and respond with warmth, interest and concern.

Spending time with babies, toddlers and early years learners is typically characterised by talking about the here and now, using language to identify what is going on and how things are happening. Before the age of three, if prompted, early years learners will begin to use language to talk about what happened before and what will happen next. This is an important intellectual shift in conversation because it creates the opportunity to use the language of text, which is always about anything other than the present—for instance, 'Once upon a time . . .' Between the ages of three and five, language develops rapidly, especially if the early years learner has someone with whom to talk. While their language may not be grammatically accurate at this stage, they are surrounded by adults who respond with appropriate forms. For instance,

Early years learner:	'When Nana coming shops?'
Mum:	'Nana will come to the shops with us tomorrow.'

The adult responds to the message, but does not 'correct' the early years learner. Not only does the early years learner get an answer to their question, they also get a model of appropriateness. Had the early years learner received the answer 'Tomorrow', they would have missed the opportunity to learn language, and about language and how it works.

A further characteristic of early language is early years learners' increasing vocabulary development. Regular words are easy to learn, but the irregular forms take a bit longer. *Try* and *tried* is easy to grasp, but *go* and *went* might take a while longer—with *goed* a frequently heard solution to this problem. The important thing from the early years learner's point of view is that they are understood and hear quantities of appropriate language forms around them. What, then, is the role of the adult with respect to early language development? Importantly, as Dickinson and Tabors (2001) point out, adults act in ways that acknowledge they understand the early years learner; the early years learner then engages and responds as they endeavour to follow the meanings that are developing through their language. In *Effective Provision of Preschool Education* (Sylva et al., 2010), the most effective preschool educators were those who engaged in what they called 'sustained shared thinking', where educators took the opportunity of 'tuning in' to early years learners' talk and engaging with them at the level of their thinking about an activity, asking questions to which they didn't know the answers and showing a genuine interest in what interested the early years learner.

Further work that helps support early years learners' sensitivity to language and how its features are patterned involves engaging early years learners in numerous language games. In particular, they enjoy rhymes and songs, and listening for words that go together because they begin in the same way or match in another way. Useful activities to build this awareness of pattern can be clapping the syllables of names, and inviting early years learners to stand and leave the group when names that begin the same way as their own are called out. In a number of these different ways, adults can support early years learners to use language for a wide range of purposes, while at the same time supporting them to familiarise themselves with the patterns of language that will help them in their later literacy development.

Early reading
Reading is complex, and any simplification—reducing it to knowledge of letters, sounds or sight words—will seriously distort early years learners' understanding of this activity. At the other extreme, defining literacy as any form of meaning-making could be equally misleading, especially for early childhood educators. While the semiotics of early years learners' lives is clearly diverse, and meaning is expressed and gleaned in numerous ways, the activity of reading print is highly specialised.

Early years learners learn about reading long before they begin formal schooling. They see people around them reading for a wide range of different purposes, and this will engage their curiosity. These texts will be rich with meaning. They can provoke action (how to use the car wash), can be shared and enjoyed (story books and emails), can give information (when to book a holiday or find out when a TV program is showing) and much more. Strickland and Schickedanz (2009), for instance, remind us just how much early years learners begin to understand about how print works, and that this will depend on their experiences of sharing texts with adults who point out how the system functions.

Typically, the bedtime story is a staple form of early reading activity shared between parents and their early years learners, even from birth. Indeed, reading at any time with an infant or toddler is a moment of shared enjoyment for both the adult and the early years learner. Holding the book in a particular orientation, turning pages, pointing to and describing the pictures—all these actions will engage the early years learner with the flow of the activity. As they grow older, pointing to the words as they are read, moving from the top of a page to the bottom, and across the lines from left to right (if reading English) will give early years learners messages about how print works. An important part of what we do as adults engaging early years learners in reading activities is to show them text and discuss what meanings different texts convey—such as a menu, a shopping list, a recipe, a poem or a list of names for a birthday party.

The language of text is typically more formal than conversational speech. Through hearing printed text read aloud, early years learners will begin to extend their understandings and expectations of the syntactic complexity of written language, to embrace the more formal genre—for instance, of stories, letter writing, explanations, descriptions and so on.

Indeed, in a print-rich culture, it would be difficult for early years learners not to become engaged with the concept of 'reading', even if they do not know how to do it for themselves. Reading food packaging, junk mail and instructions on toy boxes are all activities into which they will be drawn by surrounding adults. This has implications for the various early years settings in which early years learners participate. For instance, there will need to be a wide variety of well-illustrated books, displayed invitingly with covers facing the room, and comfortable cushions and seating arrangements for quiet enjoyment. Stories will be read aloud several times each day and educators will draw early years learners' attention to specific books that relate to their particular interests. Texts will be presented in a variety of forms, mimicking the real world of print by which early years learners are typically surrounded. Print should be displayed around the room at early years learners' eye level, in the form of information—descriptions of areas like 'This is where we paint our pictures', 'We keep our Lego here' and so on.

Vukelich and Christie (2009) point out that early literacy in the years before formal schooling is neither left to the early years learners' own devices, nor centred on skills-based explicit teaching. Rather, a nested approach should be taken, keeping reading within the everyday experiences of early years learners and building on these experiences, and engaging them in the activity while pointing out some salient features of different kinds of text, both printed on paper and through digital media. It is not enough for early years learners to notice print in their environment; they must come to understand the uses and purposes of print in their daily lives and in those of others.

Early writing

Leaving a mark is a significant human activity; it states 'I am . . .', or 'I was here . . .'. We are surrounded by this through different forms of graffiti and the significance of signing one's name, for instance. From a very young age, early years learners engage with adults as they send emails, fill in forms, write cards, note telephone conversations and the like. They show curiosity about these marks, and eventually learn that it is not just any mark that matters but that particular marks have special salience. However, a long and powerful journey takes place in this development before early years learners arrive at school. Indeed, Schickedanz and Casbergue (2009) identify three interlinked journeys that early years learners travel. The first journey takes the early years learner from expressing their meanings through oral language to creating pictures and marks, and finally recognisable writing. The second journey sees the scribble marks moving towards recognisable letters, letter strings and finally readable words. And the third journey captures the development of having a single idea to an evolving connected discourse.

Early years learners will vary in their rates of moving through these different journeys, and a key stimulus towards achieving this will be the need to *communicate*, which is fostered and supported by surrounding adults because they are interested in what early years learners think and do, and how they express this through their drawing and writing. Gradually, early years learners will want their marks to be about something, and frequently ask 'What does that say?' This gives the clue that they have discovered the purpose of mark-making as distinct from drawing. This request can be challenging, with no discernible letters available to give clues to the message encoded by the marks. At this stage, early years learners believe that what they are thinking in their head is what the marks will say, regardless of how the marks look. By engaging in conversation and genuinely eliciting the purpose and intent of the mark-making, a much richer discourse can be uncovered and made available for scribing if that is what is required. Indeed, with time, a distinction between the picture and print begins to emerge, with scribble drawing becoming quite distinct from scribble writing, as children's experience with print is increased through shared storybook reading and joining in message-making activities. This increased experience of writing is fostered through the development of, for instance, a writing centre, where children can use a range of appropriate resources, or a noticeboard for news and family information.

Early years learners continue to form different hypotheses concerning how print works. While knowing just a few letters—perhaps those in their own name—they soon realise that if their letter-like forms are to 'say' something different, they must 'look' different, so they change the order of the letters they know for each new word. Also, for some early years learners, their printed name is a personal experience and some, like Rikki (see Figure 5.1), see their written name as who they are.

Figure 5.1   'That's me and that's my name'

Rikki said 'That's me and that's my name'. This matching of words with their referent is an interesting stage, as children begin to believe that little words belong to little things—for instance, 'ant'—and big words belong to big things, like 'elephant' and 'aeroplane'. However, all these hypotheses break down as early years learners' experience of working and playing with print increases.

As early years learners develop fine motor control, they learn the strokes that form letters, with horizontal, vertical and slopes being the major players. This is why capital letters are typically the first to emerge in the early years learners' repertoire. They play with these orientations, which to them are limitless, until they begin to focus down on the forms that move from letter-like to the actual 26 letters of the alphabet in English. Budding knowledge of directionality also begins to appear during these early stages, although early years learners continue to experiment with working text in different ways for quite some time—some are indeed proud that they can 'write' both from left to right as well as right to left!

Of particular interest in these early stages of writing development is that the activity of writing slows down the whole 'literacy' process, with a specific focus on individual letters as they are created and grouped together to eventually form words. While reading needs to take place 'on the run', so to speak, if the meaning is to be maintained, writing and learning about writing can provide a much more potent opportunity to draw early years learners' attention to the specific function of letters and how their sounds can build into a word.

Literacy in the early years of school

As early years learners move into school, teaching builds on their linguistic resources as a basis for further learning. When educators consider children's prior-to-school experiences, a wide range of skills and understandings are often evident, and it is important to fully acknowledge these early language and literacy experiences. Close and careful observation of early years learners allows for focused teaching, as educators notice, record and respond to what children already know. This requires listening to early years learners talk in a range of contexts, in order to identify aspects of oral language they control and provide opportunities for them to engage with a variety of texts and resources to ascertain their understanding of the codes and conventions of texts common to the early years curriculum. In this way, educators are able to ensure a responsive classroom environment within which early years learners can continue to explore and negotiate meanings.

Language for literacy

Oral language skills make an important contribution to literacy learning, and it is widely accepted that oral language is the foundation for written language. However, more recently research evidence reviewed by Snow et al. (2005) points to the importance of certain aspects of language as impacting on literacy learning, with early years learners developing skills in vocabulary and phonological awareness, as well as decontextualised language that mirrors the complexity of written texts. Written language has been characterised as more integrated, detached and explicit than oral language, resulting in a complexity and lexical density that moves beyond the structure of spoken texts. This distinction reflects a view of language as spanning a continuum that ranges from contextualised to decontextualised discourse, with the production and comprehension of decontextualised discourse identified by Dickinson and Tabors (2001) as a language skill foundational to early literacy learning.

Contextualised language is used to talk about situations and objects that are part of the immediate context. This discourse is characterised by short exchanges that achieve an immediate purpose in the context of experiences shared by the speakers, with environmental cues and gestures assisting as meaning is conveyed. In contrast, decontextualised talk is often about things outside the immediate time and place. Meaning is conveyed as the speaker draws on specific vocabulary and elaborates ideas incorporating a variety of grammatical structures. Raban (2000) shows how this talk establishes links between ideas and experiences and fosters precision and articulation of thinking. Indeed, it is the mastery of literate language that is one of the most important challenges during the early years of schooling. This underlies the importance of children learning to use this more sophisticated form of language as a resource for early literacy.

While there are many and varied authentic contexts for children to use and learn language, book reading is a pleasurable, efficacious activity that supports language learning, particularly when this involves teaching practices that actively engage early years learners in dialogue around text reading. Reading texts to children introduces new syntactic structures to build and expand their knowledge of grammar. In addition, when this incorporates talk about text, opportunities are created for early years learners to both hear and generate more complex forms of language with growing facility. As Paris et al. (2005) point out, this talk about text is also available to build on early years learners' understanding of narrative structure as a form of knowledge that early years learners need to have as they learn to read and create texts for themselves.

As well as developing control over a range of language structures and grammatical variations, early years learners' vocabularies expand at an astonishing rate. However, Biemiller (2011) illustrates that there is also a growing awareness of differential outcomes across groups of children, reflecting their prior-to-school opportunities for learning alongside an increasing awareness of the significance of vocabulary learning to early and later literacy outcomes. Snow et al. (2005) also identify the importance of phonological awareness to early years learners' literacy learning. This accumulated evidence from research notes the need for children to hear the sounds of language and identify smaller units of sound within speech patterns. Specifically, the studies provide evidence of the significance of supporting early years learners to hear rhyme and onset and rime breaks (d/og; b/ack; f/ish; ch/ase), with phoneme knowledge acquired as children learn to read and write.

Reading to children also contributes to vocabulary learning. Hill and Launder (2010) demonstrate this clearly as they discuss the vocabulary in Sendak's (1963)

Where the Wild Things Are, a text that uses 'gnashing teeth' and 'wild rumpus', rare words generally beyond the lexical choices of everyday conversation. Again, studies like those of Beck and McKeown (2007) point to a preference for interactive reading, engaging children in conversations with explicit oral scaffolding techniques and explanations of unfamiliar words to support early years learners to acquire understanding of new words. Indeed, choosing texts with rhyme and rhythm as features of language further tunes early years learners to the patterns and sounds of oral language. When attention is directed to the print, this builds knowledge of how written language represents speech to assist reading and spelling.

Reading

Rapid and efficient word recognition that enables readers to effectively construct meaning from the printed code characterises fluent, experienced readers. Clearly, this is the ultimate aim of all reading programs; however, it would be unfortunate if educators of early years learners insisted on accurate, error-free reading and focused on word-attack drills. As noted by Harrison (2004, p. 37), '[T]his would be counterproductive, and the reason is to do with the difference between *being* a fluent reader and *learning to become* a fluent reader.' Clay (2010) reminds us that learning to read requires young children to focus on the rich and varied sources of information available in texts, and this will take time to develop fully.

Using meaningful text as the basis for learning will enable early years learners to see the purpose and function of reading. As they experience a range of texts, they become familiar with the organisation and conventions of print and develop an understanding of aspects of the printed code that assists them to know where and what they need to attend to as they begin to take increasing control of the task and develop independence in reading. Marie Clay's 'Concepts About Print' task (2002) covers many of the conventions and provides a good understanding of how a written code works within early reading books; it is a useful guide for educators as they plan to support children's learning during the early stages.

Early years learners need to draw on a range of sources of information. Clay (2001) illustrates how they extend their searching and link sources to construct complex operating systems to effectively process texts. Central to text reading is a reader's knowledge of the world. Often referred to as semantic knowledge, this store of conceptual knowledge or schema for a given topic is present in an individual's memory, and supports the ability to reconstruct information and comprehend written text. The meaning resources used to decode and understand text include knowledge of the topic, content or characters and their actions. Early years learners' understanding of language is also facilitative of early reading competence. Experience with the forms of language and the grammatical patterning of various texts provides early years learners with a knowledge of how texts are structured linguistically, and assists them to anticipate both the form and the content of the texts read. Alongside this, Paris (2005) emphasises that it is essential for early years learners to master the alphabetic principles of written language. It is widely recognised that while readers bring much to the reading task, they also require graphophonic knowledge to search for meaning in texts. For early years learners, this information source encompasses developing understandings of and familiarity with graphemes, as letters representing phonemes, and an increasing awareness of the range of letter patterns available to encode sounds.

To develop as readers, early years learners must acquire the ability to work out how to recognise words they have not encountered before. This requires them to draw flexibly across the range of information sources available to them, and ensure a precise match to the semantic, syntactic and graphophonic information available. While important, the successful identification of words is insufficient because it is also necessary to attend explicitly to teaching early years learners to reconstruct meanings from the printed code. Contemporary understandings challenge conceptualisations of teaching reading as a staged, sequenced process of decoding followed by comprehension, and acknowledge the compilation and coordination of a range of skills and strategies. The development of both decoding and comprehension, integrated into reading acquisition processes, reflects the building of complementary reading skills (Scull, 2010).

Comprehension instruction is best achieved through collaborative, conversational approaches that support a flexible, opportunistic use of strategies as discussed by Palincsar (2003). Text discussions allow educators to model comprehension strategies, and for early years learners to actively participate in conversations as text meanings are examined. Learners also need to assume increased control of comprehension processes, however, with this dependent on teaching to promote the shift from other- to self-regulation of behaviours. As educators guide early years learners towards the co-construction of text meanings, active engagement in talk interactions is central to the instructional process—before, during and after reading.

Before reading
Educators activate early years learners' prior knowledge and build background knowledge specific to the text to be read. These conversational exchanges build early years learners' skills of prediction and connections, which are key strategies in building comprehension processes.

Figure 5.2   Transcript: *Mitch to the Rescue*

T: Now this is where the adventure actually starts. OK, turn the page.

Now, there is a problem for the last duck, for the last duckling. I wonder what it might be?

C: He's too little and he's not very fast.

T: Well the water around the rocks actually goes really fast, so you could be right. Maybe it's taking him away and he can't keep up.

Do you think? Is that what you were thinking?

C: Cause all the water's going that way and he's over here, and there is the water and it's flowing.

T: OK, what's going to happen?

C: He's trapped.

T: He's trapped. Now if Mitch comes to the rescue in this story, what might Mitch do?

C: Well, he'll save it.

T: I wonder how?

C: He hops out of the boat and pops onto the rock and he gets his bucket and puts it in there with some water.

T: Well, that's a good idea, actually it is his sunhat. He was minding the sunhats. So he uses the sunhats, well isn't that a good idea?

Source: Smith, A. (1997) *Mitch to the rescue*. New Zealand: Nelson.

Skilfully, the teacher in the transcript in Figure 5.2 invites the early years learner to co-construct the text prior to reading. Her explicit use of open-ended questions such as 'I wonder what it might be?' and 'I wonder how?' involves the teacher and the early years learner in collaboratively describing the storyline as it unfolds, drawing on prior understanding and familiar concepts to articulate effectively what is known and to make connections between already known information and the new concepts in texts.

During reading
Educators' prompts during the first reading support early years learners to attend to the semantic, syntactic and graphophonic information in text, extending their

Figure 5.3   Transcript: *Rebecca and the Concert*

Text—Rebecca's cat Tiger likes to . . .

C: Rebecca's cat Tiger I (sounding first letter, child pauses)

T: What would make sense there and look right? Let's try from the beginning.

C&T: Rebecca's cat Tiger I (sounding first letter)

C: Lives.

T: Does that look right?

C: Oh likes.

T: Yes, try it again and see if 'likes' makes sense and sounds right.

Source: Smith, A. (1997) *Rebecca and the concert.* New Zealand: Nelson Price Milburn.

linking and searching systems to effectively process text. The transcript in Figure 5.3 demonstrates how educators might integrate semantic and graphophonic information to support early years learners when reading.

After reading

Discussions after reading provide distinct opportunities for early years learners to engage in talk interactions, to reconstruct text meanings and to mediate understandings gained from reading. At this early stage of reading development, the importance of negotiation and interpretation is acknowledged as impacting on comprehension processes (Skull, 2010). Contributions that challenge early years learners to review ideas, to make connections between that which was known and the new information, and to share and defend views presented are critical to positive reading outcomes. Opportunities provided to share and communicate ideas enable the 'individual student to explore and create a depth of meaning not always available to the isolated thinker' (Raban, 1999, p. 105). The transcript in Figure 5.4 is illustrative of a brief 'after' reading conversation where key concepts in the text are discussed.

Learning to write

Classrooms build on early years learners' experiences of making marks and explorations of print to further develop understandings of writing as a means of communication that is relevant and purposeful to their everyday lives. As they

Figure 5.4   Transcript: *Jonathan Buys a Present*

T: Do you think Jonathan was clever in the end?

C: Yes.

T: Why was Jonathan clever? Did he make a good choice about his present?

C: No not really, because he spent some on him and if he didn't spend it on marbles and a toffee apple he would have enough for um a toffee apple and probably a puppet.

T: For Grandad, and do you think that would have been a better present for Grandad?

C: Yes.

T: Better than the mask—why?

C: Cause he could probably get two.

T: Two presents. But do you think it was only fair that he spent some of his pocket money on himself.

C: Yeh.

T: You would, wouldn't you? Yeh, I think that's only fair.

Source: Smith, A. (1997) *Jonathan buys a present.* New Zealand: Nelson Price Milburn.

learn to read and translate printed symbols into meaningful units, they also learn to encode meaning through writing. First and foremost, early years learners need to see writing as a social activity, used to interact with others, explore ideas, and record and communicate thoughts, desires and feelings. As they manipulate the forms and functions of writing, they develop control over written language and become aware of writing as a powerful tool of influence. Wing Jan (2009) illustrates how early years learners develop an understanding of the different purposes and audiences they have for their writing and, specific to this, learn to select and use an appropriate range of text forms: recounts, reports narrative, procedures, explanations and persuasive texts. In this way, children learn to handle—with increasing control— the range of text types, and the particular linguistic structures and grammatical features, of the texts central to early learning.

As with learning to read, writing is a complex process. Writing involves going from ideas to spoken words to printed messages. The construction of messages provides a challenge for early years learners as they learn to control the differences between oral and written language. Christie (2005) identifies this challenge as being due to the fact that oral language is learned and generally used in face-to-face interactions, while writing is produced at some distance from the interaction and/or event. To support early years learners to compose texts and assist the shift from oral to written discourse structures, teacher assistance occurs through demonstration and the co-construction of texts. Learning to record conventions further challenges early years learners. However, it is often as children write that they develop greater control over the phoneme and grapheme relationships, listening to the sounds they need to record and searching for the correct letter choices. Clay (2001) notes that as early years learners explore writing, they focus closely on the features of letters and engage in their own form of segmenting sounds in words in order to write them. From these early experiences, and with teacher guidance, early years learners develop rules and strategies for spelling, noting patterns in words and using analogy to build a repertoire of known words and skill in writing new words. Correct spelling is a key skill in learning to write, and one that requires explicit attention throughout schooling.

As illustrated in Figure 5.5, this first draft text, produced electronically by an early years learner in the second year of school, shows the writer's developing control over narrative texts, with inclusion of a simple complication, signalled through her use of the connective 'but' and her resolution to the problem. We also see her use of a range of sentence structures, dialogue and punctuation, and a growing awareness of spelling patterns.

Figure 5.5   All about a girl who was very rich

Once upon a time there was a girl but had no mum or dad and was very rich. But her mum and dad was not dead.

Every day she looked and looked and never fawnd them. 'I want a mum and a dad'. But then she fawnd them in the grawnd. It took a long time to get them auwt. I lived happily ever afta.

—Annabel, age seven

As with reading, it is important that educators work though continual and recursive processes of support and handover, to enable early years learners to take increasing control of writing and develop expertise over the form and function of written texts. Teaching cycles that engage early years learners in observation and discussion of texts as models have proven to be a useful framework for teaching. These can include demonstrations of writing, followed by the co-construction or shared writing of texts, as children contribute to aspects of the writing process—the planning, composing, recording and editing of texts—before moving to independent writing.

Summary

- This chapter has emphasised the importance of oral language in the early years, and the need to build early years learners' competence as users of language for literacy learning.
- We have focused on the educator's role in specifically targeting aspects of language development and communicative variations to develop a repertoire of language resources to support learning.
- Another area that brings this work together is the integrated nature of learning to talk, read and write, as early years learners draw upon a shared range of practices and understandings to assume increased control over the demands of written text.
- We stress the importance of educators' explicit support of concept development, with clear connections across language and literacy learning, to reinforce meaningful interactions with texts.
- Knowledge of letters and words builds from early years learners' engagement with the purposeful texts they produce.
- Experience with reading texts develops a greater awareness of the semantic, syntactic and graphophonic information sources required to solve problems when constructing and reconstructing messages in text.
- Educators need to see and highlight the links across the modes of literacy as they support early years learners to apply their learning of the printed code to an increasing range of contexts and to extend their command over more complex texts in both reading and writing.
- The chapter has highlighted:
  - the purposeful, meaningful nature of early language and literacy learning with skill development nested within authentic contexts
  - the significant role educators have in providing opportunities for early years learners to explore and experiment with print and in drawing children's attention to the salient features of texts
  - the importance of early years learners' developing control over literate discourse and their increasing awareness of the sounds of language as facilitative of literacy learning

- the ways in which educators embed comprehension into literacy acquisition processes to ensure reading skill development complements the understandings gained from text reading
- the need for educators to model and support early years learners' developing control over aspects of the writing process and the range of text forms available to communicate their meanings.

Discussion questions

5.1 What kinds of resources would you make available for early years learners?

5.2 What books might you read to early years learners to build literate language?

5.3 As early years learners commence school, how might you gather information about each of them to inform your practice?

5.4 What might you emphasise in your conversations with early years learners before, during and after reading?

5.5 When would you signal concerns about the literacy development of an early years learner?

References

Beck, I.L. & McKeown, M.G. (2007). Increasing young low-income children's oral vocabulary repertoires through rich and focussed instruction. *The Elementary School Journal, 107*(3) 251–71.

Biemiller, A. (2011). Vocabulary: What words should we teach? *Better: Evidenced-based Education,* Winter, 10–11.

Christie, F. (2005). *Language education in the primary years.* Sydney: UNSW Press.

Clay, M.M. (2001). *Change over time in children's literacy development.* Auckland: Heinemann.

—— (2002). *An observation survey of early literacy achievement.* Auckland: Heinemann.

—— (2010). *The puzzling code.* Auckland: Pearson.

Dickinson, D.K. & Tabors, P.O. (eds) (2001). *Beginning literacy with language.* Baltimore, MD: Paul Brookes.

Harrison, C. (2004). *Understanding reading development.* London: Paul Chapman.

Hill, S. & Launder, N. (2010). Oral language and beginning to read. *Australian Journal of Language and Literacy, 33*(3), 240–54.

Palincsar, A.S. (2003). Collaborative approaches to comprehension instruction. In A.P. Sweet & C.E. Snow (eds), *Rethinking reading comprehension.* New York: Guilford Press.

Paris, S. (2005). Reinterpreting the development of reading skills. *Reading Research Quarterly, 40*(2), 184–202.

Paris, S.G., Carpenter, R.D., Paris A.H. & Hamilton, E.E. (2005). Spurious and genuine correlates of children's reading comprehension. In S.G. Paris & S.A. Stahl (eds), *Children's reading comprehension and assessment* (pp. 131–60). Mahwah, NJ: Lawrence Erlbaum.

Raban, B. (1999). Language and literacy as epistemology. In J.S. Gaffney & B.J. Askew (eds), *Stirring the waters: The influence of Marie Clay* (pp. 99–125). Portsmouth, NH: Heinemann.

—— (2000). Talking to think, learn and teach: The SAID classroom framework. In P. Smith (ed.), *Talking Classrooms*. Newark, DE: International Reading Association.

Schickedanz, J.A. & Casbergue, R.M. (2009). *Writing in the preschool*. Newark, DE: International Reading Association.

Scull, J. (2010). Embedding comprehension within reading acquisition processes. *Australian Journal of Language and Literacy, 33*(2), 87–107.

Snow, C.E., Griffin, P. & Burns, M.S. (2005). *Knowledge to support the teaching of reading: Preparing educators for a changing world*. San Francisco: Jossey-Bass.

Strickland, D.S. & Schickedanz, J.A. (2009). *Learning about print in the preschool*. Newark, DE: International Reading Association.

Sylva, K., Melhuish, E., Sammons, P., Siraj-Blatchford, I. & Taggart, B. (eds) (2010). *Early years childhood matters: Evidence from the Effective Preschool and Primary Project*. London: Routledge.

Vukelich, C. & Christie, J. (2009). *Building a foundation for preschool literacy*. Newark, DE: International Reading Association.

Wing Jan, L. (2009). *Write ways: Modelling writing forms*, 3rd ed. Melbourne: Oxford University Press.

6

Numeracy

Marina Papic, Joanne Mulligan and Kate Highfield

Introduction

Traditionally, adults have given early years learners little credit for their mathematical thinking and problem-solving ability. Perhaps this is because adults generally view learning mathematics as something that is quite abstract, which develops well into the formal years of schooling. Before that, it is a commonly held belief that early years learners explore basic concepts such as counting, shapes and informal measures. To some extent, this view has limited educators' expectations of early years learners' mathematics learning, and this has influenced the scope of early years programs, mathematics curricula and pedagogical practices. There is now strong research evidence that early years learners are capable of learning real mathematics very early (Perry & Dockett, 2008). They can develop a range of mathematical concepts requiring symbolic and abstract thought far beyond traditional expectations. Further, rich and effective mathematics learning experiences in the early years have been found to have a positive impact on learning in the long term.

Learning begins at birth—or some would argue even before birth. There is no difference when we consider mathematics learning. Our views about numeracy and mathematical thinking have been shaped by an understanding that mathematics learning is a continuous, dynamic process that is critical to cognitive growth and learning. We know that early years learners develop and communicate about mathematical ideas in different ways and at different rates.

In this chapter, we explore what numeracy looks like for young learners in the twenty-first century. We provide examples of:

- how early years learners develop mathematical concepts and processes in a range of contexts
- how educators can encourage and support this activity, and
- approaches to assessment and documenting learning.

What is numeracy?

The Australian Curriculum–Mathematics (Commonwealth of Australia, 2009, p. 5) defines numeracy as 'the capacity, confidence and disposition to use mathematics to meet the demands of learning, school, home, work, community and civic life'. This perspective on numeracy emphasises the application of mathematics, but the curriculum also promotes confidence and competence in learning the discipline of mathematics, and illustrates the ways in which mathematics contributes to the study of other disciplines. Current debate focuses on some important differences between numeracy and mathematics—which involves more than being numerate. Mathematics is about seeking patterns and relationships, representing them, symbolising these ideas, and eventually learning to abstract and generalise. Learning to explain and justify problem-solving processes is a critical part of learning mathematics:

> Mathematics makes a special contribution to the development of numeracy in a manner that is more explicit than is the case in other learning areas. It is important that the mathematics curriculum provides the opportunity to apply mathematical understanding and skills in context, both in other learning areas and in real world contexts. (ACARA, 2011, p. 5)

The Early Years Learning Framework (EYLF) (DEEWR, 2009) defines numeracy as:

> The capacity, confidence and disposition to use mathematics in daily life. Children bring new mathematical understandings through engaging with problem solving.

It is essential that the mathematical ideas with which young children interact are relevant and meaningful in the context of their current lives. (DEEWR, 2009, p. 38)

Clearly, the EYLF advances the idea that mathematics and mathematical thinking are integral to numeracy. 'Spatial sense, structure and pattern, number, measurement, data, argumentation, connections and exploring the world mathematically are the powerful mathematical ideas children need to become numerate.' (2009, p. 38) Thus the development of mathematical concepts beyond basic counting and arithmetic is promoted. 'Numeracy is more than counting.' (Arthur et al., 2010, p. 6) It is also about promoting patterns and relationships, and understanding the structure of concepts. This includes being able to represent, symbolise, abstract and generalise (at a simple level), and also to use argumentation to explain and justify thinking. Communication is critical to this development; therefore, literacy and numeracy are fundamentally interconnected.

Reflecting on these views of numeracy may require us to revisit its role in the twenty-first century and examine our expectations of early years learners' mathematical capacities. Becoming numerate must be considered within widely varying socio-cultural contexts and increasingly technological societies. Regardless of one's view of numeracy, early years learners possess creative and natural capabilities as mathematicians. As early childhood educators, it is imperative that we provide meaningful learning opportunities that will access and build on these capabilities.

Developing mathematical thinkers: Frameworks for learning

Advances in cognitive neuroscientific, psychological and educational research indicate that early years learners' mathematical thinking develops much earlier, and in more complex ways, than previously believed (English, 2004; Perry et al., 2008; van Nes, 2011). We now know that early forms of patterning and reasoning, abstraction and generalisation are evident in early years learners' thinking from as young as three or four years of age (Papic et al., 2011). Recent initiatives at international level in early childhood mathematics education—for example, the Building Blocks Project (Clements & Sarama, 2009), the Big Maths for Little Kids Project (Greenes et al., 2004) and the Mathematics Education and Neurosciences (MENS) project (van Nes, 2011)—provide frameworks to promote 'big ideas' in early mathematics and science education.

Frameworks for early mathematics generally include key principles for guiding concept development and mathematical thinking (DEEWR, 2009; Sarama &

Clements, 2009). Reconceptualising essential components of early numeracy takes account of new research that places mathematical content—traditionally preserved for the formal curriculum—in the prior-to-school years. Statistical reasoning and data exploration are two of these content areas. Table 6.1 lists some key concepts and principles with some examples; this is not an exhaustive list, but highlights a range of learning opportunities.

Table 6.1   Key mathematical concepts and principles

Mathematical focus	Examples of key concepts and principles	Birth to four years exemplars	Four to eight years exemplars
Number	Classification Cardinal number Numeral identification Representation Equivalence Subitising Estimation Rote, perceptual and skip counting, counting on Order, sequence and number patterns Sharing and partitioning Fractions/ proportionality Equal grouping Arithmetic strategies	Babies explore one to one correspondence by grabbing an item in each of their hands.	Kindergarten children explore counting on and counting back by playing the card game 'Snap'. Rather than 'snapping' on the same number card, children snap on one more or one less than the card displayed.
Patterns	Identifying patterns— simple repetition Unit of repeat Spatial, symmetrical, cyclic, hopscotch and growing patterns Functional thinking two- and three- dimensional patterns	Four-year-olds copy, draw, design and extend repeating patterns using various hands-on materials. Children transfer the same pattern structure into music and movement.	Year I children explore growing square number patterns using square tiles: I, 4, 9, 16. Children describe the pattern and determine the next one in the sequence, justifying their response.

continued

Mathematical focus	Examples of key concepts and principles	Birth to four years exemplars	Four to eight years exemplars
Measurement	Conservation Length Area Volume and capacity Mass Temperature Time Estimating Measuring (comparisons, informal and formal units) Comparing and ordering Recording and interpreting Proportionality	Three-year-olds explore the capacity of various containers in the sandpit. By filling various-sized containers using a number of different-sized scoopers, children develop understandings of direct comparison and units of measure.	Kindergarten children explore length using streamers. Children make comparisons and hypothesise based on their investigations— for example, the tallest child in the class has the largest foot, your arm span is equal to your height, your knee is halfway between your ankle and your hip.
Geometry	Classification of shapes Relationships between two- and three-dimensional shapes Attributes of shapes Position Directionality Uses coordinates/grids Structure and transformation of shapes (reflection, rotation, translation— flip slide turn) Symmetry Tessellation	Toddlers explore shapes, position, location and orientation as they stack blocks and build constructions.	Year 1 children use informal units to estimate and measure the mass of a cup of popping corn. Using a popcorn machine, a comparison is made between the mass of popped and unpopped corn. Children hypothesise and record findings.
Statistics and probability	Data collection Representation Interpretation Graphing Using tables and tallies Reasonableness of result Chance Likelihood of events	Three-year-olds create simple data displays by grouping their shoes according to various attributes including colour, style or size.	Kindergarten children use a digital camera to capture their favourite food items, compiling a picture graph on the IWB or blackboard.

Numeracy involves an understanding of these mathematical concepts, but more importantly requires the ability to apply them in various situations and make connections between contexts. For example, Sabina, aged four years, has a good understanding of the structure and function of three-dimensional shapes, including cubes, cylinders, spheres, cones and prisms, and an understanding of volume. She can describe the features of these shapes using everyday language and can sort them according to common attributes. Sabina's deep understanding of three-dimensional shapes became evident when she tried to repack her lunch box after removing a number of the items. She visualised the space before moving items around so that they would fit without gaps or overlaps, and so the lid would close easily. Here we see an application of a mathematical concept, with Sabina demonstrating her understanding of three-dimensional shapes and their attributes in a practical context.

Early years learners are immersed in a wide range of environments that can stimulate mathematics learning and problem-solving. These environments may not necessarily be technology rich or resplendent with ample resources for exploration. What we need to consider are the opportunities for mathematics inquiry, no matter what the context or environment may be. Multi-modal learning and multiple literacies, such as using the arts, can assist in developing mathematical ideas. Picture books and storytelling provide an avenue for mathematical discussions, explorations and problem-solving opportunities. With new technologies, mathematical concepts are emerging through techno-toys, web-based resources and other forms of digital multimedia, such as touch technologies, enabling advanced mathematical ideas to be accessible to early years learners.

The next section will provide examples of these concepts and interrelated processes: investigating, problem-solving, applying strategies, questioning, communicating, justifying, reasoning and reflecting. These examples include play experiences, games, picture books, technological resources, investigations and projects, and integrated learning—such as instances where mathematics and science are inseparable in exploratory situations.

Numeracy through play

Traditionally, the core of the early childhood curriculum has centred on children's play in the child-care context. Historically, early childhood educators have debated the role of direct or formal instruction in children's learning, particularly in the prior-to-school years, with many arguing that play is paramount to learning. Much of the early childhood literature has emphasised the value of play in a child-initiated curriculum.

Play can provide rich opportunities for mathematical learning, exploration, thinking and representation. Early years learners explore various mathematical concepts, including counting, classification, order, size, partitioning, patterns, measurement, shapes, spatial thinking and probability. Through play, they have the opportunity to construct and represent ideas, and frequently revisit ideas as a 'pattern' of experiences. This encourages them to consolidate mathematical ideas. Teachers can use their observations of early years learners engaged in play to extend their mathematical learning by scaffolding—for example, by providing resources and engaging in conversations with them (see Figure 6.1).

Figure 6.1   Example of educators extending the learning experience

One day in the play dough area, one of the children began using the dough to 'make pizza'. Several other children joined this play and also made pizzas—large ones, small ones, using a range of different play dough 'toppings'. After two days of similar play at the play dough table, the teachers decided to extend this play by providing additional materials such as baking trays, chef's hats and aprons, plastic knives and chopping boards. The children also added to this play by using a cupboard as an oven and asking for a table to be added to make it a pizza restaurant. By incorporating the pizza restaurant, children took turns being the chef, the waiter (including writing orders) and the customer. The teachers continued observing the children, seeing this play develop and documenting language, such as 'a large pizza', a 'medium sized cheese pizza' and 'half ham and pineapple please'. The children also used the language of sequencing, ordering events such as 'put the tomato on first, then the cheese'.

The educators acted as co-learners by scaffolding the process and providing resources. After playing with the dough, the children made a range of pizzas and created a recipe book. Throughout the pizza story, the children documented their experience with photos and shared the learning with their parents. Some parents also joined in, with one family who owned a bakery helping the children to make their own dough (see Figure 6.2). The children then took orders, collated their favourite pizzas and cooked them for lunch. Children cut the pizzas into eight slices, devising strategies to ensure they were an equal size. They solved the problem of how many pieces were required, and therefore the number of pizzas that were needed. They communicated their strategies, reflected on their estimations and calculations, and justified their thinking.

Learning opportunities such as these are critical in the early years, and through to formal schooling, because as educators we also need to consider how everyday

Figure 6.2   Exploring mathematical concepts and processes through cooking

experiences in the twenty-first century have changed. These experiences allow children to explore mathematical concepts, and to apply mathematical processes in a real-life context.

Numeracy through games

Games are an enjoyable way for early years learners to develop mathematical concepts. These can include concepts created by children as social activities or inherited as part of family and cultural traditions. They can be individually imaginative. They can utilise the outdoors (e.g. 'What's the time, Mr Wolf?'), or can include board games (e.g. Snakes and Ladders). Games may encompass all kinds of physical, group and team activities that develop further into formal sports and artistic endeavours or involve kinaesthetic movement. In addition to these traditional forms, technology has afforded new social norms where early years learners engage in digital games, play with techno-toys and engage in virtual environments.

Regardless of the type or complexity of the game, games create opportunities for early years learners to interact with their peers, explore mathematical ideas and language and develop problem-solving strategies. They also have the potential to develop children's dispositions for learning, including confidence, cooperation and persistence. Games can incorporate cultural perspectives as well as community events. Figure 6.3 shows an example of the game 'Bush Tucker'. Here, children roll the dice to 'catch' the corresponding number of witchetty grubs for their 'bush tucker bag'. This task enables the children to practise skills in subitising (immediate recognition of a group of objects or items in any spatial arrangement without counting), counting, addition and subtraction. Tye subitised the regular dice pattern of five and recognised that in adding the five grubs to his 'tucker bag', he had increased his total to seven.

Figure 6.3   Exploring numeracy concepts through the board game Bush Tucker

Numeracy through picture books

Picture books not only facilitate literacy; they also provide opportunities for numeracy. They often include mathematical concepts either purposefully or unintentionally, and thus provide an avenue for mathematical discussion and problem-solving.

For example, in her recent research, Marston identifies the mathematical concepts and possibilities for exploration in *Uno's Garden* (Base, 2006). According to Marston, the text was principally written for its environmental message but contains numerous mathematical concepts (see Marston & Mulligan, 2012). The illustrations support the story (and mathematics) about Uno coming to live in a beautiful forest. As more people join Uno in the forest, the number of buildings doubles with each page, and the plants and animals decrease until they realise the damage humans are causing. Using the story, children can explore counting, doubling and patterns as well as addition and subtraction ideas in an engaging and meaningful context. Children can create their own 'doubles' (and number patterns) from the theme of the book—for example, if one insect has six legs, how many legs on two insects (or double the insects).

Through picture books and storytelling, early years learners find out about the world and how mathematics is used in everyday life. They can then relate these stories and images to their own experiences and apply this knowledge to other contexts: 'If children find the context of their mathematics learning meaningful and part of their everyday lives they will be motivated, more mathematically confident, and encouraged to value mathematics more than they would otherwise.' (Marston & Mulligan, 2012, p. 212)

Numeracy through technology

Technology is constantly evolving, with new technologies presenting unique opportunities for young mathematics learners. As educators, we have to be aware of current technologies and explore their potential in mathematics learning, harnessing these tools where appropriate (Highfield, 2010). Technology use can be simple, such as using a digital camera to document children's learning and play (see Figure 6.4). Still shots of the sequence of sandcastles can also be utilised to reflect on the experience.

By capturing an image of children's work, we create an opportunity to recognise children's mathematical efforts, share them with others and help them recall and revisit their thinking.

Figure 6.4   Using a digital camera to support documentation of children's learning

When the children were allowed outside, a group of five three-year-olds rushed to the sandpit and quickly gathered digging equipment and buckets. The educator in the sandpit initially observed the children, and in particular she noted that Sam had used a small mould and was pressing wet sand out in 'cakes'. She turned to Sam and commented, 'Wow Sam, you've made so many of those.' Sam responded by saying 'One, two, three' (pointing to the first three 'cakes' out of the collection of seven) . . . (pausing) 'I made all of them!' The educator replied, 'Great counting—let's count them all together.' She then modelled the counting and said, 'You've made seven cakes.' Sam ran to a friend and said, 'Look, I've made seven cakes—see' (pointing to his sandcastles). The other children started counting their sandcastles and describing them, using statements such as, 'I've made round cakes . . . like a circle.'

Figure 6.5   Using an interactive whiteboard to make connections between concrete, symbolic and abstract ideas

During an investigation of animals, five-year-old children had been using plastic sea creatures, sorting them into groups. Initially, the children were sorting animals by type or by colour, focusing on one attribute (colour or type). The educator, aiming to extend the play, invited the children to see whether they could sort the sea creatures into two 'aquariums', providing two hoops. The children worked in pairs as discussed, then sorted the sea creatures in a variety of ways. At the end of the lesson, the children were asked to share with the group how they had sorted. They used the interactive whiteboard (with images of the creatures), dragging them into the two hoops to demonstrate their categories. One group sorted into soft and hard bodies—soft animals included sea animals such as whales, frogs and penguins; hard animals included crabs, turtles and crayfish. Another group sorted by the animal's habitat, sorting into water animals (such as the octopus and sharks) and creatures that live on land and in the water (including the turtle, penguin and frogs).

The following day, the educator provided the same task, this time altering the two groups to create a Venn diagram. This challenged the children's sorting from the previous day, causing the children to reflect on their previous thoughts and alter their strategy.

Figure 6.6   Integrated learning experience: Designing and making a rollercoaster

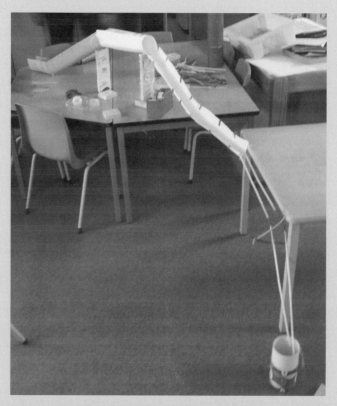

In free time, a group of six-year-old children had been investigating a marble track. Building on this play, the educator asked the children to work in groups to design and make a rollercoaster for ping-pong balls. As the educator listened to the children designing and making, he observed much more than the process of design and make. He overheard children measuring, and using direct comparison and informal measurement. They compared angles of slope and height, counted, and used trial and error. The children constantly trialled their rollercoaster, rolling ping-pong balls down to test each aspect of their ride. When their attempts failed, the children tried again, reflecting and revising their plans. As they were working in small groups throughout the process, the children communicated constantly—talking about their reasoning, the strategies they were using and evaluating their work. As each group completed the task, the class compared their constructions. In comparing constructions, mathematical language came to the fore, with comparisons of height, the number of turns and the speed of the ride (estimated by timing 'the ride'). In literacy, the children used descriptive language and wrote about their rollercoasters, typing their stories and adding digital photos of their designs.

Other technological aids include web-based resources and software, and digital games. While techno-games are widely used to practise and develop fluency in basic mathematical skills, educators should also be aware that tools that are 'drill and practice' may limit mathematical development. Mathematics learning must involve the physical processes of investigating and solving problems in practical situations (Highfield, 2010).

Interactive whiteboards (IWBs) are increasingly common in Australian contexts, and can be a useful tool to share ideas, investigate representations and manipulate resources. The following scenario (see Figure 6.5) exemplifies the use of an IWB and SMARTnotebook™ in problem-solving, using it as a tool to explore multiple solutions and as a connection between concrete, symbolic and abstract.

Enabling early years learners to share thinking (such as in the sorting example) and documenting their strategy use makes learning more transparent and promotes reflective processes. Here, the screen-based technology has the potential to bridge the gap between activities with concrete resources, and symbolic and abstract representations.

Numeracy through integrated learning and investigations

Integrated learning provides opportunities for numeracy to develop in relevant and meaningful contexts. It allows early years learners to apply mathematical concepts, understanding and processes across different curriculum areas. This approach encourages early years learners to make connections between concepts and contexts. The following scenario (see Figure 6.6) provides an example of how numeracy is enhanced through a science and technology 'design and make' experience.

The science and technology example moved far beyond a science lesson, allowing children to invent, reflect and revise. This resulted in a rich task that provided meaningful opportunities for children to investigate, problem-solve and apply mathematical concepts such as counting, measuring, shapes, angles and speed/time/distance relationships. Children communicated mathematics through representation, and frequently justified their strategies and thinking.

Becoming effective communicators

From birth, children communicate with those around them. Communication can be through various mediums, including spoken language, gestures, written words and symbols, drawings, images, pictures and sound (Arthur et al., 2010). In this new era

Figure 6.7   Four-year-old's representation of a repeating hopscotch pattern at 180 degrees

of technology, communication is through digital technology such as mobile phones, digital recorders and email. Communicating mathematical ideas and mathematical thinking is critical to the development of numeracy skills. When educators engage with early years learners, they should model appropriate mathematical language and terminology, and encourage learners to use this language when explaining their mathematical thinking and reasoning. It is also critical that early years learners are presented with regular opportunities to communicate their mathematical thinking with peers, educators, family and the wider community.

One way in which early years learners communicate mathematical thinking and their solution strategies is through their representations. Figure 6.7 shows a four-year-old representing her repeating hopscotch pattern through drawing. Sally is drawing the pattern from the teddy bear's perspective rather than her own. The teddy is positioned at 180 degrees to Sally.

The dialogue between Sally and the educator highlights her sophisticated skills of visualisation. She has the ability to view objects from different directions, perspectives and orientations. Her dialogue referring to a previously made pattern shows her ability to abstract the pattern structure and generalise it.

Sally: I have to put the green on this side.

Educator: Why that side?

Sally: Because the teddy is looking at it from the other way. I can see it this way (referring to the right of the hopscotch) but for the teddy it is on the other side (referring to the left of the hopscotch) because he is sitting on the other side. It's like backwards.

Sally: This is the same as the other hopscotch I made.

Educator: How is it the same?

Sally: See four up and four across. I made it two times. This is four up and four across too (referring to a previously made hopscotch). I made it two times too. That's the same.

Educator: How is it different?

Sally: It's different colours.

Developing educators' pedagogical content knowledge

To provide rich mathematical experiences, early childhood educators must have sound mathematical content and pedagogical knowledge. The Australian Association of Mathematics Teachers (2006) identifies the importance of educators having a strong knowledge base upon which to draw:

> Their knowledge base includes knowledge of students, how mathematics is learned, what affects students' opportunities to learn mathematics and how the learning of mathematics can be enhanced. It also includes sound knowledge and appreciation of mathematics appropriate to the grade level and/or mathematics subjects they teach. (2006, p. 2)

Professional knowledge of mathematics is also critical for early childhood educators, although the mathematics may not be considered complex. However, the professional's support for rich mathematics learning is based on their knowledge and awareness of the important mathematical 'things' to look for. This is needed right from the early years. 'Educators require a rich mathematical vocabulary to accurately describe and explain children's mathematical ideas and to support numeracy development.' (DEEWR, 2009, p. 38) Thus it is not just about vocabulary, it is about educators' understanding of the concepts themselves.

Assessing and documenting early years learners' mathematics learning

Assessing children's learning involves collecting, recording, analysing and inter-preting evidence of their mathematical knowledge, reasoning and problem-solving strategies. Assessment for children aged from birth to four years largely involves observation and questioning as they engage in experiences. Having conversations with children is a critical component of assessment in the early years. Early child-hood educators document children's learning through digital multimedia, artefacts, notes, conversation transcripts and observations. This documentation is a valuable record of the learning context and experiences, the child's process of exploring, the connections they make to previous learning and their understanding of math-ematical ideas. Documentation is also important for educator self-reflection and evaluation of their planning and teaching strategies.

Figure 6.8 provides excerpts from documentation that records a learning experience that resulted from the reading of the picturebook *Alexander's Outing* (Allen, 1994).

Assessment of mathematical development or competencies is usually insti-gated at school entry. There is much ongoing debate among educators and the community about the appropriateness of 'formal' mathematics assessment for early years learners. At an international level, the formal assessment of early numeracy or mathematics in the early years of schooling has traditionally been implemented through standardised instruments, interview-based assessments or school-based measures. Some Australian state-based testing regimes are in place, such as Best Start (NSW Department of Education and Training, 2008), a school-entry interview-based assessment. The justification for such assessments is based on the premise that early assessment can provide diagnostic indicators of chil-dren's abilities and learning difficulties so that educators can differentiate learning to meet the needs of students.

One of the limitations of these assessments is that they do not enable the depth of analysis of mathematical thinking and problem-solving strategies. For example,

Figure 6.8   Example of documentation: Investigations and problem-solving with four-year-olds

Today we read *Alexander's Outing*. While we were reading the story we discussed what was happening and several children didn't understand why Alexander was able to float—they assumed he was swimming. To extend this discussion and to provide opportunity for the children to develop an understanding of floating we set up the storybook, two jugs (one filled with water) and some floating ducks on a table. During the day, children explored this area, acting out the story and using language from the book. After a little while James exclaimed, 'It's floating—Alexander is floating!' Intrigued by this we discussed this further—and James stated, 'Well, this duck can't swim, 'cause it hasn't got legs, so he (pointing to Alexander) must have been floating too!'

As the day progressed, Mary and Chris wanted to work out if all the ducks 'could be saved like Alexander was'. They used a range of ducks on the table (small, medium and large), seeing if they could fit in the 'whole' (jug) and whether they could float like Alexander. After several trials, they worked out that only the small and medium duck could fit in the 'hole' (jug) and so mother duck, the large duck, was safe.

Throughout this activity the children developed concepts of volume and capacity, talking about the quantity of water in the jug. They used language such as: empty, full, a little bit full and nearly full. After discussion with the educator they also used language of 'half full'. In terms of literacy, the children repeated the story through play, recalling the events and sequence of events, even replicating the language of the text. The children also developed stronger concepts of floating—discussing what would and wouldn't float.

I Can Do Maths assessment (Doig & de Lemos, 2000) is a multiple-choice assessment. More recent research-based assessments focus on reasoning and move beyond basic numeracy. For example, the Schedule for Early Number Assessment 1 (SENA 1) (NSW Department of Education and Training, 2001) assesses children's number knowledge and arithmetical strategies.

With a shift to early algebraic reasoning, an Early Mathematical Patterning Assessment (EMPA) was developed, trialled and refined with pre-schoolers (Papic et al., 2011). Similarly, the Pattern and Structure Assessment (PASA) is a structured interview designed to assess a range of mathematical concepts that have common features of pattern and structure, such as repetition and equal units. The assessment components provide a framework for pedagogy using a structural approach (Mulligan & Mitchelmore, 2009).

Summary

- In this chapter we have highlighted young children's capacity for mathematical thinking. We have reviewed current perspectives on numeracy within the context of a rapidly changing technological society.
- The EYLF provides new direction for educators and the community, highlighting the importance of promoting children's mathematical development.
- We provided an overview of key concepts and processes, and some examples of these.
- Opportunities for mathematics are exemplified through play experiences, using games, picture books and technological resources.
- We raised the issue of supporting professionals in their learning about mathematics and children's mathematical thinking.
- Strategies for assessment and documentation of children's mathematical thinking are linked with the importance of educator reflection. Informal assessment strategies are contrasted with formal assessment and the development of new assessment approaches.
- We propose some implications for reforming early numeracy. As early childhood educators we may need to:
    - become more aware of the natural and spontaneous ways that mathematics is developed by children in everyday contexts
    - understand what real mathematical thinking is and how it can develop from the earliest years

- capitalise on opportunities for children to explore, represent and communicate about mathematics through play or games, literature, or other experiences
- become more attuned to new, emerging mathematical concepts and processes that are afforded by technology
- adopt a balanced perspective about policy changes in developing early childhood curriculum and assessment approaches
- pursue professional learning about mathematics that is required for effective participation in society for young children of the future.

Discussion questions

6.1 What is the relationship between early numeracy and mathematics? Can you identify similarities and differences?

6.2 If you compiled a list of key mathematical concepts and processes, what would you include? Why? How might this list have changed over the last 20 years?

6.3 What is the role of the educator in enhancing numeracy skills?

6.4 Design a numeracy experience that encourages exploration, communication and representation. Identify three key mathematical concepts that are applied and/or enhanced through this activity.

References

Allen, P. (1994). *Alexander's outing*. Australia: Penguin.

Arthur, L., McArdle, F. & Papic, M. (2010). *Stars are made of glass: Children as capable and creative communicators*. Canberra: Early Childhood Australia.

Australian Association of Mathematics Teachers /Early Childhood Association (2006). *Position paper on early mathematics*. Retrieved 20 February 2012 from <www.aamt.edu.au/Documentation/ Statements/Position-Paper-on-Early-Childhood-Mathematics>.

Australian Curriculum, Assessment and Reporting Authority (ACARA) (2011). *The Australian Curriculum: Mathematics, Version 1.2, 8 March 2011*. Sydney: ACARA.

Base, G. (2006). *Uno's garden*. Australia: Penguin.

Clements, D.H. & Sarama, J. (2009). *Learning and teaching early maths: The learning trajectories approach*. New York: Routledge.

Commonwealth of Australia (2009). *Shape of the Australian Curriculum: Mathematics*. Canberra: Commonwealth of Australia. Retrieved 20 February 2012 from <www.acara.edu.au/verve/_ resources/Australian_Curriculum_-_Maths.pdf>.

Department of Education, Employment and Workplace Relations (DEEWR) (2009). *Belonging, being and becoming: The Early Years Learning Framework for Australia*. Canberra: Commonwealth of Australia.

Doig, B. & de Lemos, M. (2000). *I can do maths*. Melbourne: Australian Council for Educational Research.

English, L.D. (2004). Promoting the development of young children's mathematical and analogical reasoning. In L.D. English (ed.), *Mathematical and analogical reasoning of young learners*. Mahwah, NJ: Lawrence Erlbaum.

Greenes, C., Ginsburg, H. & Balfanz, R. (2004). Big math for little kids. *Early Childhood Research Quarterly, 19*, 159–66.

Highfield, K. (2010). Possibilities and pitfalls of techno-toys and digital play in mathematics learning. In M. Ebbeck & M. Waniganayake (eds), *Play in early childhood education: Learning in diverse contexts* (pp. 177–96). Melbourne: Oxford University Press.

Marston, J. & Mulligan, J. (2012). *Using picture books to integrate mathematics in early learning*. In P. Whiteman & K. De Gioia (eds), *Children and childhoods 1: Perspectives, places and practices* (pp. 209–25). Newcastle upon Tyne: Cambridge Scholars Publishing.

Mulligan, J.T. & Mitchelmore, M.C. (2009). Awareness of pattern and structure in early mathematical development. *Mathematics Education Research Journal, 21*(2), 33–49.

NSW Department of Education and Training (2001). *Count Me in Too Professional Development Package (CMIT)*. Sydney: NSW Department of Education and Training.

—— (2008). *Best Start*. Sydney: NSW Department of Education and Training.

Papic, M.M., Mulligan, J.T. & Mitchelmore, M.C. (2011). Assessing the development of preschoolers' mathematical patterning. *Journal for Research in Mathematics Education, 42*(3), 237–68.

Perry, B. & Dockett, S. (2008). Young children's access to powerful mathematical ideas. In L.D. English (ed.), *Handbook of international research in mathematics education*, 2nd ed. (pp. 75–108). New York: Routledge.

Perry, B., Young-Loveridge, J.M., Dockett, S. & Doig, B. (2008). The development of young children's mathematical understanding. In H. Forgasz, A. Barkatas, A. Bishop, B.A. Clarke, S. Keast, W.T. Seah & P. Sullivan (eds), *Research in mathematics education in Australasia 2004–2007* (pp. 17–40). Rotterdam: Sense Publishers.

Sarama, J. & Clements, D.H. (2009). *Early childhood mathematics education research: Learning trajectories for young children*. London: Routledge.

van Nes, F. (2011). Mathematics education and neurosciences: Towards interdisciplinary insights into the development of young children's mathematical abilities. *Educational Philosophy and Theory, 43*(1), 75–80.

7

Science

Anne Petriwskyj

Introduction

Children's curiosity about their world offers a springboard for an exciting range of investigations in the early years, incorporating both classroom-based inquiry learning, and outdoor experimentation and excursions. With thoughtful guidance, young children can inquire into questions of genuine personal interest about the everyday natural and designed world (for example, how animals live, how the sky changes, how toys move, how cooking changes food) and community problems of real local significance (such as how to conserve water during drought or caring for the habitat of native fauna). Pedagogies that link children's guided investigation of questions of genuine interest with the structured processes of scientific inquiry foster deeper scientific understanding and positive dispositions towards science.

Science for early learners

Science inquiry for early learners aims for deep understanding and conceptual change, rather than a surface extension of interest, imitation of activities or memorisation of isolated factual scientific information. The rapid pace of change in scientific information (for instance, knowledge of the solar system or the structure of matter) means that today's 'facts' may be seen as misconceptions or errors in the near future. Therefore, the focus of science inquiry learning is on higher order thinking, including problem-solving, reflection and meta-cognition, in order to enhance early learners' capacity to thoughtfully investigate questions using a logical process (see Figure 7.1). Inquiry learning supports scientific literacy, including awareness of currently accepted scientific understandings, an awareness of scientific ways to communicate information (for example, tables, diagrams) and the development of a positive disposition towards seeking evidence rather than an unquestioning acceptance of claims.

Figure 7.1   Higher order and other thinking

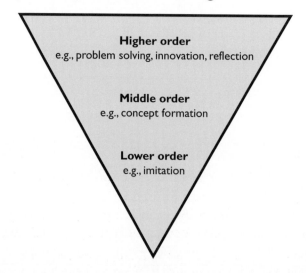

Early learners are curious about the natural and designed world, and have already formed understandings of their everyday world as a basis for science learning in early education programs (Loxley et al., 2010). Planning for science teaching that starts with children's ideas and questions includes both emergent planning or teaching within the spontaneous moment then documenting it, and projective planning or forward planning to extend children's inquiry. For early learners aged from birth to four years, this may involve spontaneously extending a child's fascination with butterflies, then planning stories, songs, movement to music, garden walks, hatching of butterflies in an empty aquarium and organising museum loans of butterfly models in the following days. However, it is not sufficient to offer resources pertinent to an observed interest; the role of the educator goes beyond the surface level to expand children's scientific awareness and to deepen their understandings and skills. Inquiry pedagogies for extending children's understandings need careful planning, implementation and evaluation to ensure that deep learning occurs.

While inquiry projects usually arise from children's interests, questions and prior understandings, there may be occasions where children's observed interests remain narrow or where educators find it difficult to ascertain clear directions for children's scientific interests. In this case, educators may sometimes use a current event (perhaps an agricultural show or a weather event such as a storm) or a recent concern in the local community (water management in a drought area; construction of an oil or gas pipeline; linking to Indigenous knowledge such as bush tucker) as a catalyst for science inquiry in order to expand children's horizons, prompt fresh interest or extend science content. For example, expectations of coverage of the curriculum strands by early years learners aged from four to eight years may prompt an educator to challenge children's narrow focus on biology into physical, chemical or earth and space sciences. In order to retain children's engagement with the inquiry questions, the educator's role is to seek children's input into the direction the investigation might take and the way they might inquire, so that children feel they have ownership of the process and become truly engaged with the topic. Children's popular culture—including television shows, internet sites, computer games and multifunctional tablet apps—offers opportunities to capitalise on what children already enjoy by drawing out the scientific content of favoured entertainment items and framing investigations around similar topics.

Ongoing monitoring and assessment of children's prior understandings and real questions can offer educators a guide as to the potential topic and specific focus of an investigation, as well as helping them to gain insights into children's possible misunderstandings that will need sensitive reframing over time. Moving from children's prior understandings and questions or from real issues in the community to hands-on, minds-on active investigations involves:

- recognition of links to curriculum expectations
- planning of engaging learning environments
- provision for collaborative negotiation of ideas
- authentic assessment of progress.

Curriculum for early years science

The shift from science curriculum documents focused on inputs such as learning tasks or activities to documents framed by learning outputs has been apparent in both the school sector and the prior-to-school early childhood education and care (ECEC) sector. Science curriculum documents for early years learners attend to three key elements, although the emphasis varies depending on the age group and the educational setting:

- processes of inquiry (e.g. observational skills)
- products or scientific understandings (e.g. life-cycles)
- values, attitudes and dispositions towards science.

Processes of inquiry

The learning of scientific inquiry processes by young children focuses on effective ways to 'find out how to find out'. Initially, these processes include asking questions, observing closely, predicting events and communicating observations. Later, they involve researching information, classifying, hypothesising and inferring from evidence collected. Early learners need to be explicitly taught how to use these processes, and to use the discipline-specific language of science processes (infer, classify) and the vocabulary of science content (metamorphosis, photosynthesis, evaporation, translucent, sedimentary). Introduction to the notion of a fair test in which only one variable is changed (such as the amount of light) and a specific aspect is measured (for example, how big a bean plant can grow from a seed), while everything else (water, nutrients etc.) stays the same, can be supported through the use of a lotus diagram to scaffold discussion (see Figure 7.2).

Figure 7.2   Lotus diagram: Fair test for growing bean seeds

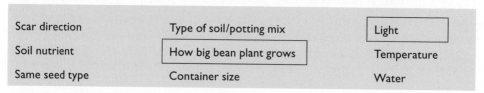

Scar direction	Type of soil/potting mix	Light
Soil nutrient	How big bean plant grows	Temperature
Same seed type	Container size	Water

Science understandings

The core areas for young children's expansion of understanding about science are often framed as science discipline content:

- biological science, or life science or life and living, such as:
  - animal structure, type, growth and habitat
  - plant structure, types, growth and environments
  - human body structure and growth
- earth and space science, or earth and beyond, such as:
  - weather and climate (e.g. water cycle)
  - earth forms, and soil or rock characteristics
  - features of the sky (e.g. moon)
- physical science or energy and change, such as:
  - push and pull forces; how toys move
  - simple machine principles: cog, lever, screw, ramp
  - magnetism, electricity, light and sound
- chemical science or natural and processed materials:
  - types of natural and processed materials
  - solid, liquid, gas states
  - change of state by heating, freezing, rusting.

While biological science may appear more accessible for early learners than some other content, educators should address the range of content areas.

Values, attitudes and dispositions
These include appreciating the work of scientists, recognising the evidence-based nature of science and demonstrating positive dispositions towards scientific inquiry and seeking information. Educator modelling is important in teaching positive dispositions towards active inquiry.

Science curriculum documents for early years learners incorporate a range of expected learning outcomes, but their framing of product outcomes can range from broad learning capacities (such as thinking or reflecting) to traditional science disciplines (biology, chemistry), depending on the age group. Dispositions such as a positive confident approach to scientific inquiry are highlighted more in curriculum documents for early years learners aged from birth to four years, while the nature of science and specific scientific content, such as understanding push–pull forces in physical sciences, are highlighted more in documents for early years learners aged from four to eight years. Attention to pedagogies also varies, although playful inquiry rather than didactic instruction is a shared focus for early years learners. Overall, there is a shift from broad inquiry learning framed by sensory exploration and play towards more explicit discipline-specific scientific understandings and inquiry processes as children move into and through school.

In Australian programs for early years learners aged from birth to four years of age, the national Early Years Learning Framework (EYLF) (DEEWR, 2009) identifies broad outcomes relevant to science, integrated with other areas of learning. These outcomes include dispositions for learning, inquiry processes and understandings such as recognising patterns in the world, and skills such as hypothesising (see Table 7.1). This curriculum specifies both broad content and effective play pedagogies supporting science inquiry. The educator's role in intentional teaching includes the provision of flexible indoor and outdoor learning environments for playful investigation, and continuity of children's exploratory play experience across the centres, homes and communities. The role includes encouragement for children to participate actively in exploration, questioning, decision-making and construction of their own learning.

In Australian school programs for early years learners aged from four to eight years of age, the national Australian Curriculum–Science (ACS) (ACARA, 2009) frames learning outcomes as inquiry skills, science understandings and science as a human endeavour (see Table 7.1), divided into year-level examples of outcomes from Foundation Year to Year 3 to indicate typical expectations. This curriculum specifies content and levels of difficulty, and suggests differentiation to cater for children with disabilities and English as a second language. The emphasis in the curriculum for K–2 is on awareness of self and the local world, using purposeful exploratory play as part of the investigation process. The content of the K–2 science curriculum includes learning the processes of classification and comparison, sharing what has been observed, recognising the work of science in everyday life and caring for the environment.

Table 7.1   Comparison of science in Australian curriculum documents

Early Years Learning Framework (DEEWR, 2009) Australian Curriculum-Science (ACARA, 2009)
Outcome 4 and 5 Skills e.g. predicting, experimenting, communicating ideas
Science Inquiry Skills e.g. observing, predicting, inferring, communicating
Outcome 4 and 5 Inquiry process e.g. thinking to solve problems, categorising, generalising about the natural world, reflective thinking to consider why things happen, recognising patterns
Science Understandings e.g. biological, physical, chemical, earth and space sciences
Outcome 4 Dispositions for learning e.g. curiosity, persistence
Science as Human Endeavour e.g. values such as appreciating the uses of science

Other curriculum documents for specific jurisdictions locate science content within a particular cultural or schooling context. For example, Foundations for Success for Indigenous early years learners prior to school (Queensland Department of Education and Training, 2008) frames learning relevant to science as thinking, inquiring and problem-solving, connecting with land and place, and representing ideas in culturally appropriate ways using home languages, Standard Australian English and traditional cultural resources (e.g. animal movements expressed in dance).

Learning environments for science inquiry

Science learning environments that support active meaningful investigation provide rich resources for multi-sensory exploration, interesting and integrated learning experiences and involvement in the broader community. For example, the fascination of children with the play of shadows on the patio could be extended through making shadow hand shapes, drawing body shadow outlines on paper taped to the wall or on the concrete pathway at various time of the day, shadow songs or poems, stories about shadows and using shadow puppets, using a torch to extend the idea of shadow from blocking the sun's light to blocking other light and talking with a photographer.

Organisation of learning environments for science involves selecting suitable materials, setting up relevant materials and planning learning centres. Classroom science-specific resources such as simple factual books or storybooks, posters, science table displays of objects, computer software or multifunction tablet apps may be extended through creative use of everyday materials, educator-made resources (see Figure 7.3) and collections of interesting found objects. Collections could include:

- items from the natural world (feathers, rocks, seed pods, pressed flowers)
- children's toys (balls, wheeled vehicles, boats, jack-in-the-box)
- kitchen or garage tools that demonstrate simple machine principles (rotary beater, tyre lever, spring-loaded clothes pegs).

The classification of resources into labelled kits (for example, magnets, light, insects and spiders) assists educators to access stored resources quickly, and supports children's developing ability to classify items into categories. The organisation of inquiry resources at classroom learning centres helps children to understand what is to be done, and presents materials in interesting ways to indicate a potential investigation. Early years learners aged from four to eight years may also be assisted in sharing ideas at learning centres by the formation of three- to four-member cooperative learning groups with assigned roles such as recorder and timekeeper.

Figure 7.3   Educator-made resource: Antarctica diorama

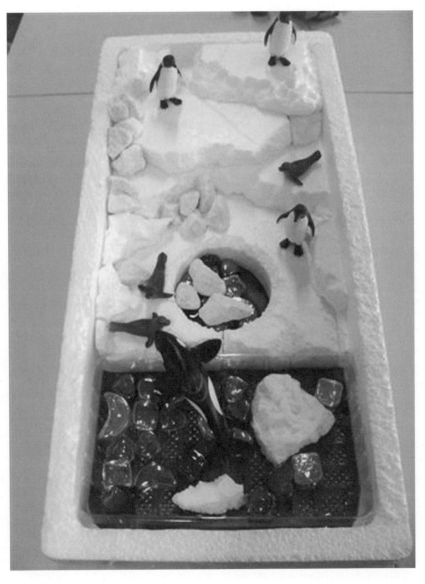

While children's innate curiosity about their world often provides sufficient opportunities for guided inquiry using everyday resources, some early years learners may prove more difficult to engage. Intriguing learning experiences (such as making a solar cooker) can provoke discussion and stimulate children's interest (Howitt & Blake, 2010). For early years learners aged from four to eight years, intriguing experiences could include:

- discrepant events—for example, an insect standing on the surface of water, a ball that doesn't bounce
- problem-based learning—imagine you are an astronaut on a space ship and you are running out of fresh water; save the duckling in the story *Alexander's Outing* before the story ends
- concept cartoons—for instance, draw a cartoon on ways of keeping a drink hot, presenting conflicting notions about heat transfer to challenge children's thinking and stimulate debate (Morris et al., 2007).

Strategies for engaging children and linking learning to their lives can also include outdoor and excursion real-world learning, projects and the application of information and communication technologies as part of science learning.

Scientific investigations that link with the real world should extend beyond the classroom into the playground (looking for insects, planting a vegetable garden, making a bark humpy) and into the use of community resources including excursions and incursions (field trips to a zoo, classroom visits by a biologist). These informal science investigation experiences, guided by educator questioning, expand children's awareness of their world (Fenichel & Schweingruber, 2010). For early years learners aged from birth to four years, growing basic vegetables and using these for cooking offers an understanding of growth of plants, an awareness of the sources of foods, an understanding of how foods are changed by processing and an appreciation of fresh foods that some children might otherwise refuse to eat (Alexander, 2006). Learning opportunities beyond the classroom extend children's experience of their environment, link classroom learning with their community and provide a fresh view of science for early years learners who are difficult to engage. For early years learners aged from four to eight years, an excursion to a science museum or an environmental centre or an incursion by a visiting science presentation group such as the CSIRO, guided by careful educator discussion and questioning, may regenerate interest in scientific inquiry.

Information and communication technologies (ICTs) extend the ways in which children inquire and represent their learning, but ICT resources should be used purposefully and should be flexible and open-ended, not drill-and-skill tasks. Children's research may be supported through information technologies such as:

- interactive whiteboard learning objects
- digital USB microscopes
- multifunction tablet apps
- webquests for safe internet searches.

Other technologies, such as digital photography, flip camera video and computer drawing tools, may be used by children to document their observations through labelled diagrams, digital photograph storyboards and science e-journals (Neumann-Hinds, 2007). For example, early years learners aged from four to eight years might use a digital microscope to observe leaf edges and veins, then save and link the images into an interactive whiteboard learning object for classifying leaves or present a digital storyboard explaining their research process to other children.

Risk management is an important element of a educator's responsibility in the science learning environment, as there is potential for harm when handling plants or animals, using potting mixes, using the internet, going on excursions or field trips, heating or freezing foods, or exploring physical forces. Each science plan should incorporate a risk evaluation and management plan to alert all staff to potential risks and to prompt preventative action. For example, on an excursion or field trip outside the school or centre, an educator would need to evaluate risks such as road traffic, sun exposure, proximity to hazards such as water, stranger danger and specific risks at the excursion site, then plan preventative strategies such as appropriate adult:child ratios, sun-safety provisions, setting of behaviour limits with the class, briefing of accompanying adults, and specific support for children who may require assistance (Table 7.2). Educator reflection following the event offers further insights into ways of making such experiences safer and more educationally relevant.

Table 7.2   Risk-management plan for environment park trip

Identified hazard	Level of risk	Management plan
Insect sting when walking in bush area; consequences, reaction by individual	Moderate risk	Long-sleeved clothing, check with parents on reactivity, insect cream for bites, Epi pen for individuals as required

The learning environment sets the frame for science inquiry and acts as a hidden curriculum. Science inquiry for early years learners adopts pedagogies that focus on active negotiated learning rather than educator-directed instruction.

Pedagogies for early years science investigations

Contemporary inquiry pedagogies in science education are framed by social constructivist and socio-cultural theories (Fleer, 2009) that emphasise co-construction of deep understandings through:

- children's active, meaningful involvement in investigations
- educator scaffolding and explicit use of scientific language
- social interaction with peers on a topic of inquiry
- connection of science to children's lives and understandings.

Inquiry approaches also embed science learning into other aspects of the curriculum, and integrate content to enrich children's learning experience. Common approaches to science inquiry for early years learners include supported discovery, and interactive or reciprocal approaches. These approaches share the characteristics of active child participation, linking of education program and home/community lives, intentional educator support and negotiation of ideas, although specific teaching strategies can vary.

Supported discovery

This approach is particularly suited to early years learners aged from birth to four years, or for the initial phases of an inquiry process for early years learners aged from four to eight years. One of the key features of this approach is the provision of a wide range of interesting resources from the natural and designed world for children to explore (for example, display table of clocks, egg timers, cog wheels, pulley models and books about how things work). However, it involves not only the provision of rich learning resources and opportunities for sensory exploration but also intentional educator support for children's personal interests and facilitation of children's own investigation. For example, a fascination with plants could prompt an investigation of types of plants, planting of a vegetable garden, harvesting of vegetables and cooking of foods that children have grown themselves (Alexander, 2006). Children could explore plant types, the structure of plants, changes in plants as they grow, sensory qualities of fresh vegetables and changes in vegetables during cooking. This set of experiences would have the added advantage of expanding the experience of those children who may have resisted eating a variety of healthy vegetables.

Interactive and reciprocal investigation

This is highly effective for early years learners aged from four to eight years and for older children in the birth to four years age range (Fleer, 2009). It involves clarification of children's prior understandings, provision of learning opportunities to support investigation, linking of inquiry to children's own home and community experiences, and both educator and peer scaffolding of investigations. For example, if questions were raised about refrigerator magnets, but children appeared to understand only attraction rather than attraction and repulsion, and used everyday language ('sticky' or 'flew up'), they could investigate what items were attracted to magnets from a sectioned box of materials, how strong various magnets were (for example, by attracting paper clips), and what happened when opposite and same poles were adjacent (using a magnetic train or magnetic construction kit). In addition to assisting children to ask researchable questions, modelling experimentation and directing children's attention towards pushes and pulls, the educator would guide children's negotiation of ideas with one another and also learn from the children.

Achieving a balance between children's own investigation and explicit educator guidance, particularly in the context of curriculum expectations in schools, presents a challenge to some educators. Intentional teaching implies that educators go beyond provision of resources and learning opportunities to help children clarify their own questions, support their inquiry processes and extend understandings about the natural and designed world. However, this approach does not mean that rigid instructional sequences heavily directed by the educator are appropriate, as these traditional transmission approaches to science teaching are quite different from supported inquiry approaches for early years learners. Teaching strategies that might be used for inquiry learning include asking guiding effective questions, offering accurate vocabulary, raising alternate ideas, making suggestions and commenting on findings.

Sustained shared thinking is built on children's own investigation and debate, and on knowledge provided from reputable sources of current scientific information. Collaborative negotiation of ideas between educators and children, and among peers, engages children in listening to alternate perspectives, communicating their own understandings to others, and researching and debating conflicting ideas. Such discussion is underpinned by the notion than opinions should be supported with evidence, and that children's own emerging ideas should be compared with those of other children and with currently accepted scientific understandings. Authentic questioning forms a key part of this sustained shared thinking process, as it aims to move children towards deeper thought and discussion. Educators should minimise or avoid closed questions with a single 'correct' answer, as this establishes a 'test' atmosphere and stifles discussion. Open and leading questions encourage deeper thinking, more extended expression of ideas and confidence in stating tentative and emerging views in an atmosphere of shared inquiry (see Table 7.3).

Table 7.3   Using authentic questioning

Minimise closed questions	Use open and leading questions
What state is the cream now?	What changes do you notice in the cream?
What colour is that?	Tell me about the colours you see.
Is that a push or a pull force?	How do you think the object moved? Why?

Provision for a diversity of learners enhances access to effective science learning for all children and supports policies of educational inclusion. Differentiating science learning for a range of abilities involves considering multiple ways of engaging with inquiry or multiple intelligences (such as using movement, viewing, reflection) and multiple levels of difficulty within learning experiences (Fraser-Abder, 2011). The importance of building on cultural understandings, including those of Indigenous Australians, is a feature of contemporary Australian curriculum documents, so the educator's role is to consider appropriate ways to incorporate these broader cultural understandings into science programs without being tokenistic. Investigations of Australian plants and animals and the use of Indigenous creation stories should involve local Indigenous community Elders if possible, to ensure authenticity. Cooperative learning strategies such as Think, Pair, Share, where early years learners are prompted to consider a question, discuss ideas with a partner then share with the class, help children to develop negotiation and social skills to participate effectively in group work during science, while ensuring that all children can have a valued role.

Integrated learning projects, rich tasks or units of work make effective use of learning time, support children's efforts to understand the world in a holistic way and engage early years learners whose immediate interest may not be scientific. For example:

- Links between literacy and science are a key component of the Primary Connections resources developed for schools by the Australian Academy of Science. Science investigations provide a real and meaningful context for children's reading, writing and explaining, so that early years learners are prompted to engage with literacy.
- Scientific drawings, such as labelled diagrams of animals or plants, flow chart drawings of an observed sequence such as shaken cream changing into butter, cross-section drawings of fruits and their seed patterns or analytical drawings of the working of an old analogue clock represent both visual literacy and scientific communication.
- The arts offer rich ways to engage children's interest (e.g. through songs and stories), to investigate understandings (e.g. how colours mix, how sounds are made, how the body moves) and to represent their understandings (e.g. through drama, movement to music and digital media). Drawing from observation offers opportunities for children to become more aware of features of items, to clarify their understandings and to communicate observations (Ehrlen, 2009).
- Links are readily made across mathematics, technology and design, and science through documenting data using graphs and tables, applying scientific understandings to design projects, and using technologies to access and present ideas. For example, measuring the distance that a toy car rolls down varying surfaces on a ramp block can involve arbitrary units (such as paper strips) or numbers, and the results can be documented on paper or in digital photographs (see Figure 7.4).

Science projects offer flexibility in child-focused investigations integrated with other areas of learning. The use of an anticipatory web or mind map of the topic at the start of a project enables an educator to plan potential resources while being flexible about diverting into varied aspects of the topic, rather than insisting that the initial investigation proceeds in a linear fashion. For example, a project about where puddles go after rain might involve inquiry into weather, evaporation, the water cycle or surface absorption, depending on specific questions children ask.

Assessment of and for learning in early years science

Documentation of children's inquiry process and product through science journals and portfolios offers authentic assessment data that have value both in

Figure 7.4 Measuring distance results using paper strips graphing

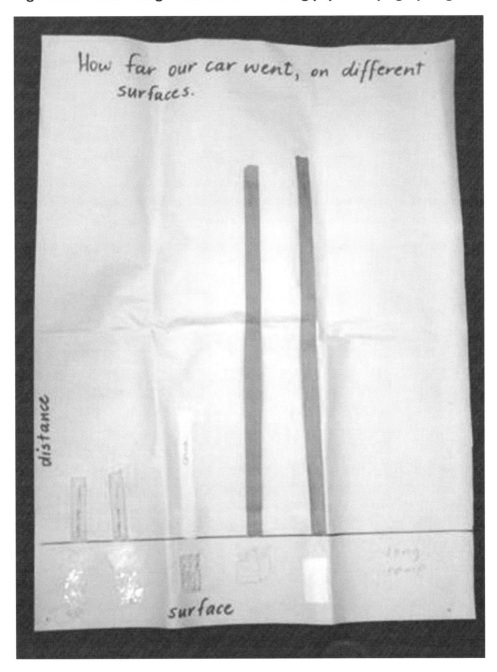

planning and in reporting on children's progress. Authentic assessment involves documentation of observational data while children are involved in investigations, and avoids decontextualised testing. The forms of data documentation may include:

- work samples (for example, labelled diagrams of insects)
- photographic documentation with accompanying notes
- narratives such as learning stories or anecdotes.

Educators need assessment data not only on the product of the investigation but also on the processes, including the context in which learning occurred. It is important that contextual data is documented alongside the children's finished product, as it provides key pedagogic information. Worksheets that frame responses as right/wrong answers should be avoided, as these act as a test with very narrow parameters. However, scaffold structures such as Y-charts (looks like, feels like, sounds like) or data tables (for example, vertebrates, invertebrates) support science-specific documentation of early years learners aged from four to eight years, and provide authentic work samples for assessment purposes.

Analysing the observational data outcomes using curriculum outcomes as a guide helps draw attention to specific understandings and inquiry skills that children might have demonstrated. However, curriculum frameworks should be utilised as guidelines for the purposes of analysis, not as a prescription or checklist, as this potentially narrows the curriculum and an educator's expectations. The grade-based structure of the ACS offers useful examples of anticipated understandings, yet this structure should be interpreted with caution, as children at a particular age might demonstrate capacities across a range of grade levels. Observational assessment that documents the context of learning enables the educator to analyse outcomes in terms of:

- new scientific understandings
- application of inquiry process skills
- use of scientific language and documentation
- enhancement of positive dispositions
- influences on learning, such as peer comments and educator questions.

Analysing this broader range of scientific learning beyond just content knowledge offers deeper appreciation of how children learn, as well as what they have learned. Influences on learning, such as peer tutoring, educator use of questions, community engagement and children's community experience with specific science content, inform educator reflection and decision-making regarding particular teaching strategies, as well as the choices of content and resources.

Summary

- Effective early years science education aims to enhance children's awareness and understanding of their world, establish systematic inquiry processes and deep thinking, frame positive dispositions towards scientific inquiry and support communication of evidence-based understandings.
- It offers opportunities to involve even those children who may appear disengaged if it:
  - focuses on active and meaningful investigations of questions children have about their own natural and designed world
  - utilises varied and engaging learning resources and inquiry opportunities, including those beyond the classroom
  - arises from children's questions or prior understandings about everyday events and phenomena, and builds on current community issues
  - differentiates to suit the range of abilities and the diversity of cultural backgrounds in inclusive classrooms
  - assesses learning in authentic ways that document understandings from multiple perspectives.

Discussion questions

7.1 Identify explorations that might arise from the fascinations of children aged from birth to four years in everyday situations (for example, food temperature change, bird flight, colour mixing). How would you extend young children's awareness and thinking about phenomena?

7.2 What forms of observation might be effective in assessing the understandings of early years learners in the birth to four years age range? How can curriculum documents assist you to interpret observations?

7.3 What teaching strategies might be effective in deepening the science understandings of children in the four to eight year age range at the same time as enhancing science inquiry skills and positive dispositions towards investigation? Why should you avoid excessive direct instruction of science information (that is, showing and telling)?

7.4 In classrooms for children aged from four to eight years, how will you differentiate the science learning experience to cater for variations in children's abilities (disabilities, giftedness), learning styles and cultural backgrounds to ensure that all children can access the curriculum and feel successful?

7.5 What opportunities exist in your community for involving community members in science learning with children, and what community resources have potential for enriching science learning?

References

Alexander, S. (2006). *Kitchen garden cooking with kids*. Ringwood: Penguin.

Australian Curriculum, Assessment and Reporting Authority (ACARA) (2009). Shape of the Australian Curriculum—Science. Retrieved 10 October 2011 from <www.acara.edu.au/verve/_resources/ Australian_Curriculum_-_ Science.pdf>.

Department of Education, Employment and Workplace Relations (DEEWR) (2009). *Belonging, being and becoming: The Early Years Learning Framework for Australia*. Canberra: Commonwealth of Australia.

Ehrlen, K. (2009). Drawings as representations of children's conceptions. *International Journal of Science Education, 31*(1), 41–57.

Fenichel, M. & Schweingruber, H. (2010). *Surrounded by science: Learning science in informal environments*. Washington, DC: National Academies Press.

Fleer, M. (2009). Understanding the dialectical relations between children's everyday concepts and scientific concepts within play-based programs. *Research in Science Education, 39*(2), 281–306.

Fraser-Abder, P. (2011). *Teaching emerging scientists: Fostering scientific inquiry with diverse learners in Grades K–2*. Boston: Pearson.

Howitt, C. & Blake, E. (2010). *Planting the seeds of science*. Fremantle: Australian Learning and Teaching Council and Curtin University.

Loxley, P., Dawes, L., Nicholls, L. & Dore, B. (2010). *Teaching primary science: Promoting enjoyment and developing understanding*. Essex: Pearson.

Morris, M., Merritt, M., Birrell, N. & Howitt, C. (2007). Trialling concept cartoons in early childhood teaching and learning of science. *Teaching Science, 52*(2), 42–5.

Neumann-Hinds, C. (2007). *Picture science: Using digital photographs to teach young children*. St Paul, MN: Redleaf.

Queensland Department of Education and Training (2008). *Foundations for success*. Retrieved 10 October 2011 from <http://education.qld.gov.au/schools/indigenous/projects/foundations. html>.

8

The arts

Narelle Lemon, Susanne Garvis and Christopher Klopper

Introduction: The importance of arts education in the early years

Arts education aims to develop children's creativity, expressive capabilities and aesthetic sensibilities through multidimensional learning activities that are grounded in arts knowledge, skills and understanding. In the early years, planning for these areas is paramount to creating learning environments that teach and nurture the arts in the areas of dance, drama, media arts, music and visual arts. Creative and imaginative experiences offer children the chance to express themselves and reflect, activities that enhance their social and emotional development. The opportunity to explore this through and with the arts develops children's understandings of their own world and other cultures. Authentic opportunities allow for the scaffolding, exploration and doing involved in fostering deep understanding of complex forms associated with innovative, imaginative thinking and problem-solving. Early years frameworks for children from birth to four years and curriculum guidelines for those aged from five to eight years in the arts highlight self-expression and presentation, and reflective thinking and responding. The language and key terminology concerning how these areas are defined in the early years change; however, underpinning these opportunities are learning experiences that develop skills with arts materials, concepts and processes, and an understanding of the arts as part of culture (Dinham, 2011). All children should be offered equal opportunities to progress, develop and engage actively with the arts to foster positive attitudes as self and with others, and attention to creativity and imagination in the early years plays an important role in this (Duffy, 1998; Ebbeck & Waniganayake, 2010; Wright, 2011). Early years thus present both a unique opportunity and a unique challenge; a part of that challenge is to engage and support all who care for and educate young children in making the arts an integrated and vital part of their earliest experiences. This chapter explores the early years in three sections, each drawing from theoretical connections and practical experiences in the learning environment to share insights into arts practice for children from birth to eight years of age.

Arts from birth to three years of age

Early years education begins the moment a child is born. Recent neuro-scientific research on infant brain development has provided reinforcement for what psychologists and educators have long believed: that experience in the first three years of life has a powerful influence on lifelong development and learning. Eisner (2002, pp. 17–18) argues that through active engagement with arts experiences, children can develop their senses and their imagination:

> The senses provide the material for the creation of consciousness, and we, in turn, use the content of consciousness and the sensory potential of various materials to mediate, transform, and transport our consciousness into worlds beyond ourselves.

A close look at what constitutes the best kind of experience for babies and infants leads quickly to the arts. Appropriate arts experiences are critical from a baby's first lullaby to a two-year-old's experimentation with play dough, and a three-year-old's dramatisation of a favourite story. For babies and infants alike, the arts play a central role in cognitive, motor, language and social-emotional development. The arts motivate and engage children in learning, stimulate memory and facilitate understanding; they also enhance symbolic communication, promote relationships and provide avenues for building competences. They provide unique ways for babies and toddlers to use movement, images, constructions and sounds along with spoken words, to express themselves, make meaning, and communicate ideas and feelings to others (Fowler et al., 2006). From this we can propose that the arts are natural for very young children. Let's explore an example. What are the young children learning?

Example 8.1: Investigating play dough

In the toddler room, the three-year-olds are investigating different colours of play dough as they mould and cut various shapes. Children are sitting at a table with different-coloured play dough, shape cutters and rollers. Through exploration, the children are building their fine motor skills, creating imaginative objects and investigating the mixing of colours.

Figure 8.1:   Investigating play dough in the early years

Now imagine two contexts with even younger children. Is it possible to have meaningful arts activities for children younger than twelve months? What can you do as an educator? Let's explore another example. Again we identify developmental learning taking place through arts experiences.

Example 8.2: Movement to music

In the six-week to six-month-old baby nursery, educators are holding the alert, awake children in their arms. They turn on a CD and begin rocking the babies to the music. They are helping to stimulate the babies through an innate sense of discovery through music by swaying to the sounds of a violin and guitar. The babies are beginning to respond to voices and music they can hear by acknowledging the educators. The educators also list the names of the musical instruments, allowing the babies to hear the names and observe modelled language.

But how do we know what constitute meaningful arts activities for babies and infants? The answer lies in an understanding of child development. When we understand the different developmental needs of young children, we can align arts activities to support children's exploration and understanding of the world. As a general summary, the following list is a guide to suitable activities.

Principles for arts activities for children aged from birth to three years

- The activities reflect a child's environment and everyday life (at home and in care) and develop these experiences into different art forms.
- The activities are language rich and centred around interactions with a significant adult. The experience reinforces early language and literacy skills as adults connect language to the young child's activities.
- The activities provide a balance of sensory stimulation (sound and movement) that is sensitive to the signals of the child.
- The arts modes are varied throughout the day and provide experiences of how meanings are transformed or revealed as they are articulated (for example, speaking, writing or drawing).
- The activities provide opportunities for the children to move to the beat of music with all parts of the body.
- They also provide opportunities for children to share their arts experiences with family and friends (an audience for the activity).

- Educators use the best-quality arts resources that can be sourced so that children learn how to use and look after valuable arts resources.

There is a common belief that educators should not interfere with the arts-making of very young children. This belief suggests children are best left unhindered in their arts development. Richards (2007) challenges this view, arguing that learning in the arts is a social, cultural and historical act. In this view, educators recognise the social and interactive nature of children's art experiences. Educators play an important role for children aged from birth to three years in helping to provide quality arts learning experiences.

Arts education for children aged from three to five years

The arts enable children to use their whole bodies for learning, and create endless opportunities for imagining and creating (Jones, 2009). Learning through the arts for three- to five-year-olds also builds self-esteem, promotes development of important social and spatial skills and contributes to well-being. While research confirms a strong link between exposure to the arts at an early age and academic performance (Ebbeck & Waniganayake, 2010; Dinham, 2011), the arts also offer children a variety of ways and opportunities to reflect on diverse approaches to learning and development in the areas of attitudes, feelings, dispositions, skills, abilities, knowledge and understanding. The arts can play a crucial role in im-proving students' abilities to learn, as they draw on a range of intelligences and learning styles—not just the linguistic and logical-mathematical intelligences upon which most school curricula are based (Duffy, 1998).

In the early years children will separate these experiences, as they are not developed in isolation; however, in planning for meaningful and authentic arts experiences, opportunities to experience different forms of representation are crucial—especially in the three to five years age group. Duffy (1998) and Dinham (2011) believe that early years educators should be using the arts and aesthetics to heighten children's sensibilities. They further suggest that creativity—the process of generating original ideas that have value—should be seen as a core element of our educational strategies in early years settings.

Arts and play are interconnected in the early years in association with young children's thinking and learning (Ebbeck & Waniganayake, 2010; Wright, 2010). For authentic experiences, children aged from three to five years of age need to be supported to:

Example 8.3: Musical instruments

Music is expressive, and opportunities that allow young children to engage with different musical instruments, their sounds, how they are played and their appearance ignite possibilities for future engagement. A show and tell moment in the classroom stimulates listening skills and promotes identification of popular children's songs. The teacher introduces the instrument to the children. Careful explanations and language are used to describe the intricacy of the shape and features that help in producing the sound. These are supported through modelling of how a musician would hold the instrument and create music. Connections to basic concepts of high/low, long/short and fast/slow are made through demonstrations. Focus, appreciation, mutual respect and what it means to participate as an audience member are also explored, and support aesthetic development in the early years. Social and cultural relationships associated with participating in the arts open up opportunities for inquiries into participation, what it means to be a musician and how one can express oneself through music.

Figure 8.2   Introducing and making available musical instruments when working with five-year-olds on listening skills and musical instrument identification

Example 8.4: Sound and light

An inquiry unit on sound and light allowed five-year-old children to connect to their interests of guitars and ukuleles through designing, creating, making and reinterpreting their notions of what and how musical instruments look like and how they generate sound. Integrating student interest aligned authentic engagement and appreciation of arts in the early years. The children were introduced to specific art materials that consisted of different textures to support their inquiry into simple weaving, printing and construction. They were encouraged to explore the use of fingers and tools to create forms that represented ideas. Careful scaffolding of ideas was undertaken through open-ended questions while the children were supported to create. The discovery through the arts ignited innovative ways of working with varied materials, allowing children to discover size, colour, shape, substance and different qualities of touch and sound, enabling them to connect to prior experiences and concepts of and questions about guitars and ukuleles.

Figure 8.3   A ukulele that a student brought into the classroom from home, and a demonstration of a guitar made during the inquiry

Table 8.1   Aspects of arts development for zero to three-year-olds to consider for learning and teaching

Arts focus	Summary of some aspects of arts development for zero to three-year-olds
Drama	• Enjoys exploring a range of narratives • Enjoys exploring character roles
Visual arts	• Explores and experiments with a range of materials • Moving into the names of primary colours and shapes
Dance	• Starts to explore with different body movements in response to music and begin to move into interpreting music • Enjoy exploring and practising movement
Music	• Developing voice control • Can name familiar songs and join in movements of song • Sings spontaneously and enjoys singing with a group • Developing control of a range of man-made and natural instruments
Media arts	• Enjoy exploring and practising language, stories and other art forms in popular media such as television, film, radio and social media

- express their thinking, knowledge and ideas
- explore, try out and create with new and different kinds of media
- experiment with colors, lines, forms, shapes, textures, designs, sound, movement and actions
- express feelings and emotions, and
- be creative.

Essentially, the communication of feeling in pre-verbal, non-verbal and verbal ways using gestures, movements, actions and making to comprehend, respond to and represent their perceptions and understandings of their world can be thought about through the adoption of their creative skills and problem-solving while they are enhancing their self-esteem and celebrating their identity (see Table 8.2 for specific unpacking of arts areas).

With arts experiences, the following principles need to be demonstrated as an early years educator working with children aged from three to five years:

- having confidence in the child's art work, communicated in a way that celebrates creativity, interpretation and imagination

Table 8.2   Aspects of arts development for three- to five-year-olds to consider for learning and teaching

Arts focus	Summary of some aspects of arts development for three- to five-year-olds
Drama	• Start to introduce narrative into their play. • Will play alongside other children engaged in same play theme. • Will play cooperatively as part of a group to act out a narrative. • Are interested in character roles. • Are able to use transitional objects. • Revisit complex narratives.
Visual arts	• Know the names of primary colours and move into naming secondary colours. • Interested in mixing own colours and move into being able to use white to make colours lighter and black to make colours darker. • Explore with materials—brushes and surfaces—and begin to use appropriate sizes for specific tasks such as a thin brush for a fine line. • Use paint to produce separate and overlapping blocks of colour. • Are able to sort and match colour shades and begin to use colour to represent realism. • Describe intentions behind visual art work. • Name marks on a page or art work. • Symbolic representation emerging. • Experiment with a variety of marks that can be made by different materials, tools and surfaces. • Use a circle and lines to represent a person moving into drawing figures, which become details. • Start to produce visual narratives. • Produce a range of shapes. • Draw shapes and figures that appear to float in space on the page. • Subdivide space on the page to show higher and lower.
Dance	• Start to explore with different body movements in response to music and begin to move into interpreting music. • Enjoy exploring and practising movement for its own sake and begin to perform simple dance steps. • March in time to music and walk on tip-toes, and begin to move with increased awareness of rhythm using skips, hops and forward jumps. • Can switch from one movement to another during dance, moving into mastering a wide range of movements.

continued

Arts focus	Summary of some aspects of arts development for three- to five-year-olds
Music	• Developing voice control. • Can play simple rhythm instruments and respond to a suggested rhythm. • Can name familiar songs and join in moving into singing with complete songs from memory and with accuracy. • Are aware of beat, tempo, melody and pitch, moving into knowing basic concepts of high versus low, long versus short, fast versus slow. • Are able to name a range of musical instruments. • Sing spontaneously and enjoy singing with a group. • Listen to recordings of music with help.
Media arts	• Enjoy exploring and practising language, stories and other art forms situated or derived from books and popular media such as television, film, radio, social media. • Media arts encourage students to imaginatively explore the possibilities for communication forms, and to learn through play and experimentation. • Students learn to experiment creatively, develop skills and communicate with a range of technologies such as digital cameras and computer software, as well as more basic technologies such as scissors and glue. • They view and listen to printed, visual and moving image media, and respond with relevant actions, gestures, comments and/or questions or with their own products. • Students begin to understand that written text, images and sound can be combined to communicate, and that media stories are made by different people and groups for different purposes.

Source: Developed from ACARA (2011); Dinham (2011); Wright (2011); Duffy (1998).

- asking questions that stimulate the child's arts ideas rather than showing or telling them what to do, or doing it for them
- accepting a child's creative products without placing a value judgement on the item
- celebrating art-making with positive comments about how the child solves a problem in relating to their work
- sharing confidence in the child's ability to make the product unique and to explore through process
- keeping arts experiences open, and engaging with free time to explore materials and ideas.

Example 8.5: Dance

The social skills highlighted through children creating dance allow for the development of problem-solving, negotiation and cooperation skills while observing others and extending interpersonal skills as they work together to create a whole-class dance where each individual's contribution is valued. Children become more confident in expressing themself through movement—exploring shapes (symmetrical and non-symmetrical), actions (locomotor and non-locomotor skills) and coordination of body parts. Children explore movement, actions, time and dynamics, as well as space and a sense of physicality. Closely interwoven dialogue allows for the three-year-olds to explore their actions to the music of 'Bananas in Pyjamas' and to discover what it means to imagine movement when being a bear. The teacher consciously models and scaffolds the children, encouraging everyone to move at the same time to the music, supporting experimentation with body movements. Marching to the music and walking on tip-toes are key movements being explored at this stage of dance development. The narrative of the music supports imaginative play as a group. Stimulated by the song lyrics, the masks assist in the children's representation of their theme for play, dance and music exploration.

Figure 8.4   Props are used to enhance the three-year-old experience— in this case, bear masks that the students have made and individualised through art work to represent their bear, which is chasing the Banana in Pyjamas

Young children's responses develop when they are exposed to a variety of aesthetics. The ability to form relationships with other people and the ability to express their feelings are just some of the important new social and emotional skills a child will develop between the ages of three and five. Children in this stage acquire several key motor skills that form the foundation of their ability to navigate the world around them. Thus embedding a variety of activities from the *arts* to enhance the expression of feelings and to promote opportunities for socialisation, as well as enhancing children's intellectual, social and emotional development, is vital.

Children aged from three to five years respond to their own and others' art works, and start to learn how to look at and participate in arts, and to talk about what they see, hear and experience—thus engaging actively as audiences. Children learn that works of art, musicians, performers, artists and designers have a place in their communities, and that specific works of art are cultural narratives about their own and others' cultures.

Through strengthening children's understanding so that they are able to explore and create in a variety of ways, guidance towards meaning-making through involvement in arts activities helps children connect to their community and understand the wider world around them.

Arts education for five- to eight-year-olds (school)

Education rich in the arts

Arts education provides children with valuable opportunities to experience and build knowledge and skills in self-expression, imagination, creative and collaborative problem-solving, communication, creation of shared meanings, and respect for self and others. Engagement in quality arts education has also been said to positively affect overall academic achievement, engagement in learning and development of empathy towards others (Cornett, 2007; Klopper & Power, 2010; Ewing, 2010; Sinclair et al., 2009). Valuing learning in diverse ways, as defined by Gardner's (1983) multiple intelligences theory, affords the potential for diverse learning to occur through arts-based learning engagement (Ewing, 2010). Thus working across the arts using a range of processes and art materials in differing contexts provides opportunities for children aged from five to eight years to find different forms of expression and various solutions. Children will have a range of preferences for expressing themselves, as Dinham (2011, p. 113) suggests, which will be encouraged 'by providing opportunities for children to work in a variety of media—and to work with different combinations of media—[this] provides children [with] more tools and opportunities to think and act creatively'.

The arts in the Australian curriculum

The Australian arts curriculum learning area gives equal recognition to the distinctiveness of dance, drama, media arts, music and visual arts, as well as to the connections between the art forms. It promotes the arts as fundamental to student learning and the capacity to 'perceive, create, think, feel, symbolise, communicate, understand and become confident and creative individuals' (ACARA, 2010, p. 2). From Years K–8, all art forms are taught through a balance of three organising strands: generating, realising and responding. In years K–2, the arts build on the Early Years Learning Framework, and a 'purposeful play-centred approach' has been recommended (2010, p. 4).

Young children learn as artists through making art works that communicate with audiences. They learn as audiences by responding critically to the arts. These actions are taught together as they are mutually dependent. Making and responding provide over-arching organising principles for the arts, and offer a consistent structure for the early years educator. Within these broad organising guidelines, each art form has its own specific terminology, concepts and processes. Students learn to use art form–specific concepts, skills and processes in their making and responding, while developing aesthetic knowledge through their arts learning (ACARA, 2011). At five to eight years of age, children benefit from working across the arts using a range of processes and art materials in differing contexts. Their engagement is heightened through different forms of expression, and finding solutions presented by meaningful connections between and through the arts.

Table 8.3   Aspects of arts development for five- to eight-year-olds to consider for learning and teaching

Arts focus	Summary of some aspects of arts development for three- to five-year-olds
Drama	• Use the elements of drama (tension, focus, mood, time, contrast, symbol, space and performance elements). • Explore relationships and narrative through dramatic play, role-play, improvisation and process drama. • Experiment with found objects, puppets and images. • Engage in spontaneous performances using their own language and devised movement. • Reflect on their own work and respond to the work of others.

continued

Arts focus	Summary of some aspects of arts development for three- to five-year-olds
Visual arts	• Use a range of equipment, materials, media and technologies to make art, craft and design works that communicate their ideas, feelings and observations. • Develop skills and processes (line, tone, colour, texture, shape, form, space and pattern). • Look at art works and talk about what they see, using the language of visual arts to share narratives about themselves and about their own and other cultures. • Recognise different purposes and contexts of art. • Understand that works of art, artists and designers have a place in their communities.
Dance	• Gain a foundational understanding of the elements of dance (action, time, dynamics, space, personal and shared space, patterns, body shapes, size, extension, levels, direction). • Improvise with the body to explore and control movement through play. • Communicate through the body to make and share performances with their peers. • Discuss and listen to opinions about their own and others' dances.
Music	• Participate in the different roles of composer, performer and audience member. • Explore and experiment with voice, instruments and sound to create their own music. • Sing, play instruments and found sound sources, and move to a range of music. • Invent and explore ways of recording musical thinking through symbols. • Use music terminology (duration, pitch, tone colour, dynamics, structure, rhythm). • Listen and respond to a range of musical works and develop their aural skills. • Respond and comment on their own music-making and that of others.
Media arts	• Experiment creatively with a range of communications technologies and digital materials. • Gain a basic understanding of the elements of media (adapting, designing, focal point, scripting, sequencing, story-building, writing). • Make simple stories using written text, images and sound. • View and listen to printed, visual and moving image media, and respond with relevant actions, gestures, comments and/or questions.

Source: Developed from ACARA (2011).

Connecting the arts across the curriculum

Connecting the arts across the curriculum has the potential to deepen learning experiences, foster creativity and enhance the ability to make meaning in diverse ways through understanding the different languages of the arts (Gibson & Ewing, 2011). 'Arts education aligns strongly with social-constructivist pedagogy and emergent process that depend on more on making judgments based on "rightness of fit" than on following formulae or set curricula.' (Wright, 2011, p. 220) When planning to connect the arts across the curriculum, one must ensure that the envisaged outcomes are authentic and that integrity is maintained within each relevant learning area. Artificial relationships should not be forged between learning areas or art forms, and the discrete knowledge, skills and understandings of each learning area or art form should not be blurred for the sake of integration. This highlights how connectivity is situated in a dichotomous tension between process of differentiation and synthesis, maintaining the integrity of the art form as a separate discipline while affirming the value of teaching for transfer with regard to shared concept and processes. Thus learning in the context of its connectivity with other learning areas becomes an optimal condition for assuring that fundamental concepts and processes shared between an art form and other domains become more deeply and broadly understood (Meyers & Scripp, 2007).

In order to successfully implement these curriculum initiatives, it has been suggested that the arts are connected across the curriculum. The nature and practice of connecting or integrating the arts is not a twenty-first century notion (Barrett, 2001; Klopper, 2009; Russell-Bowie, 2008; Snyder, 2001). 'Throughout its history, the concept of integration has operated under many labels: interdisciplinary instruction, unit teaching, the project approach, inquiry method, and whole language.' (Cornett, 2007, p. 8)

Example 8.6: Connecting the arts across the curriculum

An example of connecting the arts across the curriculum could be a learning unit based on 'hip-hop culture'. Learning experiences could include: Morning Calendar action, Alphabet hip-hop handwriting where hip-hop and rap are used with each letter of the alphabet that students practise, learning about the cultural context of hip-hop through making and responding to art, music, dance, drama and media works created during this style period and linking to history, geography and English through explorations of culture, place, time, written text and media. A researched and analysed exploration of historical events could be undertaken. Narrative text or creative writing could be utilised to illustrate the understanding of the concept of 'hip-hop culture'. This could be supported further by relevant digital or created images.

With arts experiences, it is ideal to demonstrate the following principles for arts activities for children aged from five to eight years:

- Promote and support respectful, life-enhancing relationships through group interaction.
- Practise in ways that acknowledge the child as capable and resourceful.
- Provide affirmation and a sense of belonging.
- Strive for meaning-making and making connections.
- Honour diversity.

As educators, it is important for us to be able to discern and differentiate. While the connected curriculum example might satisfy learning framework ideals and expectations, as educators we must never lose sight of the fact that all young children have an entitlement to engage with and through the arts. It is the educator who must ensure that children's artistic growth and capacity are supported. As with anything, the more knowledge, experience, skills and strategies children have, the more they can achieve.

Summary

- Creativity involves problem-setting as much as problem-solving and is closely tied to personal connection, expression, imagination and ownership (Wright, 2010, 2011).
- Meaningful arts-making reflects these aspects, and can support multiple entry and exit points for creation and appreciation. The freedom to explore, create, invent, transform, elaborate and imagine in the early years allows for children to experiment with and represent ideas and actions in multiple forms. The appeal of this process is captivating to most children as it is not strictly rule bound (Wright, 2010).
- Creating and responding through arts is a fundamental function of early cognitive, effective and social development. Through the arts, children actively construct who they are, along with their meaning of the world and how they interact with this meaning-making.
- This chapter allows for opportunities to see across the early years how:
  - young children's art-making processes open up opportunities into their realities and how they shape these

- the arts offer ways for children to share the day-to-day details of their lives with others, and allow for young children to share their inner worlds in ways that can't easily be communicated through other forms
- it is fundamental for early years educators to understand the components and meaning behind arts-making and responding to art, and to interact with children about their arts practice in association with their ideas, feelings and actions
- from birth to three years, active engagement with arts experiences can develop children's senses and their imaginations
- between the ages of three and five years, arts enhance the expression of feelings and promote opportunities for socialisation, and also enhance children's intellectual, social and emotional development
- from five to eight years, children benefit from engagement with different forms of expression and various solutions, especially meaningful integration of arts.

Discussion questions

8.1 How might you design arts learning and teaching opportunities that support children to actively construct who they are and that help them to make sense of the world around them?

8.2 How would you offer meaningful arts-making opportunities that promote and support respectful relationships?

8.3 How important are the arts to your philosophy of early years teaching?

8.4 How would you explain the importance of the arts in the early years to parents?

8.5 How can early years educators and parents work together to support a child's learning and development in the arts?

8.6 How can early years educators and community members work together to offer children a range of artistic opportunities?

References

Australian Curriculum, Assessment and Reporting Authority (ACARA) (2010). *Draft shape of the Australian Curriculum: The Arts*. Retrieved 20 December 2011 from <www.acara.edu.au/verve/_resources/Draft+Shape+Of+The+Australian+Curriculum+The+Arts-FINAL.pdf>.

——(2011). *The shape of the Australian Curriculum: The Arts*. Retrieved 20 December 2011 from <www.acara.edu.au/verve/_resources/Shape_of_the_Australian_Curriculum_The_Arts_-_Compressed.pdf>.

Barrett, J.R. (2001). Interdisciplinary work and musical integrity. *Music Educators Journal, 87*(5): 27–31.

Cornett, C. (2007). *Creating meaning through literature and the arts.* Englewood Cliffs, NJ: Pearson Education.

Dinham, J. (2011). *Delivering authentic arts education.* Melbourne: Cengage.

Duffy, B. (1998). *Supporting creativity and imagination in the early years.* Oxford: Oxford University Press.

Ebbeck, M. & Waniganayake, M. (eds) (2010). *Play in early childhood education: Learning in diverse contexts.* Melbourne: Oxford University Press.

Eisner, E. (1998). *The enlightened eye: Qualitative inquiry and the enhancement of educational practice.* Upper Saddle River, NJ: Merrill.

——(2002). *The arts and the creation of mind.* New Haven, NH: Yale University Press.

Ewing, R. (2010). *The arts and Australian education: Realising potential.* Melbourne: ACER Press.

Fowler, C., Meiners, J. & Orchard, J. (2006). Literacy is more than just words: Exploring performance literacy for very young children. Paper presented at the UNESCO World Conference on Arts Education: Building Creative Capacities for the 21st Century, 6–9 March, Lisbon.

Gardner, H. (1983). *Frames of mind: The theory of multiple intelligence.* New York: Basic Books.

Gibson, R. & Ewing, R. (2011). *Transforming the curriculum through the arts.* Melbourne: Palgrave Macmillan.

Jones, A. (2009). *Creativity and the early years of childhood: A Tasmanian Early Years Workshop Report.* Retrieved 21 December 2011 from <www.earlyyears.org.au/__data/assets/pdf_file/0005/ 118526/ TEYF_Artplay_Workshop_Report_December_2009.pdf>.

Klopper, C. (2009). The syntegrated arts education model: A non-linear approach to teaching and learning in the key learning area Creative Arts. *Journal of Artistic and Creative Education, 3*(1), 30–74.

Klopper, C. & Power, B. (2010). Illuminating the gap: An overview of classroom-based arts education research in Australia. *International Journal of Education Through Art, 6*(3), 293–308.

Meyers, D. & Scripp, L. (2007). Evolving forms of music-in-education practices and research in the context of art-in-education reform: Implications for schools that chose music as a measure of excellence and as a strategy for change. *Journal for Music-in-Education: Advancing Music for Changing Times, 1*(2), 381–96.

Richards, R. (2007). Everyday creativity and the arts. *World Futures, 63*(7), 500–25.

Russell-Bowie, D. (2008). 'Integrate or syntegrate? Models for integrating music across the primary school'. Paper presented at the International Society for Music Education Conference, Bologna, 20–25 July.

Sinclair, C., Jeanneret, N. & O'Toole, J. (2009). *Education in the arts: Teaching and learning in the contemporary curriculum.* Melbourne: Oxford University Press.

Snyder, S. (2001). Connection, correlation, and integration. *Music Educators Journal 87*(5), 32–40.

Wright, S. (2010). *Understanding creativity in early childhood: Meaning-making and children's drawings.* London: Sage.

——(2011). Arts education as a collective experience. In S. Wright (ed.), *Children, meaning-making and the arts* (pp. 194–225). Sydney: Pearson.

9

Digital technology

Narelle Lemon and
Glenn Finger

Introduction

This chapter focuses on the possibilities and potential of digital technologies for re-thinking learning in the early years. The concept of networked school communities (Lee & Finger, 2010), supported by technology trends identified in the *NMC Horizon Report 2011: K–12 Edition* (New Media Consortium, 2011), enables important relationships among early years learners, teachers, parents and caregivers. A networked school community is defined as 'a legally recognised school that takes advantage of the digital and networked technology, and of a more collaborative, networked and inclusive operational mode to involve its wider community in the provision of a quality education appropriate for the future' (Lee & Finger, 2010, p. 22). Lee and Finger (2010) acknowledge the transformational potential of digital technologies to rethink education, and propose that networked school communities are the next phase of schooling as digital technologies enable learning through a stronger, net-worked home–school nexus. This shared vision represents both parent/caregiver and educator knowledge, which articulates the hopes and dreams that they hold for children, and which establishes collaboration as central to rethinking schooling.

The meaningful and appropriate use of digital technologies in the early years also requires new expectations for educators, and these implications are discussed in relation to Technological Pedagogical Content Knowledge (TPACK) (Koehler & Mishra, 2008) and the *National Professional Standards for Teachers* (AITSL, 2011a). Two case studies are presented, with the first exploring the integration of computer interfaces as digital technologies as a way to demonstrate thinking. That case study also highlights the educational possibilities of graphical user interfaces enabled by digital technologies. The second case study refers to the digital camera, which is specifically focused upon to provide an example of the use of digital technologies in practice. Digital cameras provide portable, accessible technology with which young children can engage for early years learning. The generation of digital photographs, alongside the voice of the young photographer through reflections, forms visual narratives that communicate the intertextuality of early years perspectives on learning and teaching. With a digital camera integrated into the learning environment, a community is established whereby the children celebrate individuality to support a sense of belonging and promotion of mutual respect for insightful contributions.

Digital technologies: Rethinking learning and teaching

Life for young children in the twenty-first century is distinctly different from earlier times in relation to the technologies with which they interact. What were the technologies with which you interacted when you were young? In recollecting the technologies of your early childhood and their role in your learning, you are likely to understand that two key observations can be made. First, you are likely to understand the importance of those technologies in your learning, and hopefully remember the joy and fun of learning using those technologies. Second, depending upon your age, you can observe that young children have become immersed in increasingly rich digital, networked environments.

To illustrate this, in *Growing Up Digital: The Rise of the Net Generation*, Tapscott (1999) highlighted the ways in which young children were immersed in computers and associated technologies, and observed that the young were embracing those technologies. His subsequent work, *Grown Up Digital: How the Net Generation is Changing our World* (Tapscott, 2008), aligns with our thinking throughout this chapter and is consistent with the theme of this book, which calls for rethinking curriculum, pedagogy and assessment in teaching early years. Tapscott argues that an Industrial Age model of schooling no longer makes sense, and he explains that it is the way in which learners navigate the digital world, and what they do with the information they discover, that counts. As Tapscott explains, digital technologies both require and enable new ways of learning and teaching.

Recent curriculum documents and approaches reflect an increased understanding of the implications of digital technologies. For example, the *Early Years Learning Framework for Australia: Belonging, Being and Becoming* (Commonwealth of Australia, 2009) makes explicit the importance of technologies in Outcome 4, which states that: 'Children resource their own learning through connecting with people, place, technologies and natural and processed materials' (2009, p. 37). Technologies are defined as 'the diverse range of products that make up the designed world and extend beyond artefacts designed and developed by people and include processes, systems, services and environments' (2009, p. 46). For the purposes of this chapter, the authors have chosen to focus on 'digital technologies', which 'refer to the ever-evolving suite of digital software, hardware and architecture used in learning and teaching in the school, the home and beyond both home and school environments' (Lee & Finger, 2010, p. 15). As Lee and Finger (2010) elaborate, digital technologies are also conceptualised 'as part of a digital ecosystem that can be adapted, based on needs and context' (2010, p.15). Learners in the early years have an increasingly extensive range of digital technologies to enable communication, interaction and sharing meaning-making to deepen knowledge and understandings, which opens up possibilities and potential for rethinking early years learning.

Learning with digital technologies in the early years: Possibilities and potential

The Australian Communications and Media Authority (ACMA) report *Use of Electronic Media and Communications: Early Childhood to Teenage Years* (ACMA, 2009) provides insights and new findings about three- to four- and seven- to eight-year-olds from the Australian Institute of Family Studies study *Growing Up in Australia: The Longitudinal Study of Australian Children*. In relation to three- to four- and seven- to eight-year-old children, it reported the following:

- Television and DVDs play a substantial role in the lives of young children: 94 per cent of three- to four-year-olds watched television for an average of one hour and eleven minutes per day, and 91 per cent watched DVDs or videos for an average of 44 minutes per day.

- A sizeable proportion of three- to four-year-olds also used a computer at home (40 per cent, averaging seven minutes per day), and a minority (16 per cent) had played games using an electronic games system (averaging three minutes per day).
- Most seven- to eight-year-olds had used the internet at home at least some of the time (84 per cent), mainly for playing games. Two per cent of seven- to eight-year-olds used a mobile phone to make or receive calls, and 11 per cent used a fixed-line phone (ACMA, 2009, p. 2).

In addition to the evidence of young children having increasing access to and use of digital technologies in the home, expectations are articulated in the *Early Years Learning Framework for Australia: Belonging, Being and Becoming* (Commonwealth of Australia, 2009) that children, in being effective communicators, 'use information and communication technologies to access information, investigate ideas and represent their thinking' (2009, p. 44), and states the following:

Educators are expected to promote this learning, for example, when they:

- provide children with access to a range of technologies
- integrate technologies into children's play experiences and projects
- teach skills and techniques and encourage children to use technologies to explore new information and represent their ideas
- encourage collaborative learning about and through technologies between children, and children and educators. (Commonwealth of Australia, 2009, p. 44)

Early years educators actively enhance children's learning in ways that not only provide learning experiences and environments that are balanced and purposeful, but also provide opportunities to respond to and engage with other children and their learning. As part of the encouragement and support to explore, manipulate, play and interact with concrete materials and imaginative scenarios associations, connections can be made to and through a range of digital technologies. Learning with and through digital technologies does not replace, but complements and transforms more traditional authentic learning experiences using other technologies. As with any learning and teaching considerations, selection of the digital technology needs to be considered from an educational perspective, and the curriculum (what is taught and learned), the pedagogy (how it is taught and learned) and assessment (how do we know what has been learned) all must be carefully selected in terms of purpose, and scaffolded to be valid and meaningful (Lemon, 2011).

To strengthen our argument, the *Early Years Learning Framework for Australia: Belonging, Being and Becoming* (Commonwealth of Australia, 2009) also states that children benefit from opportunities to explore their world using technologies, and to develop confidence in using digital technologies. This can be evident, for example (as conceptualised in Figure 9.1), when digital technologies are used in the early years to support children in identifying the uses of digital technologies in everyday life; for accessing images and information, exploring diverse perspectives and making sense of their world; for designing, drawing, editing, reflecting and composing; and for engaging with digital technologies for fun and to make meaning.

Figure 9.1   Early years use of digital technologies in the learning environment

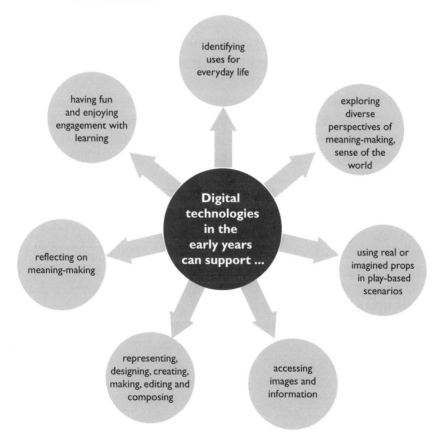

Many early years children are bringing a high level of confidence and under-standing about digital technologies because they have been interacting with and immersed in them since birth (Thelning & Lawes, 2001). These digital resources offer children other ways to play, to interact with other children and adults, to control their environments and solve problems, to be creative and to represent their ideas with words, sounds and images. Learning activities with and for digital tech-nologies can be open-ended, relevant, supportive and purposeful, and also provide immediate feedback. New ways to communicate with the real world present oppor-tunities for interacting with alternate perspectives and different world-views. Access to information for research is much broader, and allows children to locate, sort and analyse print, visual and audio information. Children can experience success because of the range of opportunities for producing multi-modal presentations and products with relative ease, and they provide extra time to engage in learning, solve problems and/or practise skills rather than explicitly focusing on the production of a product, thus validating process.

Technology trends, critical challenges and networked school communities

This section aims to make two contributions to your thinking: to draw your atten-tion to the *NMC Horizon Report 2011: K–12 Edition* (New Media Consortium, 2011), which can assist you in being aware of the latest technology trends and critical challenges; and, subsequently, to provoke thinking about the next phase of schooling as being networked school communities informed by those trends and challenges.

Initiated in 2002, the New Media Consortium (NMC) produces an annual *Horizon Report*, and identifies 'six emerging technologies or practices that are likely to enter mainstream use in the educational community within three adoption horizons over the next one to five years' (New Media Consortium, 2011, p. 3). In its 2011 report, it identified six technologies for the following three adoption horizons:

1. Time-to-adoption horizon: one year or less—cloud computing, mobiles
2. Time-to-adoption horizon: two to three years—game-based learning, open content
3. Time-to-adoption horizon: four to five years—learning analytics, personal learning environments

In addition to identifying the 'technologies to watch', the NMC Horizon Reports present key challenges. This is compelling reading for all who are interested in early years learning and digital technologies, both for becoming aware of the metatrends and for rethinking learning in the early years. For example, in the latest report, five relevant, key 'critical challenges' are articulated; these are summarised, with supporting explanation, in Table 9.1.

Table 9.1   Five critical challenges

Critical challenge	Supporting explanation
Digital media literacy continues its rise in importance as a key skill in every discipline and profession.	'As teachers begin to realize that they are limiting their students by not helping them to develop and use digital media literacy skills across the curriculum, the lack of formal training is being offset through professional development or informal learning, but we are far from seeing digital media literacy as a norm.' (New Media Consortium, 2011, p. 5)
Economic pressures and new models of education are presenting unprecedented competition to traditional models of schools.	'Creative institutions are developing new models to serve students, such as providing open content over the network . . . Simply capitalizing on new technology, however, is not enough; the new models must use these tools and services to engage students on a deeper level.' (New Media Consortium, 2011, p. 5)
The demand for personalised learning is not adequately supported by current technology or practices.	'Technology can and should support individual choices about access to materials and expertise, amount and type of educational content, and methods of teaching.' (New Media Consortium, 2011, p. 5)
A key challenge is the fundamental structure of the K–12 education establishment—aka 'the system'.	'Learners have increasing opportunities to take their education into their own hands, and options like informal education, online education, and home-based learning are attracting students away from traditional educational settings. If the system is to remain relevant it must adapt . . .' (New Media Consortium, 2011, pp. 5–6)
Many activities related to learning and education take place outside the walls of the classroom, and thus are not part of our learning metrics.	'Students can take advantage of learning material online, through games and programs they may have on systems at home, and through their extensive—and constantly available—social networks. The experiences . . . tend to happen serendipitously and in response to an immediate need for knowledge . . . having a profound effect on the way we experiment with, adopt, and use emerging technologies.' (New Media Consortium, 2011, pp. 5–6)

Source: New Media Consortium (2011).

Lee and Gaffney (2008) outline the shifts required by governments and schooling systems to understand and act upon the need for schools to become digital, and to achieve what they refer to as 'digital take-off'. In conceptualising and rethinking schooling 'beyond a digital school', Lee and Finger (2010) propose that the next shift is for schools to understand the home–school nexus enabled by digital technologies, networking learners and their homes with schooling and their wider, local and global communities. They identify some pathfinder schools already making this shift by becoming networked school communities.

The concept of the networked school community provides a response to the technology trends and critical challenges posed by the *NMC Horizon Report 2011: K–12 Edition* (New Media Consortium, 2011). It can guide the rethinking of early years learning, positioned within the context of the emerging digital technologies of cloud computing, mobiles, game-based learning, open content, learning analytics and personal learning environments. In a more practical sense, Lee and Finger (2010, p. 83) suggest that this will need to reflect the following key features:

- adopting an information age model to guide links between home and school, and to understand the scale of student access to information in the home
- becoming networked, incorporating the total school community and its homes
- recognising and encouraging a suite of changing, increasingly, sophisticated, converging and networked digital instructional technologies that connect school and home
- designing the technological architecture and infrastructure to enable a seamless, ubiquitous communication and management of digital information across and beyond the organisation.

This demands new expectations for teacher educators, and this has been well argued by Koehler and Mishra (2008) in their conceptualisation of Technological Pedagogical Content Knowledge (TPCK), now often referred to as TPACK, inferring the 'total package' needed for teaching in the twenty-first century. We support the shift needed in the design of preservice teacher education to move beyond the limitations of pedagogical content knowledge, developed by Schulman (1986) well before the internet, and applications such as Google, social media and those 'technologies to watch' discussed in the previous section of this chapter. A key set of expectations for educators in Australia is provided in the National Professional Standards for Teachers (AITSL, 2011a), and an analysis of these reveals that there are explicit TPACK expectations. An exciting, significant Teaching Teachers for the Future (TTF) Project (AITSL, 2011b), involving all 39 higher education institutions that provide initial teacher education in Australia, is strengthening the design of their initial teacher education programs using TPACK as a guiding conceptualisation, being informed by the National Professional Standards for Teachers and focusing on the Australian Curriculum in English, mathematics, science and history. According to those standards, organised in terms of standards for graduate, proficient, highly accomplished and lead teachers, *Standard 2—Know the Content and How to Teach It* has the following focus area: 'Implement teaching strategies for using ICT to expand curriculum learning opportunities for students.' Examine the career stages and statements in Table 9.2. Where do you see yourself, your classroom, and your practice positioned? What might these expectations look like in practice for learning and teaching in the early years?

Table 9.2   National Professional Standards for Teachers—ICT focus area and career stages

Standard 2: Know the Content and How to Teach It				
	Career stages			
Focus	*Graduate*	*Proficient*	*Highly accomplished*	*Lead*
2.6 Information and Communication Technology (ICT)	Implement teaching strategies for using ICT to expand curriculum learning opportunities for students.	Use effective teaching strategies to integrate ICT into learning and teaching programs to make selected content relevant and meaningful.	Model high-level teaching knowledge and skills and work with colleagues to use current ICT to improve their teaching practice and make content relevant and meaningful.	Lead and support colleagues within the school to select and use ICT with effective teaching strategies to expand learning opportunities and content knowledge for all students.

Source: AITSL (2011a).

Collectively, digital technologies and technology trends enabling networked school communities, increased expectations for educators to have TPACK capabilities, and those increased expectations evident in the National Professional Standards for Teachers require us to consider the implications for early years learning. For learning in the early years, digital tools and devices enhance learning when they reflect what is natural and familiar to early years learners, and also can introduce novelty to provoke inquiry, interest and extend thinking. Downes et al. (2001) offer guidance regarding the key requirements of educators of children from birth to eight years with regard to digital technologies. They encourage the use of open-ended digital resources that promote communication, interaction, discovery and problem-solving, and have categorised these into four main types:

- *Design and make resources*—where children can design, draw, paint, create, make, build or construct artefacts such as patterns, pictures, scenes, written texts, galleries, cards, slide shows, music.
- *Work and play resources*—where children can play, explore, investigate, look things up, solve problems and do puzzles.
- *Communicate and share resources*—where children can talk, send messages, join in a group discussion, display products of their work and play.
- *Online project resources*—where children work collaboratively on agreed tasks on and offline with children in other locations.

We encourage you to consider which activities you believe you would design, and what digital technologies you might select. Your selection, design and implementation should be informed by understanding that digital technologies should be integral to a variety of learning experiences, and are meaningfully used in the relationship between children and educator to explore meaning-making. As with all approaches in early years learning environments, a multidimensional approach supports opportunities for children to interact with many objects and devices in the classroom—for example, blocks, dolls, clay, paint, digital cameras and scanners. What is essential, though, is an awareness that the digital device often needs to be introduced to children before they can be expected to use it independently. This scaffolding assists in authentic learning experiences that allow for inquiry, questioning and meaningful use, and in turn supports enjoyment in discovery, repurposing use, transfer, reflection, understanding and success. Instructional strategies coupled with digital technologies can create powerful learning experiences. Modelling the use of those technologies in everyday life will assist children to practise skills and better understand concepts. However, we increasingly are seeing children who have enjoyed using technologies in their homes prior to entering formal schooling, and at an early age there is already diversity in access to and use of digital technologies. Indeed, some homes provide their young children with greater access to a technology-rich environment than schools.

Case study 9.1: Integrating computer user interfaces as digital technologies as a way to demonstrate thinking

The task: Using visuals and text to communicate thinking

User interfaces are defined here as the point where young children and computers interact. Since the early 1980s, we have seen the emergence of graphical user interface (GUI), which has provided wonderful educational applications. To illustrate the use of digital technologies in the early years, this case study illustrates how computer applications can be integrated into the learning environment of four-year-old learners, and used in alternative ways for them to present their thinking. The children were asked to apply and relate their thinking in visuals and text to communicate thinking about an inquiry topic as an example of an open-ended learning activity. Used in this way, computers were then seen by the educator as supporting this inquiry following open dialogue and discussions facilitated by the educator about the topic.

The role of user interfaces

An interface or program that supports mind mapping of ideas allows for children to learn about how ideas can be linked and how they can represent these in a combination of ways. Through multiliteracies, this notion of using graphic organisers is modelled. The children learn how to use the interface as a learning strategy. While doing this, they are applying and reinforcing skills associated with using such technology, such as click and drag, typing, save and print. The educator also has the ability to go back and look at the mind maps for purposes of assessment of thinking, using the program but also for monitoring the development of computer literacy.

continued

Figure 9.2   Claire engaging with a computer interface where she is required to type text, save and print in order to record her thinking

Figure 9.3   Colourful and large images are engaging for early years children when connecting to their thinking about a specific concept or idea

In the early years, children are encouraged to explore and develop relationships with others. This is crucial to providing positive experiences and a safe and stimulating environment that will encourage young children to expand their capacities and deepen their knowledge and understanding. Early years educators are thus encouraged to:

- initiate warm, trusting and reciprocal relationships with children
- provide safe and stimulating environments for children
- develop learning programs that are responsive to each child and build on their culture, strengths, interests and knowledge to take their learning and development forward
- understand, communicate and interact across cultures by being aware of their own world-view
- respect the views and feelings of each child.

The evolution of interfaces: Fourth generation interfaces

Prior to the emergence of digital technologies, early years learners were more limited to the use of more traditional technologies to present their thinking. For example, young children were often asked to read, write and draw using a variety of drawing technologies, such as pencils and paper. The images shown in Figures 9.1 and 9.2 display an expanded and enriched multimedia environment, which can include text, animation, sound and narration. We are mindful that the images show rather outdated computers, and that young children are now more likely to interact with interfaces provided by modern iPhones, iPads, tablet devices and laptops. In ensuring that early childhood learning environments are relevant, early years educators need to position themselves to accommodate and capitalise upon emerging interfaces. In summary, we have seen several generations of user interfaces, and the windows and mouse-based user interface has evolved to touch screens, and, in particular, many young children in their digital homes are experiencing rich transformations in being able to access, search for and manipulate information. There will be an ongoing challenge for learning environments to readily incorporate new user interfaces and technological changes.

Principles for engaging early years learners using digital technologies

Digital technologies can be used to enhance learner collaborations and promote young learners who can learn from each other. Networked school communities can be created to enable collaboration through effective partnerships between learning in the home and at school. Specifically, technology trends, critical challenges and the conceptualisation of networked school communities have been discussed here. We have highlighted how this requires new expectations and TPACK capabilities of educators, and encouraged innovative uses of digital technologies to engage young children for accessing information, for communication purposes, to support meaning-making and to rethink curriculum, pedagogy and assessment. There has never been a better time in relation to the suite of options and opportunities for selecting and using digital technologies to support, enhance and rethink the early years curriculum.

When engaging early years learners with digital technologies, the following principles and approaches can guide your planning to create meaningful learning and teaching in the early years:

Birth to three years
- Use digital technologies to access images and information, explore diverse perspectives and make sense of their world.
- Engage a small amount of time with various digital technologies.
- Follow moving images on the screen with eyes and fingers.
- Identify ways to turn sound on and off, press buttons and touch screen on digital devices.

Three to five years
- Identify the uses of technologies in everyday life, and use real or imaginary technologies as props in play.
- Use digital technologies as tools for designing, drawing, editing, reflecting and composing.
- Engage with digital technology for fun and to make meaning.
- Access information, investigate ideas and represent their thinking.

Five to six years
- Use a mouse to control the point on the screen to support meaningful engagement with an interface.

- Use different types of data, such as text, images and numbers, to create simple information products.
- Apply navigation skills when responding to stimulus in multimedia resources and on approved websites.
- Safely use digital technology tools, including leaving electrical connections alone, sitting upright in front of a computer, and carefully handling storage devices such as disks and memory sticks.

Seven to eight years

- Access a website to participate in a game and use drawing applications for a range of purposes.
- Cut and paste, drop and drag, drop and colour-code in order to group similar items, sequence events and identify examples that illustrate key ideas.
- Create and display students' own information products in a way that suits different audiences.
- Compose and send electronic messages such as emails.

In the following section, we outline the use of the digital camera for early years learning through providing a case study to illustrate these principles in action.

Case study 9.2: The digital camera as a digital technology in the classroom

Setting, purpose and research design

This case study is set in an early years setting in Victoria, Australia, where one of the co-authors of this chapter was educator, learner and researcher. Throughout the research, the voices of children aged between five and seven years were sought to explore their perspectives of teaching and learning through the generation of visual narratives via a digital camera, seen as a valuable m-learning tool.

The method of using a digital camera in the early years classroom evolved over time. Through the camera as an active digital technology device, others were invited into the world of the children, allowing for the recognition of the significant contribution the children could make to an understanding of learning, teaching and pedagogy. The scholarship of Margaret Carr (1998, 2001) was influential in the research design of the study, with the concept of learning stories whereby the educator creates images of children at work developed with assessment in mind. This case study extends this work, so that images and the subsequent text of learning and teaching moments are generated by the children themselves rather than by an educator or adult visiting the learning environment.

continued

Selection of digital cameras

Digital technologies are a vital contributor to the rapid expansion of learning in the twenty-first century, and the digital camera is a technology that supports this movement (UNESCO, 2005). The digital camera as a technology gives easy access to visually produced data. A strength of working visually in education is the capacity that digital technology makes available to *slow down* and *repeat observations* (Prosser, 1997) of learning environments. These movements allow multiple opportunities for deeper reflection, different perspectives, interruptions, questions, inquiries and the complexities that occur in the learning environment to be noticed. 'In today's world all these skills are necessary, in order to face rapid change in society.' (UNESCO, 2005, n.p.) This study embraces the UNESCO Four Pillars of Learning:

- *Learning to do and learning to be.* Introducing children in early years classrooms to an accessible and portable device such as a digital camera, enabling them to photograph what is important to them, and providing opportunities to reflect and share their voice.
- *Learning to know and learning to live together.* In engaging with the visual narrative process, the children are broadening their own knowledge, acknowledging and appreciating others' differing views, and developing interactive social skills that will be transferable to the workforce.

Early years children as photographic communicators of their learning

The digital camera was introduced to the young children as a technology device for learning—most importantly, a device that they would use to share their stories of learning and teaching. The aim of this study was to show that young children are capable image-makers and can engage productively with portable digital technology and generate digital photographs that share their lived experiences of teaching and learning. Careful scaffolding had to occur in order to safely use the digital camera (to wear the strap around their wrist in case of an accidental bump), take turns in sharing one camera in the classroom and show mutual respect towards what peers decided to photograph, and thus share as part of their visual narratives (Lemon, 2008).

Figure 9.4   Celia holding the digital camera with the camera strap around her wrist (taken by Hannah)

The digital camera was a part of the classroom—not an extra element on the side but an integral part of the teaching and learning taking place for all 'learners' in the classroom. The children were collaborators in the process. Throughout the year, the children were invited to use a digital camera to record events that were important to them.

Figure 9.5   'Classrooms, we'd have to work outside if we didn't have . . . We can keep our writing neat and put our pencils and glue somewhere.' (Claire)

continued

A timetable that was decided together allocated learners a specific time when each child could use the camera, with the times rotated each week. At other times, the camera was free from specific use, allowing opportunities for the children to photograph new discoveries that were unplanned. No limitations were set with regard to how many images were generated; rather, children were invited to meaningfully capture learning around them. The children themselves identified the importance of not posing or taking 'silly photos that would not make sense', as noticed by one child. After the child finished taking the photos, the images would be downloaded on to a computer where the young photographer would share their narrative, allowing for a peer to use the camera. Eventually, after scaffolding from the educator, children learnt how to download images and began to teach each other this process. Some children even explored attaching photographs to emails to send to family, as well as other programs that allowed for inserting images and typing reflections about the photographs' intentions as a way to extend their interest in digital technologies. In the sharing of photographs and the narratives that emerged, close connections were made, with ongoing reflection and links to opportunities to assess learning.

Cameron decided to print the photograph in a large format and then paste it in the middle of large poster paper. His intention was to emulate a mini-graffiti wall of reflections on learning.

Figure 9.6   Cameron invited a small group of peers to reflect on his photograph

Following scheduled sessions within the curriculum, where photographs were taken independently, the participants were invited to discuss and reflect on why they had taken the photograph(s) (intention) and what it/they meant to them. These discussions took the form of a written reflection, such as a reflective journal entry, a graphic organiser such as a mind map or a graffiti wall entry, or a one-to-one conversation with their educator, a peer, a small group of classmates or the whole class. The children always had a choice about whether they would reflect, and how they would do this and with whom. This is where the intertextuality of photographs and text, including the reflections and stories of learning, were placed together to create student-driven visual narratives.

Figure 9.7   Dan, Josh and Marco were playing the Australian animal game

'They are thinking of where they are. I think it's a memory game and you have to think hard about where the words are. When I was playing it a different day I won because I remembered where everything was I didn't get every match though because you can't play by yourself. It's Josh's turn. Only Josh and Dan's . . . is a half-face. We can only see a bit of Marco's nose and eyes.' (Emily)

continued

The digital camera became one way to promote reflection in our early years classroom. Verbal responses to photographic visuals became a regular occurrence in the classroom. The young children built on the process of using a digital camera in the classroom and reflected on their own photographs in a variety of situations. Each time, the children were encouraged to offer their photographs for learning experiences that promoted reflection through mediums such as child-directed class discussions, digital stories, vignettes of learning published in the classroom newsletter, wall displays, graffiti walls, or graphic organisers. Often in small-group or whole-class activities, a photograph was used for reflection, with sentence starters being used as both prompts and as a modelling strategy. Reflection was undertaken in written, verbal, or visual modes, providing children with an opportunity to use their preferred mode of reflection.

Figure 9.8   I have to count the feet

'Seven both sides. What does seven plus seven make [counts on with fingers] . . . fourteen. They have fourteen legs. The two brown ones are the oldest and he eats the most. I can't see him at the moment because he is hiding. They crawl on the leaves to get away from the spider. There was one in there this morning. They were all hiding under the leaves. There was a Huntsmen [spider] in there this morning. But he wouldn't eat them because they are no harm to him. But the silkworms hid because of danger.' (James)

Findings and reflections

Over time, the children gained confidence in using language to explore and describe what they had experienced. The children's generated digital photographs provide multiple perspectives on teaching and learning in their Australian classroom. From a constructivist position, these photographs allow audiences—such as parents, educators, academics, adults, community, youth or children—to discuss teaching and learning from a perspective in addition to that of the educator or from the stance of a researcher. In turn, their images support the audience to ask questions, inquire, think, discuss and look at 'us', 'self' and how the 'I' accounts for the lived experiences they capture. A fresh approach to reflective practice emerges, opening up opportunities for student-generated visual narratives and foregrounding the voices of children who are linked to digital technology (Snyder, 1999; Trinidad, 2003; Van House et al., 2004; Swan et al., 2005). This case study also demonstrates how low-cost methods can integrate digital technologies into the learning environment.

Summary

- We have established the need for all involved in early years learning to understand the implications for rethinking curriculum, pedagogy and assessment due to the transformational possibilities being enabled by digital technologies.
- The technology trends, and the insights into young children's access to and use of digital technologies in both their school and home contexts, collectively formed the basis for our encouragement of creating a stronger home–school nexus and the conceptualisation of networked school communities.
- Responses need to be formulated according to context, but we suggest that the next steps require digital technologies and rethinking early years to be seen as interrelated, and that digital technologies open up exciting possibilities.
- The critical challenges need to be well understood. In designing early years learning environments, the selection from the variety of digital technologies should be informed by educational rationales that take into account a diverse range of contexts, and understandings of individual needs.
- Various digital technologies can be selected, such as digital cameras, internet applications such as webcams, virtual tours, simulations, mobile devices, and games-based learning. These can allow children to investigate, manipulate and interact with living things, objects and materials, some of which might not be accessible otherwise.

- These rich technological applications can assist children to focus on specific features of objects and help them closely observe similarities, differences, patterns and change.
- The potential for collecting, storing and accessing electronic records for assessment purposes also opens up possibilities not explored in depth in this chapter. For example, children's work generated digitally—such as digital images, video and voice—can be stored and viewed.
- For learning in the early years, the technology trends and the critical challenges identified in this chapter demand transformational changes through rethinking early years learning. Questions relating to how, why and when digital technologies can be integral to early years curriculum, pedagogy and assessment need to be asked and addressed. We conclude with the following possibilities and potential for digital technologies to:
  - become integral to early years learning, characterised by blending technologies most appropriate for a rich variety of meaningful learning experiences
  - complement existing technologies that enable children (aged from birth to age eight) to learn through play and exploration
  - motivate and engage young children in learning that contributes to their cognitive and social development
  - enhance children's self-concept and their attitudes toward learning
  - stimulate and enhance levels of spoken, written and multimedia modes of communication
  - promote the idea of young children sharing leadership roles and initiating interactions more frequently, engaging in turn-taking and peer collaboration, and having opportunities to peer-teach transferring new ways of working with digital technologies.

Discussion questions

9.1 How might digital technologies enhance early years learning?

9.2 What are some examples of new and emerging digital technologies that you believe can enhance early years learning?

9.3 What do you think is the role of parents/caregivers in enabling access to and promoting positive participation by young children in the use of digital technologies for early years learning?

9.4 What do you think is the role of educators in enabling access to and promoting positive participation by young children in the use of digital technologies for early years learning?

9.5 By drawing upon your thinking in relation to Questions 9.3 and 9.4, in an increasingly networked world, what are the possibilities accompanying a shared vision of effective home–school partnerships through creating networked school communities?

9.6 By referring to Case Study 9.2, what are the potential and possibilities for the use of digital cameras to support and enhance early years learning?

References

Australian Communications and Media Authority (ACMA) (2009). *Use of electronic media and communications: Early childhood to teenage years.* Canberra: Australian Communications and Media Authority. Retrieved 24 October 2011 from <www.acma.gov.au/webwr/_assets/main/lib310665/use_of_electronic_media_&_comms-early_childhood_to_teenage_years.pdf>.

Australian Institute for Teaching and School Leadership (AITSL) (2011a). *National Professional Standards for Teachers.* Retrieved 24 October 2011 from <www.teacherstandards.aitsl.edu.au>.

——(2011b). *Teaching Teachers for the Future Project.* Retrieved 24 October 2011 from <www.aitsl.edu.au/ttf-project.html>.

Carr, M. (1998). A project for assessing children's experiences in early childhood settings. Paper presented at the European Conference on Quality in Early Childhood Setting. Santiago de Compostela, Spain.

——(2001). *Assessment in early childhood settings: Learning stories.* London: Paul Chapman.

Commonwealth of Australia (2009). *Early Years Learning Framework for Australia: Belonging, Being and Becoming.* Canberra: Commonwealth Government. Retrieved 24 October 2011 from <www.deewr.gov.au/Earlychildhood/Policy_Agenda/Quality/Documents/Final%20EYLF%20Framework%20Report%20-%20WEB.pdf>.

Downes, T., Beecher, B. & Arthur, L. (2001). Effective learning environments for young children using digital resources: An Australian perspective. *Information Technology in Childhood Education, 1*, 139–53.

Koehler, M. & Mishra, P. (2008). Introducing TPCK, in AACTE Committee on Innovation and Technology (ed.), *Handbook of Technological Pedagogical Content Knowledge (TPCK) for Educators* (pp. 3–29). New York: Routledge.

Lee, M. & Finger, G. (2010). *Developing a networked school community: A guide to realising the vision.* Melbourne: ACER Press.

Lee, M. & Gaffney, M. (2008). *Leading a digital school: Principles and practice.* Melbourne: ACER Press.

Lemon, N. (2008). Looking through the lens of a camera in the early childhood classroom. In J. Moss (ed.), *Research education: Visually-digitally-spatially* (pp. 21–52). Rotterdam: Sense.

——(2011). Arts and technology. In C. Klopper & S. Garvis (eds), *Tapping into the classroom practice of the arts: From inside out!* (pp. 97–132). Brisbane: Post Pressed.

New Media Consortium (2011). *NMC Horizon Report 2011: K–12 Edition*. Retrieved 18 October 2011 from <http://media.nmc.org/iTunesU/HR-K12/2011/2011-Horizon-Report-K12.pdf>.

Shulman, L. (1986). Those who understand: Knowledge growth in teaching. *Educational Researcher*, *15*(2), 4–14.

Snyder, I. (1999). Using information technology in language and literacy education: An introduction. In J. Hancock (ed.), *Teaching literacy using information technology: A collection of articles from Australian literacy educators' association* (pp. 1–10). Newark, NJ: International Reading Association.

Swan, K., van't Hooft, M., Kratcoski, A. & Unger, D. (2005). Uses and effects of mobile computing devices in K–8 classrooms. *Journal of Research on Technology in Education*, *38*(1), 99–113.

Tapscott, D. (1999). *Growing up digital: The rise of the net generation*. New York: Harvard Business Press.

—— (2008). *Grown up digital: How the net generation is changing our world*. New York: McGraw-Hill.

Thelning, K. & Lawes, H. (2001). *Discussion paper—information and communication technologies (ICT) in the early years: The connections between early childhood principles, beliefs about children's learning, and the influences of information and communication technologies*. Retrieved 24 October 2011 from <www.earlyyears.sa.edu.au/files/links/ICT_in_the_EYDiscussion_Pa.pdf>.

Trinidad, S. (2003). Working with technology-rich learning environments: Strategies for success. In M.S. Khine & D. Fisher (eds), *Technology-rich learning environments: A future perspective* (pp. 97–114). Singapore: World Scientific.

United Nations Educational, Scientific and Cultural Organization (UNESCO) (2005). *60 Years of education: Goal 3—Promote learning and skills for young people and adults*. Retrieved 24 October 2011 from <http://portal.unesco.org/education/en/ev.phpURL_ID=41579&URL_DO_TOPIC&URL_SECTION=210.html>.

Van House, N.A., Davis, M., Takhteyev, Y., Ames, M. & Finn, M. (2004). *The social uses of personal photography: Methods for projecting future imaging applications*. Retrieved 24 October 2011 from <www.sims.berkeley.edu/ ~ vanhouse /van%20house_et_al_2004b%20.pdf>.

10

Health and physical education

Danielle Twigg and Robyn Jorgensen

Introduction

Health and physical education (HPE) is an essential aspect of learning for young children. Research indicates that there is a strong correlation between academic success and student health and well-being (World Health Organisation, 2006). Generally speaking, HPE consists of three focus areas: health, physical activity and personal development. Each of these three areas contributes to early years learners' knowledge and understanding about overall health and well-being. Learning begins at birth and can be measured in various ways, including through the use of developmental milestones. This chapter will enable readers to:

- develop a solid understanding of the three focus areas of health and physical education in both prior-to-school and school settings
- identify key developmental milestones in the areas of health, physical activity and personal development for early years learners
- apply the basic principles of the three focus areas in order to design quality learning experiences for children in two age groups, including birth to four years and four to eight years

- justify the contribution HPE makes towards academic success and the overall health and well-being of early years learners.

The chapter includes a case study based on Australian research that explores the possibility that early years swimming programs may enhance the learning of young children. The chapter concludes with a summary and a set of study questions.

Health and physical education in the early years

In 1986, the first International Conference on Health Promotion was held in Ottawa, Canada. At the conference, the Ottawa Charter (World Health Organisation, 1986) for Health Promotion was developed and, more than two decades later, continues to serve as the international consensus agreement on good health-promotion practice. The Ottawa Charter provides a foundation for the development of quality health and physical education by emphasising the importance of advocating for community health education. In Australia and around the world, educators look to the Ottawa Charter as the foundation for all health and physical education curricula. Early years educators are advised to refer to the relevant curriculum (i.e. national, state) to ensure specific learning outcomes are achieved. While various curriculum-based documents may vary across contexts, it is recognised that there are some consistent themes in all HPE frameworks and curriculum guides. The three focus areas will be explored in a general way to draw attention to the main aspects of each of these areas. The three areas are health, physical activity and personal development. These focus areas are closely linked.

Health
The focus area of health emphasises the significant roles that everyday actions and environment have on healthy behaviours. In this area, early years learners focus on the multidimensional aspects of everyday health and practice by making healthy choices for their own bodies. Examples of key concepts in the area of *health* that are appropriate for early years learners may include:

- making healthy choices as an individual and community member
- understanding healthy eating habits to support growth and development
- awareness of the multiple dimensions of health, including physical, social and emotional aspects
- promotion of safety, health and well-being in everyday life.

When educating early years learners about taking care of themselves and others, it is important to use authentic examples and encourage children to learn the language of healthy habits. As a starting point in preschool, and in the early years of school, young children enjoy discussing their own personal experiences. For example, in a toddler room children might talk about brushing their teeth, whereas children in a Year 1 classroom might discuss the safe use of medications. These activities may include such activities as cooking at home, shopping for healthy foods (including fresh fruit and vegetables), visiting the doctor or helping their parent/guardian quit smoking. Conversations with primary caregivers about hygiene and healthy eating can occur with children under the age of three through daily interactions. Young children often have a natural curiosity about aspects of health, and the capacity of young learners to understand their worlds and expand their experiences should not be under-estimated. For many urban dwellers, learning where fresh foods come from is important. Misconceptions about the origins of fresh foods, while amusing to the general public, must be an important component of early years learning. Growing fresh vegetables is not only an interesting activity for early years learners, it also helps their understanding of aspects of science and cultural differences.

Physical activity
Fundamental movement skills are essential to the focus area of physical activity within health and physical education. As early years learners develop, their gross and fine motor skills will improve as a result of participation in physical activity. Some of the key concepts in the area of physical activity that will support the development of early years learners include:

- developing general body awareness through movement activities
- practising gross motor and fine motor skills
- understanding the importance of daily exercise
- learning to play games with rules and working as a member of a team.

Although children begin to develop body awareness from birth, gross and fine motor development occurs over several years. An unfortunate downside of contemporary life is that many early years learners do not have the freedom to actively engage with their physical environment. Unlike previous generations, today's early years learners are often driven to many activities, thus reducing their amount of physical activity. This makes the engagement in physical activity even more important in the early years of learning. Most early childhood education centres and schools incorporate exercise and outdoor play time into their daily timetables.

The routine of daily physical activity has many benefits for young children, including the opportunity to strengthen their own bodies in ways that cannot be achieved in the classroom. Research indicates that daily exercise contributes to higher levels of concentration, which is important for academic achievement. There are now many perceptual motor programs used in early years settings that link physical activity with cognitive activities. These programs maintain that better learning outcomes occur when physical activity is an integral part of learning. It is important for early years educators to consider the age-appropriateness and ability of all learners when planning physical activity experiences for young children.

Personal development

Self-management and social interaction are addressed within the focus area of personal development. From birth, early years learners begin to learn about their own identity, both as an individual and later as a member of society. The ways in which young children behave in various environments and how they respond to difficult personal situations are central to healthy development. Key concepts that will support the personal development of early years learners include:

- understanding one's personal identity
- respecting authority and demonstrating self-management within different environments
- practising resilience-building skills for social and emotional well-being
- learning how to communicate effectively.

Preschool children in particular enjoy learning about themselves, and should be encouraged to share their thoughts and feelings in a safe and supportive learning environment. Children in this age group need to be supported in considering the feelings of others, so the early years educator or carer must foster an environment where positive comments are reinforced and non-judgemental evaluations are encouraged. In the early years classroom, it is important to consider ways of including routines and transitions that may contribute to children's understanding of socially acceptable behaviour and consequences for poor behaviour. Self-management can be taught to very young children in prior-to-school settings through routines such as packing/unpacking school bags, managing clothing and personal belongings, and awareness of body signals (such as feeling unwell, needing a bathroom break). Early years educators should consider developing a weekly roster of jobs (one job per student) to encourage community care, effective communication and practising age-appropriate responsibility. For example, in a kindergarten classroom, each child may be allocated a job for the week, such as 'line leader' or 'classroom pet minder', to ensure that each child has the opportunity to contribute in a responsible way to the classroom. Early years educators should rotate jobs on a weekly basis to ensure each child has an opportunity to take on specific classroom jobs on more than one occasion over the course of the school year. The next section of the chapter provides suggestions for the development of high-quality HPE experiences for early years learners.

Designing quality HPE experiences for early years learners

In the early years, health and physical education must be designed to cater for diverse learners. It is a well-established fact that children grow and change at different rates over time. A child's development is likely to be influenced not only by certain stages or sequences, but also environmental factors, cultural influences and life experiences. Therefore, not all three-year-olds are alike in terms of development and ability. However, it is important to have an understanding of the impact of 'developmental milestones' on early years learners when designing quality learning activities for health and physical education. There are numerous books available that provide detailed information on child development. For the purposes of this textbook, however, an overview of the key areas of physical and social/emotional development is now provided. Being aware of these milestones is critical to the development of a curriculum that is appropriate to the needs of the learner.

Physical development

Throughout infancy and early childhood, changes in physical growth can be observed. Bodies grow at various rates and in different proportions over time. The primary factors that influence physical development are genetics and environmental factors; however, social, cultural and individual differences also contribute to the physical growth of a child. Motor development occurs as a young child's muscles and bones grow, and the child is able to move their own body.

Gross motor development typically begins between eighteen and 24 months of age. Very young children work through a number of 'milestones' as part of their gross motor development (Frankenburg, 2002), including lifting their heads (three months), rolling over (four to five months) and sitting without support (five to six months). Clark (2005) identifies six important developmental milestones, several of which occur *before* a child learns to walk:

- crawling (seven to ten months)
- walking (eleven to fourteen months)
- running (eighteen to 22 months)
- galloping (eighteen to 22 months)
- hopping (age three)
- skipping (age five)

Fine motor development occurs when a child learns to use individual body parts to manipulate and control small objects. Before a young child is able to exhibit fine motor control, the child must have developed gross motor abilities (through large muscle control) as well as hand–eye coordination. Within the first four or five months of life, an infant is able to reach for objects, through voluntary muscle control, within an arm's length distance from their own body (Harris, 2005) (see Figure 10.1). Once infants develop a *pincer grasp* (at nine to twelve months), they demonstrate their ability to pick up objects with their thumb and index finger (von Hofsten, 2005), which prepares them for using writing instruments. Historical

Figure 10.1   Infant reaching for objects

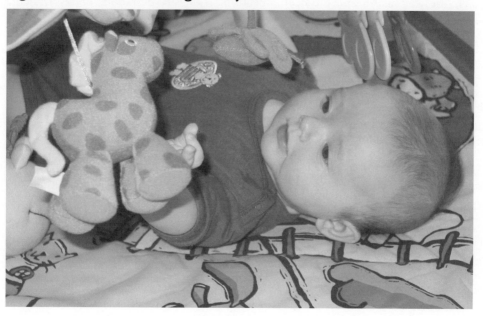

research indicates that through infancy and the first year, early learners develop hand–eye coordination that forms the basis for the use of tools and objects, and allows children to grow as contributing members of society (Goodenough, 1926). Other skills, such as copying, develop in more detail as fine motor development continues for a young child. The development of preferred 'handedness' usually occurs before the age of five years, and can be influenced by genetic and environmental factors (Harris, 2005).

Social/emotional development

Social and emotional development are critical to young children's understanding of themselves and others. Even in infancy, children learn to respond to primary caregivers in order to communicate specific needs. Babies and toddlers interact with adults through crying, gestures and babbling before learning to communicate through oral language. The significant work of Bowlby (1958) on attachment theory concludes that an understanding of the basic physiological needs of children is essential for supporting the social and emotional development of early years learners. Seminal research conducted by Parten (1932) indicates that young children learn social skills and self-management through participation in social activities, such as play and games, with peers and on their own in various settings. Early years learners begin to understand more fully rules and rights in social activities. Opportunities for early years learners to practise self-management are a key aspect of preparing young children to grow as contributors to society at large. Early years educators and carers can support young children to develop self-management skills through modelling appropriate behaviour, explicit teaching of social expectations and management of personal belongings, as well as emotional responses to various situations. Resilience education in the early years and beyond contributes to the long-term health and well-being of children, as it offers children the opportunity to test their own understandings of citizenship in a safe and supportive learning environment.

Perceptual motor programs

Many early years learning contexts use programs that unite physical development with cognition and affect. The Northern Territory Department of Education and Training (2012) summarises the perceptual motor program:

> Perceptual motor programs aim to train students to integrate auditory skills into memory retention, whilst completing physical tasks. Communication skills such as

reading, writing, speaking, and the acquisition of numeracy skills involve motor-based activities. Most of a child's initial learning occurs through the complex processes of integrating sensory systems and physical environments. (2012, p. 3)

These programs typically are implemented in the mornings, when young children are more alert and ready to learn. The programs have children engaging with activities that focus on particular physical skills—such as hopping a distance, collecting an object and then walking a beam (placed at ground level). Typically, the children circulate through a range of activities, much like a Round Robin format. By adopting this type of approach, the learners rotate through several activities in a given session and are thus exposed to a range of activities. This helps to build a wide repertoire of physical skills.

The activities used in a perceptual motor program vary, and are based on the physical development of the child. The program should include activities that cater for the development of perception (which would include control of the body, body image, directionality, awareness of space and movement through space, and rhythm); general skill development (which would include physical skills, problem-solving, language, memory and confidence); and motor skills (which would include balance, fitness, location and coordination). Motor skills include both gross and fine motor skills. Most perceptual motor programs have been developed through commercial suppliers or at the school/centre level, and their use will depend on the age of the children attending the facility.

A good perceptual motor program focuses on a range of skills, including gross motor skills; visual motor skills that require the learner to manipulate and coordinate a number of skills simultaneously; auditory motor skills where the learner coordinates auditory input with motor skills; tactile activities; activities that focus on lateralisation—that is, on one side of the body or the other (such as hopping or picking something up with one hand); and an awareness of the body and a sense of space. The program helps learners to gain a sense of posture and body awareness. At the same time, it has a strong emphasis on language, so that there is a strong correlation between language and the body. The learner may be instructed to hop in one direction on their right leg, pick up an object with their left hand and then kick a ball back with their left leg. This physical coordination with language helps to consolidate language development as well as to develop strong motor and coordination skills. In all exercises, multiple activities that coordinate both sides of the body are central to the program.

This variety of activities encourages a range of physical skills to be used, hence promoting mental stimulation in a range of areas of the brain. At the same time, the child will be required to talk about the activity or to sing songs or say rhymes, and in so doing link language and activity. This helps not only physical development but also language development. Linking physical activity with cognitive activity is thought to create stronger learning opportunities for young learners. Because children have to remember instructions for the activity, these programs also help with memory. In addition, they are thought to help with problem-solving and reasoning. There appear to be numerous benefits from well-organised programs that link physical activity with cognitive activities.

Perceptual motor programs are not meant to be remedial, but are considered to be of benefit to all students. Programs that encourage physical activity are probably more important in today's classrooms than in the past, due to the more sedentary lives of many people in today's society.

Other programs exist outside formal learning centres. In the next section, we highlight an out-of-school context where very young children are engaged in a physical activity; by so doing, they may be learning much more than just the development of gross motor skills.

Case study 10.1: Exploring the possibilities of early years swimming

Young children can participate in a range of organised physical activities—such as dance, ballet, football, or gymnastics—that extend the possibilities of learning, particularly around the enhancement of physical capacities. While the swim industry has a long history, early years swimming is a relatively new area in this sector. Like the older, more established swimming programs, most early years swimming programs have been formulated to cater for the physical developmental milestones of the child (Langendorfer, 1990). Children can commence swimming lessons from as young as three months, but most programs seem to commence around six months (see Figure 10.2), although advocates of early years swimming (such as Olympian coach Laurie Lawrence) advocate that water familiarisation—which is a key feature of early years swimming—can commence as soon as a baby is born. However, as many of the physical developments of young children are contingent on gross motor skills (such as head holding, pincer grip for grabbing items, crawling, standing unaided and walking), the appearance of these skills shapes the possibilities of what is possible in any physical activity.

What is unique about the swim environment over many other physical education contexts is that the water environment offers a degree of support for the child that is not present in other contexts. For example, a young child of six months is able to propel their body through water, whereas on land this mobility would be limited.

Figure 10.2   Nine-month-old Kyrra in a swimming class

In studies with children with disabilities, it has been found that the water context enables a degree of mobility and movement of the child that is not otherwise possible. Because of the support offered by the water, early swim programs can be structured so that activities are not limited by gross motor skills that are not yet present (such as holding the head upright unaided or being able to walk unaided). The programs have been designed to cater for these gross motor skills, but are not limited to them. This is unique to this industry, and hence may offer greater opportunities for enhanced learning.

Studies with children with physical disabilities have shown water activities can enhance mobility and aerobic strength (Fragala-Pinkham et al. 2008; Hutzler et al. 2008). Dellaratta (2002) reports increased gross motor development among under-fives with hypotonia. Similarly, Prupas et al. (2006) report improvement in gross motor skills among children with autism. At a more general level, Oates (2004) reports that participation in a swimming program helped children with disabilities enhance both their motor and affective skills so as to be more confident with their sense of self. While there has been some debate over the physical capabilities of young children in the birth to two years age range to cope with the demands of swimming, it has been reported (Zelazo & Weiss, 2006) that participation in swimming programs can accelerate motor development. In their study, Zelazo and Weiss (2006) report that

Figure 10.3   Fourteen-month-old Kyrra shows crawling and head strength in a swimming lesson

there were considerable gains in the movements required for turning 180 degrees and reaching for a wall for the sixteen- to 20-month-old children, and that this may be possible due to the reduction in gravitational forces when in the pool (see Figure 10.3).

It is reasonable to expect that young children would benefit from participating in swimming lessons prior to formal schooling. However, there are intended learning outcomes that in this case would centre on the development of particular swimming skills. Then there are the unintended learning outcomes, which are not known at the start of the teaching episodes but become evident as the learners participate in the activities. Both the intended and unintended learnings are contingent upon the quality of the learning context. The following extracts were taken from a swim lesson with three-year-old children. Here it becomes possible to see how the language used by the educator helps to introduce and consolidate learning. Many of the prepositions and spatially referential terms used in language are learnt incidentally. Within the context of swimming lessons, students are able to hear the words and move their bodies to reflect the terms. This coordination between words and actions helps in the learning of many words. The swim context enables a much richer possibility for learning many of these words. Similarly, there are many terms used in mathematics lessons that are also embedded in swim lessons. Again, the exposure to, and bodily manipulations associated with, these terms enrich the possibilities for learning language. Similarly, the interactions expose children to patterns of interacting that they will find in the school context so that they are more familiar with interactional patterns found there.

Teacher (T): Big splash with *two* feet [holds up two fingers].

T: After *one-two-three*, we are going to push *off* with our hands like a rocket.

T: Eyes *down* in the water.

T: We are kicking around in a *circle* Clinton, so kick *out* to me then around then *back* to the start.

T: Ben, arms out *straight* like a pencil.

T: Alex, *turn around* so you can kick on your back, eyes *up*.

Language skills

Through interacting with educators and the swim environment, children gain increased opportunities to develop new words and concepts. Many of these may extend beyond what is learned in the home. The language skills can vary from new vocabulary through to new ways of interacting with people. The child may have learnt how to interact with parents and family, but the patterns of language used in instructional settings are very different from those in the home or other informal settings. These patterns of language use may vary considerably from the repertoire of language they would encounter in other contexts.

Social skills

Being in social groups with peers from an early age may help in social interactions and bonding with peers. This may help young children to become more social, and to better understand and engage with social interactions as well as networking with peers. Learning to be a social person is critical for interactions in the wider society. Being able to have a go at activities—many of which are profoundly different from the non-water environment—requires confidence, trust, and some sense of adventure. The scaffolding processes of the swim environment may help young children to develop these attributes.

Intellectual dispositions

The overall participation in an instructional setting where numerous stimuli are used to promote learning may support the overall learning and capacity to learn of young children. It may be difficult to imagine how swimming may enhance intellect, but from observations of pools I have noted that there is a rich repertoire of many mathematical concepts and language. What is unique in this context is that language and concepts are closely connected—the child hears the words and these are linked with physical actions. Counting actions—one, two, three, kick—link words and actions so that the child is able to physically and cognitively make the connection. Lessons are built around this. The swim environment is also rich with a range of descriptors that are integral to mathematics, such as colour, shape and size. Asking children to 'pick up the big red ring' helps with exposure to terms commonly used in early years school mathematics. As Zevenbergen (2000, 2001) argues, such terms are commonly used in middle-class families but are of restricted use in many disadvantaged families. In studying the swimming context, Jorgensen et al. (2010) report that many aspects of mathematics are evident in the interactions between the educator and the children. As such, the swim environment offers access to many aspects of mathematical language and concepts in a friendly, non-threatening environment. This is particularly relevant given that research has shown that many families are already disadvantaged because they are not participating in swim lessons.

School skills

Exposing children to instructional practices from infancy and beyond may help them to become familiar with similar practices they will experience in more formal school-type settings such as early childhood services and/or schools. Unlike other instructional contexts, the risk for a child who is not paying attention could be profound, so educators must know what children are doing at all times in the lessons. This means that there is a strong instructional imperative in early years swimming, which often is not found in the home interactions of some familial groups. These processes—such as not running, waiting turns in a way that is safe and highly structured or focusing on the educator as they speak—may help children learn the routines they will find in school or in early childhood services.

Summary

- This chapter has outlined the ways in which health and physical education are organised in the formal educational and policy context.
- HPE is an important part of early years learning, both for overall well-being and because out-of-school contexts such as the swimming environment offer significant learning opportunities.
- The swim environment focuses primarily on gross motor skills, but within the pedagogical context other significant areas of learning are made possible.
- When considering the HPE area, the intended and unintended learnings must be considered.
- Knowing the physical milestones through which children progress provides an important organiser for the experiences of young children. These milestones form the basis for the curriculum in the early years.
- While educators may plan for particular learning outcomes, it is also important to recognise that there may be other, unexpected learning outcomes.
- Many out-of-school contexts (such as swimming) can provide an environment for enhancing HPE learning, but it is also important to recognise the other learning that may come from quality learning environments.

Discussion questions

10.1 What physical milestones would you expect to see in an eighteen-month-old child, and how would you build a quality learning experience for that child that would extend the child to achieve more?

10.2 What are the key considerations that educators make when developing the curriculum in HPE for children in the early years?

10.3 A child in your care seems to have trouble with a particular motor skill that should be emerging at their age. What might you do to assess the child and what would you do to see whether you could assist the child to learn the skill?

10.4 A parent asks your advice about whether their child should go to ballet (or dance, or swim or gymnastics) out of school time. What advice would you give to the parent?

References

Bowlby, J. (1958). The nature of the child's tie to his mother. *International Journal of Psycho-Analysis, 39*, 1–23.

Clark, J.E. (2005). Locomotion. In B. Hopkins (ed.), *The Cambridge encyclopedia of child development* (pp. 336–9). New York: Cambridge University Press.

Dellaratta, C. (2002). *Effects of a group aquatic program on gross motor development, water orientation and swimming skills in chldren with hypotonia*. Hamden: Quinnipiac.

Fragala-Pinkham, M., Haley, S.M. & O'Neil, M.E. (2008). *Group aquatic aerobic exercise for children with disabilities*. Brighton, MA: Research Center for Children with Special Health Care Needs, Franciscan Hospital for Children.

Frankenburg, W.K. (2002). Developmental surveillance and screening of infants and young children. *Pediatrics 109*(1), 144–5.

Goodenough, F.L. (1926). *The measurement of intelligence through drawing*. New York: Holt.

Harris, L.J. (2005). Handedness. In B. Hopkins (ed.), *The Cambridge encyclopedia of child development* (pp. 321–6). New York: Cambridge University Press.

Hutzler Y., Chacham, A., Bergman, U. & Szeinberg, A. (2008). Effects of a movement and swimming program on vital capacity and water orientation skills of children with cerebral palsy. *Developmental Medicine & Child Neurology, 40*(3), 176–81.

Jorgensen, R., Sullivan, P. & Grootenboer, P. (2010). Good learning = a good life: Mathematics transformation in remote Indigenous communities. *Australian Journal of Social Issues, 45*(1), 131–43.

Langendorfer, S.J. (1990). Contemporary trends in infant/preschool aquatics—into the 1990s and beyond. *Journal of Physical Education, Recreation & Dance, 61*(5), 36.

Northern Territory Department of Education and Training (2012). *Assessment of student competencies: Teacher handbook*. Darwin: NTDET. Retrieved 10 January 2010 from <www.det.nt.gov.au/__data/assets/pdf_file/0019/991/TeacherHandbook.pdf>.

Oates, M.C. (2004). *Does a recreational swimming program improve the self-esteem of children and adolescents with physical disabilities? Possible underlying mechanisms.* St John's, NL: Memorial University of Newfoundland.

Parten, M.B. (1932). Social participation among preschool children. *Journal of Abnormal and Social Psychology, 27*, 243–69.

Prupas, A., Harevey, W.J. & Benjamin, J. (2006). Early intervention aquatics: A program for children with autism and their families. *Journal of Physical Education, Recreation & Dance, 77*(2), 46–51.

Twigg, D. (2011). The heart of innovation: Arts education in the middle years. In C. Klopper & S. Garvis (eds), *Tapping into the classroom practice of the arts: from inside out!* Brisbane: Post Pressed.

von Hofsten, C. (2005). Prehension. In B. Hopkins (ed.), *The Cambridge encyclopedia of child development* (pp. 348–51). New York: Cambridge University Press.

World Health Organisation (1986). *Ottawa Charter for Health Promotion.* Ottawa: Health and Welfare Canada and Canadian Public Health Association.

—— (2006). *Creating an environment for emotional and social well-being.* Geneva: WHO.

Zelazo, P.R. & Weiss, M.J. (2006). Infant swimming behaviors: Cognitive control and the influence of experience. *Journal of Cognition and Development, 7*(1), 1–25.

Zevenbergen, R. (2000). 'Cracking the code' of mathematics: School success as a function of linguistic, social and cultural background. In J. Boaler (ed.), *Multiple perspectives on mathematics teaching and learning.* New York: JAI/Ablex.

—— (2001). Language, social class and underachievement in mathematics. In P. Gates (ed.), *Issues in teaching mathematics* (pp. 38–50). London: Routledge/Falmer.

PART III

Pedagogical practices for the early years

11

Play-based learning

Marjory Ebbeck, Hoi Yin Bonnie Yim and Lai Wan Maria Lee

Introduction

This chapter provides insights into play-based learning and what it means to practitioners working in a range of contexts with early learners in the age range from birth to eight years. Play-based learning is defined as young learners constructing knowledge as they explore, experiment, discover and solve problems in playful and unique ways. Development is linked to play and viewed as a pattern of continuous, interrelated changes that begins at birth and continues through the lifespan while learning is a change in behaviour. In the early years, it is through experience in play that learning occurs. The definition of curriculum in this chapter presents a context for young learners, demonstrating how play-based learning is fundamental to the well-being of young learners—be they infants, babies, toddlers, preschoolers or school-aged children.

The diversity of backgrounds of young learners is recognised, and provision has to be made in the curriculum for a rich diversity of learners. The chapter also considers how a socio-constructivist theoretical orientation in the curriculum can be created, with children and adults co-constructing knowledge with play-based learning as the framework.

Play and young children

For centuries, policy-makers, administrators, researchers and practitioners have demonstrated an enduring interest in the nature of play, its meaning and its role in the development of young learners. The universal significance of the value of children's play in their development has been long recognised by the almost universal acceptance of Article 31 of the United Nations (UN) Convention on the Rights of the Child, to which most countries in the world are signatories and ratifying countries. This landmark agreement recognises that the right to play is one of the basic human rights of children, thus giving serious recognition to the place of play in children's lives.

Controversy still exists today about the role of the adult in children's play, and differences in interpretation of this role occur in many cultures and contexts. However, neuroscience findings are providing convincing evidence that the early childhood years are the most critical of all stages of development, and the first three years of life are particularly crucial given the emerging architecture of the brain and its plasticity (Mustard, 2008; NICHD Early Child Care Research Network, 2005). The role of the adult in being responsive to the infant, toddler and growing child has received much prominence. This worldwide focus on neuroscience has resulted in a new interest in the importance of early experiencing, with many curriculum frameworks for the early years emerging with the catch-cry 'early experiences matter' as one of their cornerstones.

What is play?

Bruce (1994) has written a number of books about play. She proposes that:

> play is an umbrella word which causes a serious lack of agreed focus. Amongst early childhood workers, play is thought to be of central importance. In contrast, parents and those outside this specialist field often see it as recreation, relaxation and fun. It may not be well thought to contribute anything much to the learning process. (1994, p.18)

Hughes (2010, p. 3) believes that 'there is no simple definition of play and that the borderlines between play and other activities, such as work, exploration and learning are not always that clear'. In a recent publication, Ebbeck and Waniganayake (2010, p. 8) write that 'children's play is many things, joyful, engaging, pleasurable, evoking imagination, spontaneous, free flowing, sometimes involves risk taking, increases knowledge and understanding, can be individual or in interactions with children and/or adults'.

Further, play occurs across all cultures and has some universal components: play is intrinsically motivated; it needs to be freely chosen; it is deeply engaging; and it involves some form of make-believe. In addition, play is seen to be deeply embedded in culture, and cannot be separated from other parts of the social world in which children live. The short vignette below shows children playing out the customs of their lifestyles.

The class has decided to create its own Chinese Tea House in the playroom.

Ling (girl, aged five years) is very absorbed in drawing on the spoons and bowls.

Ling: 'The spoons and bowls have very pretty pictures on them. I am drawing flowers and birds on the spoons.'

Po (boy, aged six years) sits next to her; he is teaching Yan (boy, aged five years) how to make a dim sum basket.

Po: 'This is how they make the dim sum basket. Let me show you. First roll and curl the paper, and then use it as the rim. Now, add the bars below. You need the empty space to let the steam go into the basket.'

Learning through play is a frequently cited adage, but it still rings true today, for evidence abounds that children—whatever their age—learn through play. It is their primary and most fundamental way of making sense of their world. Also, in spite of obstacles put in their way, children will play and learn because of it. Play and learning are seen to be inextricably woven together, for play = learning (Hirsh-Pasek & Golikoff, 2008).

Some theoretical perspectives on play

Theoretical perspectives on play abound, and some understanding of these is essential for professionals working with children. Ebbeck and Waniganayake (2010, p. 10) present a proposition that play can be viewed through developmental prisms, and that theorists group or categorise play from a *psychoanalytic* perspective (Erikson, 1963; Freud, 1968); a *social interactionist* perspective (Howes, 1980;

Howes & Matheson, 1992; Parten, 1932; Rubin, 1980); and a *constructivist* perspective (Piaget, 1951; Vygotsky, 1967, 1978). There have been refinements of these theories, all of which lead to a recognition that there are practical implications for play that adults working with children need to apply. Theories about children's development influence our understanding about play-based learning.

Play-based learning

Play-based learning is applicable to all early learners in the early childhood age range. Children's learning is complex, and occurs when a child is deeply engaged in play, which may include any or all of the following: exploring, discovering, experimenting, hypothesising and problem-solving. By such engagement, early learners further their understanding through play as the underpinning framework. This engagement is often dramatically seen in socio-dramatic play when, through some engrossed interaction, the child will be taken further in their learning. For this to occur, there needs to be an opportunity for the child to play, and this can be in an individual way, with a peer, with an adult or in a group situation. There is no template or formula for play-based learning. However, Ebbeck and Waniganayake (2010) propose that play-based learning enables children to:

- use symbols to represent and to understand their world (Bergen, 2002; Berk, 1999; Smilansky & Shefatya, 1990; Vygotsky, 1978)
- be flexible in their thinking (Elkind, 2003; Isenberg & Jalongo, 2001; Singer & Singer, 2005)
- form meaningful relationships with peers, adults and significant others in their lives (Bronfenbrenner, 1979, 1993; Mendoza & Katz, 2008; Vygotsky, 1978)
- experience a range of emotional feelings—happiness, sadness, anger, jealousy, excitement, wonder and fear (Erikson, 1963; Van Hoorn et al., 2007; Vygotsky, 1967, 1978)
- construct their knowledge through meaningful, direct, first-hand experiences (Bruner, 1986; Dewey, 1971; Piaget, 1951, 1963)
- foster and extend their communication skills (Berk, 2006; Bodrova & Leong, 2007; NAEYC, 2009; UNESCO, 2006)
- function above their current intellectual level and further extend cognitive skills (Vygotsky, 1978).

Dockett and Fleer (1999, pp. 65–6) present a useful discussion about the Vygotskian view that play has the potential to lead development. They present three ways in which this can occur, as identified by Bodrova and Leong (2007):

- First, play creates a zone of proximal development (ZPD), and it is in this context that 'in play the child is always beyond his age, above his usual everyday behaviour; in play he is, as it were, a head above himself. Play contains in a concentrated form, as in the focus of a magnifying glass, all developmental tendencies.' (Vygotsky 1978, p. 4, cited in Dockett & Fleer, 1999, p. 65) Dockett and Fleer go on to write that 'in other words, play provides opportunities for children to use mental skills and abilities, often before these are applied in other situations. The roles adopted and the relevant rules can be enacted in ways that would not happen in reality.' (1999, p. 65)
- Second, actions and objects are separated from thought in play.
- Third, self-regulation develops through play. 'Children often show a great sense of control and self-regulation in play. When children adopt roles, and the rules that go with these, they practise self-regulation as they restrict their actions and behaviours.' (1999, p. 66)

The role of the adult in fostering play-based learning

Much has been written recently about the importance of relationships in developing effective play-based interactions: all interactions and relationships should work towards helping children to build trust and confidence in order to support the development of secure relationships, a strong identity and a positive sense of well-being. Children need to be viewed as competent, confident learners, always on a path of self-discovery and self-identity.

Kostelink et al. (2011, p. 25) comment that supportive adult–child interactions are guided by an understanding of how young children think and reason, leading adults to practise supportive interaction strategies—sharing control with the children, focusing on children's strengths, forming authentic relationships with children, supporting children's ideas, and adopting a problem-solving approach to social conflict.

In play-based learning contexts, the adult has to be sensitive to the context and know when to intervene, when not to intervene, when to be directive and when to 'back off' as the learning is proceeding without the direct intervention of an adult. Fromberg (1999, p. 68) lists a number of provisos for adults when it comes to their interactions with children's play. These include:

- *Modelling:* where adults need to model playful behaviour that stimulates development through challenge and to provide many options to the children that are exciting and attainable. Such provision denies the need for gimmicks which, unfortunately, some adults use as stimulators.
- *Questioning:* here the adult can show that there might be a number of different answers to a question, each of which is equally acceptable—thus encouraging independent thinking.

Adults need to consider that play can be an effective and enriching pedagogical tool, but their role in making this happen is crucial.

What type of curriculum facilitates play-based learning?

In any discussion on play-based learning it is essential to define a working base for a curriculum that can facilitate play-based learning. A curriculum is the sum of everything that happens as part of a child's day in an early childhood setting.

A definition of curriculum most relevant to the broad field of early childhood is that 'curriculum means all of the interactions, experiences, activities, routines and events planned and unplanned that occur in an environment designed to foster children's learning and development' (adapted from Te Wharik, in DEEWR, 2009).

When interpreting this definition, interactions are all the interpersonal communications that promote learning, caring relationships and positive self-esteem; experiences are the result of opportunities that consolidate learning and provide new and exciting challenges—they can be passive or active; and routines are the regular activities associated with the comfort, health and well-being of the children—routines promote a sense of belonging and security when they are sensitive and responsive to the needs of each child (DECS, 2005; DEEWR, 2009).

In reviewing play-based learning and the opportunities for this in a curriculum, there are some elements that span the entire age group. There are three attributes of an effective curriculum framework for young children's learning and development (OECD, 2004):

- broad developmentally appropriate guidelines and principles in order to allow flexibility for educators to meet the individual interest and needs of infants and toddlers
- core educational content and learning goals that will support program implementation, and

- curricula and pedagogical practices that ensure continuity, stability and improvement.

A socio-constructivist emphasis in the curriculum

> Socio-constructivist perspectives in early childhood education recognise the importance of viewing play as an activity where children are developing their confidence and capability for interacting with their cultural environment. (Siraj-Blatchford, 2001, p. 2)

It is important for adults to embrace the central role that families and cultural groups play in children's learning. Also, adults should create learning environments that encourage children to explore, solve problems, create and construct, by respecting relationships and providing insight into social and cultural contexts of learning and development.

Play-based learning for developmental differences

There are many individual developmental differences in children as they progress through the so-called early years from birth to age eight. However, some very broad behaviours and indicators of development can be identified. In their understanding of children, adults are not bound by so-called 'normative development', but will look for the emergence of milestones to identify children who may be at risk. There are some general characteristics found in children around broad age groups. However, it is emphasised that children are individuals, and vary greatly in their development, temperaments, dispositions and lifestyles. Often, when making provision for children in group care, educators plan for age groups along the following categories: infants who are under one year of age; toddlers from one to two years of age; preschoolers who are three to five years of age; and the early years of school, from five to eight.

Whatever the developmental level of each child, adults who work with young children need to respect them as individuals, see them as competent and, as they grow, allow them to make choices within a well-planned program. Working with children in an early childhood setting involves much more than keeping them safe, although a safe environment is the first prerequisite for play-based learning.

Provision for play-based learning for children under the age of two

For early years learners under two years of age, the following statement by Gonzalez-Mena (2005, p. 254) is appropriate, for she refers to curriculum as caregiving for children, because children:

are always learning—even when they are engaged in eating, toileting, resting, and grooming and dressing. These caregiving activities take up a good deal of program time, and can be considered a chore to those who fail to see their significance, yet they are a blessing to early childhood professionals who regard caregiving routines as a way to share an interactive moment with a child.

When planning a curriculum for babies and toddlers, it is important to be quite clear about the importance of attachment, as this relates to developing positive relationships with young children. Establishing a secure attachment is one of the ways in which caregivers in child-care centres foster positive relationships with infants/toddlers. Another important aspect in relation to play-based learning for the youngest developmental age group is including a consistent daily routine that supports active learning. This daily routine enables children to anticipate what happens next, and gives them a great deal of control over what they do during each part of their day. This is where the 'plan–do–review' process enables children to express their intentions, carry them out, and reflect on what they have done. A flexible routine is necessary even for very young children.

For this broad age group—keeping in mind the great individual developmental range—play grows out of exploration. Piaget's categorisation of sensory motor play is relevant, although his stage theory is now mainly discredited, and the dynamic systems theory (Thelen, 2001) is seen to be highly relevant as it assists us to understand how the child's mind, body and physical skills form an integrated system. Berk (2006) states that each new skill is a joint product of the central nervous system, movement possibilities and environmental support for skills. Thelen's theory is particularly important when considering the explorative play behaviour of infants, toddlers and young children.

During early infancy, from birth to six months, exploration precedes what can be described as intentional play. From birth, reflexes dominate the baby, but over the ensuing months they enjoy and bond with significant people in their world. Differentiated responses to adults can be seen when the infant holds the adult's finger, smiles spontaneously, puts objects in their mouth and sucks on them or moves a hand towards the object seen.

Considering a home context, Piers, a four-week-old baby, has just begun to smile—much to the delight of Mum, Dad and four-year-old brother Wade. In order to minimise feelings of jealousy, the mother is encouraging the older sibling to be engaged too.

Mother to Piers: 'Time to feed you again—are you hungry?'

To Wade: 'Do you want to talk to Piers while I get ready to feed him?'

Wade: 'Mum, he smiled at me, he really did!'

Mother and Wade excitedly look at Piers, whose smile at this point has disappeared but will no doubt reappear soon.

From six to twelve months, exploration continues as babies become mobile and enjoy bonds with significant people in their worlds. As physical development dominates exploration possibilities, babies hold their heads up independently, enjoy soft toys and grasp objects with the whole hand. With vision, they focus on objects near and far, enjoy brightly coloured pictures and interesting-sounding toys. They enjoy large motor activities, pull to stand, stand alone, creep. Their grasping skills increase so they are able to bring objects into play. Some babies walk from approximately nine months onwards, and this increases exploratory behaviour.

The adult in the child-care centre plays peek-a-boo with a nine-month-old baby who squeals with delight. The adult knows that this is a perennial favourite activity, along with throwing things on the floor and expecting them to be returned. The child shows interest in and enjoys noisy rattling objects and picture books made of fabric that can be grasped easily and that contain sensory features.

From one to two years playful behaviours increase, as does the social world of the child. Staff in child-care centres provide a safe environment that enables children in this age group to develop their sense of identity. They understand that many two-year-olds develop a strong sense of property rights: 'mine' is heard frequently. Sharing can be difficult—if the object is a personal thing then they see it as an extension of 'self'.

At this level of development toddlers enjoy helping, but usually want to initiate this on their own terms. With their growing use of language, they enjoy talking about pictures and like repetition of words and phrases such as those found in the books *The Very Hungry Caterpillar* and *Hairy Maclary*. In keeping with dynamic systems theory, gross motor skills develop in an integrated way. Adults plan the day with care to fit the rhythm of children, yet provide a routine with some predictability.

Shane, 20 months, and Rohan, eighteen months, were both keen to play outside, and although they did not interact together, they sat in a companionable way in the sandbox.

Shane chanted: 'dig, dig, dig' as he pushed a spade in the sand.

Rohan, less verbal than Shane, smiled but did not join in the chant; however, he also dug in the sand.

This short vignette illustrates that Shane and Rohan were secure in being together in a play context, but as yet did not interact.

Two-year-olds and beyond: Independence emerging in exploring the world

Most adults know how much energy two-year-olds expend during the day. They are constantly on the move. Their bodies also change over time as they become stronger in their muscular physique, and fine motor control develops too.

Child-care centres provide for the physical and emotional needs of two-year-olds with a carefully planned indoor and outdoor environment that is safe, but allows for limited risk-taking. Independence increases, and some elements of negative behaviour may emerge. Favourite play activities include dressing up and engaging in family activities. They often show great interest in other children, but do not always interact with them. They will often observe peers intently, imitate their actions but essentially engage in parallel play.

> Ruby and Jake sit at the table with some dough; they enjoy banging the dough with their fists. Ruby reaches for a dough cutter, but Jake wants the same one. The adult helps by suggesting that they take turns, which they do with some help.

Play-based learning in the preschool years

Many children attend preschool for either part or full day sessions. In many countries preschool begins for children at about the age of three and continues until they make the transition to school. Children are still in a pre-operational level of development, but increasingly can reason and take on the views of others. They can show empathy for others and their social competence develops through the give and take of imaginative play.

Three-year-olds: Enjoying play together

> Louise, an educator in a preschool, knows that her group of three-year-olds enjoys spontaneous play for short periods. Many of the children are very social, beginning to play cooperatively. Soon conflicts over materials and toys arise, but these are often short-lived. A favourite activity is dressing up, dramatic play that involves everyday work activities. There is an emergence of some gender and role stereotypes. 'Boys can't be nurses,' says Emily firmly to Thomas. Sometimes children in the group attempt to exclude others: 'You can't play with us, you are not our friend!'

Four-year-olds: Using language with facility and forming friendships

Greater facility with language and increased cognitive functioning make play with many four-year-olds more sustained and complex. They have often formed quite strong and enduring friendships, and they enjoy being together. Playmates at this age are very important, and an understanding of the social rules emerges. As a result, they are able to take turns, share (most of the time) and want to be with children every waking moment. They do need and seek adult approval and attention, and frequently comment: 'Look what I did.' They understand and usually comply with behavioural limits most of the time. Understanding of scientific properties emerges, with many children having developed mathematical and scientific concepts.

> Nathan and Jack begin digging in the digging patch.
>
> 'Can you see any worms?' asks Jack.
>
> 'No,' says Nathan, 'the ground is too dry and they have all wiggled away but if we water the ground there might be some here tomorrow.'

As shown in this vignette the scientific knowledge of four-year-olds is often vast and can surprise their adult carers.

Five-year-olds

Most children of this age are transitioning into the first years of formal schooling, and opportunities for play-based learning in the curriculum depend on the philosophy of the school these children attend.

The play of the five-year-old child is more visible, complex and, to the adult, more understandable—especially given the language ability of children of this age. By the age of five, children are problem-solvers. They solve problems through their play, through their discussions, through questions asked and through sensory explorations, for children are curious beings. They enjoy difficult puzzles, and stories that have a fun and nonsense element. Children's play is mostly mind-stretching and imaginative; play begins to be more complex. They often enjoy blocks, construction toys and mechanical toys such as cars, helicopters and aeroplanes, and these are often integrated into imaginative play: 'I am a helicopter pilot—can control tower give me clearance to take off?'

Children's play companions are important, as they help to prolong the play where it becomes more complex, often leading to a deeper understanding of concepts.

Most five-year-old children will enjoy painting, collage and modelling, and engage in these in a play mode with full enjoyment.

> Five-year-old Amy is alone in the play corner, playing as a hairdresser. She invites her friend Vicky to play.
>
> *Amy:* 'I can cut your hair for you.'
>
> *Vicky:* 'Yes, my hair needs a cut.'
>
> *Amy:* 'Here's a magazine for you to read.'
>
> *Vicky:* 'Oh, my mum also reads a magazine when she has her hair cut.'
>
> *Amy:* 'Look, I like to eat that!' Amy is combing Vicky's hair and looking over her shoulder at the magazine, which pictures some fruit.
>
> *Vicky:* 'Have you been to the market? Food is expensive.'
>
> The conversation changes from hairdressing to two mothers talking about rising prices for food.

Six-year-olds

At this period of development, segregation between the sexes can be very strong. Boys will seek out other boys with whom to play, although there will be many instances where both boys and girls interact happily together. Imaginative play continues to dominate the play of the six-year-old. Friendships are often constant, and these stimulate complex play-based interactions. Interest in physical activity can be strong for both girls and boys, who may enjoy swimming, hiking and cycling. There is also an increase in the use of technological toys, video games and movies. All of these are extensions of earlier play-based learning activities, and show understanding of scientific concepts.

> Three children are talking about their plan to build their own park.
>
> 'I want a garden with a swimming pool that has a conveyor belt on it, with sushi for everyone.'
>
> 'I have designed two amazing swings. Just pull the handle on the right, and they will bounce up and down.'
>
> 'I want a rocket elevator. It feels like travelling in outer space.'

Seven- to eight-year-olds

Seven-year-old children are capable of abstract thinking. They have fluent communication skills, are usually literate and are capable of high levels of cognitive functioning. Some children in this age group develop a deep interest in their scientific world, and inquiry-based learning flourishes. Cooperative play increases and can be extended for long periods of time. Some competitive and organised games can be enjoyed, depending on the dispositions of the children involved. Interest develops in team sports if these are an option at school. Both boys and girls continue to be segregated in terms of their play partners; however, although out of the formal school context they enjoy one another's company, though their interests may diverge. Some appreciation of the arts takes on a more abstract meaning, as shown below.

> The educator plays a CD of Beethoven's 'Fur Elise' to her class. After listening, the children talk about their feelings.
>
> 'Beethoven's "Fur Elise" gives me the feeling of dancing and prancing.'
>
> 'It makes me think of fish trying to escape from being caught.'
>
> 'It's like swimming in a sea of flowers.'

Play-based learning in the formal school setting tends to develop into inquiry-based learning where the pedagogy increases the amount of knowledge that children can acquire. However, many of the principles stated in this chapter still apply: children need to enjoy learning, to be able to exercise choices and to make their own discoveries.

Summary

- This chapter has focused on the importance of play-based learning and examined this in relation to the development of children in broad groupings of birth to two, the preschool years and entry to formal school from five to eight years.
- The primacy of early childhood curricula based on relationships has been emphasised, with the crucial role of the adult in a range of contexts emphasised.
- From infancy, children are viewed as competent learners, eager to find and solve problems in their quest to make sense of their world.
- Neuroscience findings provide convincing evidence that early years are the most critical of all stages of development.

- Play occurs across all cultures.
- Learning occurs when a child is deeply engaged in play.
- Adults have to be sensitive to contexts and know when to intervene (or not) in children's play.
- Adults should create learning environments that encourage children to explore, solve problems, create and construct. Whatever the developmental level of a child, adults need to respect children as individuals, see them as competent, and allow them to make choices within a well-planned program.
- When planning for babies and toddlers, note the importance of attachment, as this relates to the development of a positive relationship. Children in the preschool years can show empathy for others, and their social competence develops through the give and take of imaginative play.
- Socialisation through play is very important for four-year-olds, and the understanding of social rules emerges. Five-year-olds are problem-solvers, while imaginative play continues to dominate the play of six-year-olds. Seven- and eight-year-olds are capable of abstract thinking, sustained inquiry-based learning and competitive team sports.

Discussion questions

11.1 What are the challenges facing adults in relation to findings from neuroscience?

11.2 What are the differences between exploration and play?

11.3 What are some of the issues for adults in providing a challenging play environment for a group of four-year-old preschoolers?

11.4 Are there differences in the play environments today compared with, for example, those of 50 years ago and, if so, what are these?

11.5 Discuss how an adult with responsibility for seven toddlers might set up an outdoor play environment.

11.6 Explain how an educator of a class of seven-year-olds can stimulate interest in some inquiry-based learning.

References

Bergen, D. (2002). The role of pretend play in children's cognitive development. *Early Childhood Research & Practice*, 4(1), np.

Berk, L.E. (1999). Vygotsky's theory: The importance of make-believe play. In L.E. Berk (ed.), *Landscapes of development: An anthology of readings* (pp. 225–38). Belmont, CA: Wadsworth.

—— (2006). *Child development,* 7th ed. Boston: Pearson/Allyn and Bacon.

Bodrova, E. & Leong, D.J. (2007). *Tools of the mind: The Vygotskian approach to early childhood education,* 2nd ed. Columbus, OH: Merrill/Prentice Hall.

Bronfenbrenner, U. (1979). *The ecology of human development: Experiments by nature and design.* Cambridge, MA: Harvard University Press.

—— (1993). The ecology of cognitive development: Research models and fugitive findings. In R. Wozniak & K. Fischer (eds), *Development in context: Acting and thinking in specific environments* (pp. 3–44). Hillsdale, NJ: Lawrence Erlbaum.

Bruce, T. (1994). Seeing play for what it is: Parents and professional workers together. *International Journal of Early Years Education,* 2(1), 17–22.

Bruner, J. (1986). *Actual minds, possible worlds.* Cambridge, MA: Harvard University Press.

Department of Education and Children's Services (DECS) (2005). *We can make a difference: Learning and developing in childcare.* Adelaide: DECS.

Department of Education, Employment and Workplace Relations (DEEWR) (2009). *Belonging, being and becoming: The Early Years Learning Framework for Australia.* Retrieved 22 October 2009 from <www.deewr.gov.au/EarlyChildhood/Policy_Agenda/Quality/Documents/Final%20EYLF%20Framework%20Report%20-%20WEB.pdf>.

Dewey, J. (1971). *The child and the curriculum: The school and society.* Chicago: University of Chicago Press.

Dockett, S. & Fleer, M. (1999). *Play and pedagogy in early childhood: Bending the rules.* Sydney: Harcourt Brace.

Ebbeck, M. & Waniganayake, M. (eds) (2010). *Children's play in early childhood education: Learning in diverse contexts.* Melbourne: Oxford University Press.

Elkind, D. (2003). Thanks for the memory: The lasting value of play. *Young Children,* 58(3), 46–51.

Erikson, E.H. (1963). *Childhood and society,* 2nd ed. New York: W.W. Norton.

Freud, A. (1968). *The psycholanalytic treatment of children.* New York: International Universities Press.

Fromberg, D. (1999). A review of research on play. In C. Seefeldt (ed.), *The early childhood curriculum: Current findings in theory and practice,* 3rd ed. (pp. 27–53). New York: Teachers College Press.

Gonzalez-Mena, J. (2005). *Diversity in early care and education: Honoring differences,* 4th ed. New York: McGraw-Hill.

Hirsh-Pasek, K. & Golikoff, R.M. (2008). Why play = learning. In *Encyclopedia on early childhood.* Retrieved 15 September 2011 from <www.child-encyclopedia.com/documents/Hirsh-Pasek-GolinkoffANGxp.pdf>.

Howes, C. (1980). Peer play scale as an index of complexity of peer interaction. *Developmental Psychology,* 16, 371–2.

Howes, C. & Matheson, C.C. (1992). Sequences in the development of competent play with peers: Social and social pretend play. *Developmental Psychology,* 28(5), 961–74.

Hughes, F.P. (2010). *Children, play and development,* 4th ed. Thousand Oaks, CA: Sage.

Isenberg, J.P. & Jalongo, M.R. (2001). *Creative expression and play in the early childhood curriculum.* New York: Merrill.

Kostelink, M.J., Soderman, A.K. & Whiren, A.P. (2011). *Developmentally appropriate curriculum: best practices in early childhood education,* 5th ed. Boston: Pearson Education.

Mendoza, J. & Katz, L. (2008). Introduction to the special section on dramatic play. *Early Childhood Research & Practice, 10*(2), 1–8.

Mustard, J.F. (2008). *Investing in the early years: Closing the gap between what we know and what we do.* Adelaide: Department of the Premier and Cabinet.

National Association for the Education of Young Children (NAEYC) (2009). *Position statement on play.* Retrieved 15 September 2011 from <www.naeyc.org/positionstatements/dap>.

NICHD Early Child Care Research Network (2005). Duration and developmental timing of poverty and children's cognitive and social development from birth to third grade. *Child Development, 76*(4), 795–810.

Organisation for Economic Co-operation and Development (OECD) (2004). *Starting strong curricula and pedagogies in early childhood education and care: Five curriculum outlines.* Retrieved 15 September 2011 from <www.oecd.org/dataoecd/23/36/31672150.pdf>.

Parten, M.B. (1932). Leadership among preschool children. *Journal of Abnormal and Social Psychology, 27*, 430–40.

Piaget, J. (1951). *Play, dreams and imitation in childhood.* New York: W.W. Norton.

—— (1963). *The origin of intelligence in children.* New York: W.W. Norton.

Rubin, K.H. (1980). Fantasy play: Its role in the development of social skills and social cognition. In K.H. Rubin (ed.), *Children's play* (pp. 69–84). San Francisco: Jossey-Bass.

Singer, D.G. & Singer, J.L. (2005). *Imagination and play in the electronic age.* Cambridge, MA: Harvard University Press.

Siraj-Blatchford, J. (2001). 'Emergent science and technology in the early years.' Paper presented at the XXIII World Congress of OMEP, Santiago, Chile, 31 July–4 August.

Smilansky, S. & Shefatya, L. (1990). *Facilitating play: A medium for promoting cognitive, socio-emotional, and academic development in young children.* Gaithersburg, MD: Psychological and Educational Publications.

Thelen, E. (2001). Dynamic mechanisms of change in early perceptual-motor development. In J.L. McClelland & R.S. Siegler (eds), *Mechanisms of cognitive development: Behavioural and neural perspectives* (pp. 161–84). Mahwah, NJ: Lawrence Erlbaum.

United Nations Educational, Scientific and Cultural Organization (UNESCO) (2006). *Strong foundations: Early childhood care and education.* Paris: UNESCO.

Van Hoorn, J., Nourot, P.M., Scales, B. & Alward, K.R. (2007). *Play at the center of the curriculum,* 4th ed. Upper Saddle River, NJ: Pearson Merrill/Prentice-Hall.

Vygotsky, L.S. (1967 [1933]). Play and its role in the mental development of the child. *Soviet Psychology, 5*, 6–18.

—— (1978). *Mind in society: The development of higher psychological processes.* Cambridge, MA: Harvard University Press.

12

Transitions

Susan Krieg

Introduction

From the moment of conception, a baby is both changing and experiencing change—change is part of life. However, the effects of change are variable. Sometimes the pace and nature of the change provide the opportunity to attune to a new experience, sensation or perspective. This type of change is fundamental to learning, for it is only as we experience difference that we learn. Deleuze (1994, p. 134) says that it is as we encounter something 'not of recognition' that this 'something in the world forces us to think'. In contrast, some change is so dramatic, sudden and unexpected that there is not the same opportunity to adjust and orient, or enjoy the experience, sensation or situation. In such cases, we are confronted by a reality that is often not of our choosing, and thus we experience fear and a lack of control. For the purposes of the discussion in this chapter, it is useful to conceptualise change as being positive, but with the potential to be toxic. Along a continuum of change, as early childhood educators we would want to find a middle space—somewhere between boredom (where there is insufficient change) and trauma (where the change becomes overwhelming).

Many of the changes in contemporary children's lives involve moving within and between families, child care, preschool and school. However, it is not just 'movement' that is occurring, for the *Oxford Dictionary* defines 'transition' as 'the process or period of changing from one state or condition to another'. The use of the word 'transition' implies that there is a change in the 'way of being' as children move between family, child care, preschool and school. The research that has contributed to a better understanding of the changes that occur as early years learners move within and between these institutions has often focused on the physical environment, and on the different institutional norms and relationships (Dockett & Perry, 2007; Hill et al., 1998). The aim of this chapter is to widen this focus and broaden our thinking about transition by using different theoretical perspectives to consider our work.

I approach the topic of transition from a perspective that recognises change as part of life. The question I address here is whether we, as early childhood educators, can work with early years learners from birth to eight years in ways that celebrate and support the changes that are occurring within and around them. The chapter begins with a glimpse into the lived experience of a young child, and uses this vignette to explore new ways of thinking about transition. In the second half of the chapter, I revisit the differences between constructivism, social constructionism and critical constructivist theories. I suggest that this deeper theoretical work offers the possibility of developing a 'shared pedagogical frame' for early childhood educators working across the years from birth to age eight. This shared frame might better support children as they move between home, child care, preschool and school. This theoretical work is underpinned by beliefs about children and their positions within the social world.

Children, movement and mobility

The concept of mobility or movement is particularly relevant in any discussion of contemporary early learners' lives. Orellana et al. (2001) contend that 'it is impossible to understand the variety and complexity of childhood without a focus on movement' (cited in Prout, 2011, p. 10). This movement occurs across traditional boundaries of country and nation at an unprecedented scale alongside movement within and between families. It is timely to rethink many taken-for-granted ideas about home and stability. Prout (2011, p. 10) draws on the work of Christensen et al. (2000) to demonstrate that, for many children, 'home is now a place that is given meanings through the "comings and goings" of different family members as they move in and out of the space we call home'. Some of the ways children experience movement in and out of home are related to their chronological age. The simple fact of having a birthday often brings about change—some mandated by government, others the result of the social circumstances into which children are born. To illustrate some of these changes, I would like to introduce Josie.

It is Monday morning. Josie is tired and is having difficulty waking up this morning because yesterday the family celebrated her second birthday. Josie will be going to child care today as she has done for the past year, but because she has turned two today will be different. She will be moving into a different room with a different group of children, a different outdoor play area, more (and often different) children in the group, different adults and different routines for eating, sleeping and toileting.

Let us now shift our attention to another Monday morning three years later. Josie has just had her fifth birthday and according to the government policy (in the Australian state in which Josie's family lives) this means that today she begins school. The changes for Josie mean that she will be moving into a different and much larger institution than the centre in which she has spent the past four years. Josie will now spend most of her day in a single classroom with one educator and 20 children (according to mandated policy). This is very different from her preschool experience, where she interacted with several adults during her day and was able to move around the centre (both in and outdoors) very freely in a play-based program. Josie will now experience different daily routines. Time is now organised with a siren that signals the beginning and end of each day. During recess and lunch, Josie will play in a yard shared by many children—some much older than her. The expectations about how Josie will spend her time are now very different. In contrast to the play-based pedagogy Josie has experienced to date, she may now have much less choice and control, and there may be a much greater emphasis on more formal tasks involving reading and writing. If Josie is to make sense of these changes and find coherence in her world, she will require some support.

When we consider the changes that Josie has experienced over her first five years, the questions early childhood educators need to address are whether these changes run the risk of being overwhelming or toxic, whether they are necessary and whether they are intractable. While some of the changes are the result of mandated policy, I suggest that some are also the result of the unexamined theoretical paradigms that guide our pedagogy across the years from birth to age eight. These paradigms reflect the differences between the institutions, programs and services that are part of young learners' worlds, and the traditional purposes that underpin these institutions. Josie's experiences could be described as her negotiating her way through a 'split' system.

A split system

The differences between Australian early childhood programs, services and institutions have very long histories. It is beyond the scope and purpose of this chapter to provide a comprehensive discussion of the history of Australian early childhood care and education. However, it is impossible to address the issue of transition without reference to the importance of these histories in creating a split system. An understanding of these differences leads to a recognition of the 'increasingly complex socialisation' and 'double socialisation' occurring as young children begin to spend a large part of their daily life away from the family (Prout, 2011, p. 11). This double socialisation is compounded 'in a pluralist society when children are confronted by a range of competing, complementary and divergent values and perspectives derived from parents, school, the media, consumption practices and their peer relations' (2011, p. 11). If early childhood educators are to support early learners making sense of their worlds, it behoves them to recognise the 'double socialisation' that is occurring as children move between homes, child care, preschool and school. This support requires renegotiation of some serious faultlines in the landscape of the early childhood years.

One of these faultlines lies between child care and preschool. The distinctions between them have their beginnings in the purposes for which they were established. The establishment of child-care services in Australia was related primarily to women's participation in the labour market (Brennan, 1994). As in many other Western countries, the emphasis in child care was on health, and therefore practices focused on 'hygiene, regularity and peace' (Brostrom & Hansen, 2010, p. 89) were promoted. In comparison, preschools were 'pedagogically inspired' and had educational aims (Brostrom & Hansen, 2010, p. 89). There are many current examples of attempts to realign the purposes and pedagogy of child care and education. For example, the Early Years Learning Framework (DEEWR, 2009) is intended to provide curriculum guidance for early childhood educators working in both child care and preschools. However, as Barblett et al. (2011) demonstrate, young learners moving between long day care and preschool still often experience discontinuity and very little coherence between these programs.

Alongside the split between child care and preschool lies the split between birth to age five programs and the early years of school. Again, the history of this split is so complex and variable (between the Australian states) that it is impossible to recount here. One of the most obvious differences relates to attendance requirements. Currently, the birth to eight years age group includes both 'voluntary' attendance (often referred to as 'pre-compulsory' between birth and five years) and compulsory attendance, mandated by law as children reach the age specified by each state (commonly age six). The ratio between adults and children now increases from 1:10 in preschool to at least 1:20 in the first year of school. The different histories, purposes and governance of child care, preschool and school are evident in staffing, architecture, curriculum and pedagogy. I now turn to the pedagogic difference that currently exists across the birth to eight years age range, exploring how a deeper understanding of constructivism might contribute to minimising this difference. I argue that a shared pedagogical frame for this age group could support early learners to grow, learn and develop more effectively and equitably.

The dimensions of a shared pedagogical frame

In what ways might a shared pedagogical frame support early learners' movement between people and institutions? In its broadest sense, pedagogy relates to an interactive process whereby the educator enhances and sustains learning. The different dimensions that make up a pedagogical frame include beliefs about knowledge and the learning process that in turn construct the relationship between learners, educators and contexts. Brostrom and Hansen (2010, p. 97) refer to 'the dynamic of the pedagogue–child relation (care, empathy, acknowledgement etc); the pedagogue–content relation; the child's relation to other children and the pedagogue's relation to a group of children'. Each aspect of a pedagogical frame is equally important. However, in this chapter beliefs about knowledge are foregrounded, for I contend that these underpin the relationship between learner, educator and context. As Gergen (1995, p. 17) argues: 'Beliefs about knowledge inform, justify and sustain our practices of education.' Although not often acknowledged in many discussions of early childhood practice, beliefs about what constitutes knowledge and how it is produced underpin early childhood pedagogy—that is, beliefs about what it means to learn, what it means to know and what is worth knowing. When interacting with early learners, consciously or unconsciously we are drawing on particular knowledge and attitudes to knowledge. Ideas about knowledge are often framed covertly within statements of intent in curriculum or learning frameworks, such as the Early Years Learning Framework (DEEWR, 2009) and the Australian Curriculum (ACARA, 2010). The next section of the chapter therefore briefly revisits contemporary research into constructivism in order to illuminate the relationship between beliefs about knowledge and pedagogy.

Knowledge and constructivism

In very broad terms, debates about knowledge relate to the 'origins of human knowledge' and whether new knowledge—either individual knowledge or public discipline—is 'made' or 'discovered' (Phillips, 1995, p. 5). From an objectivist epistemological perspective, 'true' knowledge exists in an external world, and information is acquired through processes of perception and representation. From this perspective, knowledge can be transmitted 'ready made' to the learner (Wood, 1995, p. 332). However, within a view where knowledge is 'built up by the cognising subject' (constructivist) in a process where the individual 'organises' the experiential world, alternative views of 'what counts' as knowledge emerge. From a constructivist perspective, each individual (child) is engaged in a process of 'building up' knowledge as they 'organise' the experiential world (Wood, 1995, p. 337):

> The epistemological assumptions underpinning constructivism suggest that the world does not harbour unambiguous 'truths' independent of human perception, revealed to us through instruction; rather the world is knowable only through the interaction of knower and experienced phenomena. (von Glasersfeld, 1987, p. 3017)

Thus, from a constructivist perspective, learning involves a personal construction of meaning. Cognitive constructivism, the explanatory framework developed by Piaget (1959), focused on how individual learners adapt and refine knowledge based on their own experience. Piaget's (1980) depiction of the developing child as a 'lone, inventive young scientist, struggling to make independent sense of the surrounding world' (in Phillips, 1995, p. 9) has dominated early childhood pedagogy for many years. A cognitive constructivist approach to young children's learning focuses on the workings of individual mental processes. Most early childhood educators working with children aged between birth and age five would argue that they work from a constructivist paradigm with children who are actively involved in constructing their own knowledge. In the context of the discussion regarding transition, it is important to recognise that many educators working in the early years of school would also argue that they are working from a constructivist perspective. However, these educators are often working in school systems that Windschitl (2002, p. 142) contends have an objectivist epistemology as their 'default' position, where knowledge is seen to be 'transferred' from the minds of educators to the minds of learners. The tensions between objectivist and constructivist epistemological positions are enacted in the contemporary Australian context in that, while the Australian Early Years Learning Framework (EYLF) (DEEWR, 2009) outlines the expected outcomes of early childhood education for children in the birth to five years age group in broad terms, the Australian Curriculum (ACARA, 2010) uses Achievement Standards to describe much more specific learning outcomes, which are more easily measured. I argue that if we are to support early learners' transitions

Figure 12.1   Co-constructing

more effectively, early childhood educators must understand the epistemological basis of their practice, and this involves developing a deeper understanding of the different versions of constructivism.

Social constructivist, social constructionist and critical constructivist perspectives

The research into constructivism is not static; it is a work in progress. The dimensions or versions of 'constructivism' have now expanded to a point where 'philosophers have suggested more than a dozen different "constructivisms"' (Nola, 1997, in Windschitl, 2002, p. 140). While many theorists continue to take a constructivist approach and maintain an interest in the internal workings of the individual mind, social constructivist theories have emphasised the social processes involved in learning. An emphasis on the social dimensions of learning has contributed new ideas about the relationship between educators, early learners and knowledge. Within a social constructivist frame, we move our gaze from individual characteristics as explanations for learning to a focus on the social unit of activity, and regard individual higher cognitive processing as derived from that (Rogoff, 1990). Vygotsky (1978, p. 57) claimed that 'all higher (mental) functions originate as actual relations between human individuals'. Therefore, while a cognitive constructivist frame views learning as primarily individual, a social constructionist paradigm foregrounds the centrality of interpersonal relationships when considering how early learners make meaning of their worlds.

The differences between the social constructivist and social constructionist paradigms relate to their differing emphasis on either the mental processes of the individual mind as constructing knowledge from within (social constructivist) or the mind and knowledge as formed by social practices (social constructionist). Ernest (1995) uses metaphors to make some distinctions between social constructivist and social constructionist positions. He appropriates the idea of 'persons in conversation' to describe social constructivism. Here, the emphasis is on the individual mind as personal, separate and idiosyncratic, and the construction of reality occurs and then perhaps is 'adapted' in conversation with others (1995, p. 484). This can be compared with a social constructionist perspective, where the construction of knowledge is likened to individuals as 'actors in a drama'. Here, the social is prioritised over the individual, and 'to be knowledgeable is to occupy a given position at a given time within an ongoing relationship' (1995, p. 485). Social constructionist perspectives have been challenged and extended by critical constructivists, who argue that while meaning-construction is something we do as individuals, this process is 'inseparable from our culture and the power relations embedded in our culture' (MacNaughton, 2004, p. 56). MacNaughton extrapolates that: 'In education, the point of critical constructivism is to explore the effects of cultural and structural positions on how and what children can and do know and learn.' (2004, p. 47)

Understanding these different versions of constructivism enables early childhood educators to make more equitable and inclusive curriculum and pedagogic decisions, in that they offer alternative perspectives from which to consider the early learner. This understanding also offers the possibility of developing a shared pedagogic frame that might improve continuity across the services for different age groups. In the next sections of the chapter, I examine how educators working from a critical social constructionist perspective might support Josie as she moves between family, child care, preschool and school. I suggest that a critical social constructionist perspective opens up the possibility of new 'ways of being' for both Josie and the adults in her world, be they working in child care, preschool or the early years of school.

New 'ways of being' Josie

One of the ways of viewing Josie is that, from the moment of conception, she is primarily seen as 'becoming'. From this developmental perspective, Josie's growth and development is measured, recorded and assessed very carefully—and often meticulously—against a construct of what is considered 'normal' for her chronological age. She is seen as being on a single, well-defined pathway to becoming adult. This way of viewing Josie may be useful in some ways, but it also prevents other ways of knowing Josie. A critical social constructionist perspective offers some alternate ways of seeing her. First, from the moment of birth, Josie would be considered to be an active participant in her world. To come back to Ernest's (1995) metaphor, she is an 'actor in a drama'. Josie is not *preparing* to play a part, she *is* playing a part in her world. However, as critical constructivist theorists have emphasised, the power relations in the world in which Josie takes her place are not equal. The part Josie plays is primarily determined by cultural scripts: the shared meanings, attitudes and beliefs of the adults in her world (and some adults have more power than others). If we see Josie as a competent, active social participant, the lines between the learning she does in child care, pre-compulsory and compulsory educational institutions begin to blur because we see this learning as integral to Josie's participation in her social world within a social context. The routines of eating, sleeping and toileting are now no longer viewed as distinct from learning. Whether Josie is participating in planned activities, playing or having her lunch—in child care, preschool or during the early years of school—she is making meaning of her world. What is important here is how the adults interacting with Josie see their roles (and the roles of other children) as constructing this meaning with her as a value-driven process enacting the social and political imperatives of their worlds. The next section of the chapter focuses on Josie's transition from preschool to school, for it is often at this transition point that some of the different ways of viewing learning are most evident.

Blurring some binaries in early childhood pedagogy

As Josie enters the school system, she is still a competent social actor—albeit in another drama. Many of the changes she experiences in this setting are directly attributable to structural and institutional changes brought about by mandated policy. However, alongside these policy changes, the epistemological beliefs of educators in both preschool and school also contribute to the degree and nature of the changes that Josie will experience. In this section, I pursue the possibility that if Josie is to experience continuity in her learning, the pedagogical frames on either side of this transition point need to widen. For example, the differences between a child-centred, play-based pedagogy in the birth to five years age group has often been contrasted with a 'teacher-directed' and 'subject-driven' approach in the early years of school. This simplistic binary does not reflect the nuanced approaches to pedagogy that are required across the birth to eight years age range. In their study of early childhood pedagogy, Siraj-Blatchford et al. (2002) conclude that we should be moving away from such a polarised description of teaching and learning. As a result of their extensive research into early years pedagogy, these authors also argue that: 'Significant points to consider from this research are the importance of the practitioner's role in balancing adult-led and child-initiated activities, the need to engage in "sustained shared thinking" and the kinds of interactions that will guide but not dominate children's thinking.' (DfES, 2005, p. 10) This balance involves increased intentional teaching in the preschool years alongside more choice and child-initiated learning in the early years of school. This moving away from a binary between adult or child-led teaching and learning requires early childhood educators to engage in sustained epistemological work. For example, engaging with the principles of intentional teaching, co-construction, scaffolding, and the 'sustained shared thinking' identified by Siraj-Blatchford et al. (2009) would blur some of the limiting boundaries that now exist. The question is not whether Josie should have many opportunities to play—because when children are playing they are engaged and involved in ways that are hard to replicate—but whether she should also have the opportunity to experience other ways of learning as well, in both preschool and school.

There are many ambiguities in discussions of a play-based approach. Windschitl (2002) contends that these ambiguities are the result of a superficial understanding of the epistemological basis of constructivism, and have mutated into a 'predictable mythology' about what constitutes effective teaching and learning. This mythology includes such beliefs as 'activity equates to learning; children's involvement and interest are sufficient conditions for worthwhile learning; activities, as opposed to ideas, are the starting points and basis units of planning; and little thought is given to the intellectual implications of an activity' (Yinger, 1977 in Windschitl, 2002, p. 138). This mythology is evident in many discussions regarding play—for example, the debate about whether the *kinds of meaning* that children construct through play should or should not be challenged and interrogated. Where children are enacting racist or gender scripts, should the educator intervene using strategies such as modelling, describing and deconstructing in order to interrupt and alter the meanings that are being constructed? Does *what* Josie is learning matter? This is not just a question of content, but involves attitudes and dispositions. In the next section, I use examples from the Australian Curriculum to explore the issues associated with these questions.

Enacting a reciprocal pedagogical relationship: An Australian example

In the Australian context, there is significant difference between the broad, open-ended outcomes of the Early Years Framework (DEEWR, 2009) and the Achievement Standards outlined in the Australian Curriculum (ACARA, 2010). If Josie is to be supported as she moves from preschool to the early years of school, her educators need to find a path between these very different approaches. For example, the Achievement Standards from the Foundation History curriculum (ACARA, 2010) are as follows:

• By the end of the Foundation year, students identify similarities and differences between families. They recognise how important family events are commemorated.
• Students sequence familiar events in order. They pose questions about their past. Students relate a story about their past using a range of texts.

The possibility of Josie achieving these standards will depend in large part on how Josie is positioned in the learning process. Will she be an equal participant in co-constructing knowledge about 'families'? If Josie has the opportunity to play, she will experiment, improvise, rehearse, pretend and imagine different ways of being, doing and thinking in a context where other children and adults also share their knowledge and imaginings. Early childhood educators working in both preschool and school would want to retain these elements if Josie's dispositions for learning are to be enhanced and maintained. Two of the principles that characterise play are that the child has control of the 'script' and that the experience itself is intrinsically rewarding. Josie's educators can incorporate these principles in their pedagogical frame if they understand that play is a catalyst for learning and a process of discovery. If Josie's educators can engage her in sustained thinking through an inquiry-based pedagogy, they will be retaining some of the most important principles of a play-based pedagogy.

An inquiry approach to teaching and learning in the early years is consistent with an epistemological perspective that views knowledge as constructed rather than as 'truth'. Within such a frame, adults actively participate in the learning process as 'intentional mediators' (Mason, 2000, p. 347). This concept of 'teaching as mediation' reduces the oppositional positioning of 'child-centred or teacher-centred' pedagogies, and Mason contends that it is helpful to conceive of teaching as a process of *mediating* between 'what is known and what is not yet known by the learner' (2000, p. 348). Alongside this mediational role, the educator would also be critiquing and challenging existing knowledge, for critical social constructionism challenges the construct of knowledge as fixed, finite and finished, and exercises a scepticism regarding the 'certainty' of knowledge (Ernest, 1995, p. 481). Using this approach, Foucault (1980) contends that local (and, in this case, Josie's) knowledge of family is important, and that it should be 'entertained' against the claims of well-established knowledges. The word 'entertained' opens up many possibilities for thinking about pedagogy in the early years. 'Entertaining' could involve comparing, contrasting, questioning and challenging Josie's knowledge about family with the knowledge of others. This approach does not assume the dominance of one knowledge over another for, as Taguchi (2007, p. 285) argues, different knowledges are not 'valued as more or less true . . . but are put side by side and treated equally importantly as different ways of understanding'.

Vygotsky (1986) offers useful concepts for thinking about whether Josie's construction of the concept of 'family' is completely open-ended, and whether it should be. Vygotsky saw learning as a dialogic process in which later, more sophisticated (he uses the word scientific) conceptual development built on and used children's spontaneous concepts and earlier experience through interaction with others. Illustratively, Josie's knowledge of family is solely reliant on her own experience. However, one of the outcomes that we would want from her learning about family is that she understands that there are many different types of families, and this could be considered a more 'sophisticated' conceptualisation of family than the one Josie currently has. Vygotsky's perspective departed from that taken by Piaget (1959). Piaget could not reconcile the 'spontaneous character of the child's reasoning' with the development of more advanced concepts, apart from an antagonism between them. Vygotsky says of Piaget's position: 'the entire process of development appears as mechanical displacement of one mentality by the other' (1986, p. 155). Vygotsky developed an explanatory framework, where 'the development of spontaneous and of non-spontaneous concepts are related and constantly influence each other' (1986, p. 157). He states that 'the acquisition of scientific concepts is carried out with the mediation provided by already acquired concepts' (1986, p. 161). As becomes evident, within this framework the role of the pedagogue is significant. The educator has important work to do as a co-constructor, and at times a scaffolder, of knowledge, working alongside the learner, mediating between the known and the unknown. This is not a 'teacher-centred' process; it is an ongoing inquiry and negotiation of meaning. Josie and the educators with whom she is interacting will be co-constructing knowledge, working together in an inquiry process and engaged in shared, sustained thinking.

Co-construction is described by Jordan (2009, p. 46) as a process where two people interact and 'each participant listens to the other's ideas, contributes from their own, and together they develop their unique shared meaning. The child's voice is heard and valued and both participants make links between experiences, across time and distance.' Thus co-construction repositions both the early learner and the educator as working in a reciprocal relationship. Viewing learning as co-construction is premised on the belief that both Josie and the educator (or another child) with whom she is interacting see a 'context, a situation, or a phenomenon, which is "objectively" the same in qualitatively different ways' (Bowden & Marton, 1998, p. 189). By working with others, Josie will be exposed to many more ways of seeing 'family' than are available when she is working alone. As Bowden and Marton (1998, p. 189) argue, the child finding their own way into a 'landscape of ideas, concepts, terms and facts shared by others is learning. However, in this solitary process, individuals are limited by their own perspectives.' By learning how others see things, Josie will be broadening her ideas of the multiple ways in which something can be seen, and 'meaning is enriched in the process' (1998, p. 190).

Summary

- Revisiting understandings of constructivist learning and examining the differences between different versions of constructivism open up new ways to think about early childhood education.
- Teaching from a critical social constructionist perspective avoids the inherent tensions between child-centred or educator-directed approaches.
- This paradigm opens up the possibility of working from an inquiry stance for both educator and early learner in both the pre-compulsory and compulsory years. This widened pedagogical frame bridges some of the faultlines that traditionally have worked against continuity and coherence for early learners.

Discussion questions

12.1 How might our ideas about knowledge and the ways in which it is formed influence our pedagogical decisions?

12.2   What is the difference between social constructivism and social constructionism?

12.3   What contribution do critical constructivists make to our understanding of
the learning process?

12.4   What are some of the teaching techniques associated with a critical social
constructionist pedagogical frame?

12.5   What are the dimensions of a 'shared pedagogical frame'?

References

Australian Curriculum, Assessment and Reporting Authority (ACARA) (2009). The Australian
Curriculum. Retrieved 26 August 2011 from <www.acara.edu.au/curriculum/curriculum.html>.

——(2010). The Australian Curriculum. History. Retrieved 13 September 2011 from <www.australian
curriculum.edu.au/History/Curriculum/F–10>.

Barblett, L., Barratt-Pugh, C., Kilgallon, P. & Maloney, C. (2011). Transition from long day care to
kindergarten: Continuity or not? *Australasian Journal of Early Childhood, 36*(2), 42–50.

Bennett, J. (2005). Curriculum issues in national policy making. *European Early Childhood Research
Journal, 13*(2), 5–24.

Bowden, J. & Marton, F. (1998). *The university of learning: Beyond quality and competence.* London:
Routledge Falmer.

Brennan, D. (1994). *The politics of Australian child care: From philanthropy to feminism.* Cambridge:
Cambridge University Press.

Brostrom, S. & Hansen, O. (2010). Care and education in the Danish creche. *International Journal of
Early Childhood, 42*(2), 87–100.

Cole, M., John-Steiner, V., Scribner, S., & Souberman, S. (Eds.). (1978). *L.S. Vygotsky Mind in society:
The development of higher psychological processes.* Cambridge: Harvard University Press.

Deleuze, G. (1994). *Difference and repetition,* P. Patto, trans. New York: Columbia University Press.

Department of Education, Employment and Workplace Relations (DEEWR) (2009). *Belonging, being and
becoming: the early years learning framework for Australia.* Canberra: Commonwealth of Australia.

Department for Education and Skills (DfES) (2005). *Primary national strategy: Key elements of effective
practice.* London: Department for Education and Skills/Sure Start.

Dockett, S. & Perry, R. (2007). *Transitions to school.* Sydney: UNSW Press.

Ernest, P. (1995). Epistemologies in education: The one and the many. In L. Steffe & J. Gale (eds),
Constructivism in education. Mahwah, NJ: Lawrence Erlbaum.

Foucault, M. (1980). Two lectures. In C. Gordon (ed.), *Power/knowledge: Selected interviews and other
writings.* New York: Pantheon.

Gergen, K. (1995). Social construction and the education process. In L. Steffe & J. Gale (eds), *Constructivism in education.* Mahwah, NJ: Lawrence Erlbaum.

Hill, S., Comber, B., Louden, B., Reid, J. & Rivalland, J. (1998). *100 children go to school. Connections
and disconnections in literacy development in the year prior to school and the first year of school.*
Canberra: DEETYA.

Hornby, A. (ed.) (2005). *The Oxford advanced learner's dictionary*, 7th ed. Oxford: Oxford University Press.

Jordan, B. (2009). Scaffolding learning and co-constructing understandings. In A. Anning, J. Cullen & M. Fleer (Eds.), *Early childhood education: Society and culture* (2nd ed.). London: Sage.

MacNaughton, G. (2009). Exploring critical constructivist perspectives on children's learning. In A. Anning, J. Cullen & M. Fleer (eds), *Early childhood education: Society and culture* (2nd ed.). London: Sage.

Marton, F., Dall'Alba, G. & Beaty, E. (1993). Conceptions of learning. *International Journal of Educational Research, 19*, 277–300.

Mason, M. (2000). Teachers as critical mediators of knowledge. *Journal of Philosophy of Education, 34*(2), 343–52.

Phillips, D. (1995). The good, the bad, and the ugly: The many faces of constructivism. *Educational Researcher, 24*(7), 5–12.

Piaget, J. (1959). *The language and thought of the child*, M. Gabain & R. Gabain, trans. London: Routledge and Kegan Paul.

Prout, A. (2011). Taking a step away from modernity: Reconsidering the new sociology of childhood. *Global Studies of Childhood, 1*(1), 4–14.

Rogoff, B. (1990). *Shared thinking and guided participation: Conclusions and speculations*. New York: Oxford University Press.

Siraj-Blatchford, I. (2009). Quality teaching in the early years. In A. Anning, J. Cullen & M. Fleer (eds), *Early childhood education: Society and culture*. London: Sage.

Siraj-Blatchford, I., Sylva, K., Muttock, S., Gilden, R. & Bell, D. (2002). *Researching effective pedagogy in the early years*. London: Institute of Education.

Taguchi, H.L. (2007). Deconstructing and transgressing the theory–practice dichotomy in early childhood education. *Educational Philosophy and Theory, 39*(3), 275–90.

von Glasersfeld, E. (1987). Learning as a constructive activity. In C. Janvier (ed.), *Problems of representation in the teaching and learning of mathematics*. Hillsdale, NJ: Lawrence Erlbaum.

Vygotsky, L. (1986). *Thought and language*, A. Kozulin, trans. Boston, MA: Massachusetts Institute of Technology.

Windschitl, M. (2002). Framing constructivism in practice as the negotiation of dilemmas: An analysis of the conceptual, pedagogical, cultural and political challenges facing teachers. *Review of Educational Research, 72*(2), 131–75.

Wood, T. (1995). From alternative epistemologies to practice in education: Rethinking what it means to teach and learn. In L. Steffe & J. Gale (eds), *Constructivism in education*. Mahwah, NJ: Lawrence Erlbaum.

13

Partnerships

Gary Woolley and
Ian Hay

Introduction

Parents and caregivers have an important role to play in their early years learner's education by participating in varied partnerships with early childhood services and schools. This can take many forms—for example, parents can communicate with the school, volunteer, participate in decision-making, support learning at home and become active learners themselves. Indications are that children apply more attention, concentration and effort, and are more likely to seek challenging tasks, persist in the face of difficulty and experience self-satisfaction when parents demonstrate an interest in and commitment to their child's education. The quality of caregivers' involvement may vary quite considerably; however, their assistance with reading, numeracy and general homework will be more effective when guidance, training and ongoing support are provided by the early childhood service/school (Woolley & Hay, 2007). High-quality interactions will enhance the academic and social well-being of early years learners, and may contribute to building a collaborative culture of shared responsibility within the local and wider community.

Caregivers, parents, home and childhood partnerships

School authorities, policy-makers and caregiver/parent organisations have for a long time reported the benefits of developing strong home–school partnerships (DEST, 2006). For example, research shows that greater home involvement in education encourages more positive attitudes towards the early childhood service and school, improves homework habits, reduces absenteeism and enhances academic achievement. Moreover, home–school partnerships build the social capital of the community and foster an enriched early childhood service/school culture. They may also contribute to self-growth among caregivers and stimulate the professional rewards for directors or principals and school staff. However, the child should be at the centre of the learning process, with a number of other overlapping relational spheres influencing the interactions of the home and early childhood service/school (see Figure 13.1). The main relational system influencing the child and their development is the immediate family. The quality of this interaction will also be influenced by their educators and peers. The daily child care at the educational institution, the community group settings and society will also influence the level and

Figure 13.1   Relational systems of influence for the early years learner

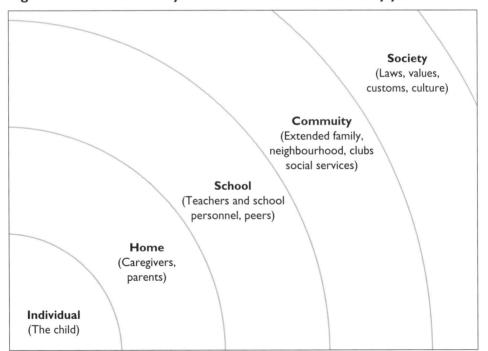

quality of these interactions. Thus educators need to understand the child within this interactive context.

In Australia, one of the significant educational policy documents reflecting a shared responsibility approach is the *Melbourne Declaration on Educational Goals for Young Australians* (MCEETYA, 2008). This declaration demonstrates governmental appreciation of the mutuality of economic prosperity and social cohesion in planning for the future, and recognises shared responsibilities in supporting children to reach their full potential. It encapsulates a more collaborative approach to supporting children and youth with attitudes and actions that connect these systems.

All partners need to be involved in shared and meaningful activities. There are six general questions that parents/caregivers need to consider (Epstein, 2011). These questions are:

1. How can I parent better?
2. What level and type of child learning/teaching should be occurring at home?
3. How do I communicate and interact with the educators?
4. Am I willing, able and confident to be a volunteer in the school?
5. Who is responsible for what home/classroom task and what information do I need to make a decision around this?
6. Am I interested in collaborating with my local community?

The responses to these questions influence the level and type of involvement. It is also important for early childhood educators to reflect on these questions, and to design activities and take actions that address each of them.

Exactly what constitutes a home and early childhood educational partnership will vary from setting to setting, from community to community and within particular cultural contexts. Even so, the evidence is that the support families provide to their early years learners at home has an impact on their children's academic achievement, educator ratings of student competence, student grades and high-stakes test scores at school (Ofsted, 2009). Moreover, children of parents who are associated with higher socio-economic status (SES) home backgrounds generally do better at school than those from low SES backgrounds. For example, Hay and Fielding-Barnsley (2006) report that book reading occurs as seldom as five times per year in some low-income families. Such findings have underpinned the need for the development of literacy programs that aim to encourage parent–child book reading in communities of low socio-economic status, and for early childhood educators to ensure that they incorporate significant language and vocabulary development within their regular programs, especially for children from families where English proficiency is an issue. Even so, when parents and caregivers are supported, this early education gap between cohorts of children begins to disappear.

In more recent years, education authorities and school systems have recognised and promoted the efficacy of this home—early childhood service/school partnership for academic and social improvement. For example, in Australia the Smarter Schools National Partnership (DESTWR, 2009) aims to increase parents' and caregivers' engagement, educational and social attainment, and the well-being of children. To provide this impetus, parents need to be actively encouraged to be involved in their child's education. This view is supported by a socio-cultural theory of human development (Vygotsky, 1978) that highlights the importance of engaging relationships for the improvement of learning. Thus children's early learning can be seen through the lens of the interplay between the values, beliefs and chosen behaviours that early years learners have learnt at home, in their cultural communities and from their interactions with others.

In particular, in terms of early childhood, the Reggio Emilia approach and philosophy is highly supportive of the partnership between early childhood educators and parents. The claim is that in this approach, parents are partners, collaborators and advocates for their children, with the educators needing to respect parents as the child's first educators and to involve parents and caregivers in every aspect of the curriculum. In general terms, the Reggio Emilia philosophy is based upon the following set of principles (Hewett, 2001):

- Children must have some control over the direction of their learning.
- Children must be able to learn through experiences of touching, moving, listening, seeing and hearing.
- Children have a relationship with other children and adults, and with material items in the world. Children must be allowed to explore, and they must have endless ways and opportunities to express themselves.

Opportunities

While it is acknowledged that the support families provide for their early years learners at home has a large impact on achievement at school, there have been increasing lifestyle pressures that can make this relationship more difficult at times. For example, there has been a shift in the balance between private and working lives in most OECD countries. Today, there are more marriage breakdowns and a greater number of mothers participating in the full-time and part-time work-force. There is also an increasing trend in the developed world towards having children later, smaller families, an ageing population, an increased focus on indi-viduality and longer working hours, with a corresponding decrease in availability for voluntary work. Moreover, many caregivers are single working mothers who struggle to maintain the balance of competing responsibilities. Even in families that have reasonably long-term and stable relationships, the interaction of fathers and mothers with their early years learners can suffer due to their increased working hours. These demographic changes can have a dampening effect on the formation of strong communication links between the home and the early learning setting.

One factor that often makes parent participation more difficult is that many parents lack the confidence and experience to participate in home–early childhood school partnerships. This is particularly the case for parents from low socio-economic communities, who may have had negative experiences with schooling in the past. Some parents are even quite hostile, and often this hostility will spring from a percep-tion of having been excluded, 'kept in the dark' or feeling 'fobbed off' when visiting educators in early childhood and formal schooling settings (DEST, 2006). In some communities, parents may not have been encouraged to help in an early learning setting. Parents and caregivers may feel intimidated when they are required to help their early years learners with unfamiliar curriculum terms and content matter. In some situations, their presence in classrooms is often perceived to be undermining rather than augmenting the educator's work. Poor handling of complaints by early childhood service/school authorities, a lack of trust and inadequate communication with parents are also major contributors to an aversion to becoming involved in early childhood service/school-based activities. This situation is often exasperated by inad-equate communication, a lack of funding and insufficient appropriate staff education to develop this important aspect of early home–school relationships.

Overcoming the challenges

The challenge for early childhood services and schools is that even though families are smaller and there are more resources that can be devoted to their children, working families have less family time, and there is a greater need to prioritise their outside commitments. Time organisation and resource constraints, a lack of infor-mation, obligations to other children, and problems with getting time off work are examples of competing demands that have to be overcome. Thus educational centres and communities need to find more creative solutions to develop supportive home–early childhood service/school partnerships that will be enduring and enhance the academic success and social well-being of their early years learners.

Low levels of involvement can be overcome when staff are welcoming, when decision-making is seen as a shared responsibility and when parents are made aware of the value of their own input (DEST, 2006). Thus early learning centres should create an environment that is inviting to parents, and investigate appropriate communication channels for caregivers. What is certain is that successful schools view early years learners' achievement as a shared responsibility, and all stakeholders—including parents and administrators, educators and community leaders—should play an important role in supporting children's learning. Often parents are more likely to come to the early childhood service/school when their child is performing, and early childhood service/schools with challenging circumstances can take advantage of these occasions to raise concerns and questions with otherwise elusive parents. Some early childhood centres have overcome many of these barriers, and have also lifted the academic and social performance of their children by going out of their way to make parents feel welcome by providing coffee mornings, English classes or after-school clubs on various issues or topics (Ofsted, 2009).

Developing partnerships

Early childhood and formal school settings need to take the initiative in forming positive relationships with parents, due to a general perception that the educational institution is in a better position to foster home–early childhood service/school partnerships (DEST, 2006). When early childhood service/schools take part in a comprehensive program of parent involvement, it should lead to a change in the culture of the early childhood service or school, and improve their relationships with families. Many parents and caregivers often do not feel comfortable attending 'parents and citizens' meetings, but are often attracted to more hands-on activities in a less formal setting that are more directly related to their child's education. Unlike more traditional notions of parent involvement as service to the early childhood service/school, some early childhood services/schools have invited parents to contribute their particular expertise to community-building through various cultural activities such as cooking, art, craft and gardening classes. For example, one school had a number of community gardens and a regular market stall where its fresh food and produce was sold (Ofsted, 2009). Such activities can be fostered by the provision of a parent meeting room so parents can socialise with one another, and to facilitate sharing of their ideas and activities. These types of initiatives demonstrate respect and concern for the general well-being of families, the gaining of the trust of parents and caregivers, and the support of their wider community.

Good family–early childhood service/school partnerships are the product of interested parents and schools that provide positive opportunities for involvement (DEST, 2006). The overriding focus should always be on the child's learning and well-being. There are many levels of involvement for parents in early childhood services and schools. For example, Epstein (1992) has developed a taxonomy of parent involvement that considers six levels of engagement: communicating; connecting learning at home and early childhood service/school; building community and identity; recognising the role of the family; consultative decision-making; collaborating beyond the early childhood service/school; and participating. Table 13.1 shows typical best practice examples of the opportunities that can be incorporated in each category.

Table 13.1   Epstein's (1992) taxonomy of parent involvement with best-practice examples

Key dimension	Best-practice examples
Communicating	• Provide personal contact; make parents feel welcome and valued; involves two-way communication that goes beyond the preschool/school newsletter; questionnaires • Email; online discussions on preschool/school issues and concerns; building supportive home environments that support early years learners' development • Support mechanisms that enable the preschool/school to inform parents about programs and early years learners' progress • Give informal parent encouragement of their early years learners • Send diaries home and seek comments from parents/carers • Preschool/school reports; work sample folders; emails; Facebook sites; preschool/school blog; e-newsletters and information pages
Building community and identity	• Formal acknowledgement of parents' input: throw a party; raising money for targeted charities; recycling activities to raise awareness and funds for students in need (e.g. subsidised uniforms) • Create programs that enable family involvement at preschool/school • A home-preschool/school liaison officer—particularly effective when a home-preschool/school liaison person is identified with a particular community and shares their cultural background • Provide libraries for parents with books, toys, computer hardware and software; clothing shop; language classes and interest workshops • Provide community support by developing or supporting a vegetable garden, market stall, native garden or building school play equipment

Recognising and supporting the role of the family	• Create a place that parents can call their own within the preschool/school site • Information sessions to help with homework, or monitoring and assisting early years learners at home with their learning activities • Programs that enable family involvement at preschool/school, such as covering library books or creating educational aids and games • Provide noticeboards where parents can wait, giving information about what they have been learning and how they can help at home • Support for athletics and swimming carnivals, art exhibitions, Grandparent's Day, Mother's Day, Father's Day, Teddy Bears' Picnics, Multicultural Food Fest, preschool/school open day, preschool/school fete, excursions, special talks, forums, speech nights, concerts, talent quests, fun days, coaching sporting teams, mentoring gifted and talented early years learners and volunteering as parent helpers
Consultative decision-making	• Establish and encourage parent organisations; conduct surveys; inform parents about issues that affect their early years learners • Create a newsletter; support parent involvement on task committees and parent committees for key events (e.g. Grandparent's Day) • Involve parents in decision-making, government and advocacy in preschool/school-related organisations • Organise committees for fetes, carnivals and special-interest days
Collaborating beyond the preschool/school	• Disseminate shared views and goals; preschool/school fetes involving community organisations; responding to natural disasters in or beyond the local community; helping parents improve their own skills • Collaborate and involve parents in preschool/school and community ventures • Grandparents or retired elders as classroom volunteers
Participating	• Understand roles; engage parents in preschool/school life; raise funds; participate in shared decision-making; working bees; volunteering as parent mentors for extension programs and sporting activities; volunteer as parent classroom helpers; take part in an audience for early years learners' performances and in various meetings and events; involvement in training of students in web page design, desktop publishing and internet etiquette • Families and preschool/school staff should be provided with the tools to develop the opportunities and build their capacity to engage meaningfully and productively • Develop ideas for family/preschool/school advisory centres; parents' radio programs; parents' multimedia presentations; parents' magazine or newsletter and parents' internet home page • Support an array of services, including homework hotlines, social services such as substance abuse or child abuse prevention, health services; refurbish preschool/school facilities; provide refreshments for and transportation to preschool/school-sponsored events

Early childhood educators

Quite often, activities that involve parents' participation in early childhood services and schools are driven by the parents themselves, but good parent–early childhood service/school relationships and communication will require thoughtful planning, creativity and concerted action (Hay et al., 2007). Early childhood educators therefore have a key role in strengthening this relationship and cultivating a positive change in the early childhood service/school community culture (DEST, 2006). When involving parents/caregivers in home–early childhood service/school programs, directors and principals should make sure that caregivers are recognised for their valuable contributions. Moreover, the school leaders also have a prime responsibility to encourage and equip educators for their important role in undertaking programs that promote parent participation.

Making parents feel welcome in the early childhood service/school is important (DEST, 2006). One common concern, however, is that in many situations educators expect education-supportive behaviour from parents, but they are not sufficiently supportive of parents. This is an attitude that may need to be changed if more effective partnerships are to be formed (DEST, 2006). Moreover, high levels of parent and community involvement in schooling will send a strong signal to young people that both the early childhood service/school and the community value formal and informal education, as well as the role of the early childhood service/school community (Hay & Fielding-Barnsley, in press).

Directors and principals should show leadership, and be visible and available to parents (DEST, 2006). For example, they could invite parents into the early childhood service/school by providing a space, such as a parent resource centre, that they can call their own in order to meet within the early childhood service/school (DEST, 2006). In such a space, parent volunteers can be invited to talk with, and offer advice to, parents. A community space within an early childhood service/school can also be a suitable venue or agency for parental self-growth (DEST, 2006). It stands to reason that when parents are encouraged to view learning as a lifelong process for themselves, they will also value education for their early years learners. For many families, this type of capacity-building is best provided by peer-educators found within the wider community. Parental capacity-building will need to focus on building parental efficacy through developing confidence in parenting and an understanding of the impact caregivers have on their child's achievement, as well as developing practical strategies, such as communicating with educators and early childhood service/school leaders, and learning how to effectively advocate for their early years learners.

Directors and school leaders are in a good position to make changes to the physical environment of their early childhood service/schools. For example, they can create formal or informal parent bodies that will support parent committees, volunteer committees and site-based management to enable parents and caregivers to take a more active role in decision-making and advice giving. When such collaborative endeavours take place, families are more likely to align their shared values (Ofsted, 2009).

Educators

Educators are often viewed as having a deep understanding of pedagogy and learning processes, and have the capacity to respond to children's diversity and their learning needs by developing positive home–school relationships. To advance this crucial role, educators will need to embrace the notion that parents are also partners in the education of the early years learner (Woolley & Hay, 2007). Educators are often hesitant to involve parents in their early years learner's academic work because they are often afraid that parents will teach concepts incorrectly or diminish their child's responsibility for their own learning. Often, what is required is a shift in thinking by educators. Educators should recognise what parents currently do at home that is effective so that better partnerships can be developed. Parents and caregivers also need to be informed about the way things are occurring in today's classrooms—for example, in science, mathematics and enabling parents in the home to develop the appropriate support and helping strategies to assist their early years learners. Quite often, a parent's or caregiver's main concern is to help their early years learners with their extension activities and even homework. It is important for educators to be aware that parents need to understand the language of learning, and that educators need to make the curriculum understandable and accessible. Thus information evenings with parents can stimulate awareness and interest, and increase home participation. Some early childhood services/schools have even encouraged educators to take on a liaison role by visiting the early years learners' homes before their early years learners start early childhood service/school, and encouraging parents to attend talks by staff about the early learners' work and educators' expectations (Ofsted, 2009).

Invitations to visit the early childhood service/school may be particularly important for the parents, who may see themselves as alienated and uninvolved. Invitations may come from the early childhood service/school, educators and students. Invitations that are generated by early childhood services/schools are seen as significant if the parent believes that the early childhood service/school is promoting a positive climate for their involvement. Invitations from educators are also important because they reinforce the notion that the engagement of parents with their child's learning will produce positive learning outcomes. Invitations from their own children are particularly significant because they convey the impression that parents' involvement will be valued. While visiting the early learning classroom, parents and caregivers should be encouraged by the educators to talk about issues of concern to them, and educators should help parents and caregivers to clarify their concerns about their children's education (Epstein, 2011).

Liaison

The Ofsted (2009) report looked at 20 outstanding schools in England that excelled against the odds despite their low socio-economic circumstances, and found that several of these schools employed a school liaison worker who was either a school employee or a parent representative. They were typically involved in enlisting parents in school activities, making home visits, conducting workshops on positive parenting, mathematics and literacy, and providing parents with a noticeboard in every classroom. In some of these schools, a school liaison worker often performed the role of a mentor who, for example, greeted parents at the school gates each morning. The liaison person was generally accessible to parents, and was often able to develop trust by providing informal advice, parenting advice, counselling and conciliation to parents. In some cases, the liaison person was not only employed to foster communication between educators and parents, but also had a positive input into school policy-making, due to their familiarity with the parents and their concerns.

Family literacy programs

The role of home and early childhood service/school–parent partnerships is considered to be a major influence on the acquisition of literacy. Many of the early family literacy programs place importance on parents and caregivers reading to early years learners at home because of the widely held belief that there is strong correlation between consistent home sharing of reading and success at school. Family literacy programs have become one of the key areas of expansion of literacy provision in the United States, Canada, the United Kingdom and Australia. There is a great deal of evidence to support the notion that family literacy programs contribute to improved literacy outcomes for many early years learners (Hay et al., 2010; Woolley, 2011).

Generally, family literacy sessions should be brief and enjoyable, and conducted in a comfortable place that is free from other distractions. An environment of mutual support and cooperation should be established by the sharing of goals and the fostering of the child's sense of enjoyment and responsibility for the reading process. Caregivers should spend time elaborating on the story plot, interesting facts and the language features of the text by explaining unfamiliar words, syntax and punctuation in a supportive dialogue context (Woolley & Hay, 2007). Caregivers' comments should be encouraging, and should emphasise meaning and story content rather than merely focusing on exact word recognition and decoding skills. The overriding concern should be to foster an enjoyment of literature and to engage rich conversations that connect the text to their child's real-life experiences. These supportive family literacy sessions can be supplemented by visits to the library and explorations in the backyard or the neighbourhood park. For example, after reading *The Very Hungry Caterpillar*, the family might search through the vegetable garden or park to look for caterpillars and bugs. This makes reading more meaningful, and will contribute to comprehension.

Literacy programs involving minority language groups

In many countries, the proportion of indigenous students and students with English as their second language (ESL) presents educators with challenges in meeting their diverse educational needs. One of the important things that educators can do is understand and acknowledge the cultural diversity, languages and cultural interactions of children. However, there is often a difference in what families do during family literacy activities, with some socio-cultural groups being much more effective than others. Thus, for early education programs to be more effective in diverse communities, schools must find creative ways to embed the cultural activities, interests and abilities of students into their classroom programs and routines. Moreover, many Indigenous and ESL parents have the competencies and the interest to help their children to achieve academically, but early childhood service/schools often overlook their potential contribution. In communities where the cultural and linguistic backgrounds are different and the children's educational needs are high, educators can make a significant difference if they engage with these cultural differences and respond with child-focused educational practice.

Intergenerational literacy programs

Intergenerational literacy programs are initiatives designed with the intention of developing the literacy skills of both adults and early years learners in the home to meet their diverse needs. It has been shown that these types of programs strengthen and encourage parental involvement, and promote a greater role in the functioning of early childhood services/schools. Intergenerational literacy programs are not without their problems, however. Rather than trying to impose the majority cultural and literacy practices, these programs should support the rich literacy and textual traditions that already exist in families. Educators therefore need to understand and support the customs and language within the subcultural group. In this context, when the overall education needs of the home are considered and the dignity of families is supported, a positive community of practice is more likely to be developed.

Summary

- The relationship between early childhood service/schools and their communities should be reciprocal.
- One of the most important objectives for educators should be the fostering of an attitude wherein parents and caregivers are viewed as equal partners in promoting their children's learning outcomes.
- This relationship implies that there is an exchange of resources to enable home–early childhood service/school partnering activities to be effective and to thrive. Thus early childhood service/schools should view parents as partners rather than clients.
- It is not always easy to develop effective, trusting and mutually respectful relationships between early childhood service/school staff and families, but family engagement in children's learning is a valuable resource for improving early years learners' long-term outcomes.
- The role of the family in supporting children's academic and social progress must be encouraged and fostered through the establishment of good channels of communication, consultative decision-making and collaboration between the home and the educational setting.
- Caregivers will respond more positively when they believe that their involvement is supportive of their child's education.
- What is certain is that positive home–school partnerships will have a lasting effect on community attitudes and student academic achievement.

- Key considerations for caregivers include:
  - diverse caregiver partnerships
  - support for learning/teaching in the home
  - open communication with educators
  - volunteering at school
  - shared responsibility and decision-making
  - community collaboration.

Discussion questions

13.1 How can early childhood educators encourage parental involvement in education activities?

13.2 Why do some early childhood services and schools in low socio-economic areas 'beat the odds' against academic under-achievement when they involve parents?

13.3 Identify differences in family literacy programs between early childhood service and primary school-aged children?

13.4 What are some very positive ways to involve parents of minority children in early childhood service or primary school partnership activities?

13.5 What are some barriers that can dampen home–school partnerships?

13.6 What are some creative ways for early learning centres to overcome these barriers?

References

Carle, E. (1969). *The very hungry caterpillar*. London: Puffin.

Department of Education, Science & Training (DEST) (2006). *Family–School Partnerships Project: A qualitative and quantitative study*. Canberra: Commonwealth Government.

Department of Education, Science & Training and Workplace Relations (DESTWR) (2009). Smarter Schools National Partnership. Canberra: Commonwealth Government.

Epstein, J.L. (2011). *School, family, and community partnerships*. Boulder, CO: Westview Press.

Epstein, J.L. & Connors, J. (1992). School and family partnerships. In M. Alkin (ed.), *Encyclopedia of educational research*, 6th ed. (pp. 1139–51). New York: Macmillan.

Hay, I. & Fielding-Barnsley, R. (2007). Facilitating children's emergent literacy using home shared reading: A comparison of two literacy models. *Australian Journal of Language and Literacy*, 3, 191–202.

—— (2009). Competencies that underpin children's transition into early literacy. *Australian Journal of Language and Literacy*, 32, 148–62.

—— (in press). Social learning, language and literacy. *Australian Journal of Early Childhood*.

Hay, I., Fielding-Barnsley, R. & Taylor, T. (2010). Facilitating young children's language and vocabulary development using a cognitive framework. *He Kupu e-journal, 2*, 37–46.

Hay, I. & Woolley, G. (2011). The challenge of reading comprehension. In T. Le, Q. Le and M. Short (eds), *Language and literacy education in a challenging world* (pp. 198–209). New York: Nova Science.

Hewett, V. (2001). Examining the Reggio Emilia approach to early childhood education. *Early Childhood Education Journal, 29*, 95–100.

Ministerial Council on Education, Employment, Training and Youth Affairs (MCEETYA) (2008). *Melbourne Declaration on Educational Goals for Young Australians.* Melbourne: Education Services Australia.

Ofsted (2009). Twenty outstanding primary schools excelling against the odds. Retrieved 11 October 2011 from <www.ofsted.gov.uk/resources/twenty-outstanding-primary-schools-excelling-against-odds>.

Vygotsky, L.S. (1978). *Mind and society.* Cambridge, MA: MIT Press.

Woolley, G. (2011). *Reading comprehension: Assisting children with learning difficulties.* Dordrecht: Springer.

Woolley, G. & Hay, I. (2007). Reading intervention: The benefits of using trained tutors. *Australian Journal of Language and Literacy, 30*, 9–20.

14

Social and emotional well-being

Danielle Twigg and
Donna Pendergast

Introduction

Promoting social and emotional well-being is a taken-for-granted aspiration of most early years programs. Importantly, it is also policy. Outcome 3 for children aged from birth to five years in the Early Years Learning Framework for Australia (DEEWR, 2009) explicitly states that 'Children have a strong sense of well-being' (2009, p. 3). Yet there is no one meaning for well-being and how it might be measured. This chapter explores the concept of well-being, and argues for the development of a culture of well-being in early learning contexts. Key strategies are shared and revolve around reducing risk factors and developing protective factors, while at the same time promoting the traits of resilience and the development of lifelong learning attributes. Examples of strategies for the early years are incorporated.

Exploring well-being

Well-being is a frequently used term, yet it is a slippery concept, multifaceted and complex in nature, and lacks a shared, common understanding. There appears to be a general acceptance of the notion that improved well-being is a desirable aspiration, and that there might be proactive initiatives to promote its development. However, measuring well-being is challenging, given the lack of clarity of definition, and there is a large body of literature that seeks to develop workable and meaningful measures of well-being related to economics, provision of housing, social services and the like. Theorists have resolved that understandings of well-being must incorporate self-definitions, thereby accepting that—like the notion of family—well-being is neither a unitary concept nor an unchanging one, such that people define well-being in different ways; furthermore, these definitions change over time. This is the idea of multiple, purposeful definitions that hold relevance and importance for the definer. Similarly, measures of well-being need to reflect the relative focus on definition in use. As a starting point, the most accessible of all definitions is the simplest: well-being is a good or satisfactory condition of existence, as defined by the individual and/or family. In the early years literature, well-being is similarly defined differently.

Nevertheless, a focus on well-being is at the forefront of policy directions in the early years in Australia. Looking to the outcomes for children aged from birth to five years in the Early Years Learning Framework for Australia (DEEWR, 2009), Outcome 3 explicitly states that 'Children have a strong sense of well-being' (2009, p. 3), with well-being defined in the glossary of terms in the following way:

> [S]ound well-being results from the satisfaction of basic needs—the need for tenderness and affection; security and clarity; social recognition; to feel competent; physical needs and for meaning in life. It includes happiness and satisfaction, effective social functioning and the dispositions of optimism, openness, curiosity and resilience. (DEEWR 2009, p. 46)

The elaboration of the Outcome links very strongly with the development of resilience. There are refined aspects specified within the Outcome: children become strong in their social and emotional well-being, and they take increasing responsibility for their own health and physical well-being. Evidence of strength in social and emotional well-being is demonstrated by, for example, humour, happiness and satisfaction; trust and confidence; enjoying solitude; and cooperating and working with others. Evidence of children taking increasing responsibility for their own health and physical well-being is demonstrated, for example, by participating in physical play; independence in physical care and hygiene; and recognising and communicating bodily needs.

Resilience

Resilience is the ability to cope with and bounce back from life's challenging and difficult events. Resilience is a mix of key skills and characteristics of a person, their social supports and the environment in which they live. Key skills can be taught from a very young age, and the development of these skills depends on the positive support of and relationships with people who surround them in the family and community. Resilience and learning are clearly connected, with learning and performing well constituting protective factors for resilience, and hence for developing a sense of well-being.

Some of the key characteristics of resilient children include:

- being socially competent—that is, flexible, caring and being able to communicate well
- having effective problem-solving skills—that is, being able to work out what the problem is, think of different ways to solve the problem and plan ahead
- being autonomous—this means having a high degree of confidence, being self-disciplined and independent
- having a sense of purpose and future—this means having goals in life, being motivated, wanting to be educated, being persistent and hopeful.

Some of the key ways of promoting resilience in children include providing caring and supportive environments, setting high but reasonable expectations and encouraging active participation.

Optimising well-being

In Australia and globally, considerable research has sought to identify how to optimise well-being. From this work, two categories of factors have been identified that impact on well-being: risk factors and protective factors. Risk factors are those that are likely to affect the achievement of a state of well-being, while protective factors are those that are likely to contribute to the enhancement of well-being. The research reveals that a number of factors impact on the well-being of children and young people in particular, and these can be grouped under five headings:

- child or personal factors
- family factors

- formal early years context (e.g. school)
- life events
- community and cultural factors.

Table 14.1 provides examples of the behaviours within each of the factors that might lead to an impact on individual well-being in the early years, but this should not be seen as an exhaustive list.

Table 14.1   Risk and protective factors impacting on well-being in the early years

Risk factors				
Child	*Family*	*Formal early years context (e.g. school)*	*Life events*	*Community and cultural*
• Low self-esteem • Poor social skills • Poor problem-solving • Difficult temperament • Lack of empathy • Homelessness • Lack of adjustment • Feelings of abandonment	• Family violence • Poor supervision of children • Harsh or inconsistent discipline • Lack of warmth or affection • Abuse and neglect • Time poor	• Learning failure • Bullying • Peer rejection • Poor attachment • Poor attendance • Deviant peer group	• Divorce and family break-up • Death of a key family member	• Neighbourhood violence and crime • Lack of support services • Social or cultural discrimination • Inconsistent community norms concerning violence

Source: Adapted from Mission Australia (2005).

Developing a culture of well-being

We propose that what we need to aim for is a culture of well-being. This is based on the proposition that self-esteem and resilience, combined with lifelong learning attributes in an environment enhanced by feeling loveable, being valued and supported and connected to self and others, lead to optimum well-being, as self-defined by the individual and the family. Key strategies to develop a culture of well-being revolve around reducing risk factors and developing protective factors, while at the same time—like all community and individual development strategies—the principles of prevention, promotion and early intervention apply. Other factors of key significance are the promotion of the traits of resilience and the development of lifelong learning attributes.

Developing resilience

After more than four decades of research on early childhood brain development, scientists from the Center on the Developing Child at Harvard University (NSCDC, 2007) have shown that early experiences determine whether a child's developing brain architecture provides a strong or weak foundation for all future learning, behavior, and health. With this in mind, we assert that early years learners need to be given the opportunity to develop skills, knowledge, attitudes and values that enhance their own resilience. From birth, children develop loving attachments with their caregivers. Even in infancy, human beings begin to develop an awareness of social well-being. Babies communicate their basic needs through crying and babbling. Throughout the various developmental stages of the early years, children begin to build upon basic understandings of social and emotional competencies through increased engagement with their own world. As children mature, they are exposed to life experiences that may prove challenging without resilience. While adults must work to provide safe and supportive environments for early years learners, as children grow, develop and gain independence there will be circumstances that they must face on their own, such as transitioning from daily life at home into a formal schooling situation, learning how to ride a bicycle or becoming a reader.

Not unlike the way in which children learn academic skills, they learn, practise and apply certain social and emotional skills by engaging in positive activities in and outside of the classroom (Zins & Elias, 2006). The Collaborative for Academic, Social and Emotional Learning (CASEL) (2003) identifies five core social and emotional learning (SEL) competencies for school and life success. These five core competencies are recognised internationally as critical to building resilience:

1. self-awareness
2. social awareness
3. self-management
4. responsible decision-making, and
5. relationship skills.

These five competencies provide a framework for early childhood educators, as well as parents, to help early years learners learn essential skills that will allow them to develop coping strategies and implement problem-solving skills when faced with the challenges of life. Table 14.2 provides the CASEL definition of each of the five core competencies.

Table 14.2   Social and emotional learning (SEL) competencies for school and life success

SEL competency	Description
Self-awareness	Accurately assessing one's feelings, interests, values and strengths; maintaining a well-grounded sense of self-confidence
Social awareness	Regulating one's emotions to handle stress, control impulses and persevere in overcoming obstacles; setting and monitoring progress towards personal and academic goals; expressing emotions appropriately
Self-management	Being able to take the perspective of and empathise with others; recognising and appreciating individual and group similarities and differences; recognising and using family, school and community resources
Responsible decision-making	Establishing and maintaining healthy and rewarding relationships based on cooperation; resisting inappropriate social pressure; preventing, managing and resolving interpersonal conflict; seeking help when needed
Relationship skills	Making decisions based on consideration of ethical standards, safety concerns, appropriate social norms, respect for others and likely consequences of various actions; applying decision-making skills to academic and social situations; contributing to the well-being of one's school and community

Source: Adapted from CASEL (2003).

Early years learners are best placed to begin developing SEL competency in safe and supportive environments, such as their own home, a child-care program or a classroom setting (Bear, 2005). The next section of the chapter provides examples of how to increase resilience in early years learners in different ways for children aged from birth to four and from four to eight respectively.

Developing SEL in children from birth to age four

From birth, parents and other adults have the opportunity to enhance the SEL competence of young children. Infants begin to develop social awareness when they begin interacting with adults and their environment. Playing games like 'peek-a-boo' and singing songs with movement activities gives infants and toddlers the opportunity to practise competencies such as self-awareness and relationship skills at a very basic level. Infants, toddlers and young children in this age cohort also may begin to practise responsible decision-making by seeking help from others for a variety of reasons (for example, to be fed or to gain assistance with tying their shoelaces), depending on their chronological and developmental age. Organisational skills and self-management activities can be modelled by nurturing adults, such as completing daily household routines (e.g. cooking, cleaning). In many cases with very young children, the adult assumes a large degree of responsibility for modelling the five core SEL competencies. However, as a child grows less dependent on the adult for basic needs, the child will be well placed to assume more of the SEL competencies on their own, as appropriate to their age and developmental stage.

Developing SEL in children from ages four to eight

As children become more independent and reach preschool age, their capacity for practising the five SEL core competencies increases dramatically. Although children between the ages of four and eight benefit highly from continued modelling by adults in their learning environment, they are far less dependent than in the previous age cohort. Early years learners in this age cohort will begin to develop self-awareness, and be able to identify key emotions (e.g. sadness, happiness, anger) as well as recognise how people respond to these emotions. Self-management for this age cohort begins with taking responsibility for personal belongings, and also beginning to learn about viewpoints and opinions. Children between the ages of four and eight develop social awareness when they work towards a common goal with their peers (such as team projects or earning rewards), or begin playing games with rules in which there is only one 'winner.' Responsible decision-making begins with friendships for early years learners in this age cohort, as they practise making compromises or resisting temptation from peers to misbehave (for example, bullying or lying). As early years learners mature, they become adept at utilising relationship skills to help with negotiation (for instance, encouraging a compromise between friends who are fighting), and they begin to see ways of applying these skills to the broader community (such as playground clean-up day or a food drive). If early years learners have the opportunity to practise these SEL core competencies under the guidance of caring adults and within a safe and supportive learning environment, they will be well placed to maximise their potential to succeed throughout the rest of their lives.

Developing lifelong learning attributes

Rapidly changing circumstances and opportunities in contemporary work, social and recreational environments demand the continuing acquisition of new knowledge, new skills and new abilities—and their efficient application. This demand can be met satisfactorily only through a process of continual learning—learning how to do, how to know, how to be and how to live together. For young people in particular, there is an urgent need to develop the confidence and know-how required to deal with the uncertainties and complex conundrums that many of them face now in adolescence. Lifelong learning focuses attention on the need for continual learning and on the sets of generic skills and capacities that will equip individuals and societies to embrace this expanded notion of learning, together with the challenges of living and working in knowledge economies and the new work order. As the Ministerial Council on Education, Employment, Training and Youth Affairs (MCEETYA) (2005, p. 5) notes in its position paper *Contemporary Learning: Learning in an Online World*, 'continuous learning with clear purpose and connection to the real-world is critical to developing the capabilities, dispositions and literacies required to participate in society and to deal with the complexity of issues and change'. One of the effects has been to refocus on engaging young people more effectively in the learning process.

What lifelong learning principles espouse is that it is no longer useful to teach a set of skills or processes or knowledge, because they will become redundant or of limited applicability within a short period of time due to the rapid progress and development of society. It means facilitation of the creation of thinking that is like an 'expert novice' (Gee et al., 1996)—that is, someone who is expert at continually learning anew and in depth. Those in the early years no longer need to become expert at any one thing. The tools with which we need to educate our young people are those that give access to communication and technical processes, and that equip individuals to be lifelong learners. Watson (2003, pp. 6–7) identifies four characteristics of lifelong learners that could set the parameters of a learning society:

- learning to *do* (acquiring and applying skills, including life skills)
- learning to *be* (promoting creativity and personal fulfilment)
- learning to *know* (an approach to learning that is flexible, critical and capable), and
- learning to *live together* (exercising tolerance, understanding and mutual respect).

By creating predictable and safe environments with caring and trustworthy relationships, educators begin to set the stage for young children to develop their own sense of agency and to function successfully as members of society. Early years learners begin to develop resilience through daily experiences in a comfortable environment, enabling them to try new things and experience challenges alongside warm and supportive adults. Research (Zins et al., 2004) indicates that children who receive explicit instruction in social and emotional learning (SEL) in school are:

- more connected to educators and school
- more engaged in learning
- more motivated to learn
- better behaved/less likely to engage in problem behaviour
- able to perform better on achievement tests and get better grades.

One study (Durlak et al., 2011) of 213 school-based, universal social and emotional learning (SEL) programs involving 270 034 kindergarten through high school students in the United States demonstrates scientific links between SEL and student gains in the following ways:

- increased social-emotional skills
- improved attitudes about self, others and school
- positive classroom behaviour
- an eleven percentile-point gain on standardised achievement tests.

The same study also indicates that these students had fewer behaviour problems, including aggressive behaviour and emotional distress. Therefore, early years educators are well placed to structure learning environments that encourage early years learners to explore new learning activities, address personal situations and build developing relationships with their peers as well as with adults. Early years learners need to feel comfortable to make mistakes and take risks in a safe learning environment in order to grow and develop. Learning how to read, for example, involves taking multiple risks and making an endless number of mistakes. Fluency comes when an individual has learned many of the conventions of language and literacy, practised these repeatedly and applied these skills and knowledge in many ways over time. A child who is fearful of making mistakes may struggle with learning how to read if they do not feel comfortable or feel safe and supported by their educators, peers or other adults—which in turn may affect the individual's ability to become a lifelong learner.

As mentioned earlier in the chapter, Outcome 3 of the Early Years Learning Framework (DEEWR, 2009) focuses on both physical and psychological well-being. The Framework asserts that children who have a strong sense of well-being will both become strong in their social and emotional well-being and take increasing responsibility for their own health and physical well-being (2009, pp. 31–2). The following section provides evidence of each of these indicators, and also includes ideas for how educators can promote a strong sense of well-being among early years learners (see Tables 14.3 and Table 14.4).

Table 14.3   Encouraging early years learners to become strong in their own social and emotional well-being

When an early years learner demonstrates . . .	Educators can promote this learning by . . .
Trust and confidence	Maintaining warm and sensitive approaches to all children, both in a group and individually
Humour and happiness	Acknowledging the child's joyful moments
Unexpected frustration in trying a new activity	Encouraging the child to use coping strategies, and/or to discuss what has led to this feeling
New ability with language as an ESL learner	Praising the child's efforts and building upon the child's new-found skills
Contributions to shared projects	Affirming the importance of cooperation and growth as a member of a group
Enjoyment of moments of solitude	Valuing the child's decision-making and awareness of personal needs

Source: Adapted from DEEWR (2009, p. 31).

Table 14.4   Encouraging early years learners to take increasing responsibility for their own health and physical well-being

When an early years learner . . .	Educators can promote this learning by . . .
Experiments with increasingly complex sensory-motor and movement skills	Including physical activities in the daily experiences of early years learners, through participatory games, and music and movement activities
Shows an increasing awareness of healthy eating and exercise	Engaging children in discussions and activities that focus on nutrition and the importance of daily exercise
Makes connections with others	Providing opportunities for children to work with various children in small groups with adult supervision
Demonstrates beginning awareness of personal hygiene and social expectations of cleanliness	Actively encouraging proper hygiene practices
Wants to rest during the day	Planning a balanced day that includes activities which require active participation along with restful activities
Shows an awareness of routines and responsibilities	Designing a daily timetable for activities, and a roster of jobs that are age-appropriate and can be completed successfully by all children

Source: Adapted from DEEWR (2009, p. 32).

Summary

- This chapter has provided an overview of social and emotional well-being for early years learners within the current policy context of Australia.
- The Early Years Learning Framework for Australia (DEEWR, 2009), Outcome 3 explicitly states that 'Children have a strong sense of well-being'. Within this chapter, we have provided evidence of the critical nature of well-being in the lives of early years learners, and offered examples of how educators can promote a strong sense of well-being among children.
- Provision of a safe and supportive learning environment designed by warm and trustworthy adults is essential to developing the social and emotional well-being of early years learners.
- Lifelong learners are required to have multifaceted skill bases that include adept problem-solving skills and advanced communication skills to meet the challenges of a fast-paced, technologically driven society.

- Well-being is an essential aspect of developing early years learners for successful lives.
- Resilient children demonstrate social competence, problem-solving skills, autonomy and a sense of purpose and future.
- Social and emotional learning (SEL) incorporates five core competencies that can be taught explicitly by educators: self-awareness, social awareness, self-management, responsible decision-making and relationship skills.
- Tools that give learners access to communication and technical processes will best equip individuals to become lifelong learners.
- Early years learners develop resilience through daily experiences in a comfortable learning environment, where they are encouraged to try new things and experience challenges alongside warm and supportive adults.
- Research has proven the benefits of SEL scientifically, including increased social-emotional skills; improved attitudes about self, others and school; positive classroom behaviour; and significant gains on standardised achievement tests.

Discussion questions

14.1 The concept of 'expert novice' is a useful way to capture the ever-changing requirements for young learners. Select another period in time—for example, the 1960s—and compare the learning needs of young people with those of children in the twenty-first century.

14.2 Name the five core social and emotional learning (SEL) competencies. Provide an age-appropriate example that can be used with the early years learners under your care.

14.3 A child in your class is exhibiting uncharacteristic and volatile emotions. How do you respond to this child's behaviour using your knowledge of social and emotional well-being?

14.4 Select one of the facets of well-being and suggest strategies for enhancing this facet in a classroom learning experience.

References

Bear, G.G., with Cavalier, A. & Manning, M. (2005). *Developing self-discipline and preventing and correcting misbehavior.* Boston: Allyn & Bacon.

Collaborative for Academic, Social and Emotional Learning (CASEL) (2003). *Safe and sound: An educational leader's guide to evidence-based social and emotional learning (SEL) programs.* Chicago: CASEL.

Department of Education, Employment and Workplace Relations (DEEWR) (2009). *Belonging, being and becoming: The Early Years Learning Framework for Australia.* Retrieved 20 February 2012 from <www.deewr.gov.au/EarlyChildhood/Policy_Agenda/Quality/Pages/EarlyYearsLearning-Framework.aspx>.

Durlak, J.A., Weissberg, R.P., Dymnicki, A.B., Taylor, R.D. & Schellinger, K. (2011). The impact of enhancing students' social and emotional learning: A meta-analysis of school-based universal interventions. *Child Development, 82*(1), 405–32.

Gee, J.P., Hull, G. and Lankshear, C. (1996). *The new work order: Behind the language of the new capitalism.* Sydney: Allen & Unwin.

Ministerial Council on Education, Employment, Training and Youth Affairs (MCEETYA) (2005). *Contemporary learning: Learning in an online world.* Melbourne: Curriculum Corporation.

Mission Australia (2005). *Developing resilience at every stage of a young person's life.* Sydney: Mission Australia.

National Scientific Council on the Developing Child (NSCDC) (2007). *The timing and quality of early experiences combine to shape brain architecture. Working Paper No. 5.* Retrieved 20 February 2012 from <www.developingchild.harvard.edu>.

Watson, L. (2003). *Lifelong learning in Australia.* Canberra: Department of Education, Science and Training.

Werner, E. & Smith, R. (2001). *Journeys from childhood to midlife: risk, resilience, and recovery.* Ithaca, NY: Cornell University Press.

Zins, J.E. & Elias, M.J. (2006). Social and emotional learning. In G.G. Bear & K.M. Minke (eds), *Children's needs III: Development, prevention, and intervention* (pp. 1–13). Bethesda, MD: National Association of School Psychologists.

Zins, J., Weissberg, R., Wang, M. & Walberg, H.J. (2004). *Building academic success on social and emotional learning (SEL): What does the research say?* New York: Teachers College Press.

15

Diversity and differentiation

Wendi Beamish and Beth Saggers

Introduction

New ways of working are being embraced by early childhood educators as they cope with demands from national reforms and changing communities. While reformers are pressing for social equity and improved outcomes for families and children, communities are diverging in terms of ethnicity, culture, language and socio-economic status. As a consequence, early childhood educators are being challenged to expand their existing repertoire of practices in order to more effectively provide quality learning experiences for every child in their care.

Practice enhancement and differentiated pedagogy are needed to address the additional needs of an increasing number of diverse learners. Community expectations are particularly focused on better educational supports for children in five cluster areas:

- culturally diverse and Indigenous backgrounds
- 'at risk' because of socio-economic and abuse conditions
- communicative, emotional and behavioural disorders

- disabilities and learning difficulties, and
- recognised gifts and talents.

This chapter focuses on some everyday practices that can be used strategically to better support all children, including those with additional educational needs. All practices are well supported in the literature and are substantiated by either research findings or strong, socially determined values. They also are very 'doable' and sustainable in today's dynamic and multifaceted early childhood settings. Seven key practices will be introduced, together with examples of how they can be applied to both enhance the learning of individual children and to strengthen a sense of group belonging. The practices are:

- having positive beliefs about all children
- learning about each child
- building meaningful relationships around the child
- creating supportive learning environments for the child
- providing engaging learning experiences for the child
- differentiating instruction for the child
- using child progress data to improve learning and teaching.

Having positive beliefs about all children

Beliefs guide our thinking and actions. As Simms (1999, p. 4) reminds us, 'what we do, and how we do it, depends on what we believe'. Beliefs comprise values, attitudes, expectations and personal convictions. They are shaped not only by personal experience but also by information gained from a broad range of sources (such as family, social networks, training and media). Moreover, they act as a filter through which we view and interpret the world around us. The beliefs that early childhood educators hold about children, teaching, learning and caring therefore matter.

Believing that all children are capable and successful learners is a necessary prerequisite to effective teaching and job satisfaction. This means, for example, expecting meaningful and function-based academic outcomes for every early years learner, including a child with multiple or intellectual disabilities. It also means believing that every child needs to be respected and accepted into the classroom community, regardless of class, culture or capabilities. Believing that parents are equal partners in the educative process and that staff collaboration yields dividends because 'none of us is as smart as all of us' (Sapon-Shevin, 1991, p. 9) are essentially building blocks to support teaching in the early years. When beliefs are positive, innovative and future oriented, problems can be solved and challenges can be overcome.

Learning about each child

Learning about individual children is core business for early childhood educators because a 'one-size-fits-all' approach does not provide effective learning outcomes for many young children. Individual-specific knowledge is the critical ingredient that allows teaching and care to be adjusted and personalised to suit each child. It enables the educator to respond in a swift, sensitive and informed manner to the emergent and ongoing needs of every child.

Learning about each child means gathering information about the child's abilities, interests and learning style. Information about what a child can and cannot do provides the fabric for strength-based teaching and learning, and for curriculum content to be broadened or reduced. Information about what a child likes and dislikes allows for the customising of objects and materials to increase child engagement, concentration and interaction. Information about the child's demonstrated patterns and approaches to learning facilitates the selection of appropriate teaching pedagogies to support the child's learning. Taken together, child-specific information of this kind enables teaching to focus on individual difference and learning to proceed along different trajectories.

Learning about each child also means gathering information about each child's family background, ethnicity and language. Family-specific information allows a child's culture to be incorporated into the everyday program, thereby facilitating culturally responsive teaching and learning. At times, knowledge about and sensitivity to family composition, social supports and available resources are vital to fostering child resilience and well-being.

Child- and family-specific information-gathering requires time, effort and cooperation (Beamish et al., 2001). The process needs to be ongoing, and confidentiality is vital in relation to 'privileged communication' (Cook et al., 2008, p. 79). Four key sources are recommended for information-gathering: families; staff and other professionals; personal interactions with and observations of the child; and documents (for example, medical, therapy and assessment reports, and education, transition, behaviour and healthcare plans).

Examples of practice

Gathering child- and family-specific information from parents of diverse learners is a purposeful activity. A sensitive and responsive approach not only fosters trusting relationships, but also uncovers unique understandings about the child.

Birth to four years

Yuson belongs to a refugee family experiencing social exclusion in the local community. At child care, Yuson uses limited English and interacts infrequently with staff and children. The educator primarily responsible for Yuson's learning and care puts aside extra time to get to know the family members and makes them feel welcome at the centre. She has begun to build a trusting relationship with the mother, and will soon attempt to gather information about Yuson's interests and what he likes to play with at home. In the meantime, she creates a safe and secure learning environment for this boy, ensures that she has a number of brief but warm interactions with him throughout the day and, whenever possible, acknowledges his contributions to the group and to other staff.

Four to eight years

Kaitlin has autism and has recently transitioned from an intensive early intervention program into Year 1. For the past year, her Year 1 teacher has been an active member of Kaitlin's transition-planning team. She and the intervention teacher have visited each other's classrooms several times and have shared a wealth of information about Kaitlin's learning and behavioural-support needs. Partnerships with Kaitlin's mother and Kaitlin's private speech therapist have been established. A data file from the intervention centre has been received by the school administration. This teacher is now well placed to coordinate Kaitlin's education and care.

Building meaningful relationships around the child

Building meaningful relationships around the child involves building a sense of trust and connectedness with each child, with the family of that child, and between the child and peers. Meaningful relationships are underpinned by warmth and respect, and stem from positive interactions and shared problem-solving. Responsive care and nurturing interactions help very young children to develop secure attachments, a sense of identity, a love of learning and an early understanding of morals, values and emotions. Close and reliable relationships with important adults and peers need to continue into the early years of schooling because relationships significantly influence ongoing development and learning, well-being and resilience, academic achievement and friendship formation.

Many diverse learners have extensive relationship needs in the early years. Personal attributes and actions often set them apart from the group, and set the occasion for poor interactions with both peers and adults. Educators, however, are well positioned to take the lead in nurturing connections with and relationships around these children. When an educator displays actions such as making the child feel consistently welcome and safe, or interacts with the child in ways that show warmth and respect, positive examples of acceptance are provided for children and staff to copy. When a supportive classroom climate is established, the child can learn without fear of being threatened or ridiculed, and friendships with peers can be fostered. When patience is coupled with clear expectations of achievement, the child is treated in the same way as other classmates, and is affirmed to be a learner.

Educators can draw on a large inventory of practical strategies to build productive adult–child relationships and positive child–child interactions in the early years. In general, a strategy should be selected or adjusted to meet the unique needs of each child, and some strategies may prove to be more effective for particular interactions or in particular settings. While several relationship-building strategies may be used at the same time, the explicit planning and ongoing evaluation of strategies and outcomes are essential.

Arthur et al. (2012) provide a useful framework to consider when selecting strategies for relationship-building. This framework clusters strategies into three groupings according to level of interaction: from low-exchange strategies (low-level interaction), through mediating strategies (moderate-level interaction), to explicit strategies (high-level interaction).

1. low-exchange strategies
   - acknowledging (for example, making meaningful comments about the child's efforts)
   - modelling (for example, modelling how to play cooperatively)
   - facilitating (for example, using some key phrases in the child's home language)
2. mediating strategies
   - supporting (for example, providing verbal or physical support in turn-taking activities)
   - co-constructing (for example, exploring and sharing experiences during group sensory play)
   - scaffolding (for example, having the child insert missing but known words during literacy learning)

- reflecting (for example, reflecting and commenting on experiences using group photographs)
- critiquing (for example, assisting the child to offer critical views on a classroom issue)

3. explicit strategies
   - demonstrating (for example, showing the child how to interrupt a conversation, step by step)
   - directing (for example, sensitively reminding the child about a classroom rule).

Examples of practice

Young children with additional needs become successful learners when they establish positive relationships and interactions with adults and other children. A caring and systematic approach is needed to nurture meaningful connections between the child and others.

Birth to four years

Lucy is a toddler who presents as self-absorbed and withdrawn. At child care, she frequently withdraws from group experiences. The use of low-interaction and mediating strategies by a caregiver who Lucy appears to like can be used to draw her into community learning. Lucy can be warmly encouraged and reassured by the caregiver to join in small-group activities (with one or two peers) and praised for any level of participation and exchange with playmates. Working at the child's level, using non-verbal encouragement and a calm voice, and suggesting that Lucy take a preferred object with her to an activity are examples of additional support strategies for building confidence and relationships.

Four to eight years

Jack is a quiet Year 3 student with serious vision difficulties related to albinism (very little pigment in the hair, skin and eyes). He is readily supported by the girls in his class, but rarely initiates exchanges with boys and often hovers on the edge of their games. With educator support, a structured approach using male peers as mediators can be used to coach Jack in how to join in small-group games (indoors and outdoors). A few peers who are socially adept can be enlisted to assist, and can be trained to facilitate and compliment Jack's approach to the group and bid for entry into particular games.

Creating supportive learning environments for the child

The learning environment can be viewed as having three interacting layers: the *socio-emotional* environment, the *behavioural* environment and the *physical* environment

(Wood, 2006). In an accepting and responsive environment, good relationships are developed, communication is promoted, and self-esteem and confidence can grow. In a safe and carefully managed environment, clear and fair behavioural expectations and positive feedback can create an atmosphere that is conducive to learning, modelling and self-regulation. In a secure and well-organised physical environment, minimal distractors and specifically chosen materials can increase child motivation, engagement and learning. Attention to each layer is important when planning and managing the classroom environment in relation to the daily schedule, activities and routines.

Supportive learning environments for young children with additional needs often require careful consideration. If these early years learners are to succeed, both academically and socially, the classroom needs to be welcoming and to be a place they want to be. In addition, the learning environment needs to promote their engagement, foster interaction and set the occasion for pro-social behaviour. Ten key recommendations for designing such environments are:

- Create safe and comfortable spaces with clear physical boundaries. Have an inviting space for leave-takings, where the child can separate and reconnect with parents and staff, and some cosy spaces to which the child can retreat if feeling anxious or angry, or for taking a break from activities or other people.
- Arrange spaces so that staff can readily observe the child's cues in order to respond effectively to emerging wants and needs.
- Allow choice and a degree of flexibility within activities and the daily schedule so that the child has some sense of control over their environment.
- Create a language-rich and communication-friendly environment where all children are encouraged to augment spoken language by using gestures, dramatic representations and electronic devices.
- Offer specific activities that allow particular staff and peers proximity and time to build positive relationships with the child, and the child to build reciprocal relationships and social skills.
- Encourage the child to learn to listen to others and, wherever possible, use small group activities for peer modelling and peer coaching.
- Set up predictable routines with clear structure and defined limits so that the child feels secure and safe.
- Establish between three and six clear and reasonable class rules for expected behaviours, provide ongoing explanations as to why each rule is important,

identify consequences for following and not following each rule, and reward the child's approximations of each rule.

- Make sure that good behaviour is encouraged and acknowledged throughout the day, and that behaviours of concern are dealt with in a planned, proactive and consistent manner by all staff.
- Design daily schedules and activities to minimise the amount of time the child spends transitioning from one activity to another and, wherever possible, intersperse preferred and non-preferred activities.

Examples of practice

Young children with additional needs are more likely to become confident and competent learners in a carefully managed learning environment. Successful learning is facilitated when children have a sense of security and belonging, and when they can participate in flexibly delivered learning experiences.

Birth to four years

Jamie has been attending child care for over six months but still experiences distress when separating from his mother. A caregiver who has a positive relationship with Jamie can be allocated to greet him by name (animated interaction) and acknowledge the parent in the classroom's arrival space. Active observation of Jamie's behaviour as he approaches the entrance allows an opportunity for the caregiver to gauge Jamie's relationship needs at that time. Following a brief farewell to his parent, Jamie can be told (at his eye level) exactly when his parent will return before being encouraged to select a favourite activity.

Four to eight years

Miriam is a precocious preschooler who defies authority, acts aggressively towards classmates and has poor verbal skills. Her young mother is a single parent who has four children under six years of age. Miriam needs to learn how to follow class rules, recognise and manage her emotions, and resolve conflicts. Pairing Miriam with a more socially skilled and verbally adept child during particular class activities and responsibilities (such as watering the class garden or taking documents to administration) may also assist in fostering pro-social behaviour, emotional regulation, peer collaboration and language learning.

Providing engaging learning experiences for the child

Early educators routinely put time and effort into creating high-quality learning environments and activities for young children in their care. Time should also be spent making sure that children engage in these environments and activities. Strong learner engagement not only facilitates a child's learning but also develops a positive tone that promotes group learning. Strong learner engagement, moreover, leads to an increased positive behaviours and improved interactions with materials and peers.

McWilliam and Casey (2008, p. 4) define engagement as 'the amount of time children spend involved with the environment (with educators, peers, or materials) in a way that is appropriate for the children's age, abilities, and surroundings'. They propose a number of different levels of engagement:

- non-engagement or unoccupied behaviour
- casual attention, a functional but unsophisticated form of engagement
- focused attention, which includes watching or listening to features in the environment
- persistence, the highest level of engagement.

Persistence, the most sophisticated level of engagement, allows the child to interact with tasks in a way that encourages attention, concentration, planning and problem-solving. These skills form the basis of cognitive development, and are crucial for learning (Landy, 2009). The provision of highly engaging experiences is therefore essential to ensure successful learning.

Engaging learning experiences require the establishment of rich learning environments that support activities for engagement. Such environments empower the child to make decisions by promoting choice-making, initiative and self-directed learning. The use of technology in the environment further supports self-direction, as well as capitalising on the interests and learning styles of particular children. In addition, technology increases the likelihood that other interactive instructional approaches will be incorporated into teaching and learning.

Engaging activities expand benefits accrued in a rich learning environment. Activity appeal is often boosted when the prerequisite skills and readiness levels of the child are taken into account during activity planning. Appeal is also increased when the child's levels of independence, learning style and motivation are used to shape aspects of the activity. Level of social competence and extent of social networks influence how well the child participates and engages in interactive learning. Therefore, the interspersing of individualised activities with small- and whole-group experiences—including those focused on cooperative learning and peer support— needs to be carefully considered when tailoring activities to a particular child.

Some rules of thumb for planning engaging activities are:

- organise the daily program by activities and routines
- plan activities that:
    - allow every child to engage in some meaningful aspect/s of the activity
    - involve purposeful actions, including some that challenge
    - promote communication and positive interactions with others
    - promote self-reliance and self-regulation
- keep track of the level of engagement displayed by individual children.

Finally, engaging learning experiences must provide multiple ways for the child to learn. Moreover, these engaging opportunities need to take place with sufficient frequency to allow the child to practise and consolidate new learning. When cumulative activities and the environment are shaped to engage the child, positive learning outcomes and success occur.

Examples of practice

Engagement is the key to learning. Creating rich learning experiences that cater for different ways of learning increases the level of child engagement.

Birth to four years

Tess is a toddler who lives with her family in the local Indigenous community, which is a considerable distance from the child-care centre. Tess comes to the centre infrequently, and when she does she always brings her 'teddy'. If left alone, this little girl will sit with teddy in the far corner of the outdoor play area for extended periods. Neither indoor nor outdoor activities have much appeal. To increase Tess's engagement with activities and her peers, some indoor play furniture, a diverse range of small toys and a collection of dress-up clothes can be brought into the area where Tess likes to sit. At times, a few peers in the toddler group can be encouraged to join Tess for short, structured play sessions in this area. At other times, this young girl and her teddy can be invited to join in or sit on the periphery of some small-group games.

Four to eight years

Daniel is in Year 1, has a diagnosis of Asperger's Syndrome and becomes extremely anxious when asked to participate in group learning activities. Daniel's strong interest in ships can be used to motivate, engage and make him more comfortable at learning centres. Visual supports and the use of choice boards can further support his in-class participation. Discussing and rehearsing a play plan prior to the lunch break can be used to foster outdoor play with a few classmates.

Differentiating instruction for the child

Differentiation is a critical element of inclusive pedagogy that enables early childhood educators to effectively support children with diverse learning needs. This type of instruction is particularly important in the early years because children present with very mixed readiness levels for learning. Differentiated instruction provides a means to shape and adjust learning experiences to maximise the likelihood of academic success and social emotional growth for individual learners. It also enables culturally responsive teaching by ensuring that group activities embrace the cultural backgrounds of all children in the group. In addition, differentiated instruction allows an educator to provide activities that safeguard against children becoming frustrated or overwhelmed while ensuring that learning experiences are engaging and challenging.

Tomlinson (2004, p. 188) describes differentiated instruction as 'ensuring that what a student learns, how he/she learns it, and how the students demonstrates what he/she has learned is a match for that student's readiness level, interests, and preferred mode of learning'. From this perspective, differentiated instruction guarantees a goodness of fit between the child's needs, learning and teaching. Goodness of fit is achieved through attention to two key elements: a planned system of organisation and management; and a delivery system for teaching and learning.

An effective planning system is at the heart of differentiation. To plan successfully, educators need to put in place a comprehensive but sustainable organisational and management system. The system can not only provide a positive and flexible context for teaching prosocial behaviours, but also help to structure the behavioural environment for learning. For example, a system can involve developing routines for giving directions, asking for help, going to the toilet, collecting and handing out materials, coming into and leaving the room, dealing with interruptions and transitioning to the next activity.

An effective delivery system is the vehicle for translating planning into effective classroom practice. A system of this kind is particularly helpful when an educator needs to determine how to differentiate and deliver instruction to a group of diverse learners. Child-specific information should be used to inform decisions about what to teach (content), how to teach (strategies) and what outcomes (product/s) should be targeted for individual children. The selection of particular strategies (teaching techniques, equipment and materials) for instruction should also be considered. Instruction can be differentiated and individualised using:

- multiple means of access (including technology)
- multiple ways of presenting content (including assessment)
- multiple levels of participation (from physical assistance to independence)
- multiple grouping techniques (including whole, small, individual, interest and independent)
- varying the depth of learning and the rate of learning
- varying instructional approaches, from child-centred learning, with acknowledging and facilitating to explicit instruction, with demonstrating and directing
- adjusting tasks (including breaking complicated tasks into smaller parts or reducing the number of steps)
- adjusting for response factors (for example, processing time, pointing instead of writing).

Examples of practice

Differentiated instruction allows for the planning and delivery of carefully tailored learning experiences to suit the learning needs of a particular child. Attention to the child's abilities, readiness skills, interests and learning style provide the starting point for matching curriculum content to learning and teaching.

Birth to four years

Maddy is a very bright three-year-old who is a proficient reader. Following collaborative discussions with her parents, it was decided Maddy's skills in literacy could be encouraged further by allowing her increased opportunities to read from a wide variety of books and electronic resources at the centre. In addition, working on individual literacy-based projects would allow her to challenge and extend her skills. Placing Maddy in a leadership role to read to a small group of peers was seen as another way of expanding her literacy experiences.

Four to eight years

Jake is a seven-year-old with physical impairment who experiences difficulties with both fine and gross motor activities. To support Jake's learning, recommendations from a private occupational therapist can be embedded into table top and outdoor activities at school. For example, Jake can be given extra time to complete any physical activity (including fine motor tasks such as writing and cutting), and have adequate rest breaks between these activities. Technological supports, such as a digital pen and an iPad, can also be used to assist his learning, and boost his confidence and self-esteem.

Using child progress data to improve learning and teaching

Another crucial aspect of learning and teaching in the early years is the evaluation of learning outcomes and achievements of children. Collecting information on child performance (such as child progress data) provides the starting point not only for measuring depth and rate of learner success but also for informing and improving educator practice. Ongoing child assessment enables this process of monitoring, review and evaluation to take place.

Data collection is an integral part of teaching. Educators need to spend time deciding what information about the child's learning should be gathered during instruction and how often this information-gathering should occur. Moreover, data collection needs to capture what the child knows and understands in multiple ways, using a mixture of formal and informal methods. When data are collected on a regular basis, child progress can be monitored continuously and learning needs can be considered carefully. Interpretation of child progress data provides direction for adjustments to the child's ongoing program of learning. It is the vehicle that allows the educator to better support the child's efforts and to teach for success. It also provides an 'index of professional accountability and serves as a vital step in the teaching/learning cycle' (Giangreco, 1998, p. 51).

In addition, child progress data should be used to understand and improve teaching. The interaction between child data and educator reflection provides the catalyst for new understandings about child learning and teaching practice. Effective reflection means moving beyond daily thinkings about children and their learning. To better understand and improve teaching and learning, effective reflection means reviewing child data and delving into precisely what the child did and did not learn, which strategies did and did not work, and which environmental supports helped and which didn't. Reflection of this nature allows for a realignment of teaching to better foster child learning in order to produce meaningful outcomes for the child.

Examples of practice

Learning is a dynamic process that needs to be systematically monitored throughout the teaching–learning cycle. Analysis of and reflection on child progress data enables both learning to inform teaching and teaching to inform learning.

Birth to four years

Lewis is a youngster who is experiencing difficulty in maintaining attention during most play-based activities. Early data collection has identified that even when Lewis is participating in a preferred activity such as outdoor play, his attention span is very brief, resulting in non-engagement or at best casual attention to engaging in play. This data can be used as a starting point to plan and implement guided water play activities in which an adult supports Lewis's participation in the activity with a selected peer. Ongoing monitoring of Lewis's concentration span during this five-minute activity, coupled with his specific responses to objects in the water and his interactions with his playmates, can provide valuable information about how to make adjustments to increase his engagement in this and some other related activities.

Four to eight years

In comparison to her Year 2 classmates, Holly presents with some behavioural concerns that impact negatively on her learning. Observations, anecdotal notes and a specific social-emotional competence checklist reveal that Holly's behaviour is more problematic just prior to transitioning to a new activity. The educator therefore decides to provide more structure for Holly during transition times. A visual chart highlighting transition times is designed for Holly, and use of the schedule is to be accompanied by a verbal reminder to Holly five minutes and then two minutes prior to each pending transition. The success of these supports can be evaluated through data collected at transition times for two days each week. Reflection on collected data should not only indicate whether Holly's behaviour is improving during transition periods, but should also provide pointers for supporting her behaviour across the school day.

Summary

- Improving practice means changing some ways of thinking and doing.
- The following 'to do' checklist related to differentiating for diversity may assist you to reflect on aspects covered in this chapter. It may also guide your actions as you adopt and adapt the seven recommended practices to suit your professional approach to teaching in the early years and the local community of children and families that you serve.
  - Scrutinise beliefs about children, learning and teaching and commit to the positives.
  - Consider all children in your care—get to know each one.
  - Observe the quality of daily interactions—build relationships and a community of learners.
  - Re-engineer the learning environment—provide socio-emotional, behavioural and physical supports.
  - Examine learning activities in action—ensure high levels of child engagement.
  - Review the effectiveness of instruction—adjust and personalise strategies.

‒   Collect ongoing child data, then interpret to enhance learning and teaching.

•   Finally, enjoy working with and learning from early years learners with diverse needs.

Discussion questions

15.1   What pre-existing beliefs do you hold that facilitate teaching and caring for early years learners with additional educational needs?

15.2   Why is it important to develop a relationship with every child in your care?

15.3   In what ways should an educator's teaching be adjusted to better suit a child's way of learning?

15.4   What is the difference between child participation and child engagement in activities?

15.5   How could you integrate the collection of child progress data into your everyday practice?

15.6   Reflect on your repertoire of existing teaching practices. List three new practices that you could use to better cater for young children with additional learning needs in your care.

References

Arthur, L., Beecher, B., Death, E., Dockett, S. and Farmer, S. (2012). *Programming and planning in early childhood settings*, 5th ed. Melbourne, Australia: Cengage Learning Australia.

Beamish, W., Bryer, F. & Wilson, L. (2001). Positive behavioural support: An example of practice in the early years. *Special Education Perspectives*, 9(1), 14–29.

Cook, R.E., Klein, M.D. & Tessier, A. (2008). *Adapting early childhood curricula for children in inclusive settings*, 7th ed. Upper Saddle River, NJ: Pearson.

Giangreco, M.F. (1998). *Quick-guides to inclusion 2: Ideas for educating students with disabilities*. Baltimore, MD: Paul H. Brookes.

Landy, S. (2009). *Pathways to competence: Encouraging healthy social and emotional development in young children*. Baltimore, MD: Paul H. Brookes.

McWilliam, R.A. & Casey, A.M. (2008). *Engagement of every child in the preschool classroom*. Baltimore, MD: Paul H. Brookes.

Sapon-Shevin, M. (1991). Cooperative learning in inclusive classrooms: Learning to become a community. *Cooperative Learning*, 12, 8–11.

Sims, M. (1999). What we believe is what we do. *Australian Journal of Early Childhood*, 24(2), 1–5.

Tomlinson, C.A. (2004). Sharing responsibility for differentiating instruction. *Roper Review*, 26(4), 188–91.

Wood, J.W. (2006). *Teaching students in inclusive settings: Adapting and accommodating instruction*, 5th ed. Columbus, OH: Pearson.

16

Gifted and talented children

*Susanne Garvis and
Donna Pendergast*

Introduction

In Queensland, Australia, education for gifted children has emerged as a key prerogative directed by the Gifted Framework (2004), with guidelines for students, educators, parents and principals. The Gifted Framework provides key identification strategies for selection of these students. Yet only very limited research has been conducted in the field of gifted education in the early years. Little is known about the types of programs that are being implemented as part of the Gifted Framework initiative. While numerous studies from the United States report on successful programs organised for preschool and preparatory age children, little is known about how these programs might operate if translated to an Australian context. There is also a gap in research about educators' knowledge of programs for gifted young children. Since many educators may be the sole provider of a gifted education program, it is important to explore individual beliefs and reflections to provide insight into early years gifted programs.

One goal of education is to enable gifted children to become autonomous learners. By supporting children who possess intellectual gifts in the early years, educators can provide them with opportunities, skills and dispositions to become creative individuals. While there is strong provision for gifted education in upper primary school and secondary school, only limited provision appears to exist in early years education (children aged from three to eight) within formal school settings. Even though a young learner aged five may be cognitively functioning at a Year 8 student level, enrichment from the classroom educator may be non-existent. Imagine learning a different letter from the alphabet each week when you can already read!

This chapter explores ways to empower young gifted children by providing enriching learning experiences in their formal schooling. Case studies are given of pull-out enrichment programs being implemented in the early years, with examples of creative writing shared by children. By providing opportunities for young gifted children, we create the conditions to enhance creativity that can later be drawn upon and maximised in adulthood. As creative adults, individuals contribute to the progress of understanding of society through either the evolution or revolution of ideas (Gardner, 1994). By supporting the elements that distinguish a creative individual (autonomy, expertise and a culture that is supportive of unconventional thought) in the early years, gifted children become empowered in their learning.

Characteristics of young gifted children

Consider that you are a Year 1 teacher with a six-year-old child in your class who has been attending for three months. You observe that when the child undertakes tasks, they are often hanging back, either not becoming engaged or flitting between a range of activities. The child does not make friends with the other children in your Year 1 class. If permitted, the child prefers to talk to adults or students in Year 7. You may consider that such a child has delayed development, but it is possible that the child might also be gifted. The child may not find the classroom activities stimulating, and prefers conversations with older thinkers compared with the conversations with Year 1 classmates. Or imagine you are the parent who is concerned because their child complains on the way home from school: 'Mummy, why do we have to keep doing the same things over and over and over again? It's so boring. The teacher knows I know it and we just keep doing it over and over. Could you please see if I can do something new?' Such a plea from a child may similarly point to a gifted young learner who is not being provided with opportunities to extend their learning.

It is usual for early years educators to wonder about the presence and identification of gifted young children in their classrooms. What are the characteristics of a young gifted child? How can an educator make sure they don't misinterpret the child's development? It is generally accepted that exceptionally gifted children exhibit a higher level of personal maturity in one or more areas than others of the same age, or others at similar stages of intellectual and emotional development (Gross, 2003). For example, some young children may begin drawing recognisable pictures or use elaborate language at two and a half years of age, or begin reading by three and read fluently by age four (Jackson, 1988, 2003). Recognising these gifts, and providing appropriate programs, are important for such children's development. According to Clark (2008), children's mental powers show rapid growth during the period from two to five years, with 'speech, mobility, and increasing social involvement all add[ing] to the fast-paced intellectual development' (2008, p. 102). It is because of this critical time period that Restak (1986, p. 91) proposes that 'the more complex the experience, the richer the environment, the more complex the brain'. Thus young gifted children benefit from appropriate gifted programs to help them reach their potential.

With an increase in women's participation in the workforce, and a subsequent increase in demand for early years formal education services, early years educators inevitably will come into contact with more gifted learners. According to Gagné's (1993) internationally accepted model of development, it is predicted that 15 per cent of children in every classroom are likely to be gifted. This means that in most early years classrooms with 24 students, at least four children in the class will be gifted. In a school of 100 children, at least fifteen students will be gifted. Given the paucity of school programs available for gifted learners, many young children travel through their schooling with limited extension of their knowledge and skills. Unfortunately, with limited opportunities for challenge, children may become disengaged from their education—and if this occurs, giftedness is unlikely to be extended into a talent.

Gifted education initiatives in Australia are organised and administered by each state and territory. Subsequently, different rules exist for early entry into formal schooling and acceleration in the early years. For example, under the current Queensland Department of Education and Training policy, children can only obtain early entry to the Preparatory Year (children generally aged five) if they have been enrolled previously in an education system in another state or territory, or in another country (Queensland Department of Education and Training, 2008a). However, early entry into Year 1 is allowed provided the child displays appropriate aptitude, ability, social and emotional competence, physical development and knowledge and understanding (Queensland Department of Education and Training, 2008b).

Given the divergence in state and territory provisions for gifted education, it is important that early years educators take an advocacy approach to gifted education. Schools can organise gifted education programs in different ways, which might include:

- a selective class for gifted young children
- after-school activities for the enrichment of gifted young children
- enrichment clusters for a group of young children with a common interest.

In the last of these options, the students meet with an adult who is an expert in the area for a few hours a week (known as the pull-out program). The adult scaffolds in-depth learning in the chosen subject-matter and works closely with the children.

While these different programs may have specified learning outcomes for the students, the foundations of each of the programs will be the same. These include the characteristics of developing autonomy, recognising and nurturing the potential of the young child and developing domain expertise. The foundation of characteristics are identified as the core for maximising creativity in individuals, leading to progression in society. Each of these three aspects will now be explored for the early years learner.

Autonomy

Autonomy is an important goal of gifted education. Once a student has been able to master a domain, they will work actively to develop that domain. Educators of gifted students are responsible for supporting young children to become masters of the domain in which they display giftedness. Autonomy is an important characteristic of adult creative individuals: creativity in new domains requires a high degree of autonomy. The importance of autonomy in creative work is evident in the case studies of seven 'creators of the modern era' who were used by Gardner (1994) to develop profiles of an exemplary creator. According to Gardner (1994, p. 156), creative individuals are marked by two contrasting trends:

A tendency to question every assumption and to attempt to strike out on one's own as much as possible, and a countervailing tendency to exhaust a domain, to probe more systematically, deeply, and comprehensively than anyone has ever probed before.

Autonomy enables individuals to generate creative products. It involves elements of expertise, thinking and problem-solving, reflectivity and a sceptical disposition towards existing ideas. To achieve autonomy, educators in the early years must support and scaffold gifted children in each of these elements. Part of the support includes demonstrating individual care and recognition of potential to establish a risk-free environment (Csikszentmihalyi, 1996). Young gifted children are often intellectually isolated in their classrooms, as they are rarely challenged by classmates. They may be less likely to contribute ideas in group discussion in classrooms, especially if their thinking and problem-solving skills are more developed than those of their peers. It is important that educators provide investigative activities that are multilayered to encourage different levels of problem-solving.

In Figure 16.1, we outline a program for preparatory students that was designed around sharing stories. The class consisted of 22 preparatory students in an enrichment cluster. In this case, the interest area was creative writing and storytelling. Reis et al. (1998) emphasise three principles of enrichment teaching and learning: (1) each student is different; (2) learning is more meaningful when students learn content and process while solving a real problem; and (3) whereas some formal instruction is necessary, a major goal is promoting knowledge and thinking skills

Figure 16.1   Enrichment cluster: Creative writing and storytelling

Case study: Creative storytelling with children aged five years

The enrichment program for children aged five years was designed for two hours a week over a four-week period, with a focus on creative storytelling and a story circle. The goal of the sessions was to encourage 'quiet' students to become part of a community of learners to share ideas. Since starting formal schooling, many of the students had lost their voice and did not share during group sessions, although they were recognised as being capable of doing so. Story circle was a time at the end of each session where every child would show an element of the story on which they had been working. Children sat in a circle on the floor with the educator, who took on the role of facilitator of conversation and encouraged children to ask questions about each other's work. Initially, the children were reluctant to talk in the group. A 'talking stick' was introduced, with only the student who held the stick permitted to talk. The students became very excited about holding the 'talking stick', and soon overcame their reluctance to contribute. After some time, the children began to depend on one another for ideas in their stories, and to support their possible plotlines. This emerged only after the children felt comfortable that they were in a 'risk-free' environment. By the end of the four-week program, the young children were actively involved in sharing their stories, supporting each storyteller and providing critical feedback.

via the application of what students have learned—they construct their own meaningfulness. These principles formed the basis of the enrichment cluster.

Recognition of potential

When creative individuals reflect on their childhoods, it is typical for them to recount the significant impact of key persons who provided support for and encouragement of their areas of giftedness. This includes educators who were sensitive and perceptive during the early years of schooling. Csikszentmihalyi (1996, p. 174) suggests that educators support children in two ways:

> First, the teachers noticed the student, believed in his or her abilities and *cared* [emphasis in original]. Second, the teacher showed care by giving the child extra work to do, greater challenges than the rest of the class received.

In the early years, educators play an essential role in supporting young gifted children, both educationally and emotionally. The key to supporting young gifted children is to provide opportunities where young children can become self-assured, engage in thinking and develop ideas.

One of the major problems with gifted education programs is that educators frequently incorrectly identify those children with gifts. This is a well recognised concern in gifted education: students may not perform in ways that reflect their potential, due to boredom and disengagement—hence a range of identification processes should be utilised. Possible identification tools to be used include:

- tests of cognitive/intellectual ability
- parent, educator or student nomination
- checklists for parents and educators developed by Michael Sayler (1994)
- the Coolabah Dynamic Assessment Model for children from diverse backgrounds (Chaffey & Bailey, 2003)
- the Harslett rating scale for teachers for intellectually gifted Aboriginal students (Harslett, 1993)
- interviews
- observation of performance
- anecdotal evidence.

Overall, Csikszentmihalyi's (1996) second element—caring about and acting on this information—is the most important aspect for the recognition of potential.

Developing domain expertise

Domain expertise is created when an individual has prolonged engagement with a domain of knowledge, is able to develop thinking skills and is enculturated into the practice of the domain. Skilled thinking is important for the development of expertise (Ericksson & Hastie, 1994). It is vital for educators of young gifted children to build awareness of the support needed for children to develop thinking beyond 'school thinking' to 'real-world thinking' (Galotti, 1989). To support young gifted children to develop thinking beyond 'school thinking', educators need to provide authentic learning experiences that are linked to the real world. Problems need to be relevant to the young child's interests and should provide opportunities for thinking outside of the norm. Good thinking involves questioning of assumptions and consideration of alternative possibilities.

The following case study examines another successful enrichment program in Australia. It provides insight into ways the educator has acknowledged the foundations of gifted education (autonomy, recognition of potential and developing domain expertise) for supporting young gifted children in their learning.

Figure 16.2   Foundations of gifted education in action

Case study: Educator reflections on an early years enrichment program

This early years multi-age gifted classroom in Brisbane caters for 25 students from Years 1–4, who meet one day a week in the school library. For the entire day, students work together and individually on various learning activities, using problem-based learning as the core approach. In the context of the gifted program, problem-based learning provides endless opportunities for gifted student learning and engagement. It incorporates many of the principles of differentiated curriculum, with some of the newer constructivist notions of learning and curriculum development. Students are placed in authentic problem situations in which there is insufficient information to comprehend and solve the problem. This approach engages students in authentic learning activities based upon professional problems of practice as the starting point, stimulus and focus for learning. The problems allow students to function and participate as members of a community of practice. There are many advantages for students engaged in problem-based learning, including the ability to construct an extensive and flexible knowledge base, develop effective problem-solving skills, build self-directed, lifelong learning skills, become effective collaborators and become intrinsically motivated to learn.

The daily timetable is shown in Figure 16.3.

Figure 16.3   Daily timetable for gifted program

Time	Activity
9.00 a.m.–9.20 a.m.	Expert for the Week (one student a week shares their expert knowledge in a presentation to the class)
9.20 a.m.–9.40 a.m.	Round Table Business Meeting of Group Tasks (What are we doing today? How is everyone going?)
9.40 a.m.–10.40 a.m.	Group tasks/work (group work on the shared project)
10.40 a.m.–11 a.m.	Morning tea
11.00 a.m.–11.10 a.m.	Thinking games and strategies
11.10 a.m.–11.40 a.m.	Focused learning
11.40 a.m.–12.40 p.m.	Individual tasks/work
12.40 p.m.–1.45 p.m.	Lunch and sport
1.45 p.m.–2.30 p.m.	Individual project
2.30 p.m.–3.00 p.m.	Reflections in different forms

Individual project

After sport, students need a quieter activity to help them refocus. During this time, students can work on their own individual interest area—one about which they would like to know more. Students can negotiate any area they like. Through guidance, students are asked to present their individual project at the end of the term, during Project Celebration Day. All students are asked to speak for ten minutes about their interest area and show/create a visual stimulus. Typical projects include the following:

- One student made a movie and reflected on what it was like to script, direct and edit it.
- Another student explored and built a mechanical bulldozer.
- A third student invented a solar panel–heated dog kennel.

These examples show that students are able to create and build their own knowledge. They then have to present this knowledge to other students. Students enjoy being given the opportunity to explore any interest area they like, and love being able to present it to the rest of the class.

Reflections in different forms

At the end of each day, students make notes in a reflection journal. For 20 minutes, students complete reflections about their own learning. Each week, students are asked to express their reflections in different modes, including writing in a diary entry format, fairytales, poetry, cartoons, narratives, storyboards, sketching and painting. At the end of reflection time, different students every week are asked to share their journey of learning so far. Students take on a presenter role, with other students becoming audience members. During this time, the audience's job is to listen to the reflection and to provide a response to and connection with their own journey in learning. At the end of the semester, all students share their learning journey.

Summary

- The field of education for gifted children in the early years is in need of advocacy.
- If you suspect a young child is gifted, your role is to empower the young child to become an autonomous learner.
- By understanding the foundations of gifted programs (intellectual autonomy, developing domain expertise and recognising the potential of the child), you can provide a supportive environment that creates the conditions to maximise creativity.
- When a gifted child reaches adulthood, they may become a creative individual, contributing to the progress of society through new ideas. As an early years educator, you will realise that you helped this adult reach their creative potential by supporting their gifts in the early years classroom.

Discussion questions

16.1 How could you support a young gifted child in their learning?

16.2 Conduct a comparison of the state and territory entry and acceleration regulations for children in the early years. Why do the rules differ?

16.3 Why is it important for an educator to recognise the characteristics of creative individuals?

16.4 What can we learn from others who work with gifted young children?

16.5 Why should we advocate for gifted education in the early years?

References

Chaffey, G.W. & Bailey, S.B. (2003). The use of dynamic testing to reveal high academic potential and underachievement in a culturally different population. *Gifted Education International, 18*, 124–38.

Clark, B. (2008). *Growing up Gifted: Developing the potential of children at home and at school*, 7th ed. Englewood Cliffs, NJ: Prentice-Hall.

Csikszentmihalyi, M. (1996). *Creativity*. New York: HarperCollins.

Ericksson, K.A. & Hastie, R. (1994). Approaches to thinking. In R.J. Sternberg (ed.), *Thinking and problem solving* (pp. 37–79). San Diego: Academic Press.

Gagné, F. (1993). Constructs and models pertaining to exceptional human abilities. In K.A. Heller, F.J. Monks & A.H. Passow (eds), *International handbook of research and development of giftedness and talent* (pp. 63–85). Oxford: Pergamon Press.

Galotti, K. (1989). Approaches to studying forma and everyday reasoning. *Psychological Bulletin, 105*(3), 331–51.

Gardner, H. (1994). The creators' patterns. In M.A. Boden (ed.), *Dimensions of creativity* (pp. 143–58). Cambridge, MA: MIT Press.

Gross, M.U.M. (2003). *Exceptionally gifted children*, 2nd ed. New York: Routledge.

Harslett, M.G. (1993). The identification of gifted Aboriginal children. Unpublished PhD thesis, University of Western Australia.

Jackson, N.E. (1988). Precocious reading ability: What does it mean? *Gifted Child Quarterly, 32*, 196–9.

—— (2003). Young gifted children. In N. Colangelo & G.A. Davis (eds), *Handbook of gifted education*, 3rd ed. (pp. 470–82). Boston: Allyn & Bacon.

Queensland Department of Education and Training (2008a). School admission and profession age 1875–2008. Retrieved 15 November 2010 from <http://education.qld.gov.au/library/edhistory/topics/age.html>.

—— (2008b). *Early entry to Year 1: Parent information*. Retrieved 15 November 2010 from <http://education.qld.gov.au/strategic/eppr/students/smspr007/pieey1.doc>.

Reis, S.M., Gentry, M. & Maxfield, L.R. (1998). The application of enrichment clusters to teachers' classroom practices. *Journal for Education of the Gifted, 21*, 310–24.

Restak, R. (1986). *The infant mind*. New York: Doubleday.

Sayler, M. (1994). *Investigation of talented students*. Denton, TX: University of North Texas.

PART IV

Assessment practices for the early years

17

Assessment and culture

Karuppiah Nirmala

Introduction

Assessment is an important aspect of teaching and learning. The purpose of assessment should be to support the holistic development of the child and to focus on building the child's confidence and the desire to learn. Assessment methods should support both the cognitive and the overall development of the child, and provide qualitative feedback on knowledge and skills in both academic and non-academic areas. In this way, reforms of assessment practices to ensure that there is both *assessment of learning* (summative) and *assessment for learning* (formative) are accepted as the standard to which we should aspire.

However, standardised or high-stakes testing is still a dominant part of the assessment landscape in many countries, including Singapore, Hong Kong and South Korea. In Australia, a renewed focus on high stakes summative assessment has recently been reignited. Hence there remains an opportunity for a stronger focus on formative or alternative assessments that are authentic, realistic and meaningful in these countries. Assessment should be conceptualised as a tool to support and improve teaching and learning. In this chapter, the experience of one country's journey is included to exemplify this.

In order to support the holistic development of young children, educators need to be empowered with suitable assessment tools that would enable them to capture information of a non-standardised nature, and help them understand the strengths, weaknesses and needs of children. This feedback also needs to be communicated constructively and effectively to both children and parents. In addition, educators need to implement these new initiatives without a fall in performance standards. They would also have to adopt culturally responsive assessment practices in order to meet the needs of young children. In the face of these challenging tasks, early years educators need to rethink their approaches towards teaching, learning and assessment.

What is assessment?

Assessment is a broad term that refers to all types of information collected and analysed, which is used for making decisions and providing feedback on the effectiveness of teaching and learning. In other words, 'assessment is a process that has a purpose, a method to achieve the purpose and an outcome', and 'the method usually involves using tools to collect the data, and specific knowledge to process the data' (Woo & Gao, 2008, p. 198).

Assessment is sometimes confused with other terms, such as 'evaluation', 'measurement' and 'tests'. Although all these terms are related, each is distinct. Evaluation is the process by which educators make specific value judgements about pupils and their work; measurement occurs when pupils' work is quantified or given a score; and tests involve formal, systematic procedures or instruments for measuring pupils' knowledge and skills (Tan et al., 2003). As these terms have different meanings and purposes they should not be used interchangeably.

With the diversity of young people in our education system and society, educators can no longer adopt a 'one-size-fits-all' approach and ignore the different cultures of the pupils in classrooms and schools. Educators must now design or select culturally responsive curricula, pedagogies and assessments that are fair and non-discriminatory against pupils of any culture.

Purpose of assessment

The purpose of assessing children varies depending on the age of the child. For example, infants and toddlers are assessed to determine whether they are developing normally or show signs of delay and require assistance or intervention; preschool children are assessed to determine whether they can be admitted to a preschool program or primary school; and primary school children are assessed to determine their achievements during a school year or whether they will be promoted to the next level. However, if these assessments are not appropriate or administered properly, they could harm instead of benefit the children concerned.

Assessment in classrooms has many purposes, which generally include the following:

- to identify a starting point for an educator in a new class
- to group pupils according to a common need
- to identifying pupils' strengths, weaknesses and needs
- to report at the parent, school and governmental levels, and
- to evaluate the effectiveness of a particular curriculum or program (Fehring, 2010).

Educators can use assessment as a tool to find out more about their pupils' progress and learning in the following ways:

- as an accountability or a reporting tool for *assessment of learning*
- as an instructional tool for *assessment for learning*, and
- as a learning tool for *assessment as learning.*

Assessment of learning occurs when educators use evidence of pupils' learning to make judgements about pupil achievement against preset goals, criteria or standards. *Assessment for learning* occurs when educators use information about pupils to inform their teaching. Finally, a*ssessment as learning* occurs when pupils reflect on and monitor their progress to inform their future learning goals. While *assessment of learning* is carried out at the end of instruction, *assessment for learning* and *assessment as learning* are carried out while instruction and learning are taking place.

When assessment is used as a reporting or accountability tool, it usually involves standardised or high-stakes testing. This is used to monitor by comparing results of pupils of certain ages and stages to position achievement and to identify changes in standards. The cumulative results are also used to evaluate educators, schools and even local authorities.

The use of such assessments for such reporting and accountability purposes can put considerable pressure on both educators and pupils, forcing them to produce 'results'; they also force schools to concentrate on teaching in the areas that are tested (e.g. literacy, numeracy and science). Hence educators focus only on preparing pupils to take tests, resulting in pupils not understanding the rationale behind tasks and activities, as well as educators feeling a loss of fulfilment and autonomy (Hall & Ozerk, 2008). Cognitive development takes centre stage, resulting in a lack of focus on social and emotional development, both of which are a part of the holistic development of the child.

Additionally, traditional assessments have a natural bias toward emphasising certain knowledge or skills, and may not be suitable for pupils of all cultures. Standardised tests measure a limited range of abilities and are also limited in making long-term predictions of pupils' learning. Educators therefore have to consider external factors such as pupils' culture and language when interpreting test scores in order to avoid biased views about their pupils' abilities, achievements and progress. Educators must also be mindful about misinterpreting or searching for signs of delay when none may exist.

In order to make good decisions and judgements, educators need information about their pupils and *assessment for learning* helps provide that information. As such, *assessment for learning* turns assessment into a process designed to support and increase pupil learning (Stiggins, 2005). Different types of assessment are available, and can be used to address some of the concerns, issues and problems related to assessing diverse children.

Types of assessment

Assessments such as standardised (paper-and-pencil) tests or examinations, worksheets, practice papers, spelling tests and essays have been—and in some cases still are—widely used in schools all over the world. Currently, there are alternative assessments that are more authentic and meaningful, and that focus more on processes rather than just products. These alternative assessments include observations, checklists, rubrics, self/peer/group assessments, projects, presentations and portfolios. However, alternative assessments are generally time-consuming and involve much effort in terms of planning, implementing, evaluating and documenting.

Nevertheless, alternative assessments are more useful than traditional classroom assessments for a number of reasons:

- Pupils are involved in creating work that is related more to real world applications.
- Pupils tend to use higher order thinking and more problem-solving skills.
- Pupils are actively involved in socially constructing their knowledge (Tan et al., 2003).

The link between teaching and learning is therefore more visible and stronger in alternative assessments than in traditional classroom assessments. Additionally, there are opportunities for pupils to incorporate their own personal and cultural experiences in their work.

There are three types of assessment: formative, summative and diagnostic. *Formative assessment* involves educators gathering information to decide where pupils are in their learning, where they need to go and how best they might get there. *Summative assessment* involves using information—usually from paper-and-pencil tests and examinations—to report on pupils at a particular time. Finally, *diagnostic assessment* involves gathering information to assess where children stand in terms of their existing learning abilities and needs.

While summative assessment takes place at the end of instruction to find out how well educators have taught and how well pupils have learnt, formative assessment takes place as teaching and learning are still going on. Diagnostic assessment takes place even before teaching occurs, in order to identify the prerequisite knowledge and skills that a pupil needs to meet an instructional objective or to identify the causes for a pupil's difficulties in meeting an instructional objective.

Assessment of pupils can be either formal or informal. Formal assessments are prepared in advance, and usually involve a disruption in the teaching and learning process—for example, paper-and-pencil tests, systematic observations and portfolios. Informal assessments, on the other hand, are usually spontaneous and carried out during the teaching and learning process—for example, conversations, interactions, questioning and cursory observations. Information gathered about pupils can be classified as *criterion-referenced* or *norm-referenced assessment*. While criterion-referenced assessment shows student's progress in their knowledge and skills relative to a pre-established standard or their previous standard, norm-referenced assessment shows their progress in their knowledge and skills relative to their peers. Standardised tests are usually norm-referenced, and are used to sort pupils according to their scores or grades. While standardised tests may have a powerful and useful place in society for such things as placement, grouping and uniform comparison across a large number of students, they should not be used excessively.

Assessment methods meant for older children should not be used for younger children, as this may result in an inaccurate assessment of the students. Assessment methods that focus on accountability (assessment of learning), or on comparison and ranking (norm-referenced) should also not be used for young children, as these methods are not appropriate and will not support their growth, development and progress. In fact, excessive use of standardised testing will place even older children—especially those from low socio-economic status families and minority populations—at a disadvantage.

Multiple sources of data are desirable, and assessments should give a complete and accurate picture of a child's progress (Wortham, 2008). However, educators must familiarise themselves with the different types of assessment and their purposes in order to select the most appropriate assessment instruments and methods for young children. Educators must also ensure that assessments are 'fair for all children' by taking into account the effects of culture, language, disability and speed of development (Wortham, 2008).

Interestingly, assessment can be viewed from a socio-cultural perspective. Cowie and Carr (2009) believe that assessment needs to be distributed across people (children and their educators, families and peers), places (the classroom and its features, structures and atmosphere) and things (artefacts and materials) in order to build a community of learners and educators, develop competence and competent learners, and support continuity in learning. Educators can make assessment culturally responsive by providing opportunities for practice and using their native language. Culturally responsive assessment should also extend beyond the classroom level to the school and national levels. Policy-makers must ensure that the tests, procedures and policies are not biased, and that they provide opportunities for pupils of different cultures to learn and succeed.

The three principles of assessment are:

- Assessment should benefit the child.
- Assessment should involve the child and family.
- Assessment should be fair for all children (Wortham, 2012).

Summative assessment

Traditionally, assessment of pupil learning has been carried out at the end of each topic or course of study, to assess and evaluate the extent to which pupils have understood and retained the information. However, retention of information is often based on rote learning and memorisation rather than understanding and internalisation of the information (Stiggins, 2005).

Information gathered from such summative assessment is used to make judgements about pupil learning and decisions affecting their promotion, retention, placement, grouping, scholarships and so on. This information does not support learning because it is not used to make changes to teaching and learning. However, if this information *is* used to make changes to teaching and learning, then summative assessment becomes formative.

Formative assessment

Formative assessment has been used successfully in classrooms in many parts of the world. It refers to the assessment of pupil progress and understanding to identify their learning needs and to adjust teaching accordingly. There are three components of formative assessment:

- communication of expectancies and success criteria
- collection of information, and
- regulation of learning (Council of Ministers of Education, Canada, 2005).

There are also three conditions for formative assessment:

- Pupils must know what is expected of them.
- Pupils and educators must know if pupils will succeed.
- The educator must prepare a range of learning strategies to ensure that all pupils progress. (Council of Ministers of Education, Canada, 2005. p. 8)

Formative assessment can be used by educators to separate pupils into groups or individually in order to better cater to their different learning interests, needs, abilities, styles and speeds. Although formative assessment can be either formal or informal it is generally less formal, and helps educators to guide or monitor pupil learning while it is still in progress, as well as plan what and how to teach.

For formative assessment to be effective, educators must provide high-quality, accurate and timely feedback. Feedback is part of the 'deliberate act of teaching', which includes 'modelling, prompting, questioning, giving feedback, telling, explaining and directing' (Parr & Limbrick, 2010, p. 587). Feedback given to pupils must be specific in order to give the child accurate information on where they are at, and lead to the pupil doing something to improve (Brookhart et al., 2010); it should also show how best to close the gap between the pupil's present performance and the desired improvement in a safe environment (Parr & Limbrick, 2010).

Communicating feedback to students seems to encourage metacognition, which enables positive student outcomes as students are more motivated to learn through self-monitoring and are more engaged in the learning process. It also seems to encourage the student to take ownership over their own development, which enables the growth of self-discipline—a key disposition required for lifelong learning. Educators who see these positive results also end up feeling motivated themselves, and as a result begin to appreciate a more balanced perspective instead of 'simply teaching in order for pupils to score well on standardized tests' (Parr & Limbrick, 2010, p. 54). However, in order to give more specific feedback, educators have to keep more detailed records. Record-keeping is a standard part of formative assessment.

Formative assessment takes two forms: *performance assessment* and *portfolio assessment*. These can be used to monitor, record and communicate the progress of pupils.

Performance assessment

Performance assessment examines pupil performance in a natural setting (such as a classroom, playground or home), using clearly defined criteria that are realistic and meaningful. Performance assessment can be used to assess pupil knowledge, reasoning, performance skills, products and dispositions.

For performance-based assessment to be effective, educators need to be able to design the task carefully and require pupils to integrate a wide range of knowledge and skills, creativity, originality and aesthetics. Educators would also have to ensure that pupils are clear about the following:

- the skills and knowledge required to complete the task
- what is going to be assessed—the product or processes involved in creating the product
- how realistic or meaningful the criteria of assessment are, and
- the assessment targets and procedures (Gronlund, 1993).

Hence educators must have the knowledge and skills to design, develop and use performance assessment effectively. However, they must also ensure that the performance tasks selected are appropriate for pupils of diverse cultures and languages.

There are two components of performance assessment: the performance task itself and a rubric for scoring that performance task. The task could require pupils to make something (e.g. a mask), produce a report (e.g. read and write or present a report on the history of masks) or demonstrate a process (e.g. search for information and organise that information to write a report or make a presentation), and could be individual, group or part-individual and part-group based (Nitko & Brookhart, 2007). In order to assess these tasks, educators would need to collect data through the use of various instruments such as observations, rubrics, checklists and rating scales.

Observations

Educators often observe children at different times and in different contexts or settings. However, these observations may not always be carried out or recorded in a systematic manner. A systematic observation involves the process of specifying the criteria or dimensions of an acceptable performance, and then observing and recording notes (Eggen & Kauchak, 2010). These notes must then be organised, analysed, interpreted and communicated to pupils and parents as feedback, or used to plan or make recommendations for future teaching and learning.

Educators can also use systematic observation to assess the holistic development of infants, preschool and primary school children, and to understand the processes that these children use to learn new knowledge rather than simply knowing the information *per se*. Observations provide educators with a good opportunity to get to know and understand the child as a unique individual rather than as a member of a group. However, educators must possess good observation skills as well as skills to make sense of and use the observations appropriately. Educators must also be aware of their own biases and use an unbiased cultural lens when observing young children.

There are many observational techniques that educators can adopt, and some of the common ones are running records, anecdotal records, time sampling and event sampling. While a running record involves a written description of the child's behaviour—exactly what the child says and does in sequence—an anecdotal record is a brief account of a selected incident or behaviour noted down soon after it occurs. Sampling observations are those in which examples of behaviours are recorded as they occur (event sampling) or at previously decided time intervals (time sampling).

The choice of observation method depends very much on the purpose of observation, as well as the observer's skills and their availability. The observer would need to carefully analyse and present the observation notes based on appropriate developmental milestones, theories of child development and current research, as well as consider the cultural context in which the observations were made. The observer would also need to be objective and prevent any personal bias from influencing both their observation and their analysis of the data. However, relying completely on observation alone may not yield desired results; observations should be coupled with instruments such as checklists, rating scales, rubrics and samples of children's work (Gullo, 2005).

Rubrics

Educators assess students' work on a regular basis. They often use rubrics to guide them in assessing or judging the quality of essays as well as performance tasks such as presentations, projects or products. A rubric is a scoring scale that describes criteria or dimensions for grading assignments, and it can help to maintain consistency and increase reliability in assessing each pupil's work (Eggen & Kauchak, 2010). These criteria or dimensions for grading assignments can be found in a checklist or rating scale.

Checklists

During assessment or systematic observations, educators can check off the desired criteria or dimensions in a checklist instead of describing them in notes. This checklist can be then used to determine whether a pupil did or did not meet a criterion or dimension of an acceptable performance.

Rating scales

Rating scales contain written descriptions of criteria or dimensions of an acceptable performance, and scales of values on which each criteria or dimension is rated (Eggen & Kauchak, 2010). Rating scales can be constructed in descriptive, graphic or numerical formats. Rating scales are similar to rubrics in their scoring, but allow for more precise information to be gathered; they are also similar to checklists in their presentation, but allow for more specific feedback to be given to pupils and parents.

Portfolio assessment

A portfolio is a collection of a student's work that is reviewed using a set of preset criteria to make judgements about a student, curriculum or program over time. It is used to showcase a pupil's *best works*, which are carefully and deliberately selected, or to show the pupil's growth, development and *progress* through work examples and samples with comments over a given period. A student's work can comprise activity sheets, artwork, journal entries, photographs, audiotapes, videotapes and so on.

For preschool and primary school children, the portfolio could track the child's development in a single subject area or across different subject areas (such as art, maths, science and language) in the key domains (such as gross and fine motor, concept, language and socio-emotional development).

The portfolio involves both the educator and pupil in the preparation, collection and organisation processes. The portfolio is assessed by the educator using a rubric that is crafted carefully to serve its purpose. Hence the portfolio is a more comprehensive presentation of information on the pupil's learning and progress than just presenting scores and grades to parents.

It should be noted here that the portfolio is not a 'scrapbook' or 'dumping ground' for the pupil's achievements and work (Nitko & Brookhart, 2007). For both the pupil's *best works portfolio* and *progress portfolio* to be effective, the educator must have good knowledge, skills and experience in both crafting and assessing the work. The educator must also ensure that the portfolio is prepared and assessed in an unbiased way, and benefits the child in their development and learning. These days, educators can share information with children and their parents on a more regular basis through electronic portfolios.

Case study 17.1: Investigating one cultural setting for assessment

In 2008, a Primary Education Review and Implementation (PERI) Committee was convened to create a dynamic lower primary education system in Singapore. The PERI Committee stressed that 'primary education should be about developing well-balanced and confident children who enjoy learning as they build strong fundamentals in both knowledge and skills during their foundation years' (MOE, 2009, p. 1). Although standardised testing will remain a part of the assessment landscape in Singapore, more formative or alternative assessment will be introduced in the lower primary years (Ng, 2009).

As a result of the PERI Report, a funded research project was carried out to identify educators', parents' and children's perceptions of existing or traditional assessments and alternative assessments in kindergarten and lower primary classrooms in Singapore by three researchers—Karuppiah Nirmala, Joanna Tay-Lim and Mercy Karuniah Jesuvadian—at the National Institute of Education, Singapore. Findings from this study could possibly be used to inform policy, training and practice regarding assessment in the kindergarten and lower primary classrooms.

Interviews with 24 educators, 128 pupils and 126 parents were conducted utilising a semi-structured questionnaire and work samples of the pupils in the areas of literacy and numeracy. Observations were also carried out in the classrooms to gain an understanding of the teaching and learning processes as well as to identify the needs of educators and pupils. Data collected from the various sources were then analysed and discussed under the following categories: variety of tasks, purposes, frequency, evaluation, feedback, use of results, impact on pupils, impact on pedagogy and documentation. Here, a summary of the key findings are presented.

The most popular notion held was to equate existing assessment with formal assessment or standardised assessment, which included worksheets, practice papers, spelling tests, compositions and examinations; and alternative assessment with informal assessments, which included show and tell, games, quizzes, field trips, learning centres, projects and hands-on activities. It seems that the participants had a somewhat fragmented and limited understanding of assessment and the different types of assessment tasks. However, they generally were more familiar with the types and frequency of standardised assessment tasks than alternative assessment tasks. Although educators had more knowledge than parents and pupils about alternative assessments, this knowledge appeared to be partial only. For example, most educators perceived that observations were merely 'moving around' the class to observe the students. None made reference to the use of observation techniques to present a more systematic record of children's development and progress.

Overall, the participants were able to distinguish the purpose of assessment practices: assessment of (summative), for (formative and diagnostic) and as learning. Dominant purposes prevailed for both the standardised and alternative assessment practices. However, the participants were able to cite more rationales for using alternative assessments rather than standardised assessments. This was a positive sign, indicating that they saw greater potential in the use of alternative assessments for the holistic development and assessment of the child. However, despite recognising the importance and benefits of alternative assessments, most parents were highly apprehensive about the changes in the modes of assessment in lower primary classrooms, which they believed would not prepare their children for Primary One (for parents of kindergarten) or for the school examinations (CAs and SAs) and national examinations (PSLE) later (for parents of lower primary children).

It is believed that, with proper documentation of children's learning, parents could be convinced that alternative assessments can do more than just prepare their children for examinations—that is, alternative assessments can also prepare their children for life and support the holistic development of their children.

Although the majority of educators were supportive of the use of alternative assessments, some of the educators expressed concerns over the practicality of implementation. Some of the concerns included the size of current classes being too big for effective facilitation, and that parents' receptiveness may not be forthcoming if alternative assessment tasks did not contribute to the grading. It was also believed that more effort and time were required for constant monitoring of the tasks; more cooperation was required among the educators; and alternative assessment tasks competed for curriculum time. These apprehensions seemed to arise from the current classroom conditions. A shift to alternative assessment practices would require adjustments to these conditions by providing greater support to educators, including equipping of educators with the necessary knowledge and skills to craft and facilitate the tasks as well as to document the students' learning; creating awareness among parents; building team support within the level; and reducing class sizes.

Summary

- Assessment practices that are culturally relevant and sensitive have an important place in the teaching and learning experience of young people.
- The world is increasingly monocultural in the sense that a wide number of heritages, belief systems and religious affiliations may be present in a typical gathering of children in the early years, making diversity the norm.
- Reforms of assessment practices to ensure there is both *assessment of learning* (summative) and *assessment for learning* (formative) is now accepted as the standard to which we should be aiming.
- The study shared in this chapter points to the suggestion that traditional assessment practices may be intimidating for the kindergarten and lower primary pupils in Singapore, as they are aware that the adults (both educators and parents) use the results to make judgements on their capabilities. It is timely that Singapore's Ministry of Education (MOE) is changing the current landscape in the lower primary classrooms by implementing the PERI's recommendations for holistic assessment, which will focus on the building of pupils' confidence and the desire to learn.
- However, there are also shortcomings with alternative assessment. Issues related to bias, culture and diversity must be considered when interpreting and evaluating data collected.

Discussion questions

17.1 Do you think young children should be assessed? If so, how early do you think they should be assessed? Why?

17.2 What is your understanding of holistic development of young children? Do you think young children should be assessed in all areas of development, or only in particular areas of development in the early years? Why?

17.3 Why do you think it is important for educators to adopt culturally responsive assessment practices with young children?

17.4 How can children and parents be involved effectively in the assessment process?

17.5 What sort of knowledge, skills and experiences do you think educators would need in order to make good decisions and judgements about teaching and learning?

References

Brookhart, S. M., Moss, C. M., & Long, B. A. (2010). Teacher inquiry into formative assessment practices in remedial reading classrooms. Assessment in Education: Principles, Policy & Practice, 17(1), 41–58.

Council of Ministers of Education, Canada (2005). *OECD study on enhancing learning through formative assessment and the expansion of teacher repertoires: Canadian report*. Retrieved 20 January 2012 from <www.cmec.ca/Publications/Lists/Publications/Attachments/78/OECD_Formative.en.pdf>.

Cowie, B. & Carr, M. (2009). The consequences of sociocultural assessment. In A. Anning., J. Cullen. & M. Fleer, *Early childhood education: Society & culture*, 2nd ed. London: Sage.

Eggen, P. & Kauchak, D. (2010). *Educational psychology: Windows to the classroom*. Englewood Cliffs, NJ: Pearson Education.

Fehring, H. (2010). Assessment in 2010 and beyond: an Australian perspective. Paper presented at the National Institute of Education, Singapore.

Gronlund, N. (1993). *How to make better achievement tests and assessments*. Needham Heights, MA: Allyn & Bacon.

Gullo, D.F. (2005). *Understanding assessment and evaluation in early childhood education*. New York: Teachers College Press.

Hall, K. & Ozerk, K. (2008). *Primary curriculum and assessment: England and other countries*. Primary Review Research Survey 3/1. Cambridge: University of Cambridge, Faculty of Education.

Harlen, W. (2007). *The quality of learning: Assessment alternatives for primary education*. Primary Review Research Survey 3/4. Cambridge: University of Cambridge, Faculty of Education.

Ministry of Education (MOE) (2009). 'Strong fundamentals for future learning: Key directions for the future of primary education'. Retrieved 12 March 2009 from <www.moe.gov.sg/media/press/2009/01/strong-fundamentals-for-future.php>.

Ng, E.H. (2009). 'FY 2009 Committee of Supply debate: 1st reply by Minister Dr Ng Eng Hen on seizing opportunities to build a world class education system'. Retrieved 27 March 2009 from <www.moe.gov.sg/media/speeches/2009/02/10/fy-2009-committee-of-supply-de.php>.

Nitko, A.J. & Brookhart, S.M. (2007). *Educational assessment of students*, 5th ed. Englewood Cliffs, NJ: Pearson Education.

Parr, J.M. & Limbrick, L. (2010). Contextualising practice: Hallmarks of effective teachers of writing. *Teaching and Teacher Education*, 26(3), 583–90.

Tan, O.S., Parsons, R.D., Hinson, S.L. & Sardo-Brown, D. (2003). *Educational psychology: A practitioner-researcher approach*. Singapore: Thomson Learning.

Smutny, J.F. & Van Frernd, S.E. (2004). *Differentiating for the young child: Teaching strategies across content areas (K–3)*. Thousand Oaks, CA: Corwin Press.

Stiggins, R.J. (2005). *Student-involved assessment for learning*, 4th ed. Englewood Cliffs, NJ: Pearson Education.

Woo, H.L. & Gao, P. (2008). Using assessment approaches effectively. In C.L. Quek, F.L. Wong & M.Y. Tay (eds), *Engaging and managing learners: Practitioners' perspectives*, rev. ed. (Ch. 12). Singapore: Pearson Education.

Wortham, S.C. (2012). *Assessment in early childhood education*, 5th ed. Upper Saddle River, NJ: Pearson/Merrill Prentice-Hall.

Wyse, D., McCreery, E. & Torrance, H. (2008). *The trajectory and impact of national reform: Curriculum and assessment in English primary schools*. Primary Review Research Survey 3/2. Cambridge: University of Cambridge, Faculty of Education.

18

Assessment

Collette Tayler and Karin Ishimine

Introduction

Assessing children's learning is recognised as highly important. Professionals use many types of assessment to support children's learning and development from birth to the early years of schooling. This chapter will address issues for early years professionals with regard to the assessment process, including some questions that are especially important in early years education: What is assessment? Why is assessment needed? What should assessment look like? We address issues that arise in assessment practice, including different forms of assessment in early childhood and school sectors. We also highlight the importance of assessment in the transition to school settings.

What is assessment in the early years field?

Within the field of early years education, we define assessment as the process of observing, recording and documenting what children do, say, make, write or draw in order to make educational decisions that will facilitate each child's progress and maximise socio-emotional and academic outcomes.

The early years field is diverse. It includes the early childhood education and care sector as well as formal schools. Across the early years, assessment appears to be understood in different ways among the professionals who are engaged with infants, toddlers and young children and their families. In terms of assessment, the early years may be divided into two age-related ranges: from birth to four years, and from four to eight years. These broadly represent the preschool phase and the early years school phase, including the Pre-K/Preparatory transition.

There is great diversity within the birth to four years workforce, in contrast to the four to eight years workforce within schools, where professionals normally hold a tertiary qualification such as a degree in education. In the early years field, the practices of assessment and reporting need to take account of a workforce with widely different types and levels of qualification, and practices need to address content that can be used to improve children's health, development and learning. All early years professionals observe children. Informally, all assess children's learning and development in everyday practices and some (nurses, early intervention specialists) assess development more formally. However, while formal assessment is not a mandatory part of early years work, assessment is foundational to scaffolding and building on children's learning. Some early years professionals may think they do not assess, even though they use skills to make judgements about child development and learning every day.

The terms 'assessment' and 'screening' are also confused across this diverse early years field. Screening is a first-stage review process of assessment intended to obtain a snapshot of how all children are faring. This is normally a more generalised process whereby a few basics of behaviour, knowledge or performance may be considered. Screening typically is followed by more detailed assessment to confirm or refute the presence of a particular condition in the case of an individual child (Meisels, 1985). Some may believe we only assess children who demonstrate particular behaviours or difficulties, while others believe that assessment is conducted only to diagnose a disability and set up remedial or intervention programs. Assessment is a systematic process that occurs in steps and involves the use of tools selected according to their fitness for purpose. What the assessor wants to investigate or know more about in the case of groups of children or an individual child should direct the selection of appropriate strategies and tools.

All children encounter assessment at some stage, and they should benefit from it. Most assessments in the early years are likely to be conducted within situations where children are playing. The Early Years Learning Framework (EYLF) confirms play as the context for learning. Play settings are therefore rich settings in which to assess children's learning and development, and to make educational decisions that facilitate progress.

Why is assessment needed?

A clearly articulated purpose for assessment is important if assessment is to be well conceived and functional (Kostelnik & Grady, 2009; Snow & Van Hemel, 2008). There are a number of purposes for assessment generally recognised across the early years, including:

- Determining an individual child's level of learning and development.
- Providing valuable feedback to children to enhance their learning.
- Highlighting what children know and can do at certain points in time.
- Screening children for potential problems that may negatively impact ongoing learning and behaviour.
- Informing parents and communities about children's development and progress.
- Guiding early childhood professionals' program decisions.
- Planning for useful interventions when children do not appear to be making satisfactory progress.
- Identifying program improvements and staff-development needs.
- Determining the overall performance of a society or group.
- Advancing knowledge of child learning and development.
- Evaluating how well a program is meeting goals for children.

Assessment for learning not only needs to provide powerful feedback to children to advance their learning (Hattie & Timperley, 2007); it also provides necessary information to families and early years professionals who are working to advance children's learning and development. Assessment for learning therefore has the capacity to promote more intentional teaching, to help professionals be more responsive to the strengths, interests and abilities of individual children. This in turn facilitates the choice of challenging learning goals, with children receptive to new challenges. In reality, *assessment for learning* is not a one-way approach from early childhood professionals to children, but a two-way communicative approach where both learn from the assessment process.

Holistic approach

Children's health and well-being, emotional and social development, language and cognitive development, and physical growth are the vital substance of all early years programs, no matter how integrated they may be at this time. Current services (for example, playgroup, long day care, family day care, occasional care, outside-school-hours care, kindergarten/preschool, primary school) have varied goals and orientations—albeit within a broad system where there is rhetoric about integrated early childhood provision. If an assessment process is articulated solely at the individual service level, each may be inconsistent with the others. Through tradition, different goals and assumed purpose, some services may espouse no place for assessment, yet build their activities on unstated or informal judgements about children, their interests and needs. This situation implies that an evolutionary shift towards more coherent and consistent assessment practices in support of child learning and development, and learning continuity, is essential. A clear purpose and rationale for the adjustment of current practices will need to be established.

In shaping the purpose of and rationale for a consistent approach towards assessment in the birth to eight years phase, two other themes—evidence-based approaches and transitions—may assist the development of a clear purpose.

Assessment continuity and coherence are genuine challenges for early years assessment practices because, no matter how much effort is made, child and family transience is a reality across the early years services. Children aged from birth to four years are encountering programs and services within a non-statutory area of provision. Unlike the school years, there is no mandate that all children will be engaged in programs at this early phase of life. Some children access programs and others do not; some experience several types of program concurrently and others experience only one program, if any. This means that some children do not participate in or cannot access assessments of their early learning and development. The families of such children may not receive reports of their children's development and learning until they reach school. Some children may experience isolated, idiosyncratic assessments in different places at different times. This situation should prompt early years professionals and families to think about who receives assessments of learning and development, and who misses important steps that may have prevented problems that could emerge later. Importantly, it points to the key role of families with regard to assessment in support of child learning and development in the birth to eight years phase of life. Families are necessary partners with early years professionals in tracing the progress of their children's physical and motor, social and emotional, linguistic and cognitive development.

How do we understand assessment?

Recent early years assessment literature (e.g. Snow & Van Hemel, 2008) supports the application of systematic assessment guidelines to help the focus, accuracy and effectiveness of identifying children's learning and development. Where important outcomes for children have been defined, clear guidelines on how best to assess in various early years programs can assist in achievement of the agreed outcomes. Commonly agreed outcomes and systematic assessment guidelines herald a shift in thinking about the anecdotal and play-based approaches that are common practices in the early years. However, the literature does not argue for the appropriation of evaluation techniques that are commonly used for older children. Rather, it supports the exploration of a variety of techniques and instruments that will ensure valid and reliable ways to measure change in children's learning and development. A clear purpose for early childhood assessment is to highlight the kinds of experiences and interactions children should have to further their learning and understandings within this phase of life.

Early years professionals have little to support them in undertaking systematic assessment (Cross et al., 2009). Meisels and Atkins-Burnett (2006, p. 545) argued that 'integrated assessment methodologies' are needed to enable early years professionals to assess different areas of learning and development as young children grow. Without a sound framework, though, there is a very real danger of misuse, misinterpretation of assessments, inconsistency of the assessment process and fragmentation of the use of assessment information.

Formalised curricula, assessment guidelines or systematic early years program evaluations generally have not been prominent in the years before schooling. The common practice of assessing young children in diverse settings, in isolation, may give some local direction about 'what to do next', but it does not realise the continuity of learning across the years from birth to formal school—the practice frequently is disjointed. In other words, current early years assessment practices, especially those involving children between birth and four years, may provide some cross-sectional detail, for example, to guide the maternal and child health system at the local level, but they can be haphazard in supplying information that scaffolds a cohesive learning program alongside children from birth. Cross-sectional information tends to support targeted short-term goals only, rather than shaping longer-term goals and a more integrated plan of development.

Children learn in many ways. To consolidate that learning, to help improve learning and to increase achievements, it is valuable to know what has been learned already, and how well children understand what they have learnt. This is a key function of assessment. Fundamentally, assessment provides feedback about what is already known, what skills are evident, and the dispositions and interests of children. Assessment in its ideal form provides clear evidence of the strengths and capabilities of children. Such feedback is important to children and families, as well as early years professionals, so that new learning and understandings can be built upon the foundations that are already clearly in place for each individual. This is the foundation for building effective ongoing learning and development programs. When early years professionals pay attention to assessment evidence, they have taken the first step towards intentional teaching: planning for each child's growth in learning and development.

What should assessment look like?

Clear principles should guide the practice of administering assessment and using different assessments in different ways according to their purpose and function. Snow and Van Hemel (2008, p. 38) argue that assessments should:

- benefit children
- meet professional legal and ethical standards
- be appropriate in form, having regard to the age and development of the child
- address educationally significant content
- be conducted in familiar contexts and situations
- be culturally and linguistically relevant so children can demonstrate their competence and strengths
- be gathered from multiple sources
- be purposefully designed and be psychometrically sound for the specific purpose
- be used to improve teaching and learning.

These principles illustrate the multiple demands placed on professionals as they work to prepare and administer well-designed and targeted assessments. High-quality practice in this area brings with it much potential for good in terms of supporting children's development and learning. Purposeful assessment design that achieves the principles noted above is an important quest for all professionals engaged in the early years field. The incorrect use and interpretation of selected, published assessment tools can have potential for minimising child learning, hampering development or causing harm—especially if the consequence is having low expectations of a child or applying inappropriate support strategies (Bowman et al., 2001).

Differentiated assessment

Children aged between birth and four years

Very young children behave and perform differently at different ages and in different contexts. As Losardo and Notari-Syverson (2001) point out, it can be difficult to maintain very young children's attention and even their cooperation in environments that are unfamiliar to them, or with other children and adults they do not already know. An adult who is known and trusted by the child is more likely to connect with them, therefore accessing what the child knows and can do. Connection with the child is a precursor of assessment. Early years professionals are usually well known to the children with whom they work. These professionals can regularly assess children's behaviours within early years settings (centres and family day care homes) using the natural behaviour of young children as they engage in play activity. Early years professionals use a mix of direct observations, recordings, interviews, rating scales and samples of natural or guided play. Such assessment is well suited to application within early years settings. These assessments can also occur in the child's home.

Early years assessments typically make use of familiar toys and other culturally appropriate materials that interest and engage the child or a small group of children, enabling them to display their true abilities, along with any difficulties they may be experiencing. Losardo and Notari-Syverson (2001) stress that low-structured, child-centred and familiar activities are needed to conduct valid, reliable assessments. The assessment activities should inherently be of interest to the child, and children's cooperation may therefore be maintained with minimal external support. Such activities form the most appropriate means of gathering accurate information naturally. This naturally derived information is likely to be representative of the child's actual abilities. The items of interest in authentic or naturalistic assessments are usually child behaviours that are functionally important to children progressing well in the setting—for example, communicating wants and needs, maintaining hygiene practices, following procedures or sequencing actions in ways that ensure successful outcomes.

Children aged between four and eight years

On the other hand, children aged between four and eight years within an early years setting are often assessed when they are in formal group situations. Children who are four years old are often still in early childhood settings such as long day care centres; however, children aged from five years often attend a school, a preschool or a kindergarten that may be attached to a formal school setting. By the time most children are six years old they are in a primary school, where the role of assessment may be more deliberate, formal and structured.

Commonly, there are two types of school-based assessment: formative and summative. Formative assessment refers to 'an assessment designed to monitor progress toward an objective and used to guide curricular and instrumental decisions' (Snow & Van Hemel, 2008, p. 427). By contrast, summative assessment is defined as 'as assessment that typically documents how much learning has occurred at a point in time; its purpose is to measure the level of child, school, or program success' (Snow & Van Hemel, 2008, p. 427). For the early years, formative assessment may be more useful for children and educators, as formalised learning is still in it early stages and working to build strong foundations is paramount. Commonly used methods in formative assessment include:

- observation by educators
- work samples—drawings, written works
- participation within a regular class, as well as in special events
- interviews with children and their families
- portfolios of the students' work.

A second category of assessment is systemic or system-wide assessment, often conducted in the form of standardised or quasi-standardised tests. Encouragement to assess children's 'performance' nationally has occurred in Australia through the National Assessment Program (NAP), a cooperative program between the Commonwealth, state and territory governments that has existed for some time. The Australian Curriculum, Assessment and Reporting Authority (ACARA), a recently created national educational authority, has been given the responsibility for testing, coordination and reporting of national basic skills tests on literacy and numeracy for all Year 3, 5, 7 and 9 students through the National Assessment Program—Literacy and Numeracy (NAPLAN), a national system-wide assessment recently implemented in Australia. In May each year, students across the country in the specified years are tested on literacy and numeracy within their schools. The results are then presented as an indicator of student performance within individual schools and school contexts. This has had the effect of applying downward pressure on students in Australian schools—and indirectly on their families—to perform well.

An unintended consequence of the Year 3 tests, when most children are eight years old, has been that NAPLAN assessment has provoked a major perceptual shift in accountability across the early years field. Forms of individual child assessment, linked with NAPLAN-type assessment, are emerging as important components of the early years curriculum in schools. These data may subsequently be aggregated to reflect the performance of early years, as is the case with schools with regard to NAPLAN assessment data. There may also be developmental links made between experiences within early years programs and children's Year 3 NAPLAN performance.

Related to systemic assessment, and in the early years phase from birth, is the Australian Children's Education and Care Quality Authority (ACECQA). Within the prior-to-school domain, ACECQA oversees the National Quality Framework, including a quality standard and an assessment and rating system for all approved early childhood education and care services. Unlike the testing of individual child literacy and numeracy led by ACARA, the ACECQA assessment process is at the service level, not the individual child level. The ACECQA assessment system addresses seven quality standards that include an educational program and practice. This form of assessment is at the system level, with data aggregated and reportable at the local service level. However, within the system early childhood educators are expected, iteratively, to plan programs for children by using their assessments of each child's learning and development.

Assessment issues

Broad abilities, specific skills or both?

There are broad and specific areas of learning and development that can be assessed. Mindes (2003) suggests that assessment yields information about all the developmental areas: motor, temperament, linguistic, cognitive and social/emotional. McGrew and Wendling (2010) argue that it is useful to understand the specific attributes of, for example, a child's cognitive skills in order to know how best to advance each child's understanding. Gullo (2005) argues that assessment should be comprehensive, and we should focus not only on current performance but also on aspects of context, children's relationships and their environment. Snow and Van Hemel (2008) suggest five specific domains that capture important aspects of children's development, while also paying attention to context and environment:

- physical well-being and motor development (health, sensory systems, growth, motor)
- social-emotional development (social competence, self-regulation, adjustment/ maladjustment)

- approaches to learning (initiative, curiosity, engagement, persistence, reasoning, problem-solving)
- language and literacy (speech, vocabulary, conversation, print concepts, writing), and
- cognitive skills, including mathematics (attention, reasoning, number and spatial sense, memory, executive function, emotional regulation, general knowledge, classification and patterning) (Snow & Van Hemel, 2008, p. 86).

Essentially, different researchers use different constructs to describe the aspects of children's learning and development. The different aspects of child development, as illustrated above, are interrelated for each individual. Some constructs assist educators to 'go deep' into an area of development and others assist them to be comprehensive. There is a need to consider a child's learning and development from different vantage points, and it is useful to know in detail how children think and whether they can perform different cognitive or intellectual operations in various social settings. Assessment of each aspect of development in individuals can produce markedly varied expression across a group of young, similar-aged children. What individual children can do, say, make, write and draw reveals much about what might come next in a learning program or set of experiences to support development and understanding. Realising, through assessment, a child's capacity in various situations can reveal the 'what' and 'how' of program 'next steps' to advance children's competency.

Professionals working with young children should address all developmental domains, notwithstanding the way that individual professionals decide to cluster the constructs within these domains. The five domains include the core skills to ensure early years learning and development. Over time, a number of instruments have been developed to assess these domains, with some far more clearly conceptualised than others. For example, there are a variety of instruments available for assessing children's language development, whereas there are relatively fewer measures developed to assess young children's mathematical understandings and skills. Furthermore, 'approaches to learning' may be poorly articulated within measurement tools because it is an elusive concept, while language development is more rigorously defined and subsequently assessed. In summary, each domain has also multiple constructs underneath it that need to become more specific. It is these more specific areas for assessment that are likely to articulate what children can do and what needs to be included in programs to help children learn and advance more effectively.

Overlapping the socio-emotional and academic

Contemporary literature confirms that effective early years programs are simultaneously rich in socio-emotional support and deep in cognitive/academic focus (Denham & Brown, 2010). This reflects the strong connection between children's socio-emotional and academic development—areas that are integrated and that support each other. Contemporary theory and evidence support the argument that a child's social and emotional skills relate to how effectively the child will learn in essential curriculum areas. This reasoning places high importance on including socio-emotional dimensions such as self-awareness, self-management and social awareness in the assessment process, and the subsequent early childhood program. The socio-emotional skills support and 'bridge the gaps' for children's improvement of academic skills (Denham & Brown, 2010). Focusing on academic development alone, in the absence of the socio-emotional dimensions of development, or vice versa, is not considered to be an optimal way to help young children achieve academic success that grows over time. The key question arising here is how we assess socio-emotional and academic skills together. It is important, as well, to analyse children's motivation and disposition, and subsequently to provide relevant experiences that are both interesting and motivating for children's learning.

Why is it necessary to take multiple readings?

Assessment is not a single outcome (though it frequently is perceived as such); it is also fundamentally a process. So how are children's learning and development captured in comprehensive and consistent ways, over time? Assessment, enacted as a process over time, involves a professional approach that assesses multiple domains through a number of different steps and strategies. Children's learning and development are dynamic, and so need to be reviewed frequently and systematically. A plan for a regular review of each child's progress allows professionals to respond to child capabilities with changes to programs, thereby ensuring that new challenges are available to children and boredom is minimised. A range of strategies and tools can be applied to record the evidence of what children can do, say, make, write and draw over time. The selected strategies and tools allow professionals to assess children formatively, and use the evidence to ensure a good match between children's capabilities and their opportunity to advance. This process is ongoing, and the evidence is used diagnostically to understand specific strengths and shortcomings in a child's capacity to operate in certain settings or situations. The process can also be used summatively—for example, at the end of a fixed period of time to document the extent of growth and change.

Assessment for learning involves taking multiple readings of children's capa-bilities. Various forms of assessment, such as systematic observations of children's behaviours, journal notes about learning episodes or events, anecdotal records of child activity, checklist completions, child portfolios (work samples) and specific competency tests, all have a place in assembling the suite of evidence about learning and development over time. When used in combination, multiple readings using varied tools provide a comprehensive yet diverse evidence base from which to make inferences about child understandings, development and learning. Puckett and Black (2008) affirm the need for assessment to occur not only cross-sectionally but at multiple points in time.

The design and selection of assessment for young children

There is a wide range of ways and tools available for collecting information about children. Selection needs to be linked with the purpose of the assessment. The assessment methods in the early years include medical procedures, observation of natural behaviour, a parent's report using checklist or questionnaires, performance in structured versions of natural tasks, and performance on standardised tests (Snow & Van Hemel, 2008).

A strength when early childhood professionals select and use a standardised tool or tools among their suite of schedules—whether they be practitioners or clinical specialists—is that such tools are validated and highly reliable for particular populations. The validity and reliability of any assessment tool that is developed or adopted are critical and central features of the tool. However, the administration of standardised tools often requires specific (specialist) training, and necessitates establishing trusting relationships between the tester and child. Most standardised tests are one-on-one testing processes for younger children and, without a trusting relationship being established first, children may not demonstrate their abilities and skills as usual. Further, standardised tools often rely on children's verbal comprehen-sion of English, and their expressive language, for the assessor to access children's levels of learning and development. Therefore, children who speak languages other than English at home may be disadvantaged through the use of some tests. This is a major weakness of using standardised English-language-delivered tools with very young children in a multicultural society like Australia.

Moreover, extra care is required to select any standardised tool. The assessment activity undertaken by any early years professional also needs to reflect the curricu-lum that is intended or in place (Scott-Little et al., 2010). Most standardised tools are developed without matching them with a particular curriculum. There is a need to assess children's outcomes based on what they have had the opportunity to learn.

Using more informal approaches (for instance, naturalistic observations, a portfolio including children's arts and craft, informal chats with children and parents) brings much potential for personalised child-focused assessment activity. Such approaches more easily accommodate children's own agency in monitoring and reviewing their progress. Children themselves have the capacity to engage in self-assessment and tracking of their developing skills and understandings, especially when this form of child behaviour is strongly encouraged by early years professionals. However, informal approaches can also result in assessment becoming less reliable and valid. The assessment information from informal approaches is best used at the individual child level, and not used to make claims about a class, community or population of young children. It is more complex to allow for comparisons with other children, and also the same children across a certain timespan. Therefore, informal and individual assessment results and reports are not likely to be used in a consistent way with regard to groups or change in groups over time.

Collaboration between practitioners and specialists in the selection and application of tools, where practicable, is likely to result in the most powerful combination of tools being put to use. Further, a functional orientation toward the best interests of the child and optimal support to the child's learning is enhanced by cross-disciplinary collaboration and sharing of perspectives.

A systematic application of assessment in any setting is important if we want to obtain useful and potentially valid information on children's learning and development. Currently, children are assessed in early years settings by using a wide array of assessment tools that have been designed for many different purposes (Snow & Van Hemel, 2008). Further, assessment tools are applied in diverse ways, including applications that do not fit with the original purpose of those tools, by a wide range of early childhood professionals who have varying levels of training. This situation can lead to the inconsistent use of assessment information by a variety of early childhood professionals (health care, education, early intervention) and across different kinds of early years settings. The diverse approaches to assessment in the early years have also facilitated a division between early childhood and school systems, preventing a smooth transition to school for many children.

A systematic and consistently applied assessment and reporting model would help to alleviate current problems in assessment and reporting, and program continuity, across the early years from birth to eight years. In light of the diverse mix of early years services and settings, a comprehensive planning model—at the least at the local neighbourhood level—would help to achieve buy-in by different professionals and effective implementation. Broadly, in regard to monitoring learning, a cyclical process of planning, implementing plans, engaging in activities, reviewing and reporting children's progress is at the heart of supporting children's optimal development and learning. This is shown in Figure 18.1.

Figure 18.1   Assessment and reporting cyclical process

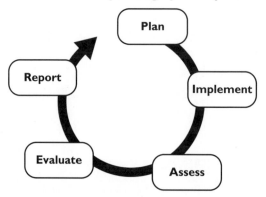

Transition to the school years

Children's development and learning constitutes a continuous process, and should be understood in this way rather than viewed as a barrier between early childhood and the school sector. The transition into school is a critical milestone for all young children. This time serves as a key point where early years professionals based in schools think carefully about the rich sources of information already available to them about each children's learning and development in the prior years. For example, parents are a vital source of detailed information about their children's behaviour, learning and achievements, as observed in different situations outside the classroom. Unless early years educators welcome and actively invite parents to share their insights—for example, through the use of a well-constructed interview tool—the rich details needed to help match learning experiences to children's interests and potential may be overlooked. When planning transition-to-school programs, it is important to consider:

- pre-existing relationships when fostering new relationships
- local knowledge about the needs of local children and their families (for example, common language spoken other than English)

- ensuring, rather than assuming, that all the relevant information is provided to families and understood fully by them
- the need to be flexible to meet the individual needs of children and families
- allowing programs to evolve in line with the needs of families, individual children and school staff, as well as in terms of logistics, dates and so on
- being mindful of making the program a part of rather than additional to, the things already being done (DEECD, 2009, p. 3.1).

Some children will have a naturally smoother transition to school than others, but all children need a positive start at school. To support this view, an effective network among early childhood professionals and primary school professionals, and the use of ECEC assessment instruments and strategies, have a critical role to play in supporting children's optimum development and learning. Assessment material should be seen as seamless, continuous and easy to translate to the school curriculum.

Summary

- In this chapter, we have discussed the importance of assessment throughout the early years from birth and raised significant issues.
- A clearly articulated purpose for assessment is important.
- Early years assessment processes vary widely, and a holistic approach is needed.
- Assessment provides feedback about what children know, what skills are evident, and the dispositions and interests of children.
- Assessment should focus on information that helps early years professionals to increase the benefits to children of engaging in continuous, supported experiences and tasks that enhance learning and development.
- Different types of assessment are utilised for children aged between birth and four years and those aged between four and eight years.
- Through assessment of a child's capacity in various, diverse situations, early years professionals match the 'what' and 'how' of programs, and can determine the 'next steps' to advance children's learning and development.
- Assessment is not a single outcome, but is fundamentally a process.
- A systematic application of assessment in any early years setting is important if we want to obtain useful information to optimise children's learning and development.

Discussion questions

18.1 How important is it for early years professionals to assess children's learning and development?

18.2 What skills and knowledge do early years professionals need to assess young children's learning effectively?

18.3 What sorts of assessment information should early years professionals provide in order to work with families and have families better understand their children's learning and development?

18.4 What kind of systematic assessments can best support the early years field to provide effective ongoing learning programs, especially across the transition from pre-compulsory early childhood services to the first years of primary school?

References

Bowman, B.T., Donovan, M.S. & Burns, M.S. (eds) (2001). *Eager to learn: Educating our preschoolers.* Washington, DC: National Academies Press.

Cross, C.T., Woods, T.A. & Schweingruber, H. (eds) (2009). *Mathematics learning in early childhood: Paths toward excellence and equity.* Washington, DC: National Academies Press.

Denham, S.A. & Brown, C. (2010). 'Plays nice with others': Social and emotional learning and academic success. *Early Education and Development, 21*(5), 652–80.

Department of Education and Early Childhood Development (DEECD) (2009). *Transition: A positive start to school resource kit.* Melbourne: DEECD.

Gullo, D.F. (2005). *Understanding assessment and evaluation in early childhood education.* New York: Teachers College Press.

Hattie, J. & Timperley, H. (2007). The power of feedback. *Review of Educational Research, 77*(1), 81–112.

Kostelnik, M.J. & Grady, M.L. (2009). *Getting it right from the start: The principal's guide to early childhood education.* Thousand Oaks, CA: Corwin Press.

Losardo, A. & Notari-Syverson, A. (2001). *Alternative approaches to assessing young children.* Baltimore, MD: Paul H. Brookes.

McGrew, K. & Wendling, B.J. (2010). Cattell-Horn-Carroll cognitive achievement relations: What we have learned from the past 20 years of research. *Psychology in the Schools, 47*(7), 651–75.

Meisels, S. (1985). *Developmental screening in early childhood: A guide,* rev. ed. Washington, DC: National Association for the Education of Young Children.

Meisels, S. & Atkins-Burnett, S. (2006). Evaluating early childhood assessments: A differential analysis. In K. McCartney & D. Phillips (eds), *Blackwell handbook of early childhood development* (pp. 533–49). Malden, MA: Blackwell.

Mindes, G. (2003). *Assessing Young Children.* Columbus, OH: Merrill.

Puckett, M.B. & Black, J.K. (2008). *Meaningful assessments of the young child: Celebrating development and learning.* Englewood Cliffs, NJ: Pearson Education.

Scott-Little, C., Cassidy, D.J., Lower, J.K. & Ellen, S.J. (2010). Early learning standards and quality improvement initiatives: A systematic approach to supporting children's learning and development. In P.W. Wesley & V. Buysse (eds), *The quest for quality.* Baltimore, MD: Paul. H. Brookes.

Snow, C.E. & Van Hemel, S.B. (2008). *Early childhood assessment: Why, what and how.* Washington, DC: National Academies Press.

PART V

Imperatives for the early years

19

Professionalism and leadership

Carmen Dalli and Kate Thornton

Introduction

Professionalism and leadership have become increasingly prominent topics in contemporary discourses about early years practice. Professionalism is assumed to be synonymous with high-quality early years education, and leadership as essential to producing it.

In this chapter, we provide an overview of a range of conceptualisations of professionalism and leadership that point to a shift in discourse that has taken hold in scholarly discussions as well as in practice. Whereas attempts to define early years professionalism historically have taken as their starting point existing definitions of professionalism as marked by qualities such as prolonged training and qualifications, and thus as residing solely or primarily in individuals, more contemporary perspectives increasingly recognise the distinctive nature of early years practice, and understand that the meaning of professionalism cannot be taken for granted. Likewise, educational leadership in the early years is no longer viewed as the sole prerogative of those holding a formal leadership position and involving power relationships between a leader and followers; instead, it is accepted that leadership can be distributed and collaborative, and that all educators can practise leadership at different times.

In educational contexts that are becoming increasingly diverse, and where compliance with mandatory regulations and standards of practice is often confused with professionalism and leadership, we argue that professionalism and leadership are complementary notions: focused on learning and teaching; embedded in collaborative relationships with children, colleagues and parents; incorporate reflective practice and openness to learning and to critique; and include advocacy at the individual, setting and sector levels.

Conceptualisations of professionalism and leadership: Shifts and convergences

Professionalism: Shifting discourses

An early trend in the professionalism scholarship was stocktaking arguments about whether early years teaching could be called a profession, with the traditional fields of law and medicine used as reference points of what established professions should look like. Lilian Katz's (1985) identification of eight common characteristics of a profession was an early example of this type of work in the early childhood sector. Listing the eight criteria of a specialised knowledge base, prolonged training, standards of practice, distance from the client, having a code of ethics, autonomy, altruism and social necessity as common characteristics of a profession, Katz used them as a basis for discussing whether early childhood education could be called a profession.

Identifying the qualities that comprise professional practice in the early childhood sector as well as the early years of school remained a popular strategy throughout the 1990s, but discourses of diversity and contextual relativity became more prominent. For example, drawing on a study of the professional activities of early years practitioners in fifteen European countries, Oberhuemer (2000) distinguished four broad roles that reflected cultural notions of what it meant to be an early years professional in different parts of Europe, with correspondingly different training foci. In Finland, Sweden and Spain, for instance, a typical role is that of the *early childhood pedagogue* who works with children aged from birth to school entry at six or seven years of age, while in nursery and primary education in France, Ireland and The Netherlands the role of *teacher* is more typical, and training is focused on children aged from three years to eleven- or twelve-year-olds. The *preschool specialist*, found in Belgium, Greece and Luxembourg, works with children in the two to three years before school entry, and the *social pedagogue* role in Denmark, Germany and Luxembourg is one that can apply to work across the lifespan. Oberhuemer highlights the historical and cultural embeddedness of both role activities and the focus of training in the different countries. She has argued that what counts as professional is a matter of interpretation and cultural discourse, as well as subject to changing societal and political dynamics.

During the early 1990s, scholarly discourses about professional practice within the Australian and New Zealand educational contexts were often bound up with discussions about ethical practice and the need for a Code of Ethics. Within each country, the early childhood sector was first off the mark in developing such a code, aimed in each case at enhancing the professional status of the sector within the broader education field and society more generally. Leadership for this initiative emerged in both instances from within the early childhood sector, with the Australian Early Childhood Association taking the lead in one country and a working group comprising academics and unionists taking the lead in the other. The aspiration—and advocacy—for this type of professional status, however, has not been unproblematic, with critical voices highlighting the limitations of Codes of Ethics—which can easily function simply as a credo rather than as a tool of practice. Others have pointed out that the structure of a profession is by its nature exclusive, and therefore creates divisions—the 'othering' of individuals and groups (Hughes & MacNaughton, 2000).

Policy tools such as regulations and accountability mechanisms—often perceived in lay debates to be indicators of professionalism—together with discourses about early education as early intervention, or investment in the future, or of cost benefits, readiness for school and best practice, are similarly criticised as neo-liberal forces that act to obscure the essentially relational nature of early years education (e.g., see Dahlberg & Moss, 2005). A response to such criticism has been the emergence of the term *democratic professionalism*. A key proponent of this view, Peter Moss (2008), suggests seven qualities that might be part of this view of professionalism: dialogue; critical thinking; researching; listening and openness to otherness; uncertainty and provisionality; subjectivity and border crossing.

More recently, local researchers have developed new lines of argument about professionalism and professional practice. For example, one of us (Dalli, 2008) has argued for recognition of educators' own perspectives of their practice in discussions of professionalism. Based on data from a 2004 national survey of qualified New Zealand early childhood educators' views of practice, Dalli proposed a ground-up definition of professionalism comprising three core components:

specialist pedagogical strategies; professional knowledge and practice; and collaborative relationships. These components are consistent with a community of learning approach to early years practice (e.g. Aitken, 2005; Scrivens & Duncan, 2003), where the focus is on cooperative forms of centre management and leadership. They also support a joint New Zealand–Australian analysis by Aitken and Kennedy (2007) that identifies the need to strengthen the knowledge and qualification base of the early childhood workforce in both countries.

Aitken and Kennedy (2007) further argue that contemporary challenges to early years professionalism include structural issues like ongoing professional development and mentoring, and increased managerialism and privatisation—which are both at odds with the strongly held value within the early years sector that education is a public good.

The ongoing marketisation of early education and care, with its corporate trappings and the reduction of 'quality' into measurable outcomes and standardised practices, has added to concerns (May & Mitchell, 2009; Woodrow & Press, 2007) that early years teaching increasingly is being pushed into technicist territory that can lead to deprofessionalisation (Codd, 2008). However, as both Osgood (2006) and Duhn (2010) illustrate, the deprofessionalisation argument may be a simplification of the complexities of neo-liberal discourses and of teachers' responses to their context. For example, Jayne Osgood showed that practitioners in England were not passive recipients of social structures, but rather active agents who could disrupt dominant discourses. Additionally, Iris Duhn's analysis of statements by New Zealand early childhood teachers in corporate and private settings demonstrates that even neo-liberal discourses of 'professionalism' differ across contexts.

Complexity, situatedness and relationality emerge from this brief overview as key concepts in discourses of professionalism. This was again apparent in a recently completed project that investigated a day in the life of six early years practitioners from different countries: Australia, England, Finland, Germany, New Zealand and Sweden (Miller, Dalli and Urban, 2012). The case studies in this project illustrated that the practitioners constructed their professionalism in relation to their actual role—*what* they did was central to *how* they defined their professionalism—and with reference to the wider social, historical, economic and political context of society as a whole. Summarising key insights from the study, we argue that understandings of professionalism are embedded in local as well as national and global contexts. We conclude that it is timely to advocate for a critical ecology of the early years profession—in other words, a stance of critical inquiry in all aspects of early years practice, including an alertness to socio-political contexts at the individual, collective and community levels.

We turn now to considering how changing views about the nature of leadership in the early years interact with discourses of professionalism.

Leadership and professionalism as converging notions

In the first edition of her seminal book *Leadership in Early Childhood*, Jillian Rodd (1994) presented a typology of qualities of an early years leader that included personal characteristics such as warmth, patience, self-awareness and knowledge; professional skills such as technical competence and effective communication; and roles and responsibilities such as developing and articulating values and vision, and acting as an advocate. While the typology remains in the book's third edition, there is acknowledgement that these characteristics, skills and roles are 'seldom attributable to one person alone' (Rodd, 2006, p. 52), and that leadership in early years settings is more likely to be collective and collaborative.

This recent shift to thinking about *leadership as a shared activity* is one of three significant changes in thinking around leadership in the field of education (Robinson, 2004). The other two shifts are a focus on *leadership practice*—rather than leadership style; and greater emphasis on *educational leadership*, in other words, leadership of teaching and learning rather than generic leadership and management skills that could apply in any context.

We return to the collaborative nature of leadership and its distribution across early years practitioners later in this section; however, it is useful to make an early note about the terminology that is used when discussing leadership roles. Two models of leadership commonly applied to the early years sector are those of *transactional* and *transformational leadership*. The key idea behind the notion of transactional leadership is that the leader either rewards or punishes followers depending on their actions; it involves the manipulation of people and situations. This type of leadership—as a transaction between leaders and followers—is not seen to encourage leadership in others. On the other hand, transformational leadership is concerned with influencing, inspiring and motivating others in order to effect change.

Within the early years sector, transformational leadership is often seen as preferable to transactional leadership; however, it has also been suggested that in the education sector we should move beyond these models, as they fail to adequately reflect the actual practices of current effective educational leaders. The term 'distributed leadership practice', in which 'leadership may be exercised by anyone whose ideas or actions are influential in the context of specific tasks and activities' (Robinson, Hohepa and Lloyd, 2009, p. 67), has been offered as an alternative. Distributed leadership can be defined as leadership that is distributed across group members, and characterised by interdependence and cooperation. Distributed leadership involves more than sharing leadership roles, as it is the collective interactions between people that are important. If educators subscribe to the model of a single leader, then they are unlikely to participate actively in leadership activities, or to feel empowered to be innovative and creative in their teaching practice, and thus contribute their knowledge and expertise in different ways. By contrast, in situations of distributed leadership, or leadership practice, leadership is not just the domain of those in formal leadership positions but extends to others in any role.

An emphasis on *leadership practice* also involves a focus on the *how* and *why* of what leaders actually do. This suggests that, rather than adopting a particular style, effective leaders take on diverse roles depending on the situation and context. We like Raelin's (2003) view of effective leadership as concurrent, collective, compassionate and collaborative, as this description accords with conceptualisations of leadership we encounter among our students and among practising educators in professional learning sessions. For instance, some metaphors for leadership offered by our students have included: geese in flight where different geese take turns to lead—an action that requires coordination and communication; conducting an orchestra—a role that involves coordinating the input of the different players; and a large tree—where the professional leader provides shelter for others, thus supporting their leadership to also grow. In our New Zealand context, the metaphor of leadership as paddling the same *waka* (a Māori word meaning a canoe paddled by a team of synchronised paddlers)—where everyone's efforts need to be synchronised to move forward—has a particularly local flavour.

Sometimes, statements have linked professionalism and leadership explicitly:

Being professional is about leading others in learning and being willing to let others lead. It's about empowering relationships in which there can be a shared vision. It's taking responsibility in caring for others.

An early years leader is a professional who advocates for children, families and their communities, and the early years sector; they are good communicators and they engage in critical thinking. They engage with the issues of the day and facilitate change.

These statements, gathered from class discussions over the last few years, illustrate how notions of leadership converge with understandings of professionalism. Not only is there an explicit link between the two terms because they are used together within the same statements; there is also a conceptual link in that the two terms are underpinned by understandings of reciprocity of action in learning and teaching, relationality in professional interactions, shared care and responsibility, advocacy for individuals as well as families and communities, and critical thinking that can result in change. Clearly, professionalism and leadership are complementary notions: embedded in pedagogy and relationships; incorporating reflective practice in collaborative settings; open to learning and critique; and including advocacy at all levels.

The rest of this chapter elaborates on these elements of professionalism and leadership, with illustrative statements by educators taken from different research projects led by the authors.

Professionalism and leadership as embedded in pedagogy and in relationships

> You recognise professionalism when the educator works at the child's level, through the body language and the facial expressions, through the tone of voice and the language used. The professional educator listens to children, follows their lead . . . and extends their learning; being interested, positive, and praising their efforts; supporting them with challenges; encouraging their independence; setting consistent expectations . . . knowing the children, their strengths, interests and needs.

> When you are a professional you are knowledgeable and able to articulate that knowledge. You know what to teach, you acknowledge diversity in learners, you are inclusive, and you lead learning. As a professional you show leadership and encourage emergent leadership in others through . . . the time and space you take and allow others—colleagues, parents and children. Active listening is part of professionalism as are laughter, humour and smiles. You need to be good communicators with children, staff, *whānau* [Māori word meaning family] and parents.

These statements identify some very specific behaviours, as well as attitudinal qualities and skills, as desirable within the pedagogical repertoire of professional early years educators. To work at the child's level requires attentive responsiveness—to know the child, their strengths, their diverse interests and their needs. The behaviours involve body language as well as a particular style of talking, including tone of voice. Attitudinal qualities are those that allow learners to take the lead that educators follow, showing interest and a positive stance that encourages and extends learning. And being professional means that one is knowledgeable about the whats and hows of teaching. Professional early years pedagogy, then—or the science of teaching and learning—is a holistic activity that engages the body as well as the mind and heart. Laughter, humour and smiles are part and parcel of being interested in others and establishing effective relationships.

Leadership, too, requires attention to others, for whom the professional educator allows time and space for listening, communicating and mutual enjoyment. The personal interest taken helps build trust and confidence, and encourages participation in leadership practice.

As in the scholarly literature, professional practice and pedagogical leadership emerge in these statements as complementary ideas focused on teaching and learning. Rather than the management or leadership of a team, leadership is that which 'causes others to do things that can be expected to improve educational outcomes for students' (Robinson et al., 2009, p. 70).

The educators' statements above highlight something about which most educators are very mindful: that relationships are critical aspects of their professional role, irrespective of whether or not they are in a formal leadership role. The need to build and sustain effective working relationships with children, colleagues, parents and management is part and parcel of professional practice, as well as part of leaderful action. One framework that has captured this awareness within the New Zealand context was developed by a teaching team in a Māori early years immersion service (Te Kōpae Piripono, 2006). The framework is based on four responsibilities that are phrased in active terms as:

- Being responsible. This relates to an individual's attitude and actions and is about being professional, acting ethically and appropriately, being honest, being positive and being open to others and to different perspectives.
- Taking responsibility. This is about courage, risk-taking, having a go, taking up the challenge and trying new things.
- Having responsibility. This relates to having designated roles and positions of responsibility.
- Sharing responsibility. This is about sharing power, roles and positions. Sharing responsibility also denotes an interaction and engagement with others, being able to listen to others' points of view, acknowledging different perspectives and both asking for and providing assistance.

This leadership framework is based on the belief that everyone involved in the early years setting—educators, children and parents—is already a leader, whether they are aware of it or not. With its strong focus on relationships, it also fits very well with the notion of collectivism expressed by Walker and Riordan (2010, p. 52) when they suggest that leadership 'is about building the capacity of the collective to make a difference'.

Reflective practice in collaborative settings

The greater focus on collaborative rather than the singular leadership mentioned earlier has multiple benefits for early years settings. An educationally powerful argument for distributed leadership is that it is necessary because of the 'breadth and depth of expertise required' to improve teaching and learning (Robinson et al., 2009, p. 210). Whereas in hierarchical leadership models the leadership activities of others are hidden, with distributed leadership everyone's knowledge, skills and dispositions can be used to contribute to the effective operation of the service:

> They are ... team players, approachable and consultative and work together to achieve best practice. They give honest, constructive 360 degree feedback; they laugh together and show enjoyment of their work in general.
>
> Professional early years educators are collaborative. They can take a leadership role if required but also know when to let others take control.

This focus on distributed leadership does not lessen the role of the professional or formal leader, but it may change its emphasis. Professional leaders in distributed models of leadership operate at the hub of a network rather than from a hierarchical position, and actively share information, ideas and resources. We have already mentioned the metaphor of a leader as an orchestra conductor, whose job it is to ensure that the orchestra members' actions are synchronised and that the skills of the musicians are heard to their best advantage. Leaders who perform this co-ordination role, promote and model respectful and collaborative relationships, and provide support and mentoring, encourage their colleagues to become involved in the leadership of the service.

A further aspect of distributed leadership is its tendency to encourage all educators to reflect on and research their practice. Educator research and self-review can be used as opportunities for professional learning for the whole teaching team:

A professional educator is someone who reflects on their practice and uses this process to improve their teaching. They are responsive to ideas that others have, while also being able to input well thought-out ideas.

Openness to learning and critique

The ability to be a reflective practitioner, willing to observe, critique and improve one's practice—individually and within a team—and the ability to undertake on-the-job research were noted within a recent OECD (2011) report, *Building a High-quality Teaching Profession*, as key skills taught in teacher education programs in educationally high-achieving countries. As one educator working in an early childhood centre wrote in a response to a question about qualities of professional educators:

> They reflect openly on their teaching and share this with colleagues . . . they are willing to learn from each other, open to learning . . . willing to offer change and experiment with change, able to take constructive criticism—and give it as well.

The importance of openness to learning and critique is also central to the notion of early years settings as professional learning communities. These have been defined as 'professional educators working collectively and purposefully to create and sustain a culture of learning for all students and adults' (Hipp & Huffman, 2010, p. 12). Shared and supportive leadership, and collective learning and application, are two of the characteristics of professional learning communities promoted by Hipp and Huffman. Practices that support collective learning and application include collective learning through open dialogue, and continuous inquiry and reflection. Professional learning communities are characterised by a high level of trust between members of the teaching team. This relational trust supports a service culture where there is robust and passionate debate of ideas and regular critique of teaching practices. Honest and constructive feedback among the team is regularly given and received. Open-to-learning conversations occur, and the professional leader listens to others carefully and encourages views that challenge rather than reinforce current ways of thinking. Conflict is embraced as an opportunity for learning and reflection. This critical team culture leads to a willingness to take risks and an openness to change.

Effective professionals and educational leaders need to be continuously open to new learning because of the pace of change in the education sector. The value of distributed leadership in implementing change and developing expertise within education settings has been emphasised in a study by Clarkin-Phillips (2009), who suggests that 'distributed leadership recognises the role that all professionals within an education setting play in implementing change, and that it is through collaboration and connectivity that expertise is developed' (2009, p. 22). An openness to learning and critique needs to be modelled by the professional leader. It is important that educators facilitate and participate in teacher learning and development opportunities, in order to encourage and support educational leadership and ensure that resources are available to adequately support teaching and learning.

Professional leaders should also encourage educators to regularly discuss their teaching practice in terms of current research, and to ensure that there is a strong focus on ensuring a rich curriculum that engages, extends and deepens children's learning. This will involve professional leaders in encouraging other educators to lead in areas where they have expertise through focusing relationships on pedagogy. Strategies that have the potential to strengthen educational leadership practice include goal-setting, problem-solving and engaging with educators' theories of action.

Professionalism, leadership and advocacy: Looking towards the future of the profession

The importance of professionalism and leadership to the quality and profile of the early years sector has been emphasised in numerous studies; however, considerable progress still needs to be made to increase our understanding of how these are conceptualised and practised. The diversity of the sector makes a common understanding of the notion of leadership problematic, and the lack of a coordinated approach to leadership development in many countries is of concern. Leadership practices differ between early years services, and whether leadership practice is strong or weak has largely been left to chance. Many professional leaders have not had the opportunity to consider their role in any depth, or to reflect on what leadership looks like in their context. They may be unaware of research around effective educational leadership practice, or distributed leadership, and may not have had the opportunity to participate in professional development related to their leadership role.

There is general agreement that those in leadership roles should be supported further through the provision of appropriate training and professional development opportunities. Characteristics of effective leadership development programs include: an emphasis on pedagogical leadership leading to improved outcomes for children and families; opportunities to reflect on leadership practice, including reflective journalling; opportunities to engage in work-based learning that allow for engagement with leadership challenges faced in everyday practice; opportunities to work alongside peers and to share experiences, ideas and challenges; opportunities to develop self-awareness and to obtain feedback from other stakeholders on leadership practice; support for the distribution of leadership, and for the development of strong professional learning communities; and confidential coaching and/or mentoring support (Thornton, 2010).

As mentioned earlier, pedagogy, relationships and advocacy are essential aspects of both leadership and professionalism in the early years, and involve reflective practice in collaborative settings as well as openness to learning and critique.

Glenda MacNaughton (2005) explains that connecting the 'critical' to reflection is about directing attention away from the individual and towards 'the operation and effects of power relationships between people' (2005, p. 7). Critical reflection is 'the process of questioning how power operates in the process of teaching and learning and then using that knowledge to transform oppressive or inequitable teaching and learning processes'. These ideas are highly pertinent in the context of looking towards the future of the early years profession.

Implications for practice arising from this view include the requirement that early years professionals should:

- be confident to advocate for children, themselves, their colleagues and for families if need be
- reflect critically on their practice, both individually and collectively, in order to strengthen teaching and learning
- actively participate in professional learning communities
- take, have and share responsibility, and act ethically and appropriately
- demonstrate willingness to speak out about policies and practices, and to promote positive change
- advocate for safe working environments and professional learning for staff
- be actively involved in the wider community, including networking and demonstrating political awareness.

Summary

- This chapter has provided an overview of a range of conceptualisations of both professionalism and leadership, and has discussed a number of elements seen as critical to both.

- Practitioners' views have been used to illustrate these notions from which implications for practice have been highlighted.
- Professionalism and leadership are complementary notions:
  - They are focused on learning and teaching.
  - They are embedded in collaborative relationships with children, colleagues, and parents.
  - They incorporate reflective practice, and openness to learning and to critique.
  - They include advocacy at the individual, setting and sector levels.

Discussion questions

19.1 To what extent is the existence of a Code of Ethics useful for the professional status of the early years sector?

19.2 In what ways do educators in your setting demonstrate their professionalism in their everyday practice?

19.3 What opportunities for advocacy exist at different levels in your work context?

19.4 How is leadership conceptualised in your setting?

19.5 To what extent does your setting operate as a professional learning community where leadership is shared and supportive, and learning is collective?

References

Aitken, H. (2005). Participation in an early childhood community of practice: The experiences of a group of newly qualified teachers. Unpublished Masters thesis, University of Waikato, Hamilton.

Aitken, H. & Kennedy, A. (2007). Critical issues for the early childhood profession. In L. Keesing-Styles & H. Hedges (eds), *Theorising early childhood practice: Emerging dialogues* (pp. 165–85). Sydney: Pademelon Press.

Clarkin-Phillips, J. (2009). Distributed leadership: Utilising everyone's strengths. *Early Childhood Folio*, *13*, 22–6.

Codd, J. (2008). Neoliberalism, globalisation and the deprofessionalisation of teachers. In V. Carpenter, J. Jesson, P. Roberts & M. Stephenson (eds), *Ngā Kaupapa here: Connections and contradictions in education* (pp. 14–24). Melbourne: Cengage.

Dahlberg, G. & Moss, P. (2005). *What ethics? Ethics and politics in early childhood education* (pp. 64–85). London: Routledge.

Dalli, C. (2008). Pedagogy, knowledge and collaboration: Towards a ground-up perspective on professionalism. *European Early Childhood Education Research Journal*, *16*(2), 171–85.

Duhn, I. (2010). 'The centre is my business': Neo-liberal politics, privatisation and discourses of professionalism in New Zealand. *Contemporary Issues in Early Childhood*, *11*(1), 49–60.

Hipp, K. & Huffman, J. (2010). *Demystifying professional learning communities*. Plymouth: Rowman & Littlefield.

Hughes, P. & MacNaughton, G. (2000). Consensus, dissensus or community: The politics of parental involvement in early childhood education. *Contemporary Issues in Early Childhood*, *1*(3), 241–57.

Katz, L. (1985). The nature of professions: Where is early childhood education? In L. Katz (ed.), *Talks with teachers of young children: A collection*. New York: Ablex.

MacNaughton, G. (2005). Doing Foucault in early childhood studies: Applying post-structural ideas. Landa: Routledge Falmar.

May, H. & Mitchell, L. (2009). *Strengthening community-based early childhood education in Aotearoa New Zealand*. Report of the Quality Public Early Childhood Education Project. Wellington: New Zealand Educational Institute–Te Riu Roa.

Miller, L., Dalli, C. & Urban M. (eds) (2012). *Early childhood grows up: Towards a critical ecology of the profession*. Dordrecht: Springer.

Moss, P. (2008). The democratic and reflective professional: rethinking and reforming the early years workforce. In L. Miller & C. Cable (eds), *Professionalism in the early years*. London: Hodder.

Oberhuemer, P. (2000). Conceptualising the professional role in early childhood centers: Emerging profiles in four European countries. *Early Childhood Research and Practice*, *2*(2), 131–41.

Organization for Economic Cooperation and Development (OECD) (2011). Building a high-quality teaching profession: Lessons from around the world. Retrieved 21 March 2011 from <www2.ed.gov/about/inits/ed/internationaled/background.pdf>.

Osgood, J. (2006). Deconstructing professionalism in early childhood education: Resisting the regulatory gaze. *Contemporary Issues in Early Childhood*, *7*(1) 5–14.

Pound, L. (2008). Leadership in the early years. In L. Miller & C. Cable (eds), *Professionalism in the early years* (pp. 75–84). Abingdon: Hodder.

Raelin, J. (2003). *Creating leaderful organizations*. San Francisco: Berrett-Koehler.

Robinson, V. (2004). *New understandings of educational leadership. Set, 3*, 39–43.

Robinson, V., Hohepa, M. & Lloyd, C. (2009). *School leadership and student outcomes: Identifying what works and why—best evidence synthesis iteration*. Wellington: Ministry of Education.

Rodd, J. (1994). *Leadership in early childhood*. Sydney: Allen & Unwin.

—— (2006). *Leadership in early childhood*, 3rd ed. Sydney: Allen & Unwin.

Scrivens, C. & Duncan, J. (2003). What decisions? Whose decisions? Issues for professional leaders in decision-making in New Zealand childcare centres. *Early Education*, *33*, 29–37.

Te Kōpae Piripono (2006). *Ngā takohanga e wha*. The four responsibilities. Retrieved 20 November 2011 from <www.lead.ece.govt.nz/CentresOfInnovation/COIDocsAndResources/SrvcSpecific DocsAndResources/NgāTakohangaeWhaTheFourResponsibilities.htm>.

Thornton, K. (2010). Lesson for leadership development: What we can learn from the UK. *Journal of Educational Leadership, Policy and Practice*, *25*(2), 29–40.

Walker, A. & Riordan, G. (2010). Leading collective capacity in culturally diverse schools. *School Leadership & Management*, *30*(1), 51–63.

Woodrow, C. & Press, F. (2007). (Re)positioning the child in the policy/politics of early childhood. *Educational Philosophy and Theory*, *39*(3), 312–25.

20

Evidence-based practice

*Gillian Busch and
Maryanne Theobald*

Introduction

An integral part of teaching, and a principle underpinning professional practice in the early years, is the importance of reflecting on and researching our own practice. For example, in Australia the Early Years Learning Framework identifies 'ongoing learning and reflective practice' (DEEWR, 2009, p. 13) as one of the five principles distilled from theories and research evidence that underpin professional practice in the early years. Recognising teaching as encompassing the role of researching pedagogical practice highlights that teaching is not simply practical or procedural, but requires intellectual work. This chapter details evidence-based practice (EBP) in early years education. It asks us to reflect upon four questions:

- What is evidence-based practice?
- What evidence do I draw on?
- How might I discern relevant evidence?
- What is my part in generating research evidence?

Educators as researchers and professionals

Being an educator requires significant intellectual work, involving thoughtful responses to the challenges and dilemmas that we encounter. The intellectual work of teaching demands that we have a genuine interest in how early years learners learn and our role in that process. Also important is a commitment to inquiry, knowledge of ourselves and our values, and a willingness to embrace the sometimes messy process of thinking and wondering. In addition, recognising educators' work as intellectual situates educators as part of an ongoing process of inquiry, where current practices are examined, outcomes evaluated and new ideas produced. Integral to the reflective process is our engagement with contemporary early years research.

Evidence-based practice supports the importance of continued 'professional renewal', which is highlighted as crucial in a number of registering authority guidelines, including those of the Queensland College of Teachers (2006). Professional renewal is supported through reflecting on and researching our own practice. Following specialised undergraduate training, you will acquire knowledge and skills that are recognised as essential for membership of the profession. The abilities, knowledge and professional values that educators demonstrate are codified as part of the professional standards, and embedded in both quality requirements and codes of ethics. Both professional standards and codes of ethics draw on particular knowledge and public expectations about what and how educators engage in their work. These standards and codes of ethics guide the professional behaviour of educators. However, emerging research contributes new knowledge, which may challenge some existing understandings and practices.

What is evidence-based practice?

Evidence-based practice (EBP) is a process that supports our engagement with emerging evidence for understanding issues relevant to our work as educators. It involves the assembling and analysis of relevant data and research, which is then used to induce improvements in teaching and learning for an individual educator or for the whole school/educational site, to achieve the best possible outcomes for early years learners (Groundwater-Smith, 2000). Evidence-based practice integrates research evidence to identify the issue and then synthesise all of the available information. Adopted by education in recent times, EBP has its origins in the disciplines of health care, including medicine and nursing. It emerged as a response to a *research-theory gap* (Trinder, 2000). One of the underpinning premises of EBP is that the actions of professionals must be based on relevant, reliable and contemporary research. Building our understandings of EBP to incorporate 'practice-based evidence' (Centre for Community Child Health, 2011) means that the expertise the professional educator brings to the inquiry process is recognised. This expertise includes existing practical knowledge drawn from prior experience and expert knowledge, perhaps acquired during undergraduate and postgraduate study. Recognising the distinction between *theory* and *evidence* helps in our understanding of EBP. *Theory* constitutes the beliefs, assumptions and premises about children and learning on which we base our work as educators. The verification of information through close investigation during the research process and via critique provides us with the *evidence* that supports ideas and theories.

Positive outcomes of EBP include the optimum use of available resources and *best practice.* While acclaimed by its advocates, critiques of EBP suggest that as an attempt to rationalise resources it is too simplistic, and may contribute to a diminution of professional autonomy (Trinder, 2000). The adoption of EBP within professions coincided with greater access to information via information technologies and increased demands for professionals to be accountable for their actions. Utilising databases—many of which relate to specific professions—professionals have quick access to contemporary research to inform their actions (Trinder, 2000). For example, medical specialists such as physicians may access research evidence during the patient consultation process.

Evidence-based practice is a cycle of inquiry involving a number of steps (see Figure 20.1) the first involves recognising a problem and then formulating a question about it. Careful composition of the question requiring investigation is important because this will inform the choice of research evidence selected to support inquiry. The second step is to pursue valid research evidence in relevant journals to support problem investigation and resolution. Within the early childhood context, organisations such as Early Childhood Australia disseminate contemporary research relevant to the early childhood context, and may provide a useful start to acquiring current research evidence. Third, the information collected needs to be analysed to assess its validity and relevance to the issue being investigated. Fourth, relevant strategies and understandings drawn from the literature are applied. Finally, the outcomes are evaluated in terms of effectiveness and suitability for their continued application (Sackett et al., 2000).

Figure 20.1   Steps in evidence-based practice

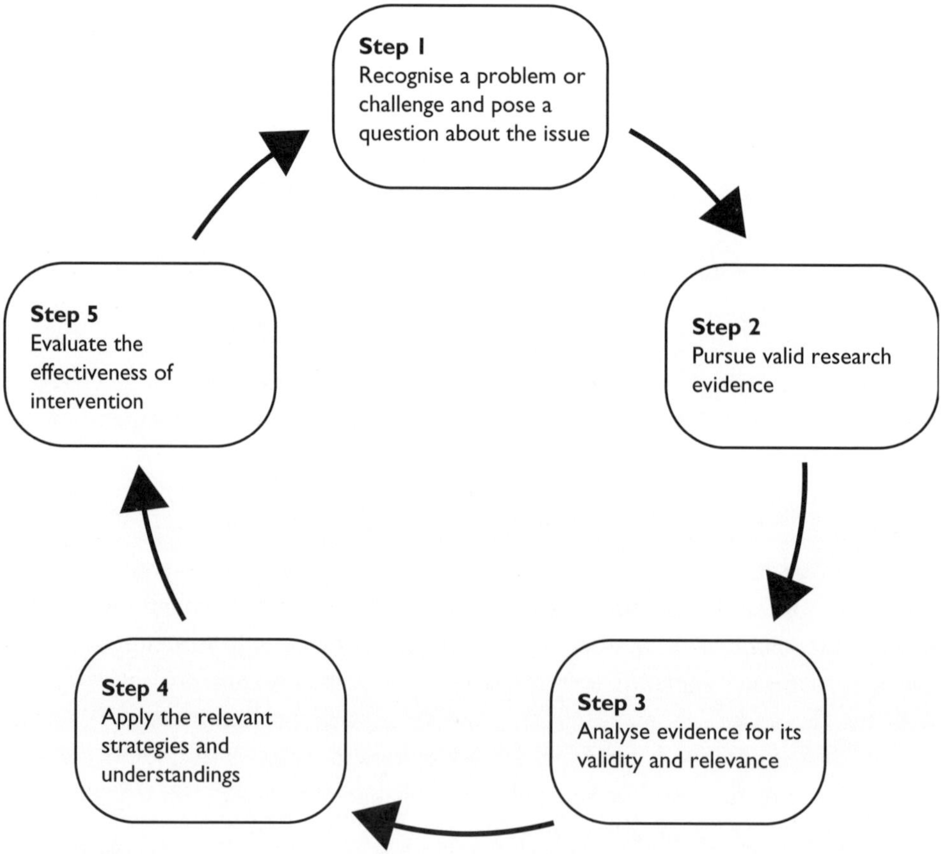

Step 1
Recognise a problem or challenge and pose a question about the issue

Step 2
Pursue valid research evidence

Step 3
Analyse evidence for its validity and relevance

Step 4
Apply the relevant strategies and understandings

Step 5
Evaluate the effectiveness of intervention

Essential dispositions and skills

The success of EBP depends on educators having a number of essential dispositions and skills. These are similar to the ones required for reflective practice and action research (Borgia & Schuler, 1998). Such dispositions include a willingness to embrace inquiry, collaboration and change. In addition, given that the investigative process may stretch over an extended period of time, it is important to be able to sustain interest in the area being investigated.

While educators may embark on the process individually, the nature of work within educational sites heightens the need for a willingness to collaborate, to listen to colleagues' contributions, to proffer thinking and queries, and to question the taken-for-granted ways of engaging in tasks. An openness to collaboration is underpinned by participant trust and respect. Given that the process results in the adoption of evidence that leads to change in existing practices, it is essential that educators have a willingness to accept change. Active participation in the inquiry process means that educators contribute to the changes that unfold, following engagement with the evidence accessed and reflection on their practice. The capacity to engage in reflective practice is crucial to the success of EBP. Critical reflection is one type of reflective practice.

Critical reflection asks us to look beyond our personal perspective and to examine issues from multiple perspectives. Engaging in critical reflection requires us to uncover the taken-for-granted assumptions on which we base our decisions. Critical reflection is a challenging intellectual task requiring that we are open to alternate views (Brookfield, 1995). Consequently, engaging in critical reflection is about unsettling the certainties with which we have lived; it therefore may be very confronting. In the reflection process, we need to consider how 'power' is acted out and embedded within our relationships with others (Fasoli & Woodrow, 1998) and how outside influences filter into educational sites and influence our practice. In so doing, we are required to consider the equity and social justice dimensions of our work. Engaging in critical reflection means careful consideration and reconsideration of research, and the implications of it for our practice. Questions include: Who is privileged? Who is disadvantaged? Who is silenced? Who retains power? What assumptions underpin my practice and do these assumptions limit how I might work with early years learners, families and other staff?

Accessing research evidence

Evidence—both qualitative and quantitative—derived from research studies, longitudinal research or systemic measures provides valuable guidance to, and justifies the importance of, the early years in terms of research, policy and curriculum agendas. As you begin to think about the evidence that you might gather as part of your EBP, you also need to consider what counts as evidence, and whether the evidence collected provides a range of perspectives about the issue under investigation. Groundwater-Smith et al. (2011, p. 325) suggest that we approach the gathering of evidence in a 'forensic way, seeking to analyse and understand an educational practice in order to improve it'. Evidence can be accessed from research of early learning settings, as well as from fields outside of education.

The fields of neuroscience and social science offer considerable evidence for our practices of teaching in the early years, and increasing greater public awareness of the contribution of early years to subsequent outcomes for early years learners. For example, brain research has highlighted the importance of supportive nurturing environments and relationships with responsive adults as an important dimension of quality early childhood environments and critical periods in children's development (Shore, 1997). Other high-profile advocates within the medical field, such as Professor Fiona Stanley (Chair of the Australian Research Alliance for Children & Youth), have highlighted the importance of the early years. For instance, Professor Stanley was influential in promoting the implementation of the Australian Early Development Index (AEDI), an instrument developed to provide a snapshot of children's development in the years before they begin school.

Evidence derived from collaborative research between the fields of law and the early years is contributing to research evidence. (Mathews et al., 2009) investigated educators' awareness of the requirements of reporting on child sexual abuse and neglect, including frequency of reporting. Their analysis proposed improvements in training for educators to build a working knowledge of child abuse indicators and their legislative duties to report on suspected cases. Along with other work in this area, this research has resulted in moves towards national legislation and policy surrounding the reporting duties of educators when reporting sexual abuse. Thus the effectiveness of using research evidence to make improvements in reporting and policy for early years learners is highlighted.

Longitudinal evidence

Longitudinal studies explore social and cultural contexts over time, and provide educators with evidence about issues that routinely have been debated and discussed within early years education. For example, research on poverty, health, family and child care provides educators with findings and recommendations that generate meanings and questions about what we do in early years and why. *Growing Up in Australia: The Longitudinal Study of Australian Children* (LSAC) (2012) produced by the Department of Families, Australian Institute of Family Studies and Australian Bureau of Statistics examines the impact of Australia's unique social and cultural environment on children (born between the late 1990s and the early 2000s). This study addresses a range of research questions about parenting, family relationships, childhood education, non-parental child care and health. By tracking children over time, the study will determine the individual, family and broader social and environmental factors affecting children's development. This work will provide evidence for educators in the early years as we make decisions about children's development and the contexts in which they live. Results from the study will also identify opportunities for early intervention and prevention strategies in early years policy areas.

Comparative evidence

Comparative studies provide valuable evidence for best practice through an examination of different education systems or models. The reports of the Organization for Economic Cooperation and Development (OECD), *Starting Strong* and *Starting Strong II* (2001, 2006) examined three cases of highly regarded early childhood models, including Reggio Emilia (Italy), Te Whāriki (New Zealand) and Lpfö 98 (Sweden). These case studies provide evidence for child participation and democratic principles to be included as key features in pedagogy and curricula in early childhood education. *Starting Strong II* (OECD, 2006) found further evidence that valuing early years learners' freedom of choice, play and creative expression leads to more successful education systems.

Childhood studies

Studies in the social sciences demonstrate how early years learners manage their everyday interactions within various educational contexts. Childhood studies stemming from the understandings of theoretical frameworks such as the sociologies of childhood and the competence paradigm (James & Prout, 1997) are starting to shape principles informing practice. These theories recognise that early years learners demonstrate their agency as they manage their everyday interactions in different educational contexts. Through research approaches, including ethnomethodology, researchers gather data to show how early years learners demonstrate their competence in shaping their everyday lives.

Ethnomethodology is an example of a social science approach that examines people's methods for producing, organising and making sense of their everyday lives (Garfinkel, 1967). This approach provides a fine-grained examination of how early years learners, through their talk and actions, demonstrate their competencies as they contribute to their everyday activities within early childhood classrooms and playgrounds. For example, Danby (2002) explored the verbal and non-verbal interactions of early years learners in a classroom. Her analysis showed how early years learners competently used communication strategies to accomplish play activities. This work challenges dominant theories about the lack of skills early years learners may have when organising their social endeavours, and provided ways for educators to reconsider early years learners' competence. Similarly, Theobald (2009), in a study of children's play during recess, shows how early years learners use telling as a tactical tool to manage their interactions with peers. These researchers have contributed empirical evidence to substantiate the theoretical propositions of agency and competence.

Recent studies demonstrate early years learners' competence in reporting on their daily experiences and their role as active participants is research. These studies provide evidence for how early years learners construct and account for what is taking place as they interact with others in their daily activities. For example, Thorpe et al.'s (2004) study of the views of Australian Foundation Year learners suggest that consulting with early years learners is critical because it uncovers matters that are important to children, but that may be disregarded by adults. Their findings reinforce the growing message about children's capabilities when it comes to expressing their own views.

Systemic evidence: The use of NAPLAN results

Another form of evidence informing the profession, and the success or otherwise of current approaches, is testing data. One component of national reforms within the Australian educational context is the implementation of the National Assessment Plan—Literacy and Numeracy (NAPLAN), which uses national scales across the areas of reading, writing, spelling, grammar and punctuation and numeracy to gauge the level of attainment in Years 3, 5, 7 and 9. The data, generated through NAPLAN tests, are positioned by the Australian Curriculum, Assessment and Reporting Authority (ACARA) as an evidence base to ascertain the effectiveness of educational programs. Similarly, in many other Western countries, statistical data generated through national testing has a powerful influence on system change and pedagogy.

As part of your thinking around 'evidence', you need to consider evidence in a number of ways. First, how will the evidence inform your practice? Second, given that you ultimately are accountable for educational outcomes, how will this evidence influence the kind of pedagogy you adopt within your setting? Third, what kinds of evidence will you privilege?

Using EBP to support practice in the early years

The Australian educational context has undergone enormous reforms as part of the 'Education Revolution' (Australian Labor Party 2009–12). An 'Education Revolution' has been rolled out within the non-compulsory and compulsory years of education, with the early years a key focus area. These initiatives draw upon the best available international research evidence to ensure optimum outcomes for early years learners. Within the context of educational reforms, opportunities abound for educators to critically reflect upon their own teaching practice. As they examine current research, educators may make changes to their practice in order to accomplish alignment with the expectations embedded in new initiatives. Some examples of educators engaged in the process of evidence-based practice are detailed below.

Example 20.1: Intentional teaching (birth to four years)

The implementation of Being, Belonging and Becoming: The Early Years Learning Framework is an important component of the Australian government's National Quality Framework for early childhood education and care. One of the eight pedagogical practices identified within the framework is intentional teaching. Anecdotal data suggest that this is one dimension of the framework with which many educators grapple, so it provides a relevant issue to investigate using evidence-based practice. Anne, an educator in the toddlers' room of a child-care centre, begins with the problem of how to implement intentional teaching. She consults current research in early years journals and relevant websites to research her question on the appropriate ways to implement intentional teaching for early years learners.

Anne finds that the research suggests that intentional teaching is best used when incorporated with the everyday activities of early years learners. She decides to make use of a conflict over a toy to implement intentional teaching. Using puppets, Anne role-plays a conflict over a toy and asks the early years learners to help the puppets take turns. Anne then reinforces this learning by demonstrating turn-taking. Anne discusses and reflects out loud the actions of the puppets as they resolve the conflict.

Example 20.2: Litterless lunch (four to eight years)

The introduction of the Australian Curriculum (ACARA, 2010), the first national curriculum for Australian schools, offers a challenge to Elizabeth, an educator of a Year 3 class. A priority across the curriculum is sustainability. Elizabeth's challenge is to find sustainable initiatives that might be worth using in her school to create a litterless lunch.

Elizabeth starts by observing existing practices at lunch time with regard to litter. She records the types of packaging being used in children's lunches. After discussing her action with others in the school, litter from the lunches is collected and sorted into two groups: lunch packaging (such as cling wrap or alfoil); and consumables (such as apple cores and sandwich crusts). The amount of litter collected is documented and measured. Plastic wrappings for sandwiches and packaging of processed foods are identified as the main contributor to the packaging litter.

In class, Elizabeth consults current research on the importance of engaging in sustainable practices and web searches about the ways to cut down on lunch-time litter with the early years learners (Pratt, 2010). Together, Elizabeth and the children find that the amount of packaging in land fill is considerable and costs are associated with making and eradicating the packaging. They also search the web for ideas implemented by other schools that have adopted the concept of the litterless lunch. Cutting down on the packaging from processed foods by buying in bulk and putting into small containers is decided on as an initiative. As well, sandwiches could be placed into containers rather than wrapped separately. Critical dialogue takes place with colleagues, early years learners and parents at the school to reflect on what could be done. These conversations are an important part of the process, and often mean Elizabeth, as part of the EBP cycle, goes back to find further research to support the initiative in relation to sustainability.

After the discussion and planning process, a school litterless lunch initiative is put into place. Ways to cut down on packaging are promoted and discussed within the school. Early years learners and parents are asked to keep a weekly journal for three weeks recording the actions they take. At the end of a four-week trial, the litter is collected and measured. A noticeable change in the amount of packaging is recorded. This initiative and the research to support the process are documented and shared with other educators and families.

Gathering our own evidence

Underpinning engagement in research are aspirations and a commitment by us as educators to make a difference in the lives of early years learners. Collaborating with colleagues and others promotes our critical reflection as we engage multiple perspectives and question the authenticity of research. Collaborating with academic researchers provides educators with another way to accumulate evidence to inform our practice. As educators, we are careful observers and listeners of early learners;

however, working with others—including researchers and peers—enables us to view another perspective of our everyday interactions. Through purposeful conversations with other staff working with early years learners, educators can explore the following questions: What evidence is available? What are the current views of evidence? How does the evidence relate to our particular setting and how we might support early years learners' contributions to gather evidence?

Example 20.3: A critical friend (four to eight years)

Within a larger research project, one of the authors video-recorded early years learners interacting with their peers in a Queensland school. Using video-stimulation, in which short excerpts of the video-recordings are shown to those early years learners in the video recording, research conversations are held. Following research approaches that position children as active participants, the author then works with the educator of the setting to unpack the early years learners' perspectives. In one conversation, several girls watch an interaction involving themselves playing school. During the interaction, three girls complain about playing a pretend game of school yet stay to play. It is revealed in the conversation that the girls seriously attend to the moral obligations of being a player in a game and their staying to play, demonstrating their obligations of friendship ahead of their participation in other activities. This conversation, along with similar research on peer interactions, provides empirical evidence to show that the girls are actually attending to the rules of the game: 'no going away'. Without the evidence, the girls' actions may be thought to be due to a lack of confidence and insufficient social skills to stand up to a more dominant child in the interaction. The educator affirms the benefits of having a third party observe and discuss the happenings of the playground with her.

The early years learner's perspective

Early years learners also can be valued participants in evidence-based practice. This might occur in relation to social and/or organisational issues in the classroom. Class meetings, where issues or problems are identified and then possible ways of approaching the issue researched and negotiated, are one example of how early years learners can be included in evidence-based practice. The adoption of this approach is underpinned by an understanding of early years learners as competent and capable of making decisions about their activities and contexts. This approach includes and trusts early years learners, and requires a willingness by us as educators to embrace the options that early years learners suggest—some of which may not necessarily be the ones that we have in mind.

Example 20.4: Planning a playground (four to eight years)

Contemporary research situates early years learners as competent decision-makers and informants in the research process. The need for a new playground provided an inner-city Brisbane school with an issue to be addressed using the steps outlined in EBP. While the educators researched playground designs and the needs of the children during outside play, the early years learners were included in the process too. As part of a class discussion, the educators ask the children what they value in a playground. The early years learners' ideas are recorded and collated. Next, the early years learners and educator research current evidence about the use of playgrounds and modern playground designs. These ideas are matched with the suggestions proposed by the early years learners, with the top five ideas being space to run, places to climb, places to talk, real animals and plants to look after. Images of the playground are drawn and then represented in 3D designs. The early years learners share their ideas and plans with the designer from the playground company. The playground designer then incorporates their ideas into the design. The resulting playground has a pen for hens, gardens for vegetables and herbs, climbing platforms, bridges and paths, and space to run. As well, positioned around the playground is quiet space for talking and wonderment.

Example 20.5: The three pigs (birth to four years)

During outdoor play time, a group of four-year-olds use a cardboard house to act out the story of 'The Three Little Pigs'. The educator sees that too many children are trying to play in the cardboard house, and overcrowding is making turn-taking a problem. The educator reflects on the problem, brings the early years learners together and asks what a possible solution could be. The early years learners are able to decide who they would like to play with, and they select one friend each in turn. A participatory approach is thus taken, offering the early years learners an opportunity to have influence and participate in the decision-making of how turn-taking in the game will be managed. In so doing, the educator promotes early years learners' agency and participation within the constraints of the institutional setting. (Theobold and Kultti, 2012)

Action research

Evidence-based practice can be achieved through action research. Central to evidence-based practice and action research is the identification of an issue or challenge to be investigated, gathering information/evidence and generating new insights about the issue, and formulating plans for action.

An action research process involves educators in a process of both action and inquiry, with the primary goal being to generate change. An action research approach employs cycles of planning, acting, reflecting and re-planning (Kemmis, 1999), which promote learning from experience. The process has phases that are interwoven, overlapping and repetitive, rather than sequentially 'fixed' or procedural. This is because participants learn from their experiences, revise directions and priorities, and introduce changes throughout the project.

The process of action research starts by identifying an issue that affects or is important to the learners or the learning setting (see Figure 20.2). Once an issue is identified, ways to investigate the issue are decided upon. Appropriate ways to gain information include holding research conversations, observing members in the learning setting, looking closely at one example, carefully studying one's own actions,

Figure 20.2   Action research

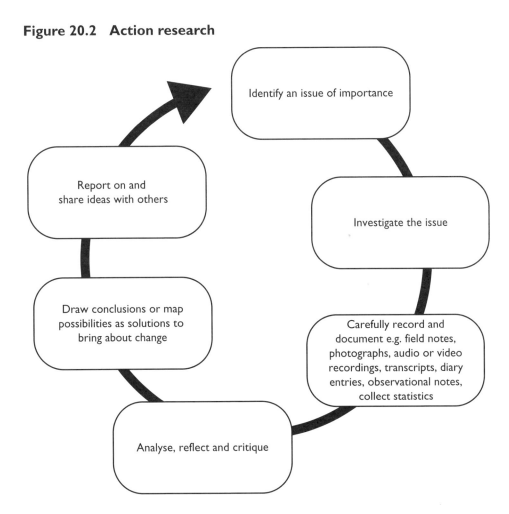

and sharing stories or ideas about the topic. Using a range of techniques to study a topic provides educators with a range of perspectives from which to examine it.

The action research process must be recorded and documented carefully. This is done in a variety of ways, including making field notes, taking photographs, making audio- or video-recordings, recording transcripts, making diary entries or writing observational notes about the members and their interactions with various elements of their settings (Borgia & Schuler, 1998). In addition, documentation is sourced through other methods, such as test scores, questionnaires and statistical records. Once information is collected, a careful process of analysis takes place. Reflection and critique are key elements of this process. We can then draw conclusions or map possibilities as solutions to bring about change. Reporting on and sharing our ideas with others are also important steps in the cyclic process.

Benefits of action research

The strength of action research includes having ownership of a project. Through action research, we acquire new skills and knowledge to examine issues/challenges from many points of view. Part of our examination of a topic includes the use of other people and research evidence. A deep understanding of the process of learning is initiated, and our professional competencies as producers of knowledge recognised. Because action research involves close analysis of practice, it becomes intertwined and embedded in the everyday practices that we are examining (Kemmis, 2010). As a result, the understandings and assumptions that underlie our everyday practices are challenged, and may be changed as much as the activities and conditions of practice themselves. Focusing on what happens as a consequence of our practice is an important part of the action research process (Kemmis, 2010).

Through accessing current research and gathering our own research, evidence-based practice enables us as educators to be both leaders and professionals. We do this as we access, conduct and evaluate research relevant to our own practice. In an age of increased accountability, educators' decisions are supported with the use of research as part of an inquiry process.

Summary

- While drawing on our professional knowledge, the detailed attention to research required to engage in evidence-based practice ensures that our decisions as educators are based upon substantiated evidence rather than beliefs or intuition.

- As we consult and research as part of the steps in EBP, we contribute to a high professional standard of education and the best possible outcomes for children. Evidence-based practice is a process that all early childhood educators can embrace.
- Following analysis of relevant evidence, EBP enables educators to uncover possibilities for resolving issues or challenges.
- Educators need to be aware of the different sources of evidence and engage in thoughtful analysis of evidence.
- Evidence-based practice may involve collaboration with children, with peers and with colleagues—including researchers.
- Evidence-based practice contributes to continual professional renewal, with the potential for educators to produce new evidence.

Discussion questions

20.1 How is participation in generating evidence part of an educator's everyday work as a professional?

20.2 Do early years learners have a part to play in the generation of evidence to support practice?

20.3 What is the place of systemic data that is generated and available publicly?

20.4 How do we assess evidence as being of a high quality?

20.5 How does the research evidence contribute to your capacity to advocate for early years learners?

References

Australian Curriculum, Assessment and Reporting Authority (ACARA) (2010). *The Australian Curriculum*. Retrieved 17 January 2010 from <www.australiancurriculum.edu.au>.

Borgia, E. & Schuler, D. (1998). Action research in early childhood. *Early Childhood Today*, 12(8), 49–51.

Brookfield, S. (1995). *Becoming a critically reflective teacher*. San Francisco: Jossey-Bass.

Centre for Community Child Health (2011). *Policy brief: Translating early childhood research evidence to inform policy and practice*. Melbourne: Centre for Community Child Health.

Danby, S.J. (2002). The communicative competence of young children. *Australian Journal of Early Childhood*, 27(3), 25–30.

Department of Education, Employment and Workforce Relations (DEEWR) (2009). *Belonging, being and becoming: The Early Years Learning Framework for Australia*. Canberra: Commonwealth of Australia.

Department of Families, Australian Institute of Family Studies and Australian Bureau of Statistics (2012). *Growing up in Australia: The Longitudinal Study of Australian Children*. Canberra: AIFS. Retrieved 20 April 2012 from <www.aifs.gov.au/growingup/pubs/asr/2011/index.html>.

Fasoli, L. & Woodrow, C. (1998). Change and criticism: Thinking critically in early childhood collaboration. *Australian Journal of Early Childhood, 23*(1), 40–4.

Garfinkel, H. (1967). *Studies in ethnomethodology*. Englewood Cliffs, NJ: Prentice-Hall.

Groundwater-Smith, S. (2000). Evidence-based practice: Towards whole school improvement. Paper presented at the Australian Association for Research in Education Conference, Sydney, December.

Groundwater-Smith, S., Ewing, R. & Le-Cornu, R. (2011). *Teaching: Challenges and dilemmas*, 4th ed. Melbourne: Cengage.

James, A. & Prout, A. (eds) (1997). *Constructing and reconstructing childhood: Contemporary issues in the sociological study of childhood*, 2nd ed. London: Falmer Press.

Kemmis, S. (1999). Action research. In J.P. Keeves & G. Lakomski (eds), *Issues in educational research* (pp. 150–60). Oxford: Pergamon Press.

——(2010). What is to be done? The place of action research. *Educational Action Research, 18*(4), 417–27.

Mathews, B.P., Walsh, K.M., Rassafiani, M., Butler, D.A. & Farrell, A. (2009). Teachers reporting suspected child sexual abuse: Results of a three-state study. *University of New South Wales Law Journal, 32*(3), 772–813.

Organization for Economic Cooperation and Development (OECD) (2001). *Starting strong: Early childhood education and care—education and skills*. Paris: OECD.

——(2006). *Starting strong II: Early childhood education and care*. Paris: OECD.

Pratt, R. (2010). Practical possibilities and pedagogical approaches for early childhood education for sustainability. In J.M. Davis (Ed). *Young children and the environment: early education for sustainability*. Pp 104–153. Melbourne: Cambridge University Press.

Queensland College of Teachers (2006). *Professional standards for Queensland teachers*. Brisbane: Queensland College of Teachers.

Sackett, D.L., Strauss, S.E., Richardson, W.S., Rosenberg, W.S. & Hayes, R.B. (2000). *Evidence-based medicine: How to practice and teach EBM*, 2nd ed. New York: Churchill Livingstone.

Shore, R. (1997). *Rethinking the brain: New insights into early development*. New York: Families at Work Institute.

Theobald, M.A. (2009). *Participation and social order in the playground*. Brisbane: University of Technology.

Theobald, M., & Danby, S. (in press) 'Well, now I'm upset': Moral and social orders in the playground. In J. Cromdal & M. Tholander (Eds.) *Morality in practice: Exploring Childhood, Parenthood and Schooling in Everyday Life*. Equinox Publishing Ltd, London.

Theobald, M & Kultti, A (2012). Investigating child participation in the everyday talk of teacher and children in a preparatory year. *Contemporary Issues in Early Childhood, 13*(3), 210–225.

Thorpe, K., Tayler, C., Bridgstock, R., Grieshaber, S., Skoien, P., Danby, S., et al. (2004). Preparing for school: Report of the Queensland 'Preparing for school' trial 2003/04. Brisbane: Department of Education and the Arts.

Trinder, L. (2000). Introduction: the context of evidence-based practice. In L. Trinder & S. Reynolds (eds), *Evidence-based practice: A critical appraisal*. London: Blackwell.

21

Gender

Scott Harrison

Introduction

> Of all the things you might remember about someone, when did you ever forget
> what sex someone was, even after the most fleeting encounter? (White, 1989, p. 17)

From the moment of birth ('It's a boy!' or 'It's a girl!'), gender takes on an important role in life. While the biological sex of an individual is usually evident at birth, we don't always understand the ways in which gender are enacted. The significance of these words, according to Doyle (1995, p. 2) lies in the 'restrictions they set, the privileges they grant and the expectations they lay down'.

One of the greatest challenges in education for both boys and girls is the way in which gender is constructed and enforced in different cultures around the world. For example, in Western cultures there is a significant body of literature indicating that girls continue to outperform boys in most areas of schooling, and that the gender gap in educational achievement is widening. Boys, recent research indicates, also undertake a narrower range of subjects and activities at school than girls. Historically, girls have been prevented from achieving in certain areas and, despite the significant gains of the feminist movement, this is still the case. It could be argued that these restrictions begin in the formative early years phase from birth to age eight.

This chapter examines the role of gender in shaping the early years. Popular literature abounds with advice about single-sex versus mixed-sex schools; separation of students on the basis of sex for particular activities; sex-stereotyping of school subjects; and the feminisation of teaching in this phase of development.

Using case studies, this chapter seeks to debunk popular myths by presenting research into the context of gender in the early years, and the gendered experiences of children in a variety of contexts. While some of the material focuses on arts-based practices, implications for other subject areas are apparent. Approaches to pedagogy and assessment feature in these cases, providing research-based applications for institutional administrators, teacher educators, educators, parents and caregivers.

Definitions and contexts

There are a number complexities involved in discussing this topic. One concerns the over-emphasis of small sex-based differences. Another is the question of the elusiveness, fluidity and complex interrelationships of biological sex, gender and sexuality.

The following definitions are drawn from the World Heath Organization (WHO): '*Gender* refers to the economic, social and cultural attributes and opportunities associated with being male or female at a particular point in time' while '*Sex* refers to the biological characteristics that define humans as female or male. While these sets of biological characteristics are not mutually exclusive, as there are individuals who possess both, they tend to differentiate humans as males and females.' (WHO, 2002, author's emphasis) *Sexuality* is the preference for male and/ or female partners and the performance of the acts associated with those preferences (Harrison et al., 2012). While sexuality is, in essence, a behavioural construction, there are societal values associated with (somewhat limited) static delineations of heterosexual, homosexual, bisexual and other identities.

Two further definitions inform the discussion to follow. *Gender congruence* is described as the extent to which an individual's personal attributes and behaviour conform to societal expectations for their gender. These attributes generally are expected to align with their biological sex within that society. In Western society, subordinate sexualities (i.e. all sexualities other than heterosexual), behaviours and choices that are perceived to be gender incongruent are, in some circumstances, met with negative social implications. *Gender differentiation* relates to the notion of over-emphasis on small differences, and is defined as the exaggeration or creation of differences where none exist. Three further concepts, *gender identity*, *gender stability* and *gender constancy*, will be unpacked later in the chapter.

The role of gender in the early years: Biological and sociological ideas

One could argue that, in an effectively organised society, each child would be allowed to identify his or her potential for the development of socially valued talents and traits. This would be followed by the cultivation of these characteristics through both formal and informal educational processes, with the eventual utilisation of these talents for the betterment of society and the well-being of the individual. This is frequently not the case due to a variety of reasons, one of which is gender. Gender is, of course, only one of the organising principles of social existence, and should be considered alongside other major mechanisms including race, religion, age and social class, as described elsewhere in this volume.

Gender differentiation, as defined above, begins almost immediately for most children. One example of this is colour-coded clothing and bedrooms for babies. This differentiation continues as children reach points at which talents and traits are assessed. Differential treatment of these characteristics often takes place on the basis of the sex of the child.

There are two basic points of view about gender difference in society: the essentialist and the constructivist. On one hand, the suggestion is made that gender differences are the result of biology, while on the other hand sits the notion that gender behaviours are acquired or constructed. Biological models have focused on the way in which innate biological differences are responsible for different behaviours in males and females. Constructivist models have reflected on the effects of socialisation of boys and girls in relation to their sex-role.

Physical differences

Recently, a number of researchers have investigated the physical differences between males and females. Table 21.1 represents a summary of the differences documented over the last 30 years.

Biological research has demonstrated that differences exist in terms of hormonal balance and reproductive processes. With regard to hormones, similar levels of

Table 21.1   Summary of male and female physical attributes

Attribute	Male	Female
Facial features	Pronounced, face and head longer	Delicate, face and head rounder
Neck	Thicker, longer	Shorter, more rounded
Shoulders	Broader, squarer	More rounded, sloping
Muscles	Bigger, more obvious	Mostly hidden under fat
Hips	Narrower	Wider, more rounded
Hands/feet	Larger, digits stronger and blunter	Smaller and narrower
Legs	Longer, bulging calves	Smoother contours
Vision	Narrower field, longer	Wider field, shorter
Hearing	More directional	Less directional, more sensitive
Taste/touch/smell	Less sensitive	More sensitive

hormone are present in male and female pre-pubescent children, yet behaviours are different. It is also known that the presence of testosterone affects behaviour, as does the presence of oestrogen.

Other differences

Researchers in the field of physical difference have also noted behavioural differences between the sexes. Some researchers claim that these are related to physical attributes, while others insist that they are purely the result of enculturation. This debate will be pursued later in the chapter. In either scenario, these differences are worth investigation.

The behaviours in Table 21.2 are commonly exhibited in each of the sexes, with the caveat that each of the behaviours represents broad generalisations.

Unpacking this a little further, the view that girls become more verbally competent than boys has been supported by research, with girls rating more highly in measures of speech production and anagrams. Girls tend to excel in spelling and grammar while boys suffer from speech difficulties (for example, a boy is three or four times more likely to suffer from stuttering than a girl) and dyslexia (five to ten times more).

Bullying is acknowledged as a contributor to the construction of gender (see Plummer, 1999; Harrison, 2008). The topic of aggression is therefore particularly

Table 21.2   Summary of behavioural differences between males and females

Male behaviours	Female behaviours
Visual spatial skills dominate, particularly in spatial rotation tasks	Verbal skills dominate—listening, qualifying and self-disclosure
Achievement-centred	Emotional, feeling-centred
Communicate information	Communicate emotions
Power oriented	People oriented
Prefer objects	Prefer faces and names
Prefer autonomous cognitive style	Prefer connected cognitive style
More verbally and physically aggressive, compete, dominate	Cooperate, listen, sensitive to verbal and non-verbal cues
Generally better at strength activities	Generally better at balance, rhythm
Generally better at gross motor skills	Generally better at fine motor skills

relevant in this chapter. Both sexes learn aggressive behaviour, but it appears young females are more inhibited about performing it. Preschool males have been found to have the highest rates of aggressive behaviours, largely due to the gender segregation that occurs because of a peer-driven difference in play style. Boys at age three are engaging in more aggressive behaviours, such as hitting and pushing. They play in large groups, outdoors, and are more likely to have a leader. Girls at this age begin to exhibit more nurturing behaviours, such as grooming and offering compliments. Boys have also been found to excel in motor performance from about age three. This could potentially have a biological base that is enhanced by training: differential treatment and practice almost certainly account for differences in agility, balance, eye–motor coordination, flexibility and reaction time.

The physical differences between the sexes shown in Table 21.1 generally are accepted as being accurate for the majority of the population. The behaviours listed in Table 21.2 are common enough for a number of researchers to agree that they can be applied to each sex. The argument of the essentialists is that these behaviours are the result of physical differences.

In summary, boys appear to excel in visual spatial activities and girls in verbal abilities. Girls generally outperform boys in creative tasks that involve words.

Boys appear to have better gross motor skills, while girls have better rhythm. While these could be seen as perpetuating traditional stereotypes, it should be reiterated that the sexes do not seem to have radical differences in abilities, but it is the enhancement of these small differences through stereotyping that leads, in part, to the construction of gender.

The construction of gender

There are two major cognitive developmental theories concerning children's developing knowledge of gender: the development of gender concept and the gender schema theory. These theories have their foundations in the burgeoning literature on gender that arose in the late 1960s and 1970s.

In gender concept theory, children develop gender identity, stability and constancy. Kohlerg (1966) summarises the development of gender concept in these terms:

> Gender identity, based on physical characteristics, is established at around age two. Gender stability, that is that gender is stable across time (once a male always a male), usually occurs between the ages of three and four while gender constancy (gender is constant across time and situations) is apparent by the age of five.

Through self-socialisation, children have knowledge of differential sex roles from an early age—certainly, according to Edelbrock and Sugawara (1978), before entering school. By the age of five, children are aware of sex stereotype traits as tested by Best et al. (1977). Women, Best says, are perceived by this age group to be gentle and affectionate while men are seen as strong and aggressive. By the age of eleven, further delineation has occurred, with other traits determined by adolescence. Urberg (1982) concurs, reporting that children aged as young as two are beginning to learn traditional sex role stereotypes, and that by the age of seven they are as accurate as adults in labelling traits or activities as stereotypically masculine or feminine.

Gender schema theory describes and explains the developing content and organisation of gender knowledge. Distinct dimensions of gender-related knowledge include behaviours, roles, occupations and traits. Of these, the orthogonal view is of interest in this discussion. This means that instead of masculine and feminine being opposite poles of the one axis, they are actually in different perpendicular dimensions and therefore independently variable. This view of gender is espoused by Bem (1981), who developed the Sex Role Inventory, still considered the standard measure for determining sex roles. This inventory includes a list of personality characteristics considered to be stereotypically male or female. For example, those considered feminine might include affectionate or gentle, while those considered male may include ambitious or assertive. The importance of the development of this inventory is that, unlike earlier scales, it deals with masculinity and femininity as two independent dimensions. According to the inventory, someone can therefore hold both masculine and feminine attitudes.

The development of gender concept and gender schema theory share two basic assumptions:

- Children's understanding of gender differs at different ages.
- The development of gender understanding parallels the development of children's growing ability to reason about other aspects of the world.

Gender role behaviour is acquired through the same process as other behaviours. Sex-typed behaviour (that is, behaviour where the sex and the gender are the same) is thought to be the result of differential reinforcement of boys and girls.

Common examples of differential reinforcement can be found in Fagot's (1978) study of children aged from 20 to 24 months. Girls were given approval for dancing, dolls and dress-ups while being discouraged from running, jumping, climbing and manipulating. Boys were more likely to be discouraged from engaging in feminine behaviour. This is a significant issue that is central to the construction of masculinity and femininity. The research of Langlois and Downs (1980) supports this view, while Lytton and Romney (1991) found that toys, games and activity choices were important aspects of gender development. Parental differences in treatment were found to decrease between the ages of two and five.

Given the early age at which stereotypes have been found to exist, parental attitude and role modelling are of considerable significance. As parents and educators are a product of their own culture, they have certain ideas that are held to be appropriate behaviour for boys and girls. The educator as role model can have positive and/or negative effects on student behaviour.

It is almost impossible to separate biological and constructed influences. Gender identity is formed through the interaction of biological, psychological and socio-cultural factors. Biology can create tendencies for boys and girls to behave differently, but it is not an absolute. For example, the 'testosterone equals aggression equals boys' viewpoint has virtually no research to support it. Cultural stereotypes and the reinforcing behaviours of other children and adults may exaggerate these small differences in biology. There is no logical reason to suggest that biology causes behaviour, or that the line of causation moves only from the biological to the social. The view being espoused here is that biological differences are a small but significant part of the construction of gender. The physical differences are significant because they form the basis for stereotypes on which the gender divide is constructed. Gender is constructed and biology, along with many other factors, contributes to this construction.

Illuminative case studies

In the second part of this chapter, fictionalised accounts of children in the early years are presented to highlight the ideas espoused above.

Case study 21.1: Emily

Emily is two. She plays equally with trucks and dolls, and wears clothing of all shapes, sizes and colours. She is a relatively quiet child who mostly plays with her sisters and cousins, all of whom are girls. Her parents are Chinese, and moved to Australia just before Emily was born. They have high expectations of Emily: her father works in information systems, and her mother spends her time at home with the children. They are quite wealthy. Emily is bilingual, takes dance lessons and is involved in a local computing club that specialises in activities for children in the early years. She will attend the local Catholic primary school and its associated co-educational secondary school. The family are quite devout, and religious observance is taken very seriously. Emily's social circle is relatively restricted to siblings and family friends, though she does interact with a variety of other children in the two hours per week she spends at the local computing club.

Case study 21.2: Brian

Brian is four. He loves fishing with his dad, and his favourite sport in summer is surfing. In winter, he plays football. His dad was a professional footballer, and there is an expectation that Brian will follow in his father's footsteps. Brian's father now works on the land, and his mother helps out as a teaching assistant at the local school. His father identifies as an Indigenous Australian and his mother is of Spanish extraction, having immigrated to Australia in the last seven years. As a result, Brian takes lessons in Latin dance and is encouraged to speak both Spanish and English at home. Brian is about to start his formal education in the preschool setting, and his parents have decided he will attend the local state school. Because his family lives in a rural location, Brian will go to a co-educational boarding school when he is twelve. This will put a serious strain on the family finances, as their income is not particularly high. He has a large circle of friends, most of whom are boys of his own age who are sons of his father's friends.

Case study 21.3: Chloe

Chloe is seven. She has a strong interest in the visual arts, but her parents also recognise the importance of her participating in sport as a way of connecting with other children. This is partly because she is an only child. She plays netball in winter and softball in summer. She has a strong sense of what is fashionable, and has highly individual tastes in her clothing choices. Most of her time at home is spent making things with found objects, cutting up paper and drawing. She is an active child and sometimes displays what some would describe as aggressive behaviours. She is physically strong, and has the capacity to overpower older children. In spite of this, she has a large group of friends, most of whom are girls. Chloe's parents are of southern European descent, and are first-generation Australians. They are not wealthy, but make huge efforts to ensure that their child is given every opportunity to participate in a variety of activities. Chloe attends a single-sex school operated by a religious order. Her parents' intention is that she will complete her schooling in this environment.

Case study 21.4: Greg

Greg is eight. He loves music. A softly spoken and gentle child, he has low muscle tone and therefore finds sport difficult. His preferred recreational activities are computer games and reading, but he has attempted a few physical activities including golf, tennis and swimming. He sings in the school choir, and has recently taken up violin. Other than his choral experience, Greg is a solitary child who enjoys his own company. The other children at his school occasionally mock him, largely because of his ineptitude in sporting endeavours. Most members of his small group of friends are girls. His parents are relatively affluent—one works as a school teacher and the other as a nurse. As such, there is a strong emphasis on education in the family setting, and an expectation of hard work. Their ethnic background is Anglo-Saxon, and Greg's grandparents were first-generation Australians. Greg attends a state school, but will go to a single-sex private school for his secondary schooling.

Commentary

The cases above serve to demonstrate how gender, biological sex and the other organising principles (race, age, religion and social class) interact. In these cases, the lines are blurred between ages, cultural background and parental income. A further influence can be noted in Brian's case: geographical location. Because of his rural upbringing, Brian's experiences will be different from those described in the other cases. This, combined with his Indigenous heritage and football experience, will play out very differently from a city-dwelling child of European descent.

A male who undertakes dance classes may be subject to some questioning from his peers in other circumstances. His involvement in sport helps to 'balance the ledger' to ensure his gender congruity remains intact. Greg, on the other hand, challenges the balance. This is due partly to his non-involvement in sport. The emphasis on the physical has its basis in the small biological differences described earlier, but has no logical bearing on gender congruity. Greg's other interests and personality traits also come into play to bring his gendered behaviours into question. For Emily, cultural background is also an important factor. At age three, her gender identity has been established, and she is in the midst of developing an understanding of gender stability. As a female, she is less likely to be confronted with the mocking to which Greg has been subjected, as family members guard the masculine identity more rigidly at this age than the feminine identity. Her family's religious affiliation will, in time, play a role in her gendered behaviours, but at this stage she and her family are content with a slight mixing of stereotypical activities. With the exception of her slightly aggressive behaviours, Chloe probably represents as close to the expected 'norm', if one were to exist. Her development of gender constancy is relatively consistent with others of her age, and her aggression could be viewed as a strength. The choice of a single-sex school for both Chloe and Greg will probably play out in different ways. Greg is more vulnerable and may benefit from the co-educational setting, while Chloe, with her involvement in a variety of activities, will no doubt thrive in any educational setting.

Implications for curriculum, pedagogy and assessment

Educational institutions typically operate on systems that reward specific behaviours, actions and successes. A casual observation of early childhood services and school functions such as assemblies places in stark relief the activities that are valued in that community. Often curricula and co-curricula offerings in athletics and the so-called 'academic' subjects such as mathematics, sciences and technologies receive greater visibility and rewards than the 'lesser' subjects—languages, studies of society and the fine arts. This has implications for children who choose to engage in the humanities and the arts, for whom less institutional significance translates to lower social and self-esteem. Educational institutions can reinforce this hierarchy by allotting greater resources (equipment, facilities and personnel) to more highly valued subjects and activities. In the home, parents and other family members can, either overtly or inadvertently, value some activities with time and levels of interest.

Children become alert to these cues early on, and therefore rationalise the activities in which they engage in order to maximise their social acceptance. Children increasingly make academic and activity choices in a gendered social context in which their choices will directly affect their social and self-esteem. Furthermore, children may choose activities that enact the behaviours that reflect their community. The hierarchy of activities by gender (Figure 21.1) illustrates the implicit system of rules and expectations for individuals' behaviour and the investment of time that influences children's and parents' decision-making about activities. The further a subject is from the masculine end of the spectrum and the closer it is to the feminine end, the less valued it is in society, and therefore in the institutional context. Subjects that present the most masculine associations also carry the greatest identity capital; conversely, subjects that present the most feminine associations carry the greatest identity liability, and increasingly are avoided by both males and females, who increasingly are competitive for places of social and academic power in their institutional interactions and beyond. For males, these subjects can also reflect the distinctly male femininity that is associated with homosexuality, and therefore carry additional identity liability. This can have serious consequence for the physical and verbal bullying of boys. For girls, the means through which acceptable behaviours are mediated are likely to be less obvious, but can be equally damaging. Social isolation is a powerful tool for both boys and girls; however, for girls, being excluded from the 'in' crowd can be devastating.

Figure 21.1   Hierarchy of activities by gender

Masculine	Feminine
Sport	Languages
Information technology	Studies of society and environment
Mathematics	The Arts
Sciences	
Trade technologies	

In relation to pedagogy, gender is, as noted earlier, only one of the organising principles to be considered, along with race, religion, age and social class. Role models form a significant aspect of the delivery of curriculum, and the exposure of children to a variety of pedagogical approaches that take account of all the variables is healthy teaching. Pedagogies that permit flexible delivery in order to account for varying interests, abilities and learning styles are to be encouraged. The scheduling of activities should be carefully considered so that children aren't forced into a choice between, for example, sport and the arts.

Pedagogies that incorporate both single-sex and co-educational activities are one of the ways in which the gendered nature of activities can be mediated. This has been particularly successful in arts-based activities, but has also enjoyed popularity in the technology sphere. This is not to say that either boys or girls should be excluded from any activity; rather, the comfort and productivity of children can be enhanced through the careful consideration of appropriate grouping of students.

Educator biases are frequently evident in pedagogical approaches. An emphasis on the individual strengths of educators is to be encouraged, but the hierarchy described above is not always the result of the top-down imposition of values and beliefs. Rather, teaching methods—including subtle messages to children about acceptable behaviours—often play an important role in shaping children's understanding of acceptable activities and behaviours.

The assessment strategies at this stage of development need to be non-judgemental. They should encourage, value and embrace all contributions, while making children aware of the ways in which they can enhance their talents and traits. Much damage can be done to children through overtly emphasising competitiveness in lieu of the achievement of standards normally associated with other children of a similar age. As noted in the chapter on gifted and talented children, this is often the age at which outstanding talent (including prodigious artistic skills) can be identified and nurtured. Diagnostic assessment that does not hold to gendered norms can play a significant role in this process.

Summary

- Gender plays a significant role in the early years. The notions of gender identity, gender stability and gender constancy are established in this period.
- The relationship between gender, sex and, to a lesser extent, sexuality are evident in children's choice of learning activities, behaviours and social interactions.
- Educators, parents and other caregivers are largely responsible for choosing and encouraging engagement in particular activities at this time. It is the values, beliefs and attitudes of these 'significant others' that can influence the gendered nature of involvement at this age, and therefore into adolescence and early adulthood.

- The responsibility for cultivation of children's talents and traits, regardless of sex and gender, rests with those who work with children in formal and informal processes.
- For institutional administrators, the provision of broad, flexible opportunities in formal and informal settings that are physically and socially safe is critical.
- Teacher educators have a responsibility to engage in research-led teaching that informs future educators about the ways in which gender can be one of the organising principles in school settings.
- For educators, a capacity to embrace diversity and nurture individual talents that may be counter to the 'norm' is vital.
- For parents, it is important to be vigilant in seeking out the most appropriate activities to enhance the natural attributes of their children, and to support endeavours and opportunities that may be considered gender-incongruent.
- For caregivers, it is necessary to ensure that informal interactions are productive without taking away the joys of play-making.

Discussion questions

21.1 What strategies can be put in place to ensure that the natural attributes of children can be enhanced, and new opportunities provided?

21.2 In what ways can awareness of the hierarchy of activities by gender (Figure 21.1) influence curriculum, pedagogy and assessment in the early years?

21.3 How can educators—both pre-service and in-service—take account of gender in designing programs that support diversity?

21.4 What steps can be taken to monitor and challenge subtle messages about accepted gender-based activities?

21.5 How can safe environments be provided for those who display gender-incongruent behaviour?

21.6 What forms of mitigation can be put in place to guard against gender-based bullying that takes place through verbal abuse, physical harassment and social exclusion?

References

Bem, S.L. (1981). *Sex role inventory: Professional manual*. Palo Alto, CA: Consulting Psychologists Press.

Best, D.L., Williams, J.E., Cloud, J.M., Davis, S.W., Robertson, L.S., Edwards, J.R., Giles, H. and Fowles, J. (1977). Development of sex-trait stereotypes among young children in the United States, England and Ireland. *Child Development*, 48, 1375–84.

Doyle, J. (1995). *The male experience.* Dubuque, IO: Brown and Benchmark.

Edelbrock, C. and Sugawara, A.I. (1978). Acquisition of sex-types preferences in pre-school aged children. *Developmental Psychology, 14,* 614–23.

Fagot, B.I. (1978). The influence of sex of child on parental reactions to toddler children. *Child Development, 49,* 459–65.

Harrison, S.D. (2008). *Masculinities and music.* Newcastle on Tyne: Cambridge Scholars Publishing.

Harrison, S.D., Welch, G.F. and Adler, A. (eds) (2012). *Perspectives on males and singing.* New York: Springer.

Kohlberg, L.A. (1966). Cognitive-developmental analysis of children's sex-role concepts and attitudes. In E.E. Maccoby (ed.), *The development of sex differences* (pp. 82–173). Stanford, CA: Stanford University Press.

Langlois, J.H. and Downs, A.C. (1980). Mothers, fathers and peers as socialization agents of sex-typed play behaviours in young children. *Child Development, 51,* 1237–47.

Lytton, H. and Romney, D.M. (1991). Parents' differential socialisation of boys and girls: A meta analysis. *Psychological Bulletin, 109,* 267–96.

Plummer, D. (1999). *One of the boys: Masculinity, homophobia and modern manhood.* New York: Harrington.

Urberg, K.A. (1982). The development of concepts of masculinity and femininity in young children. *Sex Roles, 8,* 659.

White, A. (1989). *Poles apart: The experience of gender.* London: Dent.

World Health Organization, 2002, Gender and Reproductive Rights: Working Definitions, Retrieved June 25, 2012 from http://www.who.int/reproductive-health/gender/sexual_health.html#1.

22

Communities of practice

Katherine Main

Introduction

This chapter provides information about what a community of practice is and how it can help early years educators to be more effective practitioners when they are part of such a community. A definition of a community of practice is presented that sets the context for an educator's personal learning and growth. The chapter highlights and focuses on the educators within the community and their practices. It then outlines the benefits of belonging to a community of practice, as well as facilitators and barriers to building an effective community of practice. It also demonstrates just how fundamental building a community of practice is to the professional growth of individuals and the effectiveness of early years programs, and the resultant improved outcomes for students. The three interconnected processes of community, practice and relationships that must occur simultaneously for communities of practice to be effective are considered in terms of the formation, development and maintenance of a community of practice.

What is a community of practice?

Communities of practice, teaching communities, teams and learning communities are terms that have been used interchangeably within the literature. Each term has been used to describe a type of social structure used by educators to improve their practice. However, in this chapter the term community of practice (CoP) is defined as a purposeful social structure whereby educators regularly come together to work for the collective benefit of students (Lave & Wenger, 1991). The term 'community of practice' was developed through the reconceptualising of learning theories in the late 1980s and early 1990s, whereby social anthropologists began to argue that a large portion of learning comes from our participation in social life and personal interactions (Lave & Wenger, 1991). Lave and Wenger (1991) describe a community of practice as a group of people who share a concern or a passion for something they do, and learn how to do it better as they interact regularly with each other. However, the intent behind the term goes beyond a community of learners. Within a CoP, the learning is embedded within a shared *practice* rather than just a shared learning experience. In such communities, the concept of practice is viewed as a form of ongoing learning by its members, and the process of learning is a positive trajectory of participation in practice. Thus, in an early years CoP, several individuals work together as professionals to improve both their own performance and that of their colleagues in their day-to-day practice.

Using a collaborative approach to educator practice has become more commonplace as both a top-down and bottom-up initiative as both policy and reform directives have begun to either mandate or encourage educators to move away from the traditional isolation of a single-teacher classroom (Little, 2002). As a recognised key strategy for improving practice (Fullan, 1993), CoPs and the resultant collaborative practices have been implemented as part of school-improvement initiatives. These initiatives have been seen as a means of improving outcomes for students and improving educator practice through the shared learning and individual and collective development of the community members (Fullan, 1993).

Historically, a collective approach by a 'community' in an early years setting has consisted of parents, educators and other professionals working together to meet the educational needs of each child. This approach, where communication has been encouraged and facilitated between the various stakeholders in a child's development, has always been an implicit part of working with children, and reverberates throughout early years settings (Wisneski & Goldstein, 2004). However, as Gherardi (2008) notes, the original intent of Lave and Wenger (1991), who coined the term 'communities of practice', was a focus on the 'practices' of the community. In the vast majority of literature around early years CoPs, the breadth of discussion has focused on ways to improve communication between all stakeholders, to raise awareness of best practice and the availability and role of support services. However, the purpose of this chapter is to focus on the *practices* of the *teaching* community (that is, what the educators do) and the potential benefits to both educators and early years learners of this organisational approach in early years settings.

What does a community of practice do?

Within the social structure of a CoP, educators are able to deliver programs and discuss their teaching practice and pedagogy as well as the day-to-day challenges they experience in a classroom of diverse learners. A range of practices can be undertaken collaboratively by members of a community of practice, including but not limited to planning and sharing physical space, planning curriculum, delivering the curriculum (teaching), assessing students, reporting and many of the other day-to-day tasks that are undertaken in early years settings.

Within early years CoPs, practitioners make practices such as lesson planning, personal pedagogy, assessment of and for learning, and observations overt, and also engage in joint teaching to facilitate performance-monitoring. Making these practices known establishes a sense of collaboration and community between educators within the setting. This action serves to perpetuate and further develop the established pedagogy and to look to improve practice. As such, a CoP seeks to locate the learning in the process of co-participation (building social capital) and not just within individuals (Hanks, 1991). Hence collaborative practice can become the main method of professional development for educators improving practice, and for making educators who are working together accountable to each other (Main, 2011).

Characteristics of a community of practice

Three main characteristics need to be present to identify as a CoP. First, a CoP must be defined by a shared area of interest. This shared interest is what makes a CoP move beyond a mere group of people with similar interests or connections, and where particular practices can be identified as belonging to a particular community. Where there is a claim to membership of a CoP, this membership represents a commitment to the field as well as some expertise in the area central to that field. In the case of an early years CoP, members of the community would have both a commitment to an early years philosophy and expertise in teaching early years students. Second, when working towards their interest within that field, members of the CoP may choose to collaborate to help each other and share information. This collaboration and sharing of information helps to build relationships between community members that further enhance and facilitate collaborative learning. This sharing also provides a significant amount of social and emotional support for members. Third, within the common field, there must also be a practice or a repertoire of practices that are being performed (Wenger, 1998).

These three identifying characteristics directly correlate with the three interrelated processes of *community*, *practice* and *relationships* that are necessary for the effective functioning of a CoP. As a process, *community* relates to the protocols and guidelines that set the parameters for the members, or how the community of practice functions (for example, rules, roles, goals). *Practice* processes relate the day-to-day decisions and implementation of curriculum, pedagogy and assessment of and/or learning within the context of the early years. Finally, *relationship* processes relate to the personal and professional interactions between members that facilitate the collaborative implementation of practice (Main, 2010).

Becoming a community of practice

McLellan (1996) argues that much of the learning that occurs within a context is often incidental and unintentional rather than deliberate. The CoP framework supports this notion, as it is built upon two main principles. The first is that knowledge is developed through personal experience—that is, an individual's learning is based in their day-to-day activities, with knowledge being acquired through experience. The second is that one's experience is understood through critical and analytical reflection with others (Buysse et al., 2003). Thus, as a situated theory, the value of belonging to a CoP is twofold: first, the learning is embedded in daily activities and practices whereby an individual's knowledge is gained through personal experience and observing others; and second, continued learning is a positive consequence of the social interactions and processes that require negotiation and problem-solving with others (Stein, 1998). Thus a CoP encourages ongoing personal and collective growth through personal and collective reflection, problem-solving and negotiation during day-to-day practice. However, achieving these positive outcomes requires members of the CoP to recognise the potential benefits of membership of a CoP, and the need to establish the necessary processes and protocols to achieve this.

An early years CoP can be defined as a group of early years professionals who are socially interdependent, who participate together in discussion and decision-making and who share certain practices (such as planning, teaching and assessing) that both define the community and are nurtured by it. As such, a CoP meets all the defining characteristics of a team and extends beyond that to include a shared history and constitutive narrative that is contextual and defines them as a community. However, an effective CoP takes time to develop. The process of creating a CoP that becomes a practising community, and realising the benefits of working collaboratively, involves establishing the community and maintaining it over time. Grossman et al. (2001) suggest that, once formed, a group of educators must work through a developmental process to reach their full potential. In team literature, when a team reaches its full potential, it is said to be a *performing* team. This same terminology can be applied to a CoP.

In research on team practices, it has been shown that a group of educators can go from a newly formed team to a performing team within six to eight months (Wheelan, 2005). As a CoP requires the same sense of identity, collective ownership and collective responsibility as a team, timeline parallels can be drawn between the development and progression of CoPs from forming or beginning communities to performing or mature communities. However, just as in teams, many groups of educators never achieve the goal of truly becoming a CoP and realising the associated benefits of collective participation in such a community. Table 22.1 shows the developmental phases and the identity formation and norms of interaction of a CoP.

The progression from a beginning to a mature CoP is largely dependent upon individuals changing their focus from personal growth and development towards acceptance and commitment to the collective growth and development of all members of the CoP. However, just as in teams, a CoP must move through a life-cycle of formation and development as the established norms of community, practice and relationships evolve.

The life-cyle of a community of practice

The life-cycle of CoPs can be aligned to the forming, storming, norming and performing stages of teams first described by Tuckman (1965). To work effectively together, members of a CoP must understand the characteristics of each phase of their development. Where a CoP is first formed, either as a new construct or where one or more members of the community change, the members enter the forming stage of their community. Establishing a set of guidelines for the smooth

Table 22.1   Model of the formation of teacher professional community of practice

Beginning	Evolving	Mature
1. Forming of team identity and norms of interaction		
Identification with sub-teams	Pseudo-community (some sense of unity, suppression of conflict)	Identification as a whole team
Individuals are interchangeable and easily replaceable	Recognition of unique contributions of each individual member	Recognition that the team is enriched by multiple perspectives (a sense of loss when any member leaves)
Undercurrent of incivility	Open discussion of interactional norms	Developing new interactional norms
Sense of individualism overrides responsibility to team	Recognition of need to regulate team behaviour	Shared responsibility for and regulation of team behaviour
2. Navigating faultlines		
Denial of difference	Appropriation of divergent views by dominant position	Understanding and productive use of difference
Conflict is avoided, ignored or suppressed	Conflict erupts and is feared	Conflict is an expected feature of team life, dealt with openly and honestly
3. Negotiating the essential tensions		
Lack of agreement over purposes of professional community	Begrudging willingness to let different people pursue different activities	Recognition that teacher learning and student learning are fundamentally intertwined
Different positions viewed as irreconcilable		
4. Communal responsibility for individual growth		
Belief that teachers' responsibility is to students, not colleagues	Recognition that colleagues can be resources for one's learning	Commitment to colleagues' growth
Intellectual growth is the responsibility of the individual	Recognition that participation is expected from all members	Acceptance of rights and obligations of community membership
Contributions to team are acts of individual volition		

Source: Main (2007, p. 38).

Figure 22.1   Effective practice

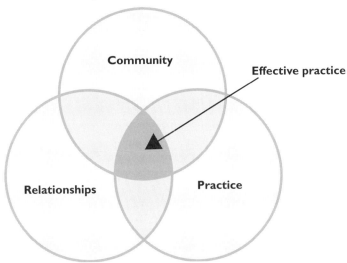

operation of the community (community), understanding the early years learner, the context and the what and how of the program to be delivered (practice), and having a commitment to foster professional working relationships (relationships) begins the journey towards the establishment of a CoP.

As tensions begin to arise or be expressed, this signals the onset of the storming stage of the CoP. Tensions relating to leadership or direction of the community, goals, roles, individual performance, personal agendas, commitment to the community goals and issues relating to inclusion can be experienced during this stage of the community's development. How these tensions are managed at this point will determine whether the budding CoP stalls at this stage of its development or progresses forward. What should be noted, however, is that tensions or conflict do not remain confined within this stage of the community's development. Tillett (1999) identifies an extensive list of constructive functions of conflict, including the prevention of stagnation of ideas and enthusiasm, encouragement of members to examine problems more closely, promotion of personal growth and confidence by challenging the individual, promotion of the community's identity and cohesion, encouragement of critical self-reflection, improvement of interpersonal communication, and building of trust among team members as thoughts, feelings, needs and opinions are expressed freely. If managed well, conflict continues to be an important facilitator throughout the next two stages (norming and performing) as CoP members work towards becoming a *performing* CoP.

Up to this point, much of the focus of members of the CoP has been on the task to be completed (that is, the program to be delivered). During the *norming* stage, a more balanced approach to community membership is developed as the focus begins to shift and there is recognition of the importance of building relationships between members. During this stage, members begin to feel a sense of belonging, shared goals begin to emerge, individuals' roles within the community become more defined, and acceptable behaviour, attitudes and work patterns start to emerge. At this point, a community is quite functional but needs to progress to the performing stage in order to realise the full potential of working collaboratively (Main, 2007).

A community can be said to have reached the *performing* stage when members have reached a balance between 'getting on with the job' and interpersonal relationships (Dwyer, 2002). When operating in this stage, a CoP has been reported to have clear goals, clear rules that are consistently followed, have an agreed decision-making process and have established performance expectations for members that are met. Members feel a strong connection to the community, and each member has a clearly defined role. Acceptable behaviour, attitudes and work patterns among team members have also been identified during this stage. As a community, a shared history is expressed through a common narrative and 'in jokes' that form the CoP's unique identity. However, it should be noted that any changes to the core membership of the community will result in the community regressing to formation stage, and having to go through previous life-cycle stages again (Main, 2007; Wheelan, 2005).

Barriers to effective communities of practice

Research has shown that creating a unified and consistent approach to program delivery in early years settings has often been stymied by the absence of team processes within a CoP. Hunt et al. (2004) identify some common barriers to the implementation of early years programs, which include: members within the CoP not having shared goals; no clear roles for CoP members; and a lack of regular meetings with a focused agenda. All of these barriers fall under the 'community' processes of the CoP. Circumventing these barriers requires the members of the CoP to take the time in their forming stage to clearly establish the roles, rules, goals and protocols of their particular CoP. Literature on team practices has shown that teams stall in the conflict or storming stage if these important community processes are not established (Main, 2010). Likewise, a CoP will stall in the storming stage of its development until such processes are defined and set in place.

Benefits of working within a community of practice

A range of benefits has been reported when educators work collaboratively. In other settings where educators engage in collaborative practices, implications have been identified for both teaching and learning (Hattie, 2004), with a number of benefits reported for both educators and students. Hargreaves (2001) argues that educators working collaboratively is a key strategy for improving the instructional effectiveness (practice) of educators. Thus, in early years settings, establishing a CoP is a strategic and purposive approach to learning and improving practice *through* practice.

Research has identified a significant number of benefits when educators work collaboratively. These include:

- educators' increased sense of efficacy (that is, increased growth, self-belief and commitment as a professional) (Ingvarson et al., 2005; Tschannen-Moran & Woolfolk-Hoy, 2007)
- reduced isolation and increased collegiality (Erb & Doda, 1989; Maeroff, 1993; Riley, 1999)
- implementation of innovative instructional/intervention strategies (Erb & Doda, 1989; Maeroff, 1993; Riley, 1999)
- increased sharing of ideas and resources (Erb & Doda, 1989)
- reduced workload (Pounder, 1999)
- capitalising on the strengths of others (Malone & Koblewski, 1999), and
- positive changes in teaching practice, including greater skill diversity (Pounder, 1999).

For students, research has also demonstrated improved academic and affective outcomes when educators work collaboratively (Newmann & Wehlage, 1995). Forming a CoP where the collaborative practices are employed effectively is therefore pivotal to improved teaching practices and learning outcomes for early years learners. However, of these benefits, an increased sense of efficacy has the potential to have the greatest influence to improve educator practice and enhance student outcomes.

Examples of a community of practice in action

Case study 22.1: Early learning centre

The members of the centre meet every afternoon to debrief and plan for the following day. Their discussion turned to three-year-old Tamara, who was finding it difficult to adjust to her new early learning centre. Tamara was quite anxious when her parents left and was not demonstrating the prosocial behaviours that would enable her to feel confident and secure within the centre. After revisiting information from previous discussions with Tamara's parents, the early years educators in the centre worked together to come up with a plan to best meet Tamara's needs. Discussions centred on the types of activities and the ways in which all staff could consistently interact with Tamara to create a predictable, consistent and secure base to help her adjust to the new setting. Throughout the discussion, the more experienced staff explained a number of strategies that they had found to be effective with Tamara in helping her to begin to develop a sense of trust and belonging.

In this scenario, the CoP is operating at the performing stage of its life-cycle. Members of the CoP share expertise and focus on the child to work collaboratively towards the best outcome. There is a balance between relationships and getting the job done.

Case study 22.2: Formal schooling setting

Working in an open-plan classroom is a new experience for Jen and Sharni. Both are very experienced educators, who have always worked within single-teacher classrooms, but both are excited about being able to work so closely with another early years educator. They both find that the other has a range of ideas and resources that will really enrich both classrooms. However, they soon realise that they have a number of areas where their previous practice as early years educators differs. They recognise that negotiating these points of potential conflict from the outset will help circumvent issues later on. They set a time to meet, and each develops her own list of personal classroom expectations and then ranks these as either 'not negotiable', 'preferred but negotiable' or 'flexible'. Working through the list and making decisions helps Jen and Sharni develop their trust with each other.

In this scenario, the CoP is in the forming stage of its life-cycle. Both educators are new to the setting, but enthusiastic and idealistic about the possibilities. They know and understand the importance of setting ground rules for the basis of their fledgling working relationship, and establish these quickly. Open and honest communication from the outset provides a framework of trust and accountability.

A teacher's sense of efficacy

Teacher self-efficacy is increasingly being accepted as the key variable influencing educator practice (process) and student outcomes (product) (Bruce et al., 2010; Ross, 1994). However, it should be noted that teacher efficacy is not a causal link but rather a mediator between process (what the educator does) and product (student outcomes) (Bruce et al., 2010). Nevertheless, a teacher's self-efficacy beliefs have been shown to be the best predictor of the amount of educator change and improved practice (Bruce et al., 2010).

Social cognitive theory argues that a teacher's self-efficacy beliefs (that is, an individual's belief that they can make a difference to students' learning) are promoted from four main sources (Bandura 1986; 1997). These are: enactive mastery experiences (past teaching successes); vicarious experiences (demonstrated by others and making inferences from social comparison); verbal persuasion (encouragement from others to believe in their capabilities); and physiological arousal (resilience). All of these sources can be experienced within the bounds of a CoP. Further, where educators were able to *see* effective practice modelled and then 'try it out', they were more likely to implement these new practices themselves (Ingvarson et al., 2005). Within a CoP, members are able to be observed and also observe practice, and then use these observations to inform and improve their own practice and increase their sense of efficacy.

Research has also shown that an individual's level of self-efficacy is not static. Teachers' self-efficacy beliefs are seen as context-specific, and an individual educator may not feel successful in all teaching situations (Bandura, 1997). This may be the case when an educator is placed in a situation for which they feel that their past training or personal experience has not adequately prepared them, or where they have been unsuccessful in a similar situation in the past. However, research has also suggested that professional development (PD) can contribute to an educator's increased sense of self-efficacy where the professional development facilitates mastery experiences or where participant interaction increases opportunities for vicarious experiences and/or verbal persuasion (Ross & Bruce, 2007). Sources such as vicarious experiences and verbal persuasion may be accessed more easily when school structures and programs promote close working relationships such as those experienced in early years CoPs, where educators are able to learn from each other (Bandura, 1997).

The need for continued learning

Early years educators' practices need to be dynamic. Early years learners are experiencing a rapidly changing world that is vastly different from the one their parents or educators experienced during their schooling years. At all levels of education, the historical paradigms of teaching and learning are being challenged. Prensky (2001) argues that there is a large discontinuity between today's students and the incremental differences, such as clothing or styles of music or entertainment, of generations in the past. Today's students are digital natives who have been immersed from birth in the digital age. Computers and video games, iPods, iPads, eReaders, video cams, mobile phones and a range of other tools and toys of the digital age are part of their world within and outside of the home. Collectively, these changes mean that early years learners are experiencing diverse cultures and rapidly changing technologies in a far more complex and uncertain world (Prensky, 2001). The challenge for early years educators is to build the foundation that will begin to prepare these early learners for the years ahead.

In practice, early years educators draw on a variety of sources to negotiate the day-to-day pragmatics of teaching, including pre-service training, early career mentoring, ongoing personal reflection and shared meaning-making through CoP. Challenging and making changes to personal conceptions of knowledge and what it means to learn place the educator in the role of learner. The notion of educator-as-learner is particularly salient, given the contextual nature of educator knowledge as well as theories around the social nature of learning (Lave & Wenger, 1991). Both the process of personal reflection and communities of practice as a means to improve individual practice and meet the developmental needs of students in the early years require educators to reflect, interpret and reconstruct their own practice using a range of complex intrapersonal and interpersonal communication skills. The need for continual professional learning through formal and informal approaches is critical to ensure early years educators are able to meet the ongoing and changing demands of early years classrooms.

In an analysis of traditional models of professional development, Robb (2000) found that traditional delivery models of professional development (that is, predominately one-day training sessions) were ineffective in meeting the diverse levels of knowledge and experience of staff or being transferred into effective practice. Robb (2007) also found that most one-size-fits-all presentations did not account for the varied contexts of the educators attending the workshop. Effective professional development has been based on the idea that professional learning needs to be continuing, social and situated within practice. Contextualising professional learning bridges the divide between theory and practice. Hence, in a CoP where educators are able to learn from each other and engage in ongoing professional dialogue, a CoP can be a very effective vehicle for ongoing professional learning and improving practice that can complement more formal modes of PD.

Realising the benefits of a community of practice

For the benefits of working within an early years CoP to be realised, members of that community also need to meet certain criteria. To truly be a community of practice, members must interact with each other—that is, they must communicate about aspects of the work that is either to be or has been undertaken. They must work together to continually improve practice through a range of planning and reflective processes, and they must be adaptive and flexible within the wide variety of contexts that cater for early years learners. McIntyre and Salas (1995) argue that working collaboratively also involves essential behaviours such as monitoring of performance (the established 'norm' of members of the community of practice to monitor their fellow members' performance and, in turn, have their performance monitored); giving effective feedback (Hattie & Timperley, 2007); closed-loop communication (where members ensure that the message received is the message intended); and backing up behaviours (where members have the ability to 'jump in' and help when they are needed). It can be seen that within an early years setting, good communication is critical for many of the benefits of an early years community of practice to be realised.

Summary

- As members of an early years CoP, educators are able to improve practice through practice—in effect being part of change in action.
- Membership of such a community requires educators to engage in personal and community reflection as a means to improve individual and collective practice.
- The potential of early years communities of practice is their ability to provide the vehicle for educators to learn from and with each other to improve program delivery, and ultimately improve the affective and academic learning outcomes of early years learners.
- However, the potential of an early years CoP can only be realised where members of the community are committed to the principles, and employ the process, required for the CoP to develop into a performing CoP.

Discussion questions

22.1   What processes do you need to consider when forming an early years CoP in order to ensure its effectiveness?

22.2   Discuss the types of activities that would best be done collaboratively by members of a CoP. What activities would best be done by individuals?

22.3   Are there differences in an early years CoP today compared with those of ten years ago? Five years ago?

22.4   What may be some of the barriers to working in an early years CoP?

22.5   What advantages can you see for early years learners in being in a setting where educators work in a CoP?

References

Bandura, A. (1986). Social foundations of thought and action: a social cognitive theory. Englewood Cliffs, NJ: Prentice-Hall.

Bandura, A. (1997). Self-efficacy. *Harvard Mental Health Letter, 13*(9), 4–6.

Bruce, C.D., Esmonde, I., Ross, J., Dookie, L. & Beatty, R. (2010). The effects of sustained classroom-embedded teacher professional learning on teacher efficacy and related student achievement. *Teaching and Teacher Education, 26*(8), 1598–608.

Buysse, V., Sparkman, K.L. & Wesley, V.W. (2003). Communities of practice: Connecting what we know with what we do. *Exceptional Children, 69*(3), 203–10.

Dwyer, J. (2002). *Communication in business,* 2nd ed. Sydney: Prentice-Hall.

Erb, T.O. & Doda, N.M. (1989). *Team organization: Promise-practices and possibilities.* Washington DC: National Education Association.

Fullan, M. (1993). *Change forces: Probing the depths of educational reform.* London: Falmer Press.

Gherardi, S. (2008). Community of practice or practices of a community? In D. Armstrong and C.V. Fukami (eds), *The Sage handbook of management, learning, education and development* (pp. 514–30). London: Sage.

Grossman, P., Wineburg, S. & Woolworth, S. (2001). Toward a theory of teacher community. *Teachers College Record, 103*(6), 942–1012.

Hanks, W.F. (1991). Foreword. In J. Lave & E. Wenger (eds), *Situated learning: Legitimate peripheral participation* (pp. 13–24). New York: Cambridge University Press.

Hargreaves, A. (2001). The emotional geographies of teachers' relations with colleagues. *International Journal of Educational Research, 35,* 503–27.

Hattie, J. (2004). Teachers make a difference. What is the research evidence? *Education Review, 7*(3), 453–65.

Hunt, P., Soto, G., Maier, J., Liboiron, N. & Bae, S. (2004). Collaborative teaming to support preschoolers with severe disabilities who are placed in general education early childhood programs. *Topics in Early Childhood Special Education, 24*(3), 123–42.

Ingvarson, L., Meiers, M. & Beavis, A. (2005). Factors affecting the impact of professional development programs on teachers' knowledge, practice, student outcomes & efficacy. *Education Policy Analysis Archives, 13*(10), 28–34.

Lave, J. & Wenger, E. (1991). *Situated learning: Legitimate peripheral participation.* Cambridge: Cambridge University Press.

Little, J.W. (2002). Locating learning in teachers' communities of practice: Opening up analysis of problems in records of everyday work. *Teaching and Teacher Education, 18*(8), 917–46.

Maeroff, G.I. (1993). *Team building for school change: Equipping teachers for new roles.* New York: Teachers College Press.

Main, K. (2007). A year-long study of the formation and development of middle school teaching teams. Unpublished PhD, Griffith University, Brisbane.

—— (2010). Teams and teaming practices. In D. Pendergast and N. Bahr (eds), *Teaching middle years: Rethinking curriculum, pedagogy and assessment,* 2nd ed. (pp. 301–16). Sydney: Allen & Unwin.

—— (2011). Teaching teams as a means of professional development to improve teacher efficacy and improve student outcomes. Paper presented at the 7th International Conference of the Middle Years of Schooling Association, Changing Curriculum, Challenging Times. 26–28 May, Gold Coast.

Malone, D.M. & Koblewski, P. (1999). A survey of professionals' attitudes and perceptions of teamwork supporting people with disabilities. *Journal of Developmental and Physical Disabilities, 11*(2), 77–89.

McIntyre, R. & Salas, E. (1995). Measuring and managing for team performance: Emerging principles from complex environments. In R. Guzzo and E. Salas (eds), *Team effectiveness and decision making in organizations* (pp. 9–45). San Francisco: Jossey-Bass.

McLellan, H. (ed.) (1996). *Situated learning perspectives.* Englewood Cliffs, NJ: Educational Technology Publications.

Newmann, F. & Wehlage, G. (1995). *Successful school restructuring.* Madison, WI: Center on Organization and Restructuring of Schools.

Portes, A. (1998). Social capital: Its origins and applications in modern sociology. *Annual Review of Sociology, 24,* 1–24.

Pounder, D.G. (1999). Teacher teams: Exploring job characteristics and work-related outcomes of work group enhancement. *Educational Administration Quarterly, 35*(3), 317–48.

Prensky, M. (2001). Digital natives, digital immigrants: Part 1. *On the Horizon, 9*(5), 1–6.

Riley, K. (1999). Managing incompetent teachers. *Management in Education, 13*(15), 15–17.

Robb, L. (2000). Redefining staff development: A collaborative model for teachers and administrators. Portsmouth, NH: Heinemann.

Ross, J.A. (1994). Beliefs that made a difference: The origins and impacts of teacher efficacy. Paper presented at the annual meeting of the Canadian Association for Curriculum Studies.

Ross, J. & Bruce, C. (2007). Professional development effects on teacher efficacy: Results of randomized field trial. *Journal of Educational Research, 101*(1), 50–60.

Rousseau, D.M., Sitkin, S.B., Burt, R.S. & Camerer, C. (1998). Not so different after all: A cross-discipline view of trust. *Academy of Management Review, 23*(3), 393–404.

Stein, D. (1998). *Situated learning in adult education.* ERIC Document Reproduction Service No. ED 418 250.

Tillett, G. (1999). *Resolving conflict: A practical approach,* 2nd ed. Melbourne: Oxford University Press.

Tschannen-Moran, M. & Woolfolk-Hoy, A. (2007). The differential antecedents of self-efficacy beliefs of novice and experienced teachers. *Teaching and Teacher Education, 23*(6), 944–56.

Tuckman, B.W. (1965). Developmental sequence in small groups. *Psychological Bulletin, 63*(6), 396–413.

Webster-Wright, A. (2009). Reframing professional development through understanding authentic professional learning. *Review of Educational Research, 79*(2): 702–39.

Wenger, E. (1998). *Communities of practice: Learning, meaning and identity.* Cambridge: Cambridge University Press.

Wheelan, S.A. (2005). *Faculty groups: From frustration to collaboration.* Thousand Oaks, CA: Corwin Press.

Wisneski, D.B. & Goldstein, L.S. (2004). Questioning community in early childhood education. *Early Child Development and Care, 174*(6), 515–26.

Index